The Origins of Early Christian Literature

Conventional approaches to the Synoptic gospels argue that the gospel authors acted as literate spokespersons for their religious communities. Whether described as documenting intragroup "oral traditions" or preserving the collective perspectives of their fellow Christ-followers, these writers are treated as something akin to the Romantic Poets speaking for their *Volk* – a questionable framework inherited from nineteenth-century German Romanticism. In this book, Robyn Faith Walsh argues that the Synoptic gospels were written by elite cultural producers working within a dynamic cadre of literate specialists, including persons who may or may not have been professed Christians. Comparing a range of ancient literature, her groundbreaking study demonstrates that the gospels are creative works produced by educated elites interested in Judean teachings, practices, and paradoxographical subjects in the aftermath of the Jewish War and in dialogue with the literature of their age. Walsh's study thus bridges the artificial divide between research on the Synoptic gospels and classics.

Robyn Faith Walsh is Assistant Professor of the New Testament and Early Christianity at the University of Miami, Coral Gables. An editor at the Database of Religious History, her articles have appeared in *The Classical Quarterly* and *Jewish Studies Quarterly*, among other publications.

The Origins of Early Christian Literature

Contextualizing the New Testament within Greco-Roman Literary Culture

ROBYN FAITH WALSH

University of Miami

CAMBRIDGE
UNIVERSITY PRESS

CAMBRIDGE
UNIVERSITY PRESS

University Printing House, Cambridge CB2 8BS, United Kingdom

One Liberty Plaza, 20th Floor, New York, NY 10006, USA

477 Williamstown Road, Port Melbourne, VIC 3207, Australia

314–321, 3rd Floor, Plot 3, Splendor Forum, Jasola District Centre, New Delhi – 110025, India

79 Anson Road, #06–04/06, Singapore 079906

Cambridge University Press is part of the University of Cambridge.

It furthers the University's mission by disseminating knowledge in the pursuit of education, learning, and research at the highest international levels of excellence.

www.cambridge.org
Information on this title: www.cambridge.org/9781108835305
DOI: 10.1017/9781108883573

© Cambridge University Press 2021

First published 2021

A catalogue record for this publication is available from the British Library.

Library of Congress Cataloging-in-Publication Data
NAMES: Walsh, Robyn Faith, 1980– author.
TITLE: The origins of early Christian literature : contextualizing the New Testament within Greco-Roman literary culture / Robyn Faith Walsh.
DESCRIPTION: Cambridge, UK ; New York : Cambridge University Press, 2020. | Includes bibliographical references and index.
IDENTIFIERS: LCCN 2020023256 (print) | LCCN 2020023257 (ebook) | ISBN 9781108835305 (hardback) | ISBN 9781108793131 (paperback) | ISBN 9781108883573 (epub)
SUBJECTS: LCSH: Bible. Gospels–Criticism, interpretation, etc. | Christian literature, Early–History and criticism. | Classical literature–History and criticism. | Christianity and literature–History–To 1500.
CLASSIFICATION: LCC BS2555.52 .W36 2020 (print) | LCC BS2555.52 (ebook) | DDC 226/.067–dc23
LC record available at https://lccn.loc.gov/2020023256
LC ebook record available at https://lccn.loc.gov/2020023257

ISBN 978-1-108-83530-5 Hardback

For my parents, Thomas and Kathleen Walsh

Contents

Preface

On January 29, 1885, a man known only as "C.B.W." traveled from Berlin to Zürich by means of a meandering train.[1] Prone to understatement and with an economy of words, he described the vistas of timber, mines, and "craggy" castles from his compartment window as he crossed the Elbe ("a large river") and the Rhine (undescribed) and arrived in Switzerland ("hilly") and, ultimately, his "handsome" destination.[2] Our mystery man was there to call upon a certain Gustav Volkmar, Professor of New Testament Exegesis at the University of Zürich, and President of the Society of Critical Historical Theology. His purpose in visiting Volkmar is unclear. But he found the professor and his daughter "so congenial" that he "determined to remain some weeks" in their company.[3]

In the course of this ambiguous residency, C.B.W. had occasion to attend a number of Volkmar's lectures. His record of these talks, and Volkmar's interactions with his students and interlocutors, is a time capsule, of sorts, of a particular kind of discourse in the European academy at the fin de siècle:

The lectures of the President to his class, were sufficient to mark him as a pronounced liberal. He took occasion in one of his lectures to explain to the class that there could not have been an eclipse of the sun at the time of the crucifixion,

---

[1] "C.B.W." is likely Charles B. Waite, according to the index of writers presented in the front matter of the volume, as I will discuss. See "Notes of Travel," *Chicago Law Times*, vol. 2, ed. Catharine V. Waite (Chicago: C. V. Waite, 1888), 326–28.

[2] Waite, "Notes of Travel," 326   [3] Waite, "Notes of Travel," 326–27.

because it was at the time of the full moon. This I thought was good science but weak theology.[4]

I confess that the phrase "good science but weak theology" pops into my head quite often. And then there were Volkmar's thoughts on the resurrection and his position in the field:

At another time, he asked the class what was the nature of the resurrection of Christ, and when one of the students answered, "Es war eine erscheinung," the old gentleman replied, "Das ist recht." On returning from class, I asked him, if the resurrection was only an appearance, how he explained the rolling away of the stone from the tomb. He replied, "There was no tomb. Jesus was put to death as a malefactor, and such were denied burial." Some of our divines would be shocked at these doctrines, but Professor Volkmar is paid by the State as a religious teacher. I asked him if the more orthodox professors did not make war upon him. He replied that they had done so in former years, but had concluded to let him alone. They went their way, and he went his.[5]

These anecdotes are from a somewhat obscure source: a back-page travelogue for the 1888 edition of the *Chicago Law Times*. I came across a scanned copy of C.B.W.'s "Notes of Travel" while researching Volkmar, and found the periodical in which it is contained to be highly eclectic in its content: a series of articles on various legal cases, as one might expect, are presented alongside gems like "Diogenes or Antipater, Which?," an article that manages to connect the Stoic wisdom of Cicero to the sale of a barren, blooded cow in Michigan. The editor of the periodical, one Catharine V. Waite, boasts an impressive résumé as an activist, suffragist, lawyer, and polymath in Chicago, leading protest movements and founding a number of literary societies, support networks for women, and, among other ventures, the seemingly short-lived *Chicago Law Times*. (Incidentally, rumor has it she was also more than capable with a six-shooter.)[6] "C.B.W." is almost certainly her husband, Charles Burlingame Waite, a lawyer appointed by President Abraham Lincoln to the Utah Supreme Court during the Civil War. His "Notes of Travel" from Paris to Berlin to Zürich and back again are, at once, absorbing and, for a fellow scholar of New Testament more than a century later, poignant.

---

[4] Waite, "Notes of Travel," 327.   [5] Waite, "Notes of Travel," 327.
[6] "Catharine Van Valkenburg Waite," in *Women Building Chicago 1790–1990: A Biographical Dictionary*, ed. Rima Schultz and Adele Hast (Bloomington: Indiana University Press, 2001), 922.

Take, for example, Waite's chronicle of one of his last conversations with the then seventy-five-year-old Volkmar:

The last day I was in Zurich, we took a long walk together … we took a seat on a bench near that magnificent lake … I told him we should probably never meet again in this life … and asked him if he did not believe in another state of existence.

The old man turned upon me his large full eye, with a suddenness that was almost startling. "Why do you ask this?" He said. I replied, I had no object except simply to know his opinion. "Well," said he, with deliberation, "that is something I know nothing about. All the teachings of Jesus related to this life. The Kingdom of God which he was seeking to establish, was to be upon the earth. To live again, is something to be hoped, but nothing is revealed to us upon the subject. The arguments in favor of a future existence must be drawn from outside the gospels."[7]

On the cusp of the turn of the century and all that lay beyond – advancing industrialization, globalization, continued imperialism, and, crucially, the world wars – Volkmar's lectures and beliefs offer a glimpse into a historical moment arguably eclipsed by the tumult of those subsequent years. The advent of Higher Criticism, a free(er) press, and the emergence of liberal politics in the latter decades of the nineteenth century allowed scholars like Volkmar to occupy positions in the European academy. Yet, as assuredly as any tide rises, an increasing concern for the secularization of society and, by extension, the university, brought forward a Protestant-Catholic backlash expressed through a variety of "repressed neoromantic narratives" and strategies. Among these strategies was an approach to the New Testament and its historical context that used these writings as a tool to reclaim and revive the "spirit" and "faith" of the middle-class in Germany, Switzerland, England, France, and beyond. Practices like *Religionsgeschichte* promised to reveal lost communities of fellow-believers, merging a "scientific" approach to antiquity with the opportunity for a "renewal of faith."[8] Scholarly and popular interest in so-called Christian origins, the layers and dates of early Christian texts, evidence for the oral traditions of a lost *Volk*, and the historical Jesus became a fairground for litigating debates old and new: Had liberal theologians and scholars neglected faith with their critical methods?

[7] Waite, "Notes of Travel," 327–28.
[8] Suzanne L. Marchand, *German Orientalism in the Age of Empire: Religion, Race, and Scholarship* (Cambridge: Cambridge University Press, 2009), 253.

Overdetermined the value of so-called orientalism? Forgotten "the people"? As the founder of Form Criticism, Hermann Gunkel, lamented at the turn of the century in *Die Christliche Welt*:

> If God had wanted me to have a voice that would penetrate the hearts and minds of every scholar of theology (*die Herzen und Gewiffen der theologilchen Forfcher dringt*), I would proclaim ... do not forget your holy duty to your people (*Volk*)! Write for the educated (*die Gebildeten*)! Do not talk so much about literary criticism (*Litterarkritik*), text criticism (*Textkritik*) ... but talk about religion (*redet über Religion*)! ... Our people thirsts [*sic*] for your words about our religion and its history (*Unfer Volk dürftet nach euren Worten über die Religion und ihre Gefchichte*)![9]

What constitutes "religion" in Gunkel's construction are the very things that the *traditionsgeschichtliche* method sought: the interests, practices, and concerns of "lost" peoples and communities, their beliefs, their lives, and their oral stories. To the extent that a piece of writing like Paul's letters or one of the canonical gospels represents a historical moment, for those sympathetic to the work of this segment of the Religions-Historical School, they also represented the "culmination of long periods in which religious ideas and practices were transmitted orally and informally."[10] Classically trained philologists had little interest in *koiné* or Silver Greek and left the theologians to it. Over time, a conceptual divide grew within scholarship between the literate, culturally and socially elite Greek and Roman writer and the humble, illiterate peasant. Increased interest in material culture, newly found papyri from places like Oxyrhynchus, and a Romantic desire to reclaim the Greco-Roman world (à la the Grand Tour) reinforced the idea that there were communities outside the text yet to be discovered. As Adolf Deissmann proclaimed in his *Licht vom Osten: Das Neue Testament und die neuentdeckten Texte aus dem hellenistisch-römischen Welt* in 1908, the "primeval prejudices of the Atticizers" had obscured "the embeddedness of primitive Christianity in folk culture (*die*

---

[9] Hermann Gunkel, "Ein Notschrei aus Anlaß des Buches Himmelsbild und Weltanschauung im Wandel der Zeiten," *Die Christliche Welt* 14 (1900): 58–61, cit. 60. I have taken some liberties with the translation of "über die Religion" above; by including the article "die" Gunkel is implying that there is one religion – Christianity – that is of primary concern. For this reason, I elected to use "our" to convey the same meaning. This quote is also cited by Marchand, *German Orientalism in the Age of Empire*, 263, albeit with a different translation.

[10] Marchand, *German Orientalism in the Age of Empire*, 266.

Volkstümlichkeit des Urchristentums)."[11] The faith and cohesion of these humble, illiterate so-called primitive Christians had much to offer the Wilhelmine and Victorian and Weimar Christian facing the threat of cultural secularization. And the development of new scholarly, *wissenschaftliche* methods made it possible to demonstrate that Christianity had been, from the beginning, a religion by and for the people. More maliciously, it would also enable scholars to link these early Christians to a pursuit of Aryan history, as I discuss in Chapter 2.

***

At its core, this book is a study of the "knowledge-making practices" of the field of early Christianity and New Testament studies, its assumptions about communities and authors, and its possible alternatives.[12] Conventional approaches to the Synoptic gospels argue that the gospel authors acted as literate spokespersons for their religious communities. Whether described as documenting intragroup "oral traditions" or preserving the collective perspectives of their fellow Christ-followers (e.g., the Markan, Matthean, or Lukan "churches"), the gospel writers are treated as something akin to the Romantic Poets speaking for their *Volk*. By contrast, Greek and Latin authors describe themselves writing within (and for) literary networks of fellow *writers* – a competitive field of educated peers and associated literate specialists who possessed the necessary training and the technical means for producing and publishing their own writings. This is a more plausible social context for the gospel writers. And it is this social context that this book examines, questioning how our understanding of early Christianity changes once we shift our frame from inherited notions of community, *Volk*, and *Geist* and, instead, bring new methods from literary theory and the broader social sciences to bear on these writings.

This monograph argues that the Synoptic gospels were written by elite cultural producers working within a dynamic cadre of literate specialists – including persons who may or may not have had an understanding of being "in Christ." Through comparison with a range of ancient *bioi* (lives), histories, and novels, this study demonstrates that the gospels are creative literature produced by educated elites interested in Judean

---

[11] Adolf Deissmann, *Licht vom Osten: Das Neue Testament und die neuentdeckten Texte aus dem hellenistisch-römischen Welt* (Tübingen: Verlag von J. C. B. Mohr Siebeck, 1908), 282; Marchand, *German Orientalism in the Age of Empire*, 269.

[12] Marchand, *German Orientalism in the Age of Empire*, xxxiii.

teachings, practices, and paradoxographical subjects in the aftermath of the Jewish War. It provides a more concrete account of the processes by which the gospels likely were written and establishes that they are in dialogue with writings and writers of their age rather than assuming that they were produced by or for "Christian communities."

Despite the title of this monograph, I do not seek "origins" for early Christianity and the gospel writers in the sense that I am not attempting to assert the uniqueness – or unique genesis – of Christianity. Likewise, I do not scrutinize dates for these writings, and I do not engage in extensive critiques of specific members of our guild. Instead, I am interested in offering a broad-based examination of how we have practiced scholarship in the field of religious studies, followed by constructive suggestions on how we might approach that practice differently. As I explain in the Introduction, a focus on writers, *their* practices, and their particular social formations is by no means a threat to our field, but an opportunity to develop a more fine-grained and historically plausible understanding of the process by which writings about Jesus were composed, shared, and contributed to the growth and eventual cohesion of a movement. As a scholar, the approach that I am advocating is not allied consciously to any present social, political, or religious objective other than a desire to better understand the dynamics of the ancient Mediterranean world. I am, however, conscious of my desire to identify and, if possible, continue to rectify any approaches and methods that have traded on the "sacred" authority of the gospels in order to advance particular religious, political, nationalistic, racist, or anti-Semitic viewpoints. In this respect, this book represents a search for origins, but the origins of our scholarly practices and their legacies. Situated as I am within a scholarly genealogy only two or three generations removed from the likes of Gunkel, Johannes Weiss, and Martin Heidegger, I am struck by the fact that we still have much work to do in reflecting on the fraught history of our field, its influences, and its influencers. I hope this monograph contributes to that work as we in the secular academy continue to strive for good science and weak theology.

Acknowledgments

In the years since I began this project, I have watched seas rise and nations fall, which is to say, it has taken me a long time. I earned my doctorate. I married my clever and loving husband, Jaswinder Bolina (and, I might add, watched him complete three books in the time it took me to write one). I gave birth to our son Taran, who is even more delightful and mischievous than I could have hoped. We said goodbye to our beloved Sarah. I moved more times than I'd like to count. I strengthened old friendships and made cherished new ones.

This project began as my PhD dissertation at Brown University under the direction of Stanley Stowers. Without Stan's intellectual generosity this book simply wouldn't exist. His influence on my thinking is evident throughout. I humbly attribute any insights here to his mentorship while maintaining that any missteps or errors are entirely my own – I am embarrassed to admit how many times he had to walk me through Bourdieu's autonomous and heteronomous poles. Stowers' brilliance and collegiality set a standard in my experience of the field, and I am fortunate to call him my Doktorvater and friend.

David Konstan served on my dissertation committee, and he and his partner, Pura Nieto Hernandez, remain very dear to me. Compassionate and unfailingly reliable, they are the sort of friends I can always call, even if it's just for help finding the right ancient reference. I admire their wisdom, energy, and drive, but, most of all, I admire their kindness.

Nancy Evans looked past my faults as an impetuous and overconfident undergraduate advisee. She helped cultivate my curiosity in the ancient world and all things Greek, and she absolutely insisted that I learn *koinē* to study the New Testament. She has shaped my life, and she remains my greatest mentor, colleague, and dear friend.

Thank you to the "Lady Cabal" – Jennifer Eyl, Erin Roberts, and Sarah Rollens – who are my daily lifeline on all things, from obscure philological questions to the latest memes. Your insights and humor are a treasure.

To my colleagues from Harvard Divinity School, Brown University, the University of Miami, and elsewhere, you are never far from my mind. I am thankful for your friendship, advice, and conversation.

To those who helped with the content of this book directly or through example, I am truly grateful: David Berger, Jonathan Brumberg-Kraus, Cavan Concannon, Chris Keith, Ross Kraemer, Gretel Rodríguez, and Stephen Young. Academia would be a lonely place without you. Anna Cwikla and Nicola Hellmann-McFarland generously edited my Fraktur transcriptions and translations. And my deepest gratitude to Beatrice Rehl, the staff at Cambridge University Press, and my anonymous readers for their guidance and critical feedback. Each of you helped make this a better book.

A number of institutions have supported me and this project over the years. The University of Miami generously provided time and funding for research and travel. I was fortunate to enjoy several stays at Fondation Hardt in Vandœuvres, Switzerland, and I am indebted to the staff and my colleagues there and I am honored to call many of you friends. A particular thank you to Gary Vachicouras and Pierre Ducrey, who welcomed an interloping New Testament scholar in among the classicists.

I appreciate the revolving members of the Redescribing Christian Origins group, especially Barry Crawford and Merrill Miller, who have offered invaluable advice and encouragement.

Thank you to the Center for the Humanities and Antiquities Interdisciplinary Research Group at the University of Miami for many helpful discussions on various iterations of this book project; I am particularly grateful for the advice I received from colleagues Jennifer Ferriss-Hill, John Kirby, Frank Palmeri, Dabney Park, Jessica Rosenberg, and Mihoko Suzuki. And I greatly appreciate my colleagues in religious studies at the University of Miami who have helped make Miami my home. A special thank you to Bill Green, Henry Green, David Kling, Michelle Gonzalez Maldonado, Justin Ritzinger, and my many students for their guidance, compassion, and for keeping me on my toes.

Among our friends and family, thank you to Maria Almeida for bringing light to every day. Brittany Cruz, Mae Smith, Angie Waller-

Guziewicz, and everyone at the Child Care Center made it possible for me to return to work; tireless, selfless, and hilarious, you also make me a better parent.

My love to our friends back in New England: Nancy Wager and the whole Wagner crew, the Doolittles, and Michael Bellofatto.

My love also to Kulwant and Ravinder Bolina for making me a part of your lives and your family, to Surinder and Sandie Bolina for answering our every call, and to the entire Bolina family in Chicago, Ann Arbor, Nashville, and elsewhere.

My husband has brought the unexpected into my life. I came to Miami contentedly on my own with no thought but for my work. Within days I met this affable, intelligent, and kind man who, within weeks, became my life partner. I confess I have no idea how you balance such creativity with unassailable logic, but I am the lucky beneficiary of your love and, crucially for the purposes of this book, your editorial eye. I have never been more filled with admiration and love for someone and I have never laughed harder.

To Taran: I don't know if or when you might read this. At this moment you are too young to recognize your own name. You wake at dawn. You pronounce bananas "my-na-nas." Your favorite word is an emphatic "more!" You destroy every puzzle. You knowingly smirk when we tell you "no." You are terrible for my work, but you make everything else feel unimportant. I adore you.

Finally, to my parents Thomas and Kathleen Walsh. You didn't bat an eye when I decided to become a religious studies major. I think I remember one conversation where you reminded me that Michael Crichton was a doctor *and* a writer, but that was about it. I had the enviable privilege of knowing that whatever school or career I entered, you would do anything it took to support me. You still do. You have sacrificed many of your own ambitions in order to give me every opportunity, and I can only hope to emulate your example. Any accomplishments in my life I attribute to you. For your generosity, I have enjoyed opportunities few are granted. I consider it my task to pay that forward now and always.

Abbreviations

References to ancient sources appear in both the footnotes and the body of the text, according to context. All ancient authors and works are abbreviated according to the conventions of the *Oxford Classical Dictionary* (4th ed.), unless otherwise noted. Journals and related sources are referenced in accordance with *L'Année philologique*. The following abbreviations are used for frequently cited works, book collections, reference materials, and so forth.

ANRW	*Aufstieg und Niedergang der römischen Welt*
CIL	*Corpus inscriptionum latinorum* (volume and item number)
DK	H. Diels and W. Kranz, eds. *Die Fragmente der griechischen Historiker*. Berlin, 1952.
FHG	*Fragmenta historicorum graecorum*, 5 vols. Ed. C. Müller and T. Müller. Paris, 1843–70.
IG	*Inscriptiones graecae*. Berlin, 1873– .
LCL	Loeb Classical Library
OCD	*The Oxford Classical Dictionary*, 4th ed. Ed. S. Hornblower et al. Oxford, 2012.
P. Oxy.	*The Oxyrhynchus Papyri*, Egypt Exploration Society. London, 1912–.
PI	*The Philo Index: A Complete Greek Word Index to the Writings of Philo of Alexandria*. Ed. P. Borgen et al. Eerdmans; Brill, 2000.
PMG	*Poetae Melici Graeci*. Ed. D. L. Page. Oxford, 1962.
SBL	Society of Biblical Literature
SEG	*Supplementum epigraphicum graecum*, vols. 1–42. Amsterdam.

Note on the Text

All translations, both ancient and modern, are my own unless otherwise noted.

At times, I cite scholars within this monograph who have been accused of or charged with crimes and other serious offenses, or who have known ties to prejudiced organizations (e.g., the National Socialist Party in Germany). It is my strong preference not to offer these individuals professional acknowledgment given the nature of their actions and associations. That said, it would be intellectually misleading for me to omit entirely reference to certain works and persons, particularly as it pertains to my critique of German Romanticism and its legacies of anti-Semitism and racism. Therefore, I have endeavored only to cite such individuals when absolutely necessary to my argument and the conventions of the field.

Introduction

"Diamonds in a Dunghill": Seeking New Approaches in Early Christian Studies

When Thomas Jefferson took up a razor to piece together his *Life and Morals of Jesus of Nazareth*, his goal was to strip away, quite literally, the vestiges of ancient philosophy and so-called gnosticism that had convoluted the work of the "simple evangelists." In a letter to John Adams, he boasted that the "primitive simplicity" of early Christianity was as plain as "diamonds in a dunghill." Strategically pasting together passages from the canonical gospels, he imagined himself liberating the text from the "logos and demiurges, aeons and daemons" of Christian Platonists. This "Jefferson Bible" intended to lay bare the pure teachings of a remarkable, ancient moralist.[1] While Jefferson's assembled text illustrates the extent to which scripture is "good to think with," as Claude Lévi-Strauss once said, it also stands as evidence for how scripture, in a sense, changes over time.[2]

Jonathan Z. Smith charged, somewhat ironically, that the historical-critical study of the Bible suffers from an antiquarian bias. This bias is exemplified by the tendency of scholars to begin their evaluations of ancient materials from the point of a text's prehistory "but never its

---

[1] Cited from Daniel Boorstin, *The Lost World of Thomas Jefferson* (Chicago: University of Chicago Press, 1993), 159. On the influence of Jefferson's works and letters on the study of Christianity, see Jonathan Z. Smith, "On the Origin of Origins," in *Drudgery Divine* (Chicago: University of Chicago Press, 1990), 1–35. Also see Suzanne L. Marchand, *German Orientalism in the Age of Empire: Religion, Race, and Scholarship* (Cambridge: Cambridge University Press, 2009), 287.

[2] Wilfred Cantwell Smith, "The Study of Religion and the Study of the Bible," *Journal of the American Academy of Religion* 39, no. 2 (1971): 131–40.

subsequent history."[3] Our earliest writings about Jesus are not only artifacts of the ancient Mediterranean but also artifacts of second-eighteenth-, nineteenth-, and twentieth-century thought.[4] Others such as Wilfred Cantwell Smith have made similar claims noting that scholars of Christian origins should approach their source material "not merely as a set of ancient documents or even as a first- and second-century product but as a third-century and twelfth-century and nineteenth-century and contemporary agent."[5] The Jefferson Bible is a fine example of the subsequent handling of scripture in the service of gaining insights into Christian history. Such activity need not be literal as with Jefferson and his razor, but it can be evident in the frameworks, terms, and methods used to describe the beginnings of Christianity.

Jefferson's larger correspondence reveals that his stitchery was a well-intentioned attempt at historiography. Jefferson and his cohort perceived that the gospel writers had injected popular philosophy into their accounts of Jesus' life in order to make his teachings more palatable to a Roman (i.e., "pagan") audience.[6] The notion that the so-called primitive Christians would have been in any way "philosophical" agitated against a strongly held vision of Jesus as a humble moral teacher tailed by his "unlettered apostles." Chief among these incursions was a breed of Platonism that, in Jefferson's view, smacked of Trinitarianism. He cautioned that "it is too late in the day for men of sincerity to pretend they believe in the Platonic mysticisms that three are one and one is three." Jefferson's planned "euthanasia for Platonic Christianity" remained fixed on this particular motif.[7]

Hindsight suggests that Jefferson's terms and methods were greatly influenced by eighteenth-century Deist and anti-Catholic polemics in

---

[3] Jonathan Z. Smith, *On Teaching Religion*, ed. Christopher I. Lehrich (New York: Oxford University Press, 2013), 30.

[4] J. Z. Smith raises this same issue in the case of the "J" and "Q" sources in *On Teaching Religion*, 30.

[5] Smith, "The Study of Religion," 134; Smith, *On Teaching Religion*, 30. Also see Smith, "On the Origin of Origins," 1–35. I also cite this quote from W. C. Smith in Robyn Faith Walsh, "Q and the 'Big Bang' Theory of Christian Origins," in *Redescribing the Gospel of Mark*, ed. Barry S. Crawford and Merrill P. Miller (Atlanta: SBL Press, 2017), 483–533, cit. 483.

[6] Jefferson's conversation partners on Christianity include John Adams and Joseph Priestly. See E. P. Smith, *Priestly in America: 1794–1804* (Philadelphia: Blakiston, 1920), 122–24, 145–46. This source is also cited in Smith, "On the Origin of Origins," 3, n. 2.

[7] Smith, "On the Origin of Origins," 9; L. J. Cappon, ed., *The Adams-Jefferson Letters: The Complete Correspondence between Thomas Jefferson and Abigail and John Adams* (Chapel Hill: University of North Carolina Press, 1959), 1–2, 2:433.

which he was something of a participant-observer.[8] Working from an Enlightenment vocabulary, he reinscribed binary categories of orthodoxy and heresy, theology and philosophy, Judaism and Hellenism in his evaluations while simultaneously professing to offer a more accurate representation of the first century C.E.[9] Related arguments against "pagan imprinting" on the historical Jesus would continue to have enormous influence on subsequent studies of early Christianity and late antiquity.[10] Ultimately, Jefferson's ambition may have been to reconstruct the sayings of the historical Jesus to his liking, but his efforts revealed more about Jefferson's own interests than those of his subject – as is often the case.[11]

The conceit of the Jefferson Bible was that the gospel writers manufactured *lives* about Jesus and his followers reflective of certain aims and sensibilities. For Jefferson, the gospels' so-called paganism revealed that they were constructed narratives whose purpose lay beyond offering a historically authentic account of the earliest stages of the Jesus movement. The irony of Jefferson's charge is thick, but he was correct in positing that early Christian literature was not strictly concerned, to paraphrase

---

[8] Smith, "On the Origin of Origins," 9; Cappon, *The Adams-Jefferson Letters*, 2:385.

[9] The false dichotomy between Judaism and Hellenism is addressed in more detail by Troels Engberg-Pedersen in his 2001 *Paul beyond the Judaism/Hellenism Divide*. In that edited volume, Engberg-Pedersen explains that the ideological implications of each term have served to create artificial distinctions between the people, practices, and language of Judea and the rest of the Greek and Roman world. As I argue in Chapter 2, this interpretation has roots in Romantic thinking about the peoples and places of the ancient Mediterranean (including political and anti-Semitic leanings). Engberg-Pedersen acknowledges influence from the *Religionsgeschichtliche Schule*; however, he convincingly argues that the territories "conquered and held by Alexander the Great and his successors and then by the Romans" constituted more of a "cultural melting pot" than is usually recognized. As such, we should understand Judaism as one of a number of "traditions with roots before the Hellenistic period proper," like the traditions of Greece and Rome that experienced significant interface and overlap with one another. Engberg-Pedersen also effectively argues that the Judaism/Hellenism divide maintains traditional, theological readings that render early Christian writings and, particularly, Paul as "pawns in a power game." This "game" views the representative texts and practices of Christianity not as fully integrated within Mediterranean society but as incomparably unique and "new" within its historical, cultural, and literary context. See Troels Engberg-Pedersen, ed., *Paul beyond the Judaism/Hellenism Divide* (Louisville: Westminster John Knox, 2001), 1–4.

[10] Smith, "On the Origin of Origins," 13.

[11] A recent example of personal narrative evidently informing critical theses is Matthew D. C. Larsen, *Gospels before the Book* (New York: Oxford University Press, 2018), see xiii–xv. Invoking Bakhtin, Larsen conflates modern forms of writing practices and publication (his own) with antiquity.

Plutarch, with writing histories.[12] Jefferson intuited that the gospel writers were, first and foremost, *writers* functioning within a particular medium and employing known and conventional tools of their trade. Their literary choices rendered an idealized vision of Jesus and his life using details more strategic than historical. As Celsus recognized centuries before Jefferson, in reading these works one quickly realizes that their content "may or must be mendacious."[13] For various reasons, the gospels were suitable for use as a canonized origin story for the Jesus movement, but by modern standards of veracity, they ultimately reveal little about the beginnings they profess to relate. Rather, the gospels reveal more about the *writers* who created them and the subsequent generations of readers who have endorsed and perpetuated Christianity's own myth of origins.

THE PARADIGM OF EXCEPTIONALISM

Jefferson's struggle is emblematic of certain tensions that undergird studies of the New Testament and Christian history: When reconstructing the past on the basis of creative literature like the gospels, how can we meaningfully distinguish between fiction and history?[14] Has the ongoing desire for details – any details – about the reputed origins of this still actively practiced religion led scholars to tread too far into speculation or, in the words of Burton Mack, "fantasy" in their assessments of these texts?[15] In contradistinction to a field like classics – where few of the gods and practices described are still believed – "religious" writings are freighted with a significance that does not attend other kinds of historical

---

[12] Plut. *Vit. Alex.*, 1.2: "For it is not histories we are writing (ἱστορίας γράφομεν) but lives (βίους). It is not always the most famous deeds which illuminate a man's virtues and vices (ἀρετῆς ἢ κακίας); often a clearer insight into a man's character is revealed by a small detail, a remark, or a joke (πρᾶγμα βραχὺ... ῥῆμα... παιδιά), than by battles where tens of thousands die, or by the greatest of conflicts, or by the siege of cities." Greek taken from Bernadotte Perrin, *Plutarch Lives*, VII, LCL (Cambridge, MA: Harvard University Press, 1919).

[13] Celsus is quoted by Origen, *Contra Celsum*, cit. 2.55; cited in G. W. Bowersock, *Fiction as History: Nero to Julian* (Berkeley: University of California Press, 1994), 7.

[14] The category distinction between fiction and history, both ancient and modern, is discussed in Bowersock, *Fiction as History*, passim, as well as M. David Litwa, *How the Gospels Became History: Jesus and Mediterranean Myths* (New Haven: Yale University Press, 2019), 1–45.

[15] Burton L. Mack, *A Myth of Innocence: Mark and Christian Origins* (Minneapolis: Fortress Press, 1988), 9.

data; the gospels are read by some as a faithful account of what happened to Jesus and his followers. They are also, in part, responsible for the formation of Western concepts of morality and law. Consequently, vignettes about – and particular understandings of – the teachings of Jesus are broadly familiar to popular audiences, and familiarity can breed critical complacency. Within the secular academy, we have inherited certain methods for reading these "sources" that are specific to our fields and not easily challenged, for both professional and personal reasons. With such high stakes, it is little wonder that the study of religion tends toward reifying tradition.[16] What we ascribe to these texts is so extraordinary; how could we expect them to have been produced in an ordinary way?

This book argues against approaches to the Synoptic gospels that treat them principally as religious texts. Such approaches impede our ability to evaluate these works as we would any other kind of Greco-Roman literature. While these methods are born of our desire for a more concrete understanding of Christian beginnings, they have led us to presume the existence of cohesive religious groups and theological diversity, all the while uncritically invoking the language of "community."[17] Scholarship that insists on reclaiming the social networks of the gospel writers has been particularly troubled. We know a great deal about Mediterranean and West Asian writers and writing practices, yet analyses of the gospels continue to muddle their social circumstances in order to speak of oral traditions, Christian communities and their literate spokesmen, or the gospels "before authors."[18] We continually look for evidence of socially marginal, preliterate Christian groups in these works, treating the gospel

---

[16] I am influenced here by Elizabeth Clark, who says of microhistory/*Alltagsgeschichte*: "the personal quality of its subject matter encouraged a too-easy identity with the people represented and their emotions, obscuring the 'otherness' of the past." Here she is summarizing common critiques of the *Alltagsgeschichte* movement in Germany. This statement also anticipates, to some degree, her later criticism of British Marxist historiography. See Elizabeth A. Clark, *History, Theory, Text* (Cambridge, MA: Harvard University Press, 2009), cit. 78–79. A student of Clark's work may recognize in my hypothetical questioning above her reflections on the state of historiography in the twentieth and twenty-first centuries. See, in particular, her "The Territory of the Historian," in *History, Theory, Text*, 63–85.

[17] Stanley K. Stowers, "The Concept of 'Community' and the History of Early Christianity," *Method and Theory in the Study of Religion* 23 (2011): 238–56; Karen L. King, "Factions, Variety, Diversity, Multiplicity: Representing Early Christian Differences for the 21st Century," *Method and Theory in the Study of Religion* 23, nos. 3–4 (2011): 216–37.

[18] Larsen, *Gospels before the Book*, 3.

writers not as rational actors but as something more akin to Romantic
Poets speaking for their *Volk*. Few if any disciplines that study the ancient
Mediterranean describe their subjects as having such myopic concerns.
Why, then, do we treat the gospels so idiosyncratically?[19]

While it is the case that writers compose their works with certain
audiences in mind, the way scholars of early Christianity have emphasized
the *religious* communities of these authors is at the very least parochial, if
not ahistorical. Greek and Roman authors routinely describe themselves
writing within (and for) literary networks of fellow *writers* – a competitive field of educated peers and associated literate specialists who engaged
in discussion, interpretation, and the circulation of their works. These
networks could include learned individuals from a variety of social back-
grounds, but each member possessed the necessary training and the
technical means for producing or publishing various forms of writing.
Each was also bound by certain expectations and conventions of training,
reading, composition, and literary exchange; while capable of innovation,
they were still beholden to the dictates of genre, citation, and allusion in
order to demonstrate knowledge of and engagement with other works
within their literary field.

It stands to reason that the gospel authors were similarly trained and
positioned, working within cadres of fellow, cultural elites.[20] Some of
their associates may or may not have even had an understanding of being
"in Christ"; the act of writing itself was the principle and guiding sphere
of influence. In such a historical context, the gospel writers are not the
"founding fathers" of a religious tradition – at least not in their historical
moment. They are rational agents producing literature about a Judean
teacher, son of God, and wonder-worker named Jesus. This particular
subject matter offered numerous possibilities for employing literary techniques and motifs in conversation with other writings (and writers) of the
milieu – including discourses on gods, Judean practices, philosophy,
politics, and paradoxography. In short, the gospels represent the strategic
choices of educated Greco-Roman writers working within a circumscribed field of literary production.[21] It is this social network of literate
cultural producers that we should examine in our scholarship, aiming for

---

[19] On Christian exceptionalism, also see Maia Kotrosits, *Rethinking Early Christian
Identity: Affect, Violence, and Belonging* (Minneapolis: Fortress Press, 2015), passim.

[20] As I will explain, cultural elitism does not necessarily correspond to social and economic
privilege in Greco-Roman antiquity.

[21] Here I am invoking the language of Pierre Bourdieu, which features prominently in
Chapter 3.

descriptions that are both practical and plausible given the kinds of social engagement and expertise we know to be typical of such specialists. To be clear, I am not advocating that we exchange one "community" (a gospel community of early Christians) for another (a community of writers); rather, I am offering a critique of how the term "community" has been ascribed to these particular writings historically. Moreover, the social formations of readers and writers that I describe, and for which I offer abundant evidence, are not the idealized communities of the Romantic imagination. I replace a notion of community that lacks effective utility in social analysis, and is supported by little or no historical evidence, with a model widely deployed in historical and sociological scholarship.

Likewise, the rhetorical claims, themes, and narrative structure of the Synoptic gospels are artifacts of certain traditions of imperial-age *literature*, and not evidence of their reliability and "incomparable uniqueness" as religious texts.[22] It may no longer be novel to say that the gospels were not sui generis literature in the first and second centuries, but this has not stopped the field from largely treating them – and their authors – as if they are exceptional.[23] To illustrate this point, apropos of Jefferson, we know that the gospel writers are heavily influenced by the Middle Platonists, Stoics, and other popular philosophies of the period; yet philosophical terminology and allusion (e.g., *eidos, pneuma, logos, pistis*) are still often translated with Western Protestant Christian theological vocabulary (e.g., "spirit").[24] We know that attributing authorship to divine forces or authorial anonymity are common rhetorical habits in this period, but when this occurs within the gospels, the tactic is associated with the adaptation of an oral tradition, memory, or "collective authorship."[25] We know Greek and Roman authors routinely offer fanciful paradoxographical or topographical descriptions of their subjects in order to indicate (most often falsely) firsthand knowledge; for the gospels, these references are often taken as literal in some measure (e.g., contact with

---

[22] Stanley K. Stowers, "Kinds of Myths, Meals, and Power: Paul and Corinthians," in *Redescribing Paul and the Corinthians*, ed. Ron Cameron and Merrill P. Miller (Atlanta: Society of Biblical Literature, 2011), 105–14, cit. 105.

[23] For more on the history of this tendency in the field, see Marchand, *German Orientalism in the Age of Empire*, 252–91.

[24] See Jennifer Eyl, *Signs, Wonders, and Gifts: Divination in the Letters of Paul* (New York: Oxford University Press, 2019).

[25] Larsen, *Gospels before the Book*, 11.

"eyewitnesses" in Luke's preface).[26] Scholars have long noted parallels between the canonical gospels and works like the Greek novel or the *Satyrica*, including the shared *topoi* of ritual anointing, crucifixion, a disappearance off the cross, a cannibalistic fellowship meal, (implied) resurrection, and the motif of the empty tomb; yet comparisons between these ancient *corpora* are few and far between.[27]

Our narrow approaches are largely a function of the subsequent use of the gospels as documents of Christian origins. Others have described this inclination as the New Testament's domination by the "internal perspectives of Christian theology" or "academic Christian theological modernism."[28] Because Christianity has exerted such a strong influence on Western politics, philosophy, and ethics, there is a tautological tendency to view the so-called early Christians as being "just like us." This view was concretized by scholarly practices like *Religionsgeschichte* and the idea that the gospels represent a retrievable and embedded "folk culture" – that the gospels are texts written "by and for the people," so to speak.[29] Whether conscious or habitual, this interpretive anachronism unmoors New Testament writings from their historical context in service of later theological needs. As a result, we perpetuate a still-extant mythology about the rapid institutionalization, diversity, cohesion, and unparalleled origins – the "Big Bang" – of the Jesus movement. We also reach for details on the social world of a community of people – early Christians – not sustained in the text, while functionally ignoring the one social network we can concretely examine from a historical standpoint, that of ancient writers. I discuss these issues of translation and interpretation further in Chapters 1 and 2.

Such readings are reinforced when a work lacks literary refinement, thus inviting associations between it and the interests of nonliterate practices or social formations (e.g., oral tradition and "churches") or obscure or particularized forms of writing (e.g., *hypomnēmata*). These kinds of associations may well be category mistakes born of modern

---

[26] On the generic conventions of ancient approaches to geography, see, e.g., Richard F. Thomas, *Lands and Peoples in Roman Poetry*, Cambridge Philological Society Supp. Vol. 7 (Cambridge: Cambridge Philological Society, 1982).

[27] Notable exceptions: Ilaria Ramelli, "The Ancient Novel and the New Testament: Possible Contacts," *Ancient Narrative* 5 (2007): 41–68; Richard I. Pervo, "Wisdom and Power: Petronius' *Sat.* and the Social World of Early Christianity," *Anglican Theological Review* 67 (1985): 307–25; Sławomir Poloczek, "Pusty grób Kalliroe i Chrystusa," *U schyłku starożytności - Studia źródłoznawcze* 13 (2014): 9–32.

[28] Stowers, "Kinds of Myths," 106.

[29] Marchand, *German Orientalism in the Age of Empire*, 269–70.

assumptions about class and economics that do not correspond with the ancient world. To argue that literacy is directly related to class in antiquity is itself something of an anachronism; high education and knowledge of *paideia* did not necessarily correspond to economic or social standing as we understand these categories today. As demonstrated by the satirical *deipnosophistae* or the *Satyrica*'s Trimalchio, participation in dominant literary culture did not guarantee that one possessed the ability to read and write. Likewise, one did not necessarily require wealth, high class, or even free status to be a literate cultural producer, as was the case with Epictetus, a former slave. And certain genres of writing (e.g., *commentarii*) are not firm predictors of the education, relative skill, or elitism of an author.[30] Thus, scholars who speculate that the gospels clearly represent collective authorship, memoranda, or the work of less-educated or socially marginal writers are speculating beyond the limits of our evidence. More often than not, these interpretations take the gospels' descriptions of the humble, illiterate masses, rural non-elites, and imperial resisters as representative of the prototypical "early Christian." That the gospel writers might actually represent Roman literary elites writing about supernatural interests and foreign and bucolic landscapes and peoples seems contrary to how we have imagined Jesus' followers for millennia. But this idealized version of the early Christian story confuses the subject matter of the gospels with their authors.

In a similar vein, certain rhetorical approaches deployed in the gospels contribute to the notion that they are somehow exceptional. These writers tell us that Jesus is divinely authorized through his birthright, teachings, and wonder-working as a son of God – a powerful figure, even if a social underdog. He is portrayed in turns as a riddler and purveyor of esoteric knowledge or an ethical teacher and miracle-worker. And, unlike the notable statesmen, poets, and philosophers who populated civic biographies, Jesus' extraordinary wit and otherworldly superpowers reveal his authority and status. In combination, these features communicate that Jesus is an unparalleled figure and suggest that the gospel genre is an innovative departure from previous literary forms. Yet when compared

---

[30] See Richard Last, "The Social Relationships of Gospel Writers: New Insights from Inscriptions Commending Greek Historiographers," *Journal for the Study of the New Testament* 37, no. 3 (2015): 223–52, and Andrew M. Riggsby, *Caesar in Gaul and Rome: War in Words* (Austin: University of Texas Press, 2006), 134: "One of the most striking things about the *commentarius*, in contrast to most literary genres of antiquity, is its wide range of authorship. Known writers are spread broadly in time, space, and social status."

with other first-century literature, the Jesus of the gospels can be fruitfully compared with the Cynics, Aesop, the pastoral heroes of the Greek novel, or witty underdogs in the biographical tradition, the subject of Chapter 5. Moreover, many of the *topoi* used by the gospel writers convey Jesus' special standing, but they do so through familiar literary allusions – the empty tomb, for instance, is found throughout Greek and Roman literature and material culture (e.g., the novel and numerous paradoxographical fragments) to indicate supernatural status. Even strategic omissions, like anonymity, are common tricks of the trade among imperial writers and can be understood without associations with memory traditions or communal authorship, as I discuss in Chapter 4.

It is certainly the case that the gospels present strong ideas about certain kinds of social formations – including communities of disciples and *ekklēsia*. If one takes for granted that these groups correspond with the author's social world in some measure, then it is little wonder that the field devotes so much attention to the idea of "Christian communities." Traditional approaches to the Synoptic gospels are instructive. The explosive growth of early Christianity in Luke is often taken as descriptive, not apologetic. Matthew lacks the same focus on institutionalization and rapid growth, but his sustained interest in group dynamics and an ideal Israel are taken as evidence of his lived aspirations. Mark makes an interesting contribution to this paradigm in that his ornery Jesus is more often misunderstood than revered; his account offers little in terms of communities and rapid institutionalization – this is, after all, the gospel that originally ended with the women fleeing from Jesus' empty tomb, bewildered and afraid, saying "nothing to anyone" (οὐδενὶ οὐδὲν εἶπαν; Mark 16:8). Yet discourse about communities and related early Christian social formations routinely get projected back onto Mark (e.g., the Markan "community of the new age"),[31] thus revealing the idiosyncrasies of

---

[31] See Howard Clark Kee, *Community of the New Age: Studies in Mark's Gospel* (Macon: Mercer University Press, 2000). Dwight N. Peterson illustrates this confusion well in the case of the gospel of Mark: "Mark's community has not yielded a controlled field of interpretation. The reason for this is that virtually every scholar who discovers a Markan community behind the gospel – that is, the community for which the gospel was written, and which is supposed to serve as a control for a reading of Mark – discovers a different Markan community. The community behind the Gospel of Mark lived either before 70 [C.E.] or after 70 [C.E.], either in the tense times leading up to the destruction of the temple or in its immediate aftermath. It lived in Rome, or in Galilee, or in Southern Syria. It was a Gentile community, or a mixture of Jews and Gentiles or a Jewish community. Its interests were primarily to establish itself in opposition to a discredited Jerusalem Christianity ... to forge a new, apocalyptic community ... to steer a mediating political

the community-reconstruction method. Not every subject explored by an author represents something concrete about their social experience, but it can be illustrative of their training, interests, and narrative imagination. That the Synoptic gospels also contain similarities in content and subject matter can just as easily indicate competition between individual writers as it does shared memory traditions preserved by disparate groups of Christians. I focus on the Synoptics in this study for this reason.

Eventually placed together in circulation (or, more accurately, canon), the Synoptic gospels helped to construct a cohesive and legitimizing history for Christianity. Accounts of healings, resurrections, miraculous mass conversions, and angelically abetted prison breaks in the Acts of the Apostles fortified this remarkable chronicle of the origins and development of Christianity. Miraculous beginnings and powerful figures communicate a demand to be taken seriously. When laying claim to a storied past, only "august roots" will do.[32] Indeed, Acts' treatment of Paul as the miracle-working apostle to the Gentiles and authoritative founder of a number of early Jesus movement *ekklēsiai* reinforced the idea that early Christianity was institutionally sound and widespread. Paul as figurehead and martyr would carry through later writers such as the authors of the Pastoral Epistles, the Acts of Paul, Marcion, and Irenaeus, despite the fact that Paul's own letters reveal that his activity stood on far more contested ground – in 1 Corinthians, for example, Paul attempts to evoke a sense of unity among his addressees by invoking rhetoric about established groups.[33] It does not follow that this supposed group was, in fact, cohesive. Yet the "churches" and other communities described in Paul and

path between Roman imperialism and Jerusalem hegemony ... to distance itself from Judaism in the Roman imagination because of the recent destruction of the temple ... to forge a new myth of Christian origins out of a variety of disparate traditions ... to explain to Mark's Jewish-Christian community why the temple was destroyed and replace Israel with Mark's Jewish-Christian community in God's plan." See Dwight N. Peterson, *The Origins of Mark: The Markan Community in Current Debate* (Leiden: Brill, 2000), 152.

[32] See William E. Arnal, "The Collection and Synthesis of 'Tradition' and the Second-Century Invention of Christianity," *Method and Theory in the Study of Religion* 23, no. 3 (2011): 193–215, cit. 199: "even modern groups seeking to define themselves and their identity in the *present* do so by inventing or laying claim to an ancestral identity which unifies, identifies, and gives them august (or respectable, or congenial) roots" (emphasis in original).

[33] As the sociologist Rogers Brubaker cautions: "We must ... take vernacular categories and participant's understandings seriously, for they are partly constitutive of our objects of study. But we should not uncritically adopt the engaged *categories of ethnopolitical practice* as our *categories of social analysis*." Rogers Brubaker, *Ethnicity without Groups* (Cambridge, MA: Harvard University Press, 2004), 10 (emphasis in original).

Acts remain *the* model for understanding early Christian social networks in the first century. This includes the authors of the gospels and related writings (e.g., Q, John, the Gospel of Thomas).

Collated and canonized "Christian" writings have come to tell an origin story for the Jesus movement – "instant-aging" Christianity – creating a foundation from which to claim continuity.[34] In other words, writings like the gospels, Acts, and Paul's letters, placed in combination, have invented a tradition.[35] Following a long process of consensus-building, the writings of the New Testament are considered the represen-tative account of Jesus' life, the Jesus movement, Paul's mission, and the founding of the early church. We are aware of the historiographical issues that attend the gospels; few scholars debate that these are documents written at least one or two generations after Jesus' death. Yet even one of the most widely used textbooks in the field places its discussion of the gospels before the letters of Paul, inferring that they represent a reliable history of some kind.[36] Oral tradition theory has helped create a justifi-cation for this approach; if the gospel writers are recording the oral, folk traditions of the early Christians, at least some of these details or sayings must be "genuine."[37] Likewise, if the most formative group for the gospel writer is his community of fellow Christians, then the content of these writings is not unduly sullied by "outside" literary influences or competi-tion. One strategy that helps maintain this thesis is the speculation that the gospel authors are including certain stories or teachings to serve the religious community for which they are presumed to be writing. These approaches read the gospels as particular kinds of social history that have more to do with present interests than the usual processes for writers in antiquity. Uniting these texts into a conceptual whole has also had the effect of creating narrative coherence and a historical trajectory out of

---

[34] Willi Braun, "Schooled Intelligence, Social Interests, and the Sayings Gospel Q," paper presented at Westar Seminar on Christian Origins, Santa Rosa, CA, October 2007, 55. Cited from Arnal, "The Collection and Synthesis of 'Tradition,'" 201.

[35] The phrase "invented tradition" or "the invention of tradition" stems from the work of Eric Hobsbawm, which is discussed further below. See Eric Hobsbawm, "Introduction: Inventing Traditions," in *The Invention of Tradition*, ed. Eric Hobsbawm and Terence Ranger (Cambridge: Cambridge University Press, 2010), 1. I am referencing Hobsbawm in a somewhat narrow sense in this section. For a critique of his larger project and Marxist influence, see Clark, *History, Theory, Text*, 83–85.

[36] Bart Ehrman, *The New Testament: A Historical Introduction to Early Christian Writings*, 6th ed. (New York: Oxford University Press, 2016).

[37] This is the central task of organizations like the Jesus Seminar, which seeks to identify which of these sayings or passages are most likely authentic.

what was otherwise an amorphous beginning. Read through a lens that perpetuates Christianity's own myth of origins, we no longer easily understand the gospels as "normal" ancient literature produced by educated, elite members of Greco-Roman society. The theological and ideological aims of subsequent generations have reinforced that we read these works as affirming community, cohesion, conversion, and stability.

By establishing a more historically plausible context for the writers of the gospels, this monograph opens up numerous possibilities for reimagining their social worlds. This includes offering a more concrete description of their probable writing processes, an expanded view of possible conversation partners within their literary networks (both Christ-followers and not), a broader range of literary *comparanda*, and a new view on how to classify the gospel genre. To this end, I situate these writings within the biographical tradition of Greco-Roman literature, which commonly features a marginal or subversive figure forced to succeed through the use of their wits or wonder-working skills. By bringing so-called early Christian texts into closer conversation with the larger canon of ancient Mediterranean literature and literary practices, my project traverses an artificial divide that has persisted for generations between academic disciplines that study ancient texts. When compared side by side, the *bioi* (lives) written by the gospel authors are no more remarkable than writings like Lucian's *Demonax*, the *Satyrica*, other Greek and Roman novels, or later works like Apuleius' *Metamorphoses* (a.k.a. The Golden Ass), among others. Thus, I illustrate the need for our academic fields to reconsider why we classify certain texts either as part of religious canon or as Greek or Latin classics. Such reconsideration also invites us to examine any data we may have overemphasized or overlooked by implicitly retaining preconceptions about these texts.

This project also considers how New Testament scholarship has arrived at such idiosyncratic conclusions about the gospels and related works when compared with allied studies of classical literature. I begin this investigation by turning to German Romanticism and its influence on the critical study of biblical literature. Much like the efforts of the Brothers Grimm to reclaim a unified Germanic past through the oral stories of the common people or nation (*Volk*), scholars of early Christianity interested in trying to understand the social roots of the Jesus movement have treated the gospel writers like the Romantic Poet chronicling the spontaneous and miraculous origins of a people. I identify the trajectory within the field that has allowed this interpretative model to perpetuate, reaffirming the second-century invention of Christianity featured in texts like Acts and the discourses of the church fathers.

Overall, my critique demonstrates that, if we want to describe accurately the Jesus movement of the first century, new scholarly approaches are needed that focus on the practices, motivations, and social interests of the gospel authors qua authors, not on how these writings are reliable chronicles of the historical Jesus. The following five chapters offer various alternatives to our traditional methods for reading Christian literature. After laying out the problématique in Chapter 1, Chapter 2 questions how New Testament scholars came to read the gospels as records of "oral traditions" about Jesus and argues that, unlike allied fields like classics, they have not yet come to terms with their intellectual inheritance from Romantic understandings of the author. Chapter 3 offers an overview of what we know about Mediterranean book culture and literary networks and demonstrates how a focus on the "habitus" of writers (and away from religious "communities") opens up numerous possibilities for rereading the gospels as imperial literature. Along these lines, Chapter 4 posits that many seemingly unique elements of the gospels are fully intelligible within the context of other first-century Greco-Roman writing strategies. I highlight three features in particular. First, I argue that the gospels' descriptions of Judea engage a familiar literary trope that looks to exotic or bucolic settings to discuss the relative virtues and vices of Roman imperialism. I suggest that this kind of literature often appears in the aftermath of military conflict, which helps explain the emergence of – and general interest in – the gospels following the Judean War.[38] Second, I reexamine several *topoi* central to Jesus' *bios* (e.g., crucifixion, empty tomb, fellowship meals) and establish that they are well attested elsewhere in first- and second-century literature, including the often overlooked *Satyrica*. Finally, I argue that the gospels engage in a certain "anti-intellectualism" that denies traditional *paideia* in favor of supernatural inspiration, offering examples of other writers making similar claims – particularly when their subject matter includes talk of the gods, pastoral or "natural" locations, or rural people. Chapter 5 builds on this approach by mapping out how one can understand the gospels as a form of "subversive biography" that inverts the expectations of civic lives by focusing on social underdogs who get by on their wits and/or

---

[38] This is a subject I explore in more detail in Robyn Faith Walsh, "IVDAEA DEVICTA: The Gospels as Imperial 'Captive Literature,'" in *The Bible and Class Struggle*, ed. Robert Myles (London: Lexington Books, 2019), 89–114.

wonder-working, rather than military strength or brawn (e.g., *The Alexander Romance*, Aesop). In combination, these literary strategies help us understand why the subjects of Judea, Judaism, Jesus, and his death were interesting to imperial writers and ultimately compelling to a broad audience – without invoking the language of (or assumptions about) Christian communities.

PREMISES AND DEBTS

Any study that combines close reading of primary texts with metacriticism of its field is charged with certain influences and assumptions. Among the various premises that this project takes for granted, a few stand out that may strike my readers as somewhat unusual. First, because I am advocating for an approach to these writings and history that foregrounds concrete data without appealing to inherited assumptions and methods to "fill in the blanks," this monograph accounts for Christian beginnings from the perspective of Occam's razor: What is the simplest solution given the evidence we have at our disposal? This approach includes consciously limiting ourselves to analysis and comparison using what is patently in front of us without aspirational appeals to imagined communities, diversity, social formations, and processes. For the gospels, we have knowledge of Roman writing practices, the relative education levels and social networks of writers, and we have Greek texts written during the imperial period. Therefore, I treat the gospels as one would any other literature of this era.

Given the above, I focus almost exclusively on evidence for education and writing practices from elite Roman book culture. This decision is largely due to the fact that we do not have enough extant evidence for educational training from outside this cadre (e.g., among Pharisees) without appealing to much later material. Historians of education tend to rely on the accounts of Quintilian, Seneca, Pliny, and Plutarch to help reconstruct these practices. My study does not diverge substantially from this data set, although I do, on occasion, turn to Paul and Philo as "case studies" in order to add their literary activities to a body of evidence from which they are traditionally excluded. I also cite data from material culture in order to contextualize the technical processes of writing. I maintain throughout that we must not confuse elitism with social capital per se – as noted previously, there is no firm connection between education and class in antiquity. Many of our extant authors were, in fact, slaves, freedmen, or born into humble circumstances (e.g., Antisthenes, Cleanthes, Epictetus); similarly, many figures with high status were what we might term illiterate (e.g., Tiberius' astrologer, the oracle at Colophon). In this respect, when I speak of "elite cultural producers" or "literate cultural producers," I do not necessarily mean the ruling classes or aristocracy in the strictest sense.

Ultimately, my goal is to offer a more thoroughgoing account of what it took to be able to read and write in the imperial period in order to demonstrate that it was a labor-intensive and specialized skill. Recognizing literacy and the production of literature in this manner also helps avoid the false impression that I am projecting onto the past the assumptions and models of the present; in other words, I am aware that the networks of writers I am proposing look, to some extent, suspiciously like the educated elites, professionals, and academics who are of a background and disposition to be interested in this subject and this book. Literacy, specialization, and the ability to publish may have been the purview of few, statistically speaking, in the ancient Mediterranean world, but the composition of a literary network had the potential to be as socially diverse as the model found in the fanciful Scipionic Circle: a former slave and his charges, an educated solider, interested members of the aristocracy, a competitive playwright, and a Stoic. Unfortunately, our ability to reconstruct the exact contours of the literary circle of the gospel writers is fraught with some difficulty. This leads me to my second caveat.

I understand the gospel authors as creative writers dynamically engaging with their subject matter; they are not biographers or historians as we understand the categories today. As such, there is only so much we can determine in terms of their motivations, conversation partners, audiences, and so forth. What I offer here are educated guesses as to their social location and sources, but I am also content with the possibility that we are limited in what we can reliably know or reconstruct. This means I will not be speculating about these writing groups beyond what we know was typical for the age and what the gospels themselves reveal about known *topoi*, rhetorical strategies, vocabulary, and so forth. Such ambiguity may strike some of my readers as uncomfortable or unfulfilling – particularly for a field largely built on attempting to reconstruct "origins," as I discuss in my Preface. For example, when I argue in Chapter 4 that the author of the *Satyrica* is a member of Pliny's intellectual circle and perhaps aware of Christians and/or the Synoptics, I do not insist that this is the only way to read the *topoi* that these sources share. Given the current state of what survives, and what we know about the dating of these texts, it is futile to make a firm determination in one direction or another. I endeavor not to stretch these works beyond what the evidence allows. This includes being extremely cautious about not replacing speculation about one group (i.e., "the Christian community") for another (i.e., "networks of authors") without justifying my position on the basis of available historical data.

Moreover, when I scrutinize categories like "religion" or "community" it does not signal that I think these concepts are not useful to us or must be disregarded entirely. When I describe religion as a second-order category in Chapter 1, I do so in order to demonstrate that religion, when clearly and discretely defined, can help us avoid zero-sum understandings of social practices like writing about supernatural subjects (e.g., the gods or their sons). Writers need not be a part of a religious community in order to write about Jesus, for example, but they must be a part of a social network that is in a position to circulate or publish their works. Whether such a network also counts among its members what we might call "Christians" in part or in full is something the field will continue to interrogate. What I am proposing is that we step away from assuming that hypothetical *religious* communities are the sole or most formative influences on our authors, particularly given what we know about writing practices. Similarly, I do not have a problem with the term "community" per se. What I resist is the conceptual baggage we have inherited from German Romanticism that tends to associate the gospel writer's "community" with religious, illiterate, and socially marginal *Volk* like the characters that populate the gospels themselves. I map this inheritance, its fault lines, and its perils in Chapter 2. Thus, what I am proposing are alternative social networks that take the elite cultural producers who were necessarily a part of the production of the gospels into account. Redescribing the gospels not as folk tradition but as normal ancient literature opens us up to an entirely different history for these texts, one grounded in data, not theological hope.

On the subject of terminology and classification, my readers will also note that I use the terms "writer" and "author" (and their variants) more or less interchangeably. A recent move in the field questions the degree to which the term "author" is anachronistic. These critiques suggest that "the author" is a modern category born of assumptions about the degree to which any piece of writing is considered "bound" or "finished"; thanks to the printing press, we possess a contemporary bias for "the book" and see all forms of writing through this prism when there are ample examples from antiquity of unauthored or "less finished" forms of writing.[39] Inspired by poststructuralist anti-authorialism, "the author" is considered a construct and distinct from the writer – writers perform acts of writing while the author is a product of discourse. Directly related to the "death of the author" debate of the twentieth century, this approach has been roundly critiqued within literary theory for the ways it wrests agency away from the author as a rational actor, foregrounding the reader and language in the process, and ultimately attributing authorship to amorphous and fuzzy signifiers like *audience, readers, communities, culture*, or to later redactors who are still not properly *authors*. I critique this approach in Chapter 2 when I discuss how the "death of the author" debate reinforces the Romantic idea of the author-genius as the mouthpiece of the collective and reinforces the notion that cultures write texts, not people. In short, ignoring the role of the author in a work's composition and reception allows the scholar to create a king worthy of the killing; a lack of specificity about the technical aspects of writing allows the "author" to be replaced with whatever social construct, literary form, or hypothetical audience works best for the scholar's ideal analysis.[40] In the case of the gospels, it allows for communities, redactors, oral speech, and so on to function as the primary authorial agents. Consequently, if one assumes that something like oral speech is responsible for the content of the gospels, this will dictate the processes by which the scholar imagines the text in question was created (e.g., recorded memory tradition). It is a distinction without a difference from the usual approaches employed in early Christian studies that evoke communities as authors.

Also, because I am challenging what I term "Christian exceptionalism" in this book, I do not capitalize the word "gospel" unless in direct reference to the name attributed to a specific piece of writing (e.g., the Gospel of Mark). This move consciously violates the recommendation of a number of style guides that indicate that the term be lowercase only in reference to the literary genre; however, not emphasizing these works in

---

[39] Eva Mroczek, *The Literary Imagination in Jewish Antiquity* (New York: Oxford University Press, 2016); Larsen, *Gospels before the Book*, which relies heavily on the model established by Mroczek. I also discuss Mroczek's work in Robyn Faith Walsh, "Revisiting Paul's Letter to the Laodiceans: Rejected Literature and Useful Books," to appear in volume dedicated to François Bovon, ed. Brent Landau et al. (Tübingen: Mohr Siebeck), forthcoming.

[40] See Seán Burke, *The Death and Return of the Author: Criticism and Subjectivity in Barthes, Foucault and Derrida*, 3rd ed. (Edinburgh: Edinburgh University Press, 2010), 25.

any way that reinforces that they are set apart or intrinsically unique is at the core of my methodology and literary analysis. In most cases the term "gospel" will refer to the Synoptic gospels (my primary object of study).

Finally, this monograph represents a new conversation in the field. It is itself a beginning that suggests we can give writings like the Synoptics new life if we are willing to consider influences and social networks outside of religious communities, Christian history, collective memory, and the like. Remaining attentive to how and why we have made assumptions about communities helps us see past the accretions that faith, tradition, and inherited interpretation have deposited onto these materials. Such attention permits us to reassess the gospel writers on their own terms – what Jefferson illustratively described as seeking "diamonds in a dunghill." By incorporating these writings back into the panoply of ancient Mediterranean literature and practice, our future directions are bountiful.

I

The Myth of Christian Origins

Truly it is a good thing to have heard a bard (ἀοιδοῦ)

Such as this, resembling the gods in voice (θεοῖς ἐναλίγκιος αὐδήν).

For I say there is no more graceful end (τέλος χαριέστερον)

Then when joy (εὐφροσύνη) holds the entire people (δῆμον),

And guests (δαιτυμόνες) throughout the halls listen to a bard,

Sitting in rows, and the tables beside are filled

With grain and meat, and the cupbearer (οἰνοχόος), drawing wine

From the mixing vessel (κρητῆρος) carries it about and pours it into cups.

This seems to me the most beautiful (κάλλιστον) of things.

(*Odyssey* 9:3–11)

Analyzing Odysseus' speech on the art of poetry, Bruce Lincoln suggests that the "ideological justification and idealized self-representation" embedded in the speech's meta reflection is "a myth about myth: a story poetry tells about itself as a means to define, defend ... romanticize ... legitimate, exaggerate, mystify, modify and advance its own position."[1]

---

[1] See Bruce Lincoln, *Theorizing Myth: Narrative, Ideology, and Scholarship* (Chicago: University of Chicago Press, 1999), 21. For a more in-depth examination of ancient discourses on poetry, see Peter T. Struck, "The Genealogy of the Symbolic," in *Birth of the Symbol: Ancient Readers at the Limits of Their Texts* (Princeton: Princeton University Press, 2004), 1–20. Struck also addresses the influence of Romanticism on contemporary understandings of poetry and allegory in "The Symbol among the Romantics," in *Birth of the Symbol*, 272–77.

The concept of myth is multivalent; however, Hesiod's meaning of *mythos* is instructive: "an assertive discourse of power and authority ... to be believed."[2] Whether from the edge of Thomas Jefferson's razor or Acts' portrait of the first century, *mythos* on the history – and prehistory – of early Christianity is ideologically freighted.[3] If the gospels and Acts function as myths that Christianity tells about itself, scholars must be careful not to reinscribe those myths as history. Or, as Lincoln irreverently states in his epilogue: "If myth is ideology in narrative form, then scholarship is myth with footnotes."[4]

One idealized representation of early Christianity that is continually retold is that there were no authors before the second century CE. That is to say, scholarship on early Christianity tends not to ascribe autonomous authorship to writers until the second century. For first-century CE texts like the Synoptic gospels, authorship is often described using the language of community.[5] Even if an individual writer or redactor is acknowledged, the author is imagined to be functioning within and for a group of fellow Christians akin to the illiterate and socially marginal Christ followers found in the gospels themselves. In such scholarship, these so-called primitive Christians are remarkably cohesive and uniform in their concerns: the apocalyptic Markan community living in exile, the Jewish-Christians in Matthew breaking with the local synagogue, the Lukan community's loyalty to Paul.[6] The collective memories – the oral traditions – of these groups are recorded by their spokespersons and reinforced in each gospel with talk of ideal social formations or presuppositions about cohesion. Rarely considered are the technical and

---

[2] Lincoln, *Theorizing Myth*, 17.

[3] My reference to Thomas Jefferson here recalls my Introduction.

[4] Lincoln, *Theorizing Myth*, 209.

[5] Because the community approach is so pervasive, it would be tedious to list multiple examples. Some useful representative pieces that discuss this problématique (with bibliography) include John G. Gager, *Kingdom and Community: The Social World of Early Christianity* (Englewood Cliffs: Prentice-Hall, 1975); Dwight N. Peterson, *The Origins of Mark: The Markan Community in Current Debate* (Boston: Brill, 2000), esp. chapter 5, "What Gospels Do: A Critique of Markan Community Construction," 151–94; Erin Roberts, *Emotion, Morality, and Matthew's Mythic Jesus* (Oxford University Press, forthcoming); Richard S. Ascough, "Matthew and Community Formation," in *The Gospel of Matthew in Current Study: Studies in Memory of William G. Thompson*, ed. David E. Aune (Grand Rapids: Eerdmans, 2001), 96–126; Luke Timothy Johnson, "On Finding the Lukan Community: A Cautious Cautionary Essay," in *Contested Issues in Christian Origins and the New Testament: Collected Essays* (Leiden: Brill, 2013), 129–43.

[6] The concept of the "primitive Christian" is discussed at length in Chapter 2 with examples from scholarship.

practical processes involved in producing literature in the imperial period – at least, apart from justifying the existence of these imagined communities. Prevailing Roman book culture dictates that the gospel writers were educated elites working within social networks of similarly positioned cultural producers. And the content of their writings reveals deep engagement with contemporary literary tropes and trends of that book culture, not the common "traditions" of an unacknowledged religious community.

This chapter reexamines this pervasive "community" framework for understanding the social world of early Christianity. Sometimes referred to as the "Big Bang" theory of Christian origins, it is characterized by three predominant assumptions: that the early Jesus movement grew explosively, that it was well established institutionally, and that its followers comprised almost miraculously bounded communities.[7] Different early Christian texts have contributed to this (modern) myth of the early Christian Big Bang. However, this vision of the early Christian landscape reaches an apex with Acts and its origin story, detailing the miraculous founding, growth, and development of the Jesus movement.[8] The approach I outline in this chapter proposes an alternative to the Big Bang model. I begin by "rectifying our categories," which is to say, I reexamine

---

[7] Some scholars who have used this terminology include N. T. Wright, *The New Testament and the People of God* (Minneapolis: Fortress Press, 1992), 452; Burton L. Mack, "On Redescribing Christian Origins," *Method and Theory in the Study of Religion* 8 (1996): 247; Michael F. Bird, "Sectarian Gospels for Sectarian Christians? The Non-Canonical Gospels and Bauckham's *The Gospels for All Christians*," in *The Audience of the Gospels: The Origin and Function of the Gospels in Early Christianity*, ed. Edward W. Klink III (London: T&T Clark, 2010), 32; John S. Kloppenborg, "Greco-Roman *Thiasoi*, the *Ekklēsia* at Corinth, and Conflict Management," in *Redescribing Paul and the Corinthians*, ed. Ron Cameron and Merrill P. Miller (Atlanta: Society for Biblical Literature, 2011), 189. While each of these scholars uses the term "Big Bang," they do not all use it in the same way that I do in this chapter.

[8] The origin story of Acts is adapted and perpetuated by the Pastoral Epistles, Irenaeus, and others. Later leaders within the church would construct a similar kind of "miraculous founding" using stories of violence and martyrdom against early Christians. Tales of the Great Persecution were a mechanism for reconsidering (and amplifying) the role of "the Church" within its own early history. Moreover, self-styled historians such as Eusebius, claiming to rely on eyewitness accounts, chronicled the unjust persecution of emperors and other leaders, mobs, and rogue citizens against early Christians in order to herald the bravery, virtue, and obedience of these martyrs. For a recent study on these issues, see Candida Moss, *The Myth of Persecution: How Early Christians Invented a Story of Martyrdom* (New York: HarperCollins, 2013).

scholarly vocabulary on the subject of early Christian social formations.[9] I also examine the notion of "invented tradition" in more detail with an analysis of the influence of second-century texts like Acts on our understanding of Christian origins.[10] This examination leads into a discussion of Paul and the shortcomings that attend adopting his "categories of ethnopolitical practice as our categories of social analysis" for the study of early Christianity.[11] Finally, I propose that our modern adaptation of the mythic Big Bang of Christian origins is informed, in part, by Romantic-era thinking on the inspired folk speech of primitive communities, which is also the focus of Chapter 2.

RECTIFYING OUR CATEGORIES: TERMINOLOGY, VOCABULARY, AND ANACHRONISM

Without attention to the motivations and operational categories of those who interpret early Christian writings, the field risks uncritically adopting

---

[9] "Rectifying our categories" involves a careful description of one's subject, divorced as much as possible from adopting traditional, and potentially misleading, *doxai*; comparison between the object of study and similar social phenomena from other time periods and/or cultural contexts, allowing similarities and differences to reveal further detail; a redescription based on the description and comparison performed that reflects on the seemingly simple questions the object of study evokes (e.g., what kinds of meals are Jesus people engaging in); and, finally, an approach that acknowledges that language is not disinterested and our descriptive terms require (re)examination. See Smith, "On the Origin of Origins," 1–35; Burton L. Mack, *The Christian Myth: Origins, Logic, and Legacy* (New York: Continuum, 2001), 70–74; Stanley K. Stowers, "Kinds of Myths, Meals and Power: Paul and Corinthians," in *Redescribing Paul and the Corinthians*, ed. Ron Cameron and Merrill P. Miller (Atlanta: Society of Biblical Literature, 2011), 143.

[10] Dating Acts to the second century is not uncontested, with some scholars dating it to the late first century. I follow the arguments of Arnal and others, who suggest that Acts demonstrates a familiarity with the later works of Josephus, as well as the Pastoral Epistles and Polycarp, all dated to the early to mid-second century. See Richard I. Pervo, *Dating Acts: Between the Evangelists and the Apologists* (Santa Rosa: Polebridge, 2006); Margaret Y. MacDonald, "Rereading Paul: Early Interpreters of Paul on Women and Gender," in *Women and Christian Origins*, ed. Ross Shepard Kraemer et al. (New York: Oxford University Press, 1999), 236–52, cit. 237.

Also, my language in this study takes for granted that "Luke" authored Acts, although this is also contested. Whether or not the same author penned Acts, or an author closely imitated the literary form and style of Luke's gospel, it does not substantially alter my larger observation about the later "invention of tradition" for Christianity's origin myth. For more on the history of Luke circulating with Acts and its attribution to Luke (which begins as early as the late second century), see François Bovon, *Luke 1: A Commentary on the Gospel of Luke 1:1–9:50*, trans. Christine M. Thomas, ed. Helmut Koester (Minneapolis: Fortress Press, 2002), 9.

[11] Rogers Brubaker, *Ethnicity without Groups* (Cambridge, MA: Harvard University Press, 2004), 10.

frameworks that are themselves artifacts of the scholar's milieu and not that of the object of study. Any examination of the ancient world must necessarily include an evaluation of the history of vocabulary – not only the vocabulary of the text in question but also the inherited vocabulary or "language" of Christian theology, the Enlightenment, and post-Enlightenment philosophy that we use to characterize and describe our sources. More than a Gadamerian *Wirkungsgeschichte* that seeks the history of interpretation or effect of biblical texts at particular historical moments, such an approach is part and parcel of a larger project of redescription for the study of religion aimed at demystifying objects of study and treating social phenomena as ordinary human processes.[12] As discussed in the Introduction, we must approach early Christian writings not only as first- and second-century CE Mediterranean artifacts but also as artifacts of eighteenth-, nineteenth-, and twentieth-century European thought.[13] Taking this caution into account entails contending with three interrelated obstacles that impede proper analysis of our historical data: terminology, translation, and anachronism.

Our analyses and descriptions of the ancient world are thrown off course with the use of categories and terminology that are representative of the *scholar's* social world and not that of antiquity. Recalling the Introduction, when Thomas Jefferson makes continual references to the "Platonizing Christianity" of the gospel writers, for instance, he is doing so through a particular lens. This terminology is specific to Enlightenment-era concerns about the Hellenization of early so-called Jewish Christians and Jefferson's own anti-Catholic anxieties. The word "Platonism" acted as a stand-in for "the generic notion of 'heathen' or 'pagan idolatry' or ... that of 'superstition' employed with respect to Catholic cult practices in the early reformers."[14] This anti-Trinitarian fervor led Jefferson to conclude that the teachings of Jesus had been corrupted by "his inept and superstitious biographers," "conniving

---

[12] Hans-Georg Gadamer, *Truth and Method*, 2nd rev. ed. (New York: Continuum, 2004), 300–2.

[13] J. Z. Smith raises this same issue in the case of the "J" and "Q" sources in *On Teaching Religion* (New York: Oxford University Press, 2013), 30. This paradox is also crystallized in the case of the hypothetical saying-source Q; Q is not a first-century CE "Palestinian artifact" but is quite literally an artifact of the late eighteenth and early nineteenth century.

[14] Smith, *Drudgery Divine*, 17.

Platonists," and, later, "illogical Calvinists" and underhanded priests.[15] He bemoans:

> The Christian priesthood, finding the doctrines of Jesus ... too plain to need explanation, saw in the mysticisms of Plato, materials with which they might build an artificial system which might ... admit everlasting controversy, given employment for their order, and introduce it to profit, power, and pre-eminence.... It is fortunate for us that Platonic republicanism has not obtained the same favor as Platonic Christianity; or we should now have been all living, men, women, and children, pell mell together, like beasts of the field or forest.[16]

In short, while Jefferson may have intended to use "Platonic Christianity" as a historical description, the terminology did not exist in antiquity and possessed strong pejorative connotations for Jefferson and his ilk. Even the category of "Christianity" requires analysis – particularly before being applied to sources, persons, or circumstances that do not explicitly claim the moniker (even then, taking such claims for granted is problematic). If scholars fail to recognize the ideological or conceptual baggage that can attend categories like these, it inevitably leads to imprecision and assumption. In many cases, such lemmas are folk designations that cannot be taken uncritically or literally.

Terms such as *origins*, *identity*, *experience*, *ethnicity*, *diversity*, and *community* are among the problematic signifiers that contribute to misleading descriptions of the ancient world.[17] Even *religion* is a fraught analytical category; the way it is employed in scholarship on the ancient world is necessarily anachronistic and is often enmeshed with modern

[15] Carl J. Richard, *The Founders and the Classics: Greece, Rome, and the American Enlightenment* (Cambridge, MA: Harvard University Press, 1995), 189.

[16] Lester Jesse Cappon, ed., *The Adams–Jefferson Letters: The Complete Correspondence between Thomas Jefferson and Abigail and John Adams* (Chapel Hill: University of North Carolina Press, 1959), 433. For more on Jefferson's position on the corruption of Jesus' teachings and its implications for historical study and contemporary Protestant thought, see Richard, "Philosophy," in *The Founders and the Classics*, 168–95.

[17] On the concept of Christian origins, see Mack, *The Christian Myth*; William E. Arnal, "The Collection and Synthesis of 'Tradition' and the Second-Century Invention of Christianity," *Method and Theory in the Study of Religion* 23, no. 3 (2011): 193–215. On early Christian "diversity," see Keith Hopkins, "Christian Number and Its Implications," *Journal of Early Christian Studies* 6, no. 2 (1998): 185–226; Stanley K. Stowers, "The Concept of 'Community' and the History of Early Christianity," *Method and Theory in the Study of Religion* 23, nos. 3–4 (2011): 238–56, cit. 243; Karen L. King, "Factions, Variety, Diversity, Multiplicity: Representing Early Christian Differences for the 21st Century," *Method and Theory in the Study of Religion* 23, nos. 3–4 (2011): 216–37.

ideas of individual experience.[18] This incongruity has to do, in part, with the development of the term in Western intellectual history. A product of Enlightenment-era thinking, *religion* is largely understood in terms of private or personal belief and, thus, discussed as if wholly separate from other spheres of civic, legal, political, or other activity. As such, it has no neat equivalent in the ancient Mediterranean where activities involving the gods and other non-human forces permeated many facets of daily social life. How should one classify, for instance, a binding spell (*dēfixiō*) that fails to invoke any specific deity[19] or haruspices called upon by Rome to interpret a loud noise heard on the outskirts of the city?[20] These classifications are further complicated when folded into questions of ethnicity. Juvenal, for instance, suggests that Judeans will "sell you whatever [interpretation] you want of a dream" (*qualiacumque voles Iudaei somnia vendunt*; Juv. 2.6.540) for a fee.[21] The *Satyrica* and, later,

[18] Approaches to the study of religion (both ancient and modern) that focus on the question of an individual's personal experience have been roundly critiqued in the field on a number of fronts. Among the issues that arise from such studies is the tendency for scholars to treat the question of "experience" as an implicit category. By "implicit category," I mean to say a concept understood to be somehow innate to human beings and, therefore, highly subjective and often described in critical literature with mystifying language such as "belief" or "the sacred." Not only does such scholarship fail to achieve the kind of definitional clarity prized by history and the social sciences, its results tend to lack propositional content, therefore, risking simply reproducing the practitioner's own folk understandings of their activities, rather than treating them as objects of social analysis. See Robyn Faith Walsh, "Religion Is a 'Private Matter,'" in *Stereotyping Religion: Critiquing Clichés*, ed. Craig Martin and Brad Stoddard (London: Bloomsbury, 2017), 69–82.

Also see Wilfred Cantwell Smith, "The Study of Religion and the Study of the Bible," *Journal of the American Academy of Religion* 39, no. 2 (1971): 131–40; Jonathan Z. Smith, "Religion, Religions, Religious," in *Relating Religion: Essays in the Study of Religion* (Chicago: University of Chicago Press, 2004), 179–98. On the anachronistic, Christian importation onto this analytical category, see Talal Asad, *Genealogies of Religion: Discipline and Reasons of Power in Christianity and Islam* (Baltimore: Johns Hopkins University Press, 1993); Stanley K. Stowers, *A Rereading of Romans: Justice, Jews, and Gentiles* (New Haven: Yale University Press, 1994), 26–27; J. Z. Smith, "Bible and Religion," in *Relating Religion*, 197–215; Brent Nongbri, *Before Religion: A History of a Modern Concept* (New Haven: Yale University Press, 2013). On religion as a discursive second-order category, see Stanley K. Stowers, "The Ontology of Religion," in *Introducing Religion: Essays in Honor of Jonathan Z. Smith*, ed. Willi Braun and Russell T. McCutcheon (Oakville: Equinox, 2008), 434–49, cit. 436; Kevin Schilbrack, "Religions: Are There Any?," *Journal of the American Academy of Religion* 78, no. 4 (2010): 1112–28; Nongbri, *Before Religion*, 154–59.

[19] Stephen G. Miller, "Excavations at Nemea, 1979," *Hesperia* 49 (1980): 196–97; *SEG* 30.353.

[20] In 56 BCE a loud boom was heard near Latium; Cic. *Har. resp.* 1.93; 2.26–53.

[21] Juv. 2.6.540.

Apuleius' *The Golden Ass* reference itinerant experts who offer various kinds of specialized interpretations and skills – the little Greek mathematician named Serapa "who knew the secrets of the gods" (*Graeculio, Serapa nomine, consiliator deorum*; Apul. *Met.* 76–77) or Zatchlas the Egyptian who animates avenging corpses (Apul. *Met.* 2.28). Such activities do not take place in conceptual or practical isolation but are a piece of a larger and more complex panoply of social engagement.

One strategy in recent years has been to dismiss the category of religion altogether as a tool for describing ancient data; if the ancients did not participate in activities that fit our contemporary notion of religion, then perhaps religion is not something that can apply to their practices and understandings.[22] But this approach fails to recognize the utility of the term as a category for scholarly use. By focusing on practices, religion can function as a taxonomy for specific kinds of action having to do with the supernatural (e.g., gods, non-obvious beings) and related anthropomorphisms (e.g., ancestors). Theorizing religion along these lines also recognizes it as a kind of human activity with particular contours that can be described and analyzed. Creating such second-order categories permits scholars to assess a variety of social practices in terms of their organization and how they are bundled with one another. In his work on the ontology of religion, Stanley Stowers suggests that "there are an unlimited number of ways that religious practices can connect with other religious practices and practices that are not religious," and the extent to

---

[22] For example, see Brent Nongbri, "Dislodging 'Embedded' Religion: A Brief Note on a Scholarly Trope," *Numen* 55 (2008): 451: "If our reading of the textual and material evidence is correct, what the Romans did was not religion, at least not in the sense that the term is generally used. Ceding this point should in no way lower our opinion of the Romans; it should only reinforce the idea that Romans were different from us in this regard. In spite of this urge to grant the Romans religion, neither the appeals to ancient discussions of *religio* nor an expanded definition of religion is an effective means of claiming that Romans had the modern concept of religion." Nongbri would later soften this approach in his 2013 *Before Religion*. After rehearsing the history of the concept of religion from antiquity to the present, he effectively agrees with the earlier work of Jonathan Z. Smith and Stanley Stowers: "When Stowers writes that 'the definition [of religion] ought to be an explicitly second-order conception,' he seems to me to take for granted something very much like the arguments put forth in this book" (Nongbri, *Before Religion*, 158). He ultimately proposes disaggregating the term "religion" in order to "correspond better to ancient peoples' own organizational scheme … We will end up not with slightly tweaked books on ancient Greek religion or on Roman religion, but with books on Athenian appeals to ancestral tradition, Roman ethnicity, Mesopotamian scribal praxis," and so on (Nongbri, *Before Religion*, 159). Of course, the difficulty with Nongbri's proposal is that terms like "tradition" and "praxis" can be equally contested.

which *religion* is the predominant driver of a particular action would be "a matter of more and less."[23] Thus, an Etruscan haruspex called upon by the ruling elite to decipher an omen would be performing a state-sponsored action as an ethnic specialist in interpreting supernatural phenomena. The degree to which this specialist is performing a religious act would depend on context – again, a matter of "more or less." Exploring multiple social dimensions provides a much more thorough-going and dynamic understanding of our data. Such an approach is also sufficiently flexible so as to engage a range of time periods and cultural milieus, without the ideological and conceptual baggage that can attend studies bound by uncritical scholarly or folk categories of religion.[24]

Applied to the gospel writers, we need not deny that they may have had some firsthand knowledge of individuals or groups associated with the Jesus movement, but this would need to be demonstrated and not assumed. Moreover, any knowledge of or engagement with practices associated with the Jesus movement would need to be held in tension with other spheres of social influence, such as professional or political interests. It is these overlapping spheres of influence, training, and com-mitment that dictate how to account for the content of the gospels and not a vague or exclusive appeal to religious groups.

A theorization of religion along these lines has the additional purchase of revealing how categories of religion are routinely imagined as inextric-ably tied to self-evident and uniform social formations. Language that focuses on putative and bounded social groups has had enormous impli-cations for early Christian studies. In terms of folk conceptions, accept-ance of Christianity's later claims to cohesion is central to its Big Bang origin myth. Acts, for instance, makes continual reference to miraculous deeds inspiring spontaneous conversions – "the great number of the ones having believed (δὲ πλήθους τῶν πιστευσάντων) were of one heart and one mind/soul (ἦν καρδία καὶ ψυχὴ)" (Acts 4:32) – resulting in the rapid development of Christian communities: "Fear (φόβος) came to every mind/soul (ψυχῇ), because many wonders and signs (τέρατα καὶ σημεῖα) were happening through the apostles. And all of the believing ones (πιστεύσαντες) were together and had all things in common (εἶχον ἅπαντα

---

[23] Stowers, "The Ontology of Religion," 444.

[24] For more on religion as an emic category for scholars, see Russell T. McCutcheon, *Critics Not Caretakers: Redescribing the Public Study of Religion* (Albany: State University of New York Press, 2001), 10–12.

κοινά).... And from day to day ... the Lord (κύριος) added to the ones being saved (τοὺς σῳζομένους)" (Acts 2:43–47).

Even if one recognizes the extra-ordinary or fantastic nature of Christianity's founding and development in Acts, the "Christian community" remains a tantalizing prism through which to make sense of passages that employ language about groups. When Matthew invokes references to a chosen *ethnē* ("the kingdom of God will be ... given to a people [ἔθνει] producing the first fruits of the kingdom," Matt. 21:43; "go therefore and make disciples of all people [τὰ ἔθνη]," Matt. 28:19) or Luke speaks of the new Israel and the fate of the *oikoumenē* (Luke 2:1, 4:5, 21:26), it can be difficult to separate these claims from projections of social reality.[25] But the existence of religious groups cannot be uncritically accepted as they may be literary devices or simply aspirational; "what Paul and other writers thought some population had miraculously become and ideally ought to be is not good evidence for actual community."[26] Again, we must resist taking our subjects literally or adopting their self-descriptions as evidence of fact.

Building on this foundation, whenever social groups are invoked as normative in scholarship, we must question why. As with Jefferson's Platonizing Christians, we need to ask where and how we have inherited these terms and typologies. For contemporary studies of the New Testament and early Christianity, we must contend with our propensity for reinscribing classifications that are heavily influenced by German Romanticism. Chief among these is the concept of "community," which is rooted in anti-Enlightenment and Romantic notions of a cohesive *Volk* inspired by the "spirit" or *Geist* of a group's oral teachings. To assume that sources like the Synoptics emerged from the folk speech of established early Christian groups presumes a social environment for these writers that agitates against what is known about ancient authorship practices. It privileges a presumed social formation (religious communities) over an axiomatic one (networks of literate specialists) without demonstrating why such a move is warranted. Moreover, religion is not a matter of "more or less" in this scholarly construction; it is a matter of "only": the author's assumed religious community is the only considered social

---

[25] On Luke–Acts as a "memory theater" for "a new (Christian) Israel," see Laura Salah Nasrallah, *Christian Responses to Roman Art and Architecture: The Second-Century Church amid the Spaces of Empire* (Cambridge: Cambridge University Press, 2010), 117.

[26] Stowers, "The Concept of 'Community,'" 24.

context, leaving more plausible associations – like broad networks of elite cultural producers – largely unexamined.

Related to the question of terminology is the problem of theologically interested vocabulary affecting the translation of ancient sources. Similar to importing presumed or anachronistic social contexts onto historical evidence, translations have the potential to skew our understandings of an author's literary environment and strategic intentions. As a discipline, the act of translation itself presents numerous methodological challenges – this is arguably even more so the case with texts still used in contemporary religious practice. Just as religion can be a matter of more or less, when a word has present theological significance, it can be extremely difficult to divorce the concept from the way it functions in that religious discourse. For example, in recent years the translation of *ekklēsia* as "church" has been roundly critiqued; Jennifer Eyl, for instance, argues the term refers not to cohesive groups in the letters of Paul but the Septuagint's concept of the "day of the *[ekklēsia]*" and the processes by which gentiles are adopted into the kinship of Judea.[27] Such specificity is occluded when texts continue to carry the interpretive freight of subsequent generations. Terms like *ta ethnē* (pagan), *hamartia* (sin), *pneuma* (spirit), *pistis* (faith), and *metanoia* (conversion) are particularly susceptible to historically imprecise and, ultimately, mythologizing translations because of their role in later theological formulae. For early Christianity, anachronistic translations directly affect our understanding of the origins and social development of the Jesus movement. As Eyl explains, there is a great risk of inscribing "a later Christianized understanding of Christian beginnings" when certain kinds of language are treated as self-evident.[28] As such, rectifying or reexamining our categories includes attention to terminology that can reify anachronisms about the breadth and cohesion of those with an interest in Jesus in the first two centuries CE.

Correspondingly, there is no identifiable and stable origin for the movement that becomes known as Christianity. The designation of "Christian" for texts like the gospels is not representative of any social categorization or explicit claim made by the authors of these texts themselves. It is not an emic category, and the writers do not demonstrate a concrete awareness that they are participating in something we might call

---

[27] Jennifer Eyl, "Semantic Voids, New Testament Translation, and Anachronism: The Case of Paul's Use of *Ekklēsia*," *Method and Theory in the Study of Religion*, 26, nos. 4–5 (2014): 315–39.
[28] Eyl, "Semantic Voids," 316.

religion. In fact, many scholars have reasonably concluded that evidence for something like Christianity, distinct from Judaism, begins to emerge only in the second century CE.[29] Thus, it is unclear whether the gospels constitute a representation of Christian beginnings or Christian "origins" in anything but the weakest sense. It is not until the second century that actors invested in developing a coherent tradition for the history of Christianity begin to codify earlier "sources" as Christian. Given this, we must be cautious when using terminology that has the potential to reinscribe the kind of myth of origins found in Acts. By evaluating works like the gospels independent of their later role as narrative tokens of the early Jesus movement, we are able to better locate their content – and vocabulary – within the scope and tradition of Roman imperial literature.

THE INVENTION OF TRADITION

The relationship that develops between writings like the gospels and what comes to be known as Christianity in the second century represents an invented tradition. By "invented tradition," I mean the factitious development of continuity between an institution, state, or other social group and a historic narrative, ritual, symbol, or figure. Invented traditions are designed to link groups to "a suitable historic past"[30] and largely adhere to the following principles: "a) ... establishing or symbolizing social cohesion or the membership of groups, real or artificial communities, b) ... establishing or legitimizing institutions, status or relations of authority, and c) ... whose main purpose was socialization, the

---

[29] For example, Arnal, "The Collection and Synthesis of 'Tradition,'" 193–215.

[30] Eric Hobsbawm, "Introduction: Inventing Traditions," in *The Invention of Tradition*, ed. Eric Hobsbawm and Terence Ranger (Cambridge: Cambridge University Press, 2010), 1. In the case of practices, Hobsbawm describes a repetitive process of "formalization and ritualization, characterized by reference to the past" – for example, the choice of Gothic-style architecture for the British parliament in the nineteenth century and then again in the rebuilding campaigns following the Second World War (Hobsbawm, "Introduction," 1–2). Other examples that appear in his edited volume *The Invention of Tradition* are the institution of the bagpipe and kilt as representative of Scottish heritage following the union of Scotland and England in the early eighteenth century or the reinstitution of the "traditional" English folk carol among "middle-class collectors" centuries after it had remained dormant and neglected; see Hugh Trevor-Roper, "The Invention of Tradition: The Highland Tradition of Scotland," in *The Invention of Tradition*, 15–41. Certain elements of the following argument appeared in an earlier form in Robyn Faith Walsh, "Q and the 'Big Bang' Theory of Christian Origins," in *Redescribing the Gospel of Mark*, ed. Barry S. Crawford and Merrill P. Miller (Atlanta: SBL Press, 2017), 483–491.

inculcation of beliefs, value systems and conventions of behavior."[31] This process of invention seeks to build a legitimizing foundation for present interests through reference to the past, whether that past be the adaptation of a particular ritual action (e.g., the horsehair wigs of English barristers), the elevation of a relatively marginal or subversive figure to the center of an august ancestral inheritance (e.g., Vercingetorix in France), or the reclamation of a previously neglected or forgotten artist or artwork, song, or writing as a representative cultural product (e.g., the collected folktales of the Brothers Grimm in Germany or the paintings of El Greco in Spain).[32] In antiquity, similar attempts at "laying claim" to status by making reference to the past are found in the divine genealogies of Roman emperors, the Atticisms of the Second Sophistic, the post-Aristotelian writings and biographies of Pythagoras, and later rabbinic collections of "oral Torah," to name a few.[33]

The search for Christian origins participates in an invention of tradition. The second century established a legitimizing history through first-century artifacts such as the gospels, letters, and figureheads like Paul and Peter.[34] By pulling these disparate stories, teachings, and characters together into a collective narrative, the compilers and redactors of the second century sought to develop a myth of Christian origins that was sufficiently unifying and novel so as to be worthy of a place among the panoply of already-established Mediterranean intellectual and religious traditions. To fail to recognize these efforts as the strategic maneuvers of later inventors or myth-makers – in other words, to believe Christianity's own myth of origins – is to begin our analyses from a limiting perspective that accepts the first-century Jesus movement as a recognizable and cohesive social formation. This kind of classification is both uncritical and misleading; as William Arnal notes: "we continue to speak and act as

---

[31] Hobsbawm, "Introduction," 9. Also see Pascal Boyer, *Tradition as Truth and Communication: A Cognitive Description of Traditional Discourse* (Cambridge: Cambridge University Press, 1990), vii: "repetition or reiteration of tradition implies complex processes of acquisition, memorization and social interaction which must be described and explained."

[32] On Vercingetorix, see Michael Dietler, "'Our Ancestors the Gauls': Archaeology, Ethnic Nationalism, and the Manipulation of Celtic Identity in Modern Europe," *American Anthropologist* 96, no. 3 (1994): 584–605. On the late influence of El Greco on Pablo Picasso, see Jonathan Brown, *Picasso and the Spanish Tradition* (New Haven: Yale University Press, 1996) and John Richardson, "Picasso's Apocalyptic Whorehouse," *New York Times Review of Books* (April 23, 1987): 40–46.

[33] Arnal, "The Collection and Synthesis of 'Tradition,'" 200.

[34] Arnal, "The Collection and Synthesis of 'Tradition,'" 201.

though 'Christianity' represents a coherent, sensible, and informative classification for *what* we are studying when we study the writings of the New Testament, and this assumption continues to circumscribe what we regard to be thinkable."[35] Among the assumptions authorized by an uncritical acceptance of Christianity's myth of origins is precisely that the "Christianity" of the first century was spontaneous, cohesive, diverse, and multiple.

It is important to pause at this juncture to clarify that there are two distinct but related observations I am making about how tradition is invented for early Christianity and how the concept of community becomes a normative social construction. While the activities and interests of the second century inform how we have come to read the New Testament and other early Christian literature, this does not mean that we are unable to say anything concrete about the first century and, specifically, the social context of the authors of these texts. However, it does require that we disaggregate our approach to this literature from the model of *religious* community that has been so pervasive.

First, there is the active and ongoing process of invention and myth-making that begins in the second century CE. This invention takes place on numerous fronts, including the process of assembling a canon of literature with the joint circulation of certain texts. It also takes place through writings like Acts, which takes the figure of Paul and composes a narrative establishing continuity for the Jesus movement in the aftermath of Jesus' death. This strategy establishes Paul as a "pan-Christian hero":

> Multiple gospels alongside the letters and Acts show that Paul is part of a larger story still, that of Jesus, and specify and elaborate the objects of his "faith." Bringing them all together both domesticates and authorizes the letters, verifies Acts, and interprets the gospels, which in their turn show us that Paul's community organizing and rule-making was *about* Jesus; and so gives us a picture whose whole is greater than the sum of its traditional parts.[36]

This, for all intents and purposes, "Hero-Paul" is not celebrated as a novel interpreter of the scriptures and philosopher. On the contrary: one of his speeches drones on for so long in Acts that he inadvertently kills a man who dozes off and falls out of a third-story window (Acts 20:9). Hero-Paul is a founder, a martyr, and a miracle worker. Biographical

[35] Arnal, "The Collection and Synthesis of 'Tradition,'" 195.
[36] Arnal, "The Collection and Synthesis of 'Tradition,'" 206.

details about the man function as meditations on Paul's virtues and vices, explicated through minor details.[37]

More important to the author of Acts is to establish a life of Paul that "domesticates" him.[38] Acts spackles over the messiness of Paul's real-life mission – as evidenced in his letters – and instead offers him a prominent role on par with the disciples in the establishment of the Jesus movement. Acts also applies the Big Bang paradigm to this invented tradition in order to offer an account of the founding and development of "the church" through Paul. Crucially, as Paul was heralded as the founder of Gentile Christianity and its proto-orthodox communities, the idea of "Christian communities" became increasingly normative. And, as other second-century figures like Irenaeus began to circulate the gospels alongside Paul's letters, it added to a synthetic sense of Christian history whereby "[t]wo distinct *anthologies* are ... juxtaposed, each imagined to comment on, and serve as an interpretive filter for, the other."[39] Thus, a reader of the gospels and Acts may turn to Paul's letters and accept that his addressees represented cohesive groups.

Recognizing this second-century invention of tradition helps scholars avoid some of the anachronisms, vague categories, and assumptions that have been the drivers of previous descriptions of Christian origins. The true origins of Christianity are in how its canonical texts were later collated, circulated, and established as authoritative, not in the mythic constructions we find described in the writings themselves.[40] In other words, we should not confuse the aspirations of the second century for

---

[37] Acts demonstrates some awareness of Paul's letters – for example, in its description of his missionary activity (e.g., 2 Corinthians 11 and Acts 9; 1 Thessalonians 2–3 and Acts 17), the role of women in positions of leadership, the names of Paul's "co-workers," and certain linguistic and thematic parallels (e.g., Galatians 2 and Acts 15). Scholars have long agonized over the issue that, if the author of Acts was aware of Paul's correspondence, he often chose to ignore them. See, for example, Pervo, *Dating Acts*, 54–55. Also see a review of the debate and substantial bibliography in Joseph B. Tyson, *Marcion and Luke–Acts: A Defining Struggle* (Columbia: University of South Carolina Press, 2006), esp. chapter 1, "The Date of Acts," 1–23. In my estimation, given that the ability to write literature or letters was the purview of so few in antiquity, and given what is evidently the wide circulation of Paul's letters, the author of Acts may have had only a few written materials at his disposal; therefore, I judge that it is reasonable to think that some of Paul's correspondence was among them.

[38] Arnal uses the word "domesticates" in reference to Irenaeus' use of the Areopagus speech in Acts 17:22–31 in *Ag. Her.* 14–15; Arnal, "The Collection and Synthesis of 'Tradition,'" 205, n. 25.

[39] Arnal, "The Collection and Synthesis of 'Tradition,'" 204. Emphasis in original.

[40] See Arnal, "The Collection and Synthesis of 'Tradition,'" 202.

the realities of the first. However, this theoretical approach has its short-comings if scholars fail to hold it in tension with the need to evaluate early Christian literature beyond imagined first-century communities. For example, some have looked to the letters of Paul and, continuing to misunderstand his talk of cohesive social groups as actual and not aspirational, suggest that we must class *all* of his letters as second-century forgeries.[41] In the case of the gospels, others have proposed that we pivot from attempting to speak of specific churches (e.g., the Lukan community, Matthean community, and so on) and instead reimagine the gospels as literature written for "all Christians" throughout the Empire.[42] There has also been a move toward suggesting that the gospels were "less 'bookish' texts" and akin to "memory more than writing" without true authors.[43] Each of these alternative approaches continues to assume a mystified and miraculous beginning for Christianity in which religious communities are regarded as normative, multiple, and cohesive.

Rather than begin by positing a religious community behind these works, a focus on literate practices dictates a new starting point that directly engages Roman book culture. While it is possible that the authors of the Synoptic gospels were associated in some measure with a group of persons either interested or actively participating in practices pertaining to the Jesus or Christ movement (e.g., meeting in assemblies, sharing in eucharist meals, praying together, interpreting sacred Judean texts), this ultimately remains conjecture. That these writings survive at all means that they circulated according to a set of discrete social conditions. Recent work by scholars like AnneMarie Luijendijk increasingly gives us a better idea of what these social conditions may have been, which I discuss further in Chapter 3.[44] With limited literacy rates, limited means of publication, and defined parameters of language and genre, we can speak of the gospel writers' literary networks with some specificity. Evidence for strategic literary decisions is evidence for engagement with particular

---

[41] For example, Hermann Detering, "The Dutch Radical Approach to the Pauline Epistles," *Journal of Higher Criticism* 3, no. 2 (1996): 163–93. This article first came to my attention through Arnal, "The Collection and Synthesis of 'Tradition,'" 203.

[42] Richard Bauckham, *The Gospel for All Christians: Rethinking the Gospel Audiences* (Grand Rapids: Eerdmans, 1998).

[43] Matthew D. C. Larsen, *Gospels before the Book* (New York: Oxford University Press, 2018), 11.

[44] AnneMarie Luijendijk, "The Gospel of Mary at Oxyrhynchus (P. Oxy. L 3525 and P. Ryl. III 463): Rethinking the History of Early Christianity through Literary Papyri from Oxyrhynchus," in *Re-Making the World: Christianity and Categories*, ed. Taylor G. Petrey (Tübingen: Mohr Siebeck, 2019), 391–418.

kinds of expertise and, therefore, particular kinds of interpretive networks. Stowers explains:

In antiquity, only a tiny fraction of the population was literate at all and a much smaller fraction literate enough to write and interpret literature. Networks or fields of writers, interpreters of writings, and readers educated in particular niches of the fields all formed highly specialized social arenas that produced and contested their own norms, forms of power, practices, and products of literacy. Banishing individual persons as writers from the account of Christian beginnings mystifies interests.[45]

Approaching the gospels in this way transforms them from *lives* documenting the theologies of each "church" or "community" into an individual author's account of the last days of a notable philosopher, such as the *Phaedo*, a collection of *chreia* in the style of *Demonax*, a depiction of the figure of Jesus as a teacher of ethics, or a Jesus as an epic hero establishing divine lineage and authority in style of the *Aeneid*, and so on.[46] Attention to the strategic literary decisions of these authors opens up entirely new avenues of investigation that focus on the sort of networks that fostered this kind of literature, not the type of mirror reading onto communities characteristic of Romantic methodologies.

Writing networks are not the social formations that scholars of the New Testament are typically looking for when they speak of seeking Christian origins in either the first or second century. Thus, some questions naturally arise from this approach; chief among them is how to make sense of the groups to which Paul is writing. After all, Paul is our earliest source for evidence of the Jesus movement. Are his letters not evidence that there are some recognizably Christian "communities" in the first century? Paul's letters offer an interesting case study in how assumptions about community have affected scholarship on Christian origins. Acts' "Hero-Paul" elevated him from one among many interpreters of sacred books in a competitive field of first-century religious specialists to

---

[45] Stowers, "The Concept of 'Community,'" 250.

[46] Scholars have already recognized parallels between the gospels and Q and literary forms like *chreiai* or dialogues like the *Phaedo*. What I am proposing is that by disaggregating these writings from notions of church or community, we are better able to consider why the authors of these texts are choosing to engage these particular forms of literature and, thereby, better explore their interests in exchanging these kinds of writings with one another. On Jesus as a teacher of ethics, see Erin Roberts, "Anger, Emotion, and Desire in the Gospel of Matthew" (PhD diss., Brown University, 2010). On Luke–Acts as epic, see Marianne Palmer Bonz, *The Past as Legacy: Luke–Acts and Ancient Epic* (Minneapolis: Fortress Press, 2000).

the founder of Gentile Christianity. However, a reexamination of the rhetoric of group dynamics in Paul's letters reveals that Hero-Paul is also a mythic construction.

"HERO-PAUL": A CASE STUDY

The New Testament, a product of second- and fourth-century development, constructs a myth of origins for Christianity that continues to be immensely influential in both theological and secular circles. The contours of this account are familiar: following Jesus' death, the disciples established the first church, and then, an apostolic mission of teaching and conversion spread the movement rapidly throughout the Empire. This missionizing activity culminated in the founding and development of the so-called early churches. Acts informs this perspective by continually invoking groupist rhetoric.[47] This tandem reading reinforces the idea that the practices, interpretive innovations, and writings of what comes to be known as Christianity emanated from an identifiable, powerful genesis. Implicit in this theory is the premise that Christianity materialized in a manner otherwise unprecedented in comparison with the origin stories of other "new religious movements."[48] Certainly, in order for there to have been thousands converted in a single day, as claimed by Acts 21:20, the growth rate of the movement would have to have been nothing short of miraculous.[49]

A similar account can be brought to bear on the letters of Paul – despite scholarship increasingly recognizing Paul's strategic license in constructing a myth of origins for his audience. While Paul boasts of the numbers of those "in Christ" (Rom. 12:5), it is far from clear that these people share a mutual awareness or acceptance of this designation. What is clear is that Paul was actively engaged in an ongoing struggle, both to obtain authority and to coalesce disparate social actors into a more cohesive unit. Among the many methods in his toolkit were the authority and interpretation of Mosaic law (e.g., Rom. 3–4; Gal. 3), appeals to popular

---

[47] Acts brings this full story together. Paul's letters and Matthew are centrally "organized" by Acts in order to produce this narrative.

[48] I borrow the concept of "new religious movements" from Rodney Stark's work on Mormonism. See Rodney Stark, *The Rise of Mormonism*, ed. Reid L. Neilson (New York: Columbia University Press, 2005). For a comprehensive guide on the history of scholarship on so-called NRMs, see James R. Lewis, ed., *The Oxford Handbook of New Religious Movements* (New York: Oxford University Press, 2008).

[49] Hopkins, "Christian Number and Its Implications," 243.

philosophical motifs (e.g., Rom. 7; 1 Cor. 12), shared narratives on cultural decline (e.g., Rom. 1–3), instruction on the performance of particular ritual actions like baptism (e.g., Rom. 6), requests for sponsorship and funds (e.g., 2 Cor. 9), the use of highly charged conceptual categories such as *ekklēsia*, and moments of pique when news of quarrels and rupture seemingly goad him into invective (e.g., Gal. 3:1). Many of these rhetorical strategies are constituent of Paul's larger project of religious and ethnopolitical group-making. He proposes that God's *pneuma* is intrinsically shared among his addressees, binding them together.[50] The reception of his message appears to have varied. While Paul was corresponding with assemblies that may have self-identified as cohesive, his letters reveal that these associations were dynamic and variable rather than stable and organized.

In his work on estimating early Christian populations, Keith Hopkins avers that "most ancient observations about Christian numbers, whether by Christian or pagan authors, should be taken as sentimental opinions or metaphors, excellently expressive of attitudes but not providing accurate information about numbers."[51] Relatedly, Paul's continual use of language aimed at group formation can be understood as largely performative. When "ethnopolitical entrepreneurs" reify categories like community, assembly, or congregation, it is often in pursuit of *"invoking* groups they seek to *evoke* ... summon them, call them into being."[52] In other words, the deployment of certain categories in the course of constructing new social identifications may be part of a strategy for further fostering such relationships.[53]

---

[50] See Caroline Johnson Hodge, *If Sons, then Heirs: A Study of Kinship and Ethnicity in the Letters of Paul* (New York: Oxford University Press, 2007).

[51] Hopkins, "Christian Number and Its Implications," 243.

[52] Brubaker, *Ethnicity without Groups*, 10. Emphasis in original.

[53] Following the critique of Rogers Brubaker on identity theory, the concept of identity "bears a multivalent, even contradictory theoretical burden" in the academy today (Brubaker, *Ethnicity without Groups*, 35). For instance, in the case of issues of race, ethnicity, and nationality, the term can be a puzzling appellation when it is employed without a clear and defined rubric of complementary meaning and analysis. Some recent proposals for rectifying this issue have suggested using the term "identification," which encourages specificity as to the agents and practices involved in the act of identifying. Both relational and categorical acts of identification, in this sense, are "intrinsic to social life" in a way identity alone is not (Brubaker, *Ethnicity without Groups*, 41). Language, gender, citizenship, and ethnicity would be examples of categorical identifications that call for analysis of the practices or other interplays involved in establishing self-understanding and/or persons or institutions ascribing categorization onto others. This

Paul's coaxing in Galatians 3 is a useful example: chiding his recipients collectively as fools and "bewitched" (3:1, 3), he launches into a series of rhetorical questions that serve as hopeful reminders that they are supposed to be one in Christ, unified by *pneuma*, their "experiences" (*pathē*) and miracles (3:4–5, 26–28). Paul then outlines his myth of origins for Gentiles baptized "in(to) Christ" – namely, that they are coheirs with Christ and adopted into the patrilineal line of Abraham (4:1–7). He is able to draw a new ethnic map for Gentiles that ties them back to a shared ancestor, which emphasizes their mutuality. Attendant practices such as ritual meals or baptism serve to affirm and inculcate these ties further. This newfound affiliation asks that its members recognize a kinship in both genealogy and shared *pneuma*.

Paul also continually emphasizes their participation in a fated, Empire-wide movement as he describes his own mission. In Galatians, 1 Corinthians, and Romans he reminds his readers that he received the gospel from the risen Christ and not from human origins (e.g., Gal. 1:11–12; 1 Cor. 15:1ff.; Rom. 15) and that he has been tasked with winning "obedience from the Gentiles, by word and deed, by the powers of signs and wonders (ἐν δυνάμει σημείων καὶ τεράτων), by the power of the *pneuma*." Moreover, he claims that "from Jerusalem and as far around as Illyricum, I have fulfilled the gospel of Christ (πεπληρωκέναι τὸ εὐαγγέλιον)" (Rom. 15:19). One can see the roots of the Big Bang paradigm amplified by Acts in such passages with their focus on supernatural motivation, exceptionalism, and expansion.

Paul's ethnically coded language demonstrates that individuals are capable of shifting their religious and ethnic identifications according to situational need.[54] For Paul – a religious and ethnopolitical entrepreneur functioning remotely in a competitive field – ethnicity is not a blunt instrument; it is an authoritative frame for achieving cohesion among participants, and one that calls for a sense of shared mind and practice. It does not necessarily follow that he was successful. Participants are capable of ranking their affiliations into hierarchies, establishing varying levels of association, breaking these associations altogether when prudent, or never fully grasping or accepting a message like Paul's.[55]

---

latter "mode" in particular I judge to be exceptionally helpful for thinking about religions.

[54] Hodge, *If Sons, then Heirs*, 118.

[55] Brubaker, *Ethnicity without Groups*, 18; Hodge, "Negotiating Multiple Identities," in *If Sons, Then Heirs*, 117–36.

Even Paul variously calls upon his standing as a *Ioudaios*, a Pharisee, and one among the Gentiles (Gal. 4:3) when doing so proves advantageous (1 Cor. 9:20ff.). With such mutable social ties, it can be difficult to determine when information about a group is representative or rhetorical.

Despite a mounting scholarly awareness of Paul's precarious entrepreneurial undertaking, religious "community" – and the rhetorical implications of that term – remains a common framing for speaking about early Christianity. This can be attributed, at least in part, to our lack of concrete data; Paul's letters arguably represent our best insight into first-century *ekklēsiai*, and therefore, if we want to say anything at all about these associations, it is tempting to engage in an interpretive tautology that relies on Paul.[56] In such cases, his idealized portrayal of his audience as a community bounded by shared *pneuma*, participation in Christ, and moral perfection is accepted as genuine or actual. Scholars who uncritically accept Paul's letters as representative of established groups tend to question why and to what degree these early Christians are following the guidelines of their titular leader. For example, the Corinthian letters are often treated as "poster child[ren] for the danger of divisions in the community" and not evidence that this group was only loosely affiliated.[57] The Corinthians likely never possessed the kind of commonality in mind and practice characteristic of a community. Rather than accept that Paul was only variously successful in his attempts to coalesce those to whom he was writing, scholars often focus on the possibility that "outsiders" inveigled the Corinthians away from Paul's brand of proto-Christianity. This assumption trades on notions of orthodoxy and heresy, the initial acceptance of Paul's message, and spontaneous social organization.[58]

On the whole, the mass conversions and miraculously established churches of Acts tend to receive more scrutiny than Paul's *ekklēsiai*. It is not uncommon to find scholarship pondering the "Christ-believing influencers in the Galatian communities" muddying Paul's message among his

[56] Hodge, *If Sons, then Heirs*, 46, discusses this circular reasoning in Romans.

[57] Stowers, "The Concept of 'Community,'" 243.

[58] A similar point was raised by Iris Marion Young in her feminist critique of the concept of community: "The ideal of community, finally, totalizes and detemporalizes its conception of social life by setting up an opposition between authentic and inauthentic social relations." See Iris Marion Young, "The Ideal of Community and the Politics of Difference," in *Feminism/Postmodernism*, ed. Linda J. Nicholson (New York: Routledge, 1990), 302.

people.[59] In this construction, the Galatians are a formerly strong group that had been sullied by an outsider and made weak, underlined by moments in the letter in which Paul asks "to whom are you bewitched (ἐβάσκανεν)" (3:1) and "who prevented you from being persuaded by the truth (ἀληθείᾳ μὴ πείθεσθαι)"? (5:7).[60] Scholars seeking information about the composition of these communities will ask questions such as to what degree does the group consider themselves Gentile Christian or Jewish Christian. It is also common to find studies that hypothesize the existence of multiple Pauline communities in one location "in communication and cooperation."[61] Even if scholars disavow the aspirational or mythic account of Acts, acceptance of Paul's rhetoric about communities in Galatia – or Corinth, Philippi, and Thessaloniki, for that matter – reinforces the same myth of origins. This misstep with Paul reinforces the perils that attend taking any of our ancient authors literally without pausing to reflect on the strategic function of constructions like "community."

Among the problems with this approach, two concerns are particularly significant. First, as is often acknowledged when noting the occasional nature of Paul's letters, ancient letter writing was an activity conducted by social actors according to particular needs or in response to particular situations. Letters are not simply containers of information. They reflect social hierarchies, contain carefully crafted attempts at persuasion, and follow well-established rhetorical and literary conventions. As such, Paul cannot be spared from scrutiny with respect to the categories he employs in his descriptions of social relationships. Paul's descriptions of the *ekklēsiai* he addresses must be held in tension with his rhetorical claims.

Second, rather than gloss over messy processes like group formation, attention to individual acts – such as writing and what we know about the social networks that involve this kind of activity – provides an opportunity to establish a less mystified and more fine-grained historical analysis. Such an approach is not limited to "normative theological concepts parading as descriptive and explanatory social concepts" but is based on what is customary for the era and subject in question.[62] In the case of

---

[59] Mark D. Nanos, *The Irony of Galatians: Paul's Letter in First-Century Context* (Minneapolis: Fortress Press, 2002), 138.

[60] I am using adapted language from Mary Douglas. On "Group/Grid" dynamics, see Mary Douglas, *Natural Symbols: Explorations in Cosmology* (New York: Routledge, 2003).

[61] Nanos, *The Irony of Galatians*, 30.

[62] Stowers, "The Concept of 'Community,'" 245–46.

Paul, he is one among a number of figures touting themselves as specialists in textual interpretation, divination, and other so-called religious practices. An investigation along these lines would situate Paul in a highly competitive field of self-styled apostles, super-apostles, and so forth, illuminating a dynamic social landscape for the early stages of the Jesus movement in which something like the cohesion of the participants would need to be demonstrated.[63]

DEMYSTIFYING EARLY CHRISTIAN LITERATURE

The gospel writers' interest in social formations – if they possess any such interest at all – does not offer a plausible account of the development of the Jesus movement(s) into what is now called Christianity. Indeed, concerns about the boundaries of normative Christianity are more akin to debates about orthodoxy and heresy that emerge in subsequent centuries of Christian history.[64] A brief survey of Q and the canonical gospels – the texts that traditionally constitute early Christianity's myth of origins – demonstrates very little by which to trace the development of the social practices that must have constituted the institutionalization and spread of Christianity.

The hypothetical sayings-source Q is often cited by scholars as a genesis for the Big Bang, a now-lost source used by Matthew and Luke that may have dated back, in some proposals, to some of the earliest oral traditions of the Jesus movement. There is very little, if any, evidence within Q for concrete social groups. Some scholars attempt to identify community language in passages like Q 12:33–34 and 16:13, which focus on issues of wealth and ethics:

Do not treasure for yourselves treasures on earth where moth and [an insect's] nibbling (βρῶσις) destroy and where robbers break in nor steal, but treasure for yourselves treasures in heaven, where neither a moth nor [an insect's] nibbling

---

[63] See Jennifer Eyl, *Signs, Wonders, and Gifts: Divination in the Letters of Paul* (New York: Oxford University Press, 2019); Heidi Wendt, *At the Temple Gates: The Religion of Freelance Experts in the Early Roman Empire* (New York: Oxford University Press, 2016).

[64] See, for example, Karen L. King, *What Is Gnosticism?* (Cambridge, MA: Harvard University Press), 7: "The writings of the ancient Christian polemicists fostered the search for a single origin based on their claim that heresy had one author, Satan.... Scholars accepted in principle that all manifold expressions of Gnosticism could be traced to a single origin, but they searched for the source in more historical places, like heterodox Judaism."

destroy and where robbers do not break in or steal. For where your treasure is, there will also be your heart (καρδία). (Q 12:33–34)[65]

No one can serve two masters (Οὐδεὶς δύναται δυσὶ κυρίοις δουλεύειν); for a person will either hate (μισήσει) the one and love (ἀγαπήσει) the other, or be devoted (ἀνθέξεται) to the one and disdain (καταφρονήσει) the other. You cannot serve God and mammon (οὐ δύνασθε θεῷ δουλεύειν καὶ μαμωνᾷ). (Q 16:13)

John Kloppenborg describes these passages as focusing on the "hoarding activities of the elite" and suggests that the message behind them is that the "Q folk" – an interesting turn of phrase Kloppenborg repeats frequently – are "not of the urban classes in which the Jesus movement eventually spread, but the villages and towns of the Galilee, where God's actions and reign had everything to do with the basics of life." He suggests that these passages "circulated not among urbanites, but among the rural poor, not in the Gentile cities of the east, but in the towns of Jewish Galilee."[66] Yet he does not explain in detail how this material was circulated among these "folk" or how "this utopian vision was eventually effaced by the editing of Matthew and Luke."[67]

Broadly, Q scholarship has focused on an itinerancy hypothesis, that is, Q's internal "rhetoric of uprootedness" of implied social upheaval.[68] Gerd Theissen, for instance, proposes that "the ethical radicalism of the sayings transmitted to us [in Q] is the radicalism of itinerants" who lived under extreme stress.[69] Theissen's reading of Q was influenced by an

---

[65] Q passages cited from James M. Robinson, Paul Hoffmann, and John S. Kloppenborg, eds., *The Critical Edition of Q* (Leuven: Peeters, 2000). The repetition in this particular passage corresponds with this and other critical editions of Q.

[66] John S. Kloppenborg, *Q: The Earliest Gospel: An Introduction to the Original Stories and Sayings of Jesus* (Louisville: Westminster John Knox, 2008), 97. Emphasis in original. Kloppenborg suggests that "texts such as Q were composed to function more like musical script for performance than a textbook to be read" and that "oral-scribal interactions" account for the transmission of Q to other gospel writers (ix).

[67] Kloppenborg, *Q: The Earliest Gospel*, 96.

[68] William E. Arnal, *Jesus and the Village Scribes: Galilean Conflicts and the Setting of Q* (Minneapolis: Fortress Press, 2001), 157.

[69] Gerd Theissen, "The Wandering Radicals: Light Shed by Sociology of Literature on the Early Transmission of the Jesus Sayings," in *Social Reality and the Early Christians: Theology, Ethics, and the World of the New Testament*, trans. Margaret Kohl (Minneapolis: Fortress Press, 1992), 40. Theissen even goes so far as to suggest that Jesus himself did not intend to establish communities of Christians but to establish a band of "travelling apostles, prophets and disciples who moved from place to place and could rely on small groups of sympathizers in these places." Later Theissen describes these "sympathizers" or, as he also calls them "sedentary sympathizers," in terms that resemble a "community" of Christians, using the Essenes as a comparable example to what he has in mind in terms of their eventual hierarchical construction, leadership, etc. He also

itinerancy thesis within the field that extends back to Adolf von Harnack's work on the *Didache*. Harnack argued that the *Didache* offered a
set of regulations for wandering and impoverished prophets who traveled
from Christian community to Christian community, seeking shelter, food,
money, and other goods.[70] This imagined class of "professionally home-
less preachers of the Christian message" is first encountered with the
"missionary journeys on the part of Jesus' disciples . . . the wandering of
Jesus himself, and Acts and Paul's letters."[71] In other words, it maps the
same kind of explosive beginnings advanced by the Big Bang paradigm.
While these studies attempt to give some idea of the kind of social
formation that may have acted as a delivery system for Q and other
Christian materials, they fail to explain the concrete processes by which
the messages and teachings of these itinerant charismatics and preachers
would have been received and understood, why they would be appealing
in the first place, or how they are then instituted by the supposed existing
communities they encountered, and so forth. Even if one wishes to argue
that Paul's mission and travel support the itinerancy model often associated with Q, Paul's evident struggle to establish cohesive communities
hardly supports the expansive growth and stable formations imagined
by Acts.

Relatedly, Mark's gospel is of little help for those seeking details about
Christian groups. Mark's Jesus is an elusive, ornery figure. A purveyor of
esoteric teachings, Jesus does little to inculcate community – Mark's
emphasis is on secrecy and silence (e.g., "And he warned them not to tell
anyone about him," 8:30). Jesus' own disciples are unable to comprehend
who he is or nearly any of his teachings. This so-called Messianic Secret
greatly troubles those looking to uncover the Markan community behind

---

suggests that these "sympathizers" are banded together by Hellenistic "community
organizers" like Paul; however, he continues to see the activities of the itinerants and
the "community organizers" as fundamentally distinct. See Gerd Theissen, *Sociology of
Early Palestinian Christianity*, trans. John Bowden (Philadelphia: Fortress Press, 1978), 8,
18–21, 115.

[70] Adolf von Harnack, *Die Lehre der zwölf Apostel* (Leipzig: Hinrichse, 1884). Arnal also
identifies the Harnack thesis as a foundation for work on Q. See Arnal, *Jesus and the
Village Scribes*, 14–18.

[71] Arnal, *Jesus and the Village Scribes*, 13. Arnal does not hold the same strong association
to Cynic-like wandering charismatics as does Theissen. He does away with the strict
itinerancy hypothesis and suggests instead that the travel implied by "itinerancy,"
following Kloppenborg, should be imagined more like a morning walk around the Sea
of Galilee than travel across long distances. See Arnal, *Jesus and the Village Scribes*,
71, 94.

the text. Representative scholarship debates how "the gospel grew out of a christological conflict within the church" as Mark attempted to "correct what it considered to be the dangerous or false Christology ... Mark's Christology is a Christology of the cross and is closely related to the title 'Son of Man.'"[72] Such concerns are more characteristic of later debates among church leaders than anything Mark indicates to his readers.

Matthew offers a Jesus who calls for a worldwide mission (e.g., 28:18–20). Matthew is also concerned with *ekklēsia* (e.g., 16:18, 18:17), and his selection of the word *ekklēsia* over *synagōgē* is often cited as evidence of the "Matthean Christians" wanting "to 'differentiate' themselves from Jewish groups."[73] A similar argument is advanced citing Matthew 21:43, with some proposing that Matthew wishes to establish the followers of Jesus as the new Israel. Among other first-century writers, *ethnē/ethnos* is a technical designation; Strabo identifies the Jews as one among four *ethnē* in Palestine, while Josephus and Philo also use the term for the Jewish people.[74] More broadly, it designates "a variety of specialized groups such as guilds and trade associations." *Ethnē* also has precedent in speaking of idealized communities. Plato, for instance, uses *ethnē* in *Republic* 421c to speak of various groups within his utopian city.[75] To ignore these referents and conclude that Matthew is talking about a divide between Judaism and the rise of a new, "truer" Israel is to ignore the function of this term in its milieu and is tantamount to importing issues of orthodoxy and heresy back onto the text.

---

[72] Adam Winn, *The Purpose of Mark's Gospel: An Early Christian Response to Roman Imperial Propaganda* (Tübingen: Mohr Siebeck, 2008), 12. In this chapter, Winn is drawing on the work of a number of notable early Christian scholars and their positions on Mark, including William Wrede, Rudolf Bultmann, and Ludwig Bieler. See William Wrede, *The Messianic Secret*, trans. J. C. G. Greig (Cambridge: J. Clarke, 1971); Rudolf Bultmann, *Theology of the New Testament*, trans. Kendrick Grobel (New York: Scribner, 1951); Ludwig Bieler, *Theios Aner: Das Bild des "Göttlichen Menschen" in Spätantike und Frühchristentum* (Vienna: Höfels, 1935).

[73] Ascough, "Matthew and Community Formation," 113.

[74] See Strabo, *Geogr.* 16.2. Philo's use of the term and its derivative is vast; an excellent resource is *The Philo Index: A Complete Greek Word Index to the Writings of Philo of Alexandria*, ed. Peder Borgen, Kåre Fuglseth, and Roald Skarsten (Grand Rapids: Eerdmans; Leiden: Brill, 2000), 104–5. Also see Nicola Denzey Lewis, "The Limits of Ethnic Categories," in *Handbook of Early Christianity: Social Science Approaches*, ed. Anthony J. Blasi et al. (Walnut Creek: Rowman AltaMira, 2002), 489–507, cit. 496.

[75] Anthony J. Saldarini, "Reading Matthew without Anti-Semitism," in *The Gospel of Matthew in Current Study: Studies in Memory of William G. Thompson*, ed. David E. Aune et al. (Grand Rapids: Eerdmans, 2001), 166–84, cit. 172.

Matthew does not require a religious community to speak of questions of *ekklēsia* or an ideal Israel. Among the source material at Matthew's disposal are the Septuagint, possibly Q, Paul, and Mark. It is evident that one of Matthew's prime objectives is to clarify, via an interpretation of Jewish scripture, the mysteries presented by Mark's obfuscating Jesus. Recent studies on Matthew have also noted that his Jesus can be read through a Stoic lens.[76] Matthew's Jesus is a teacher of ethics who reexamines Judean law and engages in the same kind of intellectual interpretive practices we see among other Judean writers like Philo or Paul. Moreover, it is also quite possible that Matthew received his ideas about *ekklēsia* from his knowledge of Paul. None of this literary activity requires the primacy of a Matthean community. In fact, given the tautological nature of arguments that attempt to read Matthew's language as a portrait of his fellow Christians (i.e., studies that use Matthew's language to reconstruct an imagined community and then interpret Matthew through the lens of that community), reevaluating the literary precedents for his use of terms like *ekklēsia* and *ethnē* reveals that Matthew's group-talk is a rhetorical signpost rather than evidence of literal communities behind the text.[77]

---

[76] Erin Roberts, "Anger, Emotion, and Desire in the Gospel of Matthew" (PhD diss., Brown University, 2010); Roberts, *Emotion, Morality, and Matthew's Mythic Jesus*; Stanley K. Stowers, "Jesus the Teacher and Stoic Ethics in the Gospel of Matthew," in *Stoicism in Early Christianity*, ed. Troels Engberg-Pedersen, Tuomas Rasimus, and Ismo Dundenberg (Grand Rapids: Baker Academic, 2010), 59–76. Interestingly, and as Jefferson's objections attest, the observation that the gospels and Paul had parallels with philosophical movements of the first century was made very early on in historical critical reviews of this literature – albeit in the context of citing the imposition of those paradigms on the original "primitive Jewish Christian eschatology" of the Jerusalem church. See, for example, Rudolf Bultmann, "Primitive Christianity as a Syncretistic Phenomenon," in *Primitive Christianity: In Its Contemporary Setting*, trans. R. H. Fuller (London: Thames & Hudson, 1956), 210, 211: "Christian missionary preaching was not only the proclamation of Christ, but, when addressed to a Gentile audience, a preaching of monotheism as well. For this, not only arguments derived from the Old Testament, but the natural theology of Stoicism was pressed into service."

[77] Although, as I continue to argue, this does not preclude the existence of some kind of "religious" group among Matthew's social network. I simply question the primacy of any such group over other formative associations, like other writers. As noted above, Dwight N. Peterson makes a similar argument concerning the dubious nature of assuming that all potential "communal" references within a text are in reference to a concrete fellowship of Christians, stating that the method overall is aimed at establishing a "means of attaining interpretive control ... in order [for the scholar] to achieve desired results" from the text in question. Peterson enumerates several of what he calls "unjustified assumptions which are entailed within the drive to construct communities behind documents." Of these critiques, three are particularly striking and, in my view, relevant to the broader study

The same observations made about Acts throughout this chapter also apply to Luke. Luke's communal language is wrapped up with its presentation of a larger myth of origins. Luke presents Jesus as a figure akin to other well-known Greco-Roman literary characters and heroes. In many respects, Luke writes "more like a normal Hellenistic author" and, thus, "the idea of something that suggest[s] communal authorship [is] exposed for its oddness."[78] In her work on Luke–Acts, for instance, Marianne Palmer Bonz notes the parallels between Luke–Acts and the *Aeneid*'s efforts to bring "the Augustan present directly into contact with the heroic past." Vergil's epic "incorporated a complex synthesis of patriotic, moral, and religious themes in its mythologizing history of archaic Roman origins and of the divine prophecies that would read their eschatological fulfillment in the Golden Age of Augustan rule."[79] The same themes of genealogy, eschatological fulfillment, cosmic destiny, and mythologizing of origins takes place in Luke–Acts and, for that matter, in Paul's letters. And Luke was not alone in penning a "Hellenized Jewish" epic when considered alongside Philo, Theodotus, Ezekiel's *Exagoge*, and the fragments of an epic poem recorded by Alexander Polyhistor (preserved by Eusebius).[80] While not in meter, Luke nonetheless

---

of the Synoptic gospels and Q: first, that "community constructors" assume to be able to understand an author's psychology, "as if one can reconstruct the intention of an author when one has no information about who the author was, or what that author wrote, other than that abstracted from the document one is reading," cautioning that the "intentionality of a document is not the basis of interpretation, but the result"; second, he denies that one can assume to know the condition of the audience of the gospels and, furthermore, that this audience is "somehow constitutive of the meaning of the text"; third, he proposes that the exercise of attempting to retrieve the historical Markan community, for example, "obscures the interests of the reader of Mark behind a screen of alleged historical 'objectivity.'" This then allows the interpreter to impose on the text any number of socio-historical reconstructions, utilizing preferred methodological devices in order to achieve desired interpretive results. He rightly likens this method to a house of cards that "has the potential to be quite beautiful and complex ... but all one needs to do is to turn on a fan." Peterson, *The Origins of Mark*, 156–61.

[78] Stowers, "The Concept of 'Community,'" 240.

[79] Bonz, *The Past as Legacy*, 23–24. It is important to note that, while Bonz recognizes these parallels, she continues to subscribe to a Big Bang paradigm of Christianity's social development. Interestingly, however, she remains aware of the implausibility of that social model, even if she does not address it directly. Phrases such as "[Christianity's] proclamation had met with a surprising degree of success" and "Equally as stunning as the rapid success of the Christian mission among Gentiles, however, was the finality of the rupture of the church with its religious past" are found throughout her monograph (Bonz, *The Past as Legacy*, 25).

[80] Bonz, *The Past as Legacy*, 27–29.

can be situated within an established genre of foundational epic, *bioi*, and the novel, as I will discuss.

While the subject of this monograph is the Synoptics, it is worth noting that the Gospel of John elicits a dynamic and complex set of discussions about social formations, including references to Samaritans (e.g., 8:48, 52), Pharisees (e.g., 7:45–48, 12:42), and the synagogue (e.g., 9:22, 16:2, 20:19). Scholarship on the imagined Johannine community represented by these references links it to "Paul's Jewish-Christian opponents in Corinth," "the emergence of motifs that had a later flowering in Gnosticism," or "inner-community controversy ... in a period after the conflict with the synagogue had begun to subside."[81] Of the four canonical gospels, John is arguably the gospel least associated with offering an account of the historical Jesus given its more cryptic and difficult teachings. Yet because of its strong presentation of group, it is frequently associated with the historical circumstances of its supposed community. Again, the vast and complex scholarship on this gospel is beyond the scope of this study; its role in evolving debates about the historical Jesus in the Romantic and Victorian eras – and the continued influence of these debates – is arguably a book in and of itself.[82] However, it is notable that John's discussion of social formations does *not* lend itself to a sense of a worldwide movement. Compellingly, John concludes with a reference to the culture of books: "And there are also many other things that [risen] Jesus did which, if every one of them were written down (γράφηται), I think that the cosmos itself could not contain the books that would be written (οὐδ'αὐτὸν οἶμαι τὸν κόσμον χωρήσειν τὰ γραφόμενα βιβλία)" (21:25). With this ending, John invokes ancient writers, not mythic Christian communities. In other words, John reflects on a social activity in which he himself is engaged, not on an account of the mythic beginnings of Christianity.

Bruce Lincoln notes that, much like with religious communities, it is common for those studying myths to associate them with "specific, ethnically and linguistically defined populations" and that this orientation takes for granted that nations, "cultures," and/or *Völker* (depending on the speaker's discourse) are primordial, bounded, unproblematic entities

---

[81] Robert Kysar, "The Contribution of D. Moody Smith to Johannine Scholarship," in *Exploring the Gospel of John: In Honor of D. Moody Smith*, ed. R. Alan Culpepper and Carl Clifton Black (Louisville: Westminster John Knox, 1996), 3–17, cit. 4.

[82] For more on the significance of historical Jesus research at the fin de siècle, see Suzanne L. Marchand, *German Orientalism in the Age of Empire: Religion, Race, and Scholarship* (Cambridge: Cambridge University Press, 2009), 252–91.

and that myth is the equally primordial voice, essence, and heritage of that group. Myth and group are understood to be linked in a symbiotic relation of co-production, each being simultaneously producer and product of the other.[83] Lincoln recognizes that this treatment of myth in contemporary scholarship has roots in the anti-Enlightenment elevation of *völkisch* and the national reclamation projects of men like Johann Gottfried Herder and the Brothers Grimm. These Romantic-era projects possessed a strong political element, aimed at generating a sense of national identification; however, in the process they reinterpreted the myths they selected as the "reinstation of something ancient, eternal, and authentic." Romantic studies on the *Volksgeist* of the German people, James Macpherson's *Ossian*, or Herder's meditations on Shakespeare or the *Geist* of the Hebrew scriptures were myth about myth: "It is not always the case that myths are the product and reflection of a people who tells stories in which they effectively narrative themselves ... myths are stories in which some people narrate others, and at times the existence of those others is itself the product of mythic discourse."[84]

Indeed, Herder and the German Romantics occupy outsized standing in the intellectual genealogy of the study of New Testament and early Christianity. Herder in particular had significant influence over the History of Religions School and a number of the scholars discussed in the Preface: Hermann Gunkel, founder of Form Criticism, and Johannes Weiss, teacher of Rudolf Bultmann, who was the *Doktorvater* of Helmut Koester, who remains a great influence on the field today. In the next chapter, I examine the influence of German Romanticism on our approaches to the early Christian Big Bang and the concept of community. This study reveals that more than a product of Christianity's own second-century invention of its origins, the persistence of the community model within the field has strong, and not always immediately evident, ties to eighteenth-, nineteenth-, and twentieth-century political and philosophical thought. Recognizing our inheritance from the Romantic movement helps us to see how we have arrived at such an idiosyncratic place in our evaluation of the gospels in order to begin to reconsider these writings more properly within their intellectual milieu.

[83] Lincoln, *Theorizing Myth*, 210.   [84] Lincoln, *Theorizing Myth*, 211.

2

The Romantic "Big Bang"

German Romanticism and Inherited Methodology

In August 1837, Ralph Waldo Emerson delivered the annual address of the Phi Beta Kappa Society at the First Parish Church in Cambridge, Massachusetts. Titled "The American Scholar," it was regarded by the Fireside Poet Oliver Wendell Holmes, Sr., as America's "intellectual Declaration of Independence" from Europe, proclaiming the scholar or "Man-of-Letters" to be the principal voice of society writ large.[1] Borrowing imagery from Empedocles, Emerson opened his pioneering oration by musing on the so-called divided Man:

You must take the whole society to find the whole man ... this original unit, this fountain of power, has been so distributed to multitudes, has been so minutely subdivided and peddled out, that it is spilled into drops, and cannot be gathered. The state of society is one in which the members have suffered amputation from

---

[1] A related discussion of Emerson also appears in the open-source journal *Relegere* for a special edition on "Pre-Critical Readers and Readings: The Bible in the Eighteenth and Nineteenth Centuries"; Robyn Faith Walsh, "The Influence of the Romantic Genius in Early Christian Studies," *Relegere* 5 (2015): 31–60. Also see Robyn Faith Walsh, "Q and the 'Big Bang' Theory of Christian Origins," in *Redescribing the Gospel of Mark*, ed. Barry S. Crawford and Merrill P. Miller (Atlanta: SBL Press, 2017), 483–533.

All translations in this chapter are my own unless otherwise noted. The majority of German cited initially appeared in Fraktur typescript; I have occasionally modified spelling to aid in readability.

Ralph Waldo Emerson, "The American Scholar," in *The Annotated Emerson*, ed. David Mikics (Cambridge, MA: Harvard University Press, 2012), 72–92. Oliver Wendell Holmes' quote cited from Mikics, *The Annotated Emerson*, 72. Also see John Patrick Diggins, *The Lost Soul of American Politics: Virtue, Self-Interest, and the Foundations of Liberalism* (Chicago: University of Chicago Press, 1986), 198.

the trunk, and strut about so many walking monsters – a good finger, a neck, a stomach, an elbow, but never a man.[2]

Of this divided man, according to Emerson, "the scholar is the delegated intellect ... [i]n the right state, he is, *Man Thinking*."[3] This Man Thinking is unfettered by the dogmas and philosophies of others, and he is not among the bookworms and "bibliomaniacs of all degrees."[4] Man Thinking is inspired purely by nature, and it is through him that the "active soul" gives birth to genius and creates truth. Although universal to every human, the active soul is hindered – "unborn" – save within Man Thinking.[5] His creation is "proof of divine presence." As Emerson avers, "if man create not, the pure efflux of the Deity is not his" and one is rendered unable, as he states further along in his speech, to "read God directly."[6]

Despite the fact that Emerson, Holmes, and their kind viewed this address as the American scholar's liberation from the perceived shackles of European culture and influence, Emerson's language betrays the very indebtedness he seeks to shed. His notion of a divinely inspired and universal soul or spirit that is shared by humankind and finds its expression in the mouthpiece of the scholar – this "Man Thinking" – owes itself to certain lines of European Romantic thought. Emerson's predecessors in

---

[2] This imagery of "walking monsters" and dismembered body parts appears throughout Greek literature, usually with reference to Empedocles. See Arist. *fr.* 57, *Cael.* 300b25–31, *De an.* 430a28–30; Simpl. *in Cael.* 587, 1; and Empedocles, *fr.* 376: ἧ πολλαὶ μὲν κόρσαι ἀναύχενες ἐβλάστησαν, γυμνοὶ δ'ἐπλάζοντο βραχίονες εὖνιδες ὤμων, ὄμματά τ'οἶ' ἐπλανᾶτο πενητεύοντα μετώπων ("There many heads sprouted up without necks, arms staggered naked, unattached to shoulders, and eyes wandered, lacking foreheads"). Greek text from *The Presocratic Philosophers: A Critical History with a Selection of Texts*, 2nd ed., ed. G. S. Kirk et al. (Cambridge: Cambridge University Press, 1983), 303.

Among German Romantic thinkers, we also see this imagery in the works of Friedrich Hölderlin (*Tod des Empedokles*) and Friedrich Nietzsche (*Also sprach Zarathustra: Ein Buch für Alle und Keinen*). Nietzsche was greatly influenced by Emerson, considering him his "Brother-Soul" (Friedrich Nietzsche to Franz Overbeck, December 24, 1883, in *Briefwechsel: Kritische Gesamtausgabe* 3, 1, ed. Giorgio Colli and Mazzino Montinari (Berlin: de Gruyter, 1975–2004), 463. For more on Emerson's influence on Nietzsche, see Jennifer Ratner-Rosenhagen, *American Nietzsche: A History of an Icon and His Ideas* (Chicago: University of Chicago Press, 2012), 1–9; Mikics, *The Annotated Emerson*, 74, n. 6.

[3] Emerson, "The American Scholar," 74. Emphasis in original.

[4] Johann Gottfried Herder maintains a similar anti-intellectualism when he refers to what Isaiah Berlin terms "tranquil philologists" and "detached literary epicures who turn over ... pages idly." See Isaiah Berlin, *Three Critics of the Enlightenment: Vico, Hamann, Herder*, ed. Henry Hardy (Princeton: Princeton University Press, 2013), 241.

[5] I am paraphrasing Emerson's words in this section: "This every man is entitled to; this every man contains within him, although in almost all men, obstructed, and as yet unborn" (Emerson, "The American Scholar," 77).

[6] Emerson, "The American Scholar," 77, 79.

Germany, for instance, conceived of a divine Spirit, or *Geist*, working among the people, the *Volk*, as a revelatory source of creativity, genius, and God's word.[7] For Emerson, Man Thinking was – as he termed elsewhere – the poet: an interpreter of nature in both poetry and prose who stands "among partial men for the complete man."[8] To borrow a phrase from the French sociologist and philosopher Pierre Bourdieu, the poet was an elite "producer of cultural goods" and represented in literature the collective voice of an otherwise disjointed communal body.[9]

At the core of political Romanticism and German Idealism was the notion that human beings and human culture cannot exist outside a community or state.[10] The early Romantic poet Novalis (1772–1801), for instance, argued, "In order to become and remain human, [man] needs a state (*Staats*).... A man without a state is a savage (*Wilder*). All culture arises from the relationships between man with the state (*Alle Kultur entspringt aus den Verhältnissen eines Menschen mit dem Staate*)."[11] This sentiment is also expressed in the work of Romantic

---

[7] Emerson declared in the inaugural issue of the Transcendentalist periodical *The Dial* (1840): "Those who share in it have no external organization, no badge, no creed, no name" but are united by the "spirit of the time." Despite this protestation, among Emerson's influences, Platonism, Neoplatonism, and Hindu philosophy were particularly formative. As an early member of the American Transcendentalist movement, he also engaged with the works of German Idealism and early Romanticism. Herder had particular influence among New England Transcendentalists more broadly, following the publication of James Marsh's translation of *On the Spirit of Hebrew Poetry* in 1833. Indeed, Emerson's passage on "Man Thinking" has many resonances with Herder's writings on the physiognomy of wholes.

[8] Mikics, *The Annotated Emerson*, 200.

[9] Pierre Bourdieu, *The Field of Cultural Production: Essays on Art and Literature*, trans. Randal Johnson (New York: Columbia University Press, 1993), 115.

[10] The question of what the category "Romanticism" encompasses is complex. It is widely accepted that it designates philosophical and theological lines of thought that emerge following the work of Friedrich Schlegel; however, one occasionally finds secondary material that refers to the German intellectual movements of the eighteenth and nineteenth centuries as a period of Romantic thought, subsuming the Idealists (e.g., J. G. Fichte, F. W. J. Schelling, G. W. F. Hegel) under the Romantic banner. In some measure, this is a misleading designation that fails to appreciate the degree to which Romanticism proper emerges as a counter to post-Kantian idealist views, yet the term nonetheless acknowledges the complex of political, social, and intellectual change that characterized the Romantic era following the American, French, and so-called Copernican revolutions. Admittedly, I have used the term to encompass a variety of anti-Enlightenment positions in Germany.

[11] Novalis, *Schriften. Die Werke Friedrich von Hardenbergs*, vol. 3: *Das philosophische Werk II*, ed. Richard Samuel, Paul Kluckhohn, Gerhard Schulz, and Gabriele Rommel (Stuttgart: Kohlhammer: 1968), 548. In this case, Novalis' use of the term "savage" (*Wilde*) is pejorative; however, particularly in later German Romantic thought, the idea

thinkers Friedrich Schlegel (1772–1829) and Johann Adam Möhler (1796–1838), who maintained that the "authentic Christian consciousness belongs not only to the solitary *homo religious* . . . [it] is fundamentally collective and communal, the *sensus communis* of the faithful."[12] Möhler explicitly amalgamates the "Christian consciousness (*christliches Bewusstsein*) of the individual . . . with the consciousness of the whole Church (*Kirche*)."[13] Moreover, he held that a divine Spirit or communal *Geist* imparts revelation onto its members and binds this community together. Thus, the notion of what Emerson terms "Man Thinking" is found in scripture through the writings of the so-called Hebrew poets and the evangelists. In the case of the canonical gospel writers, their chronicles of Jesus' life and death were directives of the *Heilige Geist* or Holy Spirit, embodying the sacred tradition of the church, while simultaneously representing the interests and needs of their fellow Christians. As Möhler explains, "we have received the infallible Word (*untrügliches Wort*) . . . [but] in this reception, human activity (*menschliche Tätigkeit*) . . . necessarily has a part."[14]

Although divided by a generation and oceans apart, Emerson, Schlegel, and Möhler all present a similar notion pervasive in German Romantic thought: the author is synecdochical both of a unifying, inspirational *Geist* and of the community in which (usually) the author is writing. While Emerson did not participate directly in the development of early Christianity studies, Bruce Lincoln's observation regarding the Romantics – and Johann Gottfried Herder (1744–1803) in particular – is instructive: "[They are] highly influential well beyond romantic and nationalist circles and arise whenever myths and peoples are understood as mutually – and unproblematically – constitutive."[15] In this way,

of the "noble savage" would take hold – a man who is uncorrupted by civilization's ills. I will discuss Herder's position on the so-called savage later in this chapter.

[12] James C. Livingston, *Modern Christian Thought*, 2nd ed., vol. 1: *The Enlightenment and the Nineteenth Century* (Minneapolis: Fortress Press, 2006), 193.

[13] Johann Adam Möhler, *Die Einheit in der Kirche, oder das Princip des Katholicismus: dargestellt im Geiste der Kirchenväter der drei ersten Jahrhunderte* (Tübingen: Laupp, 1825), 43; Livingston, *Modern Christian Thought*, 193. The notion of a "sensus communis" was widespread and persistent in both Enlightenment and German Romantic thought. See Gerald Ernest Paul Gillespie, Manfred Engel, and Bernard Dieterie, eds., *Romantic Prose Fiction* (Philadelphia: Benjamins, 2008), 517.

[14] Johann Adam Möhler, *Symbolik, oder, Darstellung der Dogmatischen Gegensätze der Katholiken und Protestanten nach ihren öffentlichen Bekenntnissschriften* (Mainz, 1888), 354.

[15] Bruce Lincoln, *Theorizing Myth: Narrative, Ideology, and Scholarship* (Chicago: University of Chicago Press, 1999), 211. I discuss Lincoln's work on myth further

German ideas about the state, theory of knowledge, and value theory (e.g., moral and political philosophy and aesthetics) that emerged as a response to the Enlightenment and the French Revolution have had significant and persistent influence over European and American intellectual life. One might even say that the works of Romantics like Herder constituted their own Big Bang in approaches to historiography, philology, and linguistic theory.[16] Some of these fields openly acknowledge their connections to Romantic thought in that their terms, methods, and dominant discourses take derivative or innovative turns (e.g., literary theory). However, the study of early Christianity remains as unwittingly steeped in Romantic influence as Emerson appeared to be in his 1837 address to his fellow scholars.[17]

This chapter proposes that critical scholarship of the New Testament – a field that emerged within the Romantic philosophical, political, and cultural movement – has inherited from German Romantic and Idealistic thought a number of presumptions about the social formation of early Christianity and the role of early Christian authors within their presumed communities. Such presumptions have contributed to the development of approaches to early Christian writing that are idiosyncratic when compared with allied studies of ancient literature. Specifically, save certain lines of nineteenth-century Homeric Analyst–Unitarian scholarship, the canonical gospels tend to be the only ancient sources in which scholars posit a community behind their production.[18] As this illustrative quote

along in this chapter. On Herder's influence on the academy, see Berlin, *Three Critics of the Enlightenment*, 7–25, 208–300.

[16] See, for example, Georg G. Iggers, *The German Conception of History: The National Tradition of Historical Thought from Herder to the Present* (Middletown: Wesleyan University Press, 1983). Of course, any treatment that attempts to link such diverse lines of thought into a tidy framework is, by nature, something of an oversimplification. I do hold, however, that the parameters I have outlined here are, in the main, descriptive of developmental trends in the academic fields under consideration.

[17] This is not to say that Emerson was "unwittingly" Romantic in his thinking. As Harold Bloom observed: "Emerson is to American Romanticism what Wordsworth is to the British or parent version." See Harold Bloom, *The Ringers in the Tower* (Chicago: University of Chicago Press, 1971), passim, cit. 297. For more on what is often called Transatlantic Romanticism, see Russell B. Goodman, *American Philosophy and the Romantic Tradition* (Cambridge: Cambridge University Press, 1990), 34–57.

[18] The Analyst debate was itself couched in Romantic ideas about oral traditions and national ethos. Some examples include Ulrich von Wilamowitz-Moellendorff, *Homerische Untersuchungen* (Berlin: Weidmann, 1884), and Karl Lachmann, who attempted to trace the "stemma" (genealogy) of the narrative strands of Homer, comparing the *Iliad* to the German *Nibelungenlied*. See Karl Lachmann, "Liedertheorie," in *Betrachtungen über Homers Ilias* (Berlin, 1847).

from the previous chapter avers: "Classicists do not approach Vergil's or Philodemus' writings as the products and mirrors of Vergil's or Philodemus' communities."[19] Yet for early Christianity, the community is too often taken as normative. This is not to argue that every time "community" is mentioned in early Christian studies it is in direct or self-conscious reference to the Romantics. But the use of this often ill-defined term signals an issue of conceptual clarity that continues to trouble the field: namely, the tendency to invoke ahistorical Romantic ideologies about the author.

There are less mystified ways to describe the beginnings of gospel literature that do not involve appealing to the notion of Christian communities. Based on our historical knowledge of writing practices in antiquity writ large, it is not amorphous communities but an author's network of fellow writers that is the most plausible and influential social environment for the production of literature. The subsequent chapters will demonstrate this historical context, including how to read the gospels as conventional Greco-Roman literature. Anticipating that discussion, this chapter elucidates the tight interrelation between the field of New Testament/early Christian studies and German Romanticism (hereafter, simply Romanticism[20]) that has done much to throw our evaluations down a dubious path. In particular, Romantic theorists Herder and Möhler contributed much to the idea that communities are the presumptive social environment of "the poet" or, in this case, of the early Christian author. A close reading of their work reveals a clear trajectory from Romantic methodologies for reading literature to the Form Criticism (*Formgeschichte*) and Redaction Criticism (*Redaktionsgeschichte*) that continue to undergird approaches to the New Testament today. In short,

---

[19] Stanley K. Stowers, "The Concept of 'Community' and the History of Early Christianity," *Method and Theory in the Study of Religion* 23 (2011): 238–56, cit. 247. Of course, an author like Vergil is recognized as belonging to a social network of Augustan-era poets like Horace, Ovid, Propertius, and Tibullus that one might term a "community" of a sort. This is precisely the kind of alternative social formation that I seek to identify for the gospel writers.

[20] This chapter focuses on German Romanticism in the interest of particularity, as this movement has more directly influenced the field of New Testament/early Christian studies. That said, there are certainly strong connections between the themes and methods I discuss here and other Romantic movements, notably in Britain and in the work of thinkers like Blake and his *Marriage of Heaven and Hell*, "Introduction" to *Songs of Experience*, and the Preface to *Milton*. This is a subject to which I hope to return in the future. For more on Coleridge and the futility of a too-literal reading of the Bible, see Elizabeth A. Clark, *History, Theory, Text: Historians and the Linguistic Turn* (Cambridge, MA: Harvard University Press, 2004), 165ff.

and as I discuss in the Preface, I judge that the field has lost sight of its roots in Romanticism and that appeals to this legacy are now not only largely unconscious but also persistent.[21]

Before delving into the work of Herder and Möhler, broader themes in Romantic thinking about the ancient world and the role of the poet/author are worth rehearsing. In order to understand the intellectual ethos that contributes to scholarly imagination about the gospel writers and the early Christians, one must first understand the institutional and political contexts that characterized historical inquiry within Germany. It is also necessary to understand how the Romantics' ideas about both societal structure (sometimes referred to as theories of organic form) and language played a role in their reading of ancient literature. The sections that follow establish a more concrete connection between Romanticism and current methodologies within the broader discipline of religious studies and within the study of the New Testament in particular. Given the relative rarity with which these historiographic issues are treated in the field, I have taken the liberty of reviewing these matters in some detail.

Among the issues under (re)consideration is a neoclassical revival that, in Germany, took the form of what others have termed a "longing for myth."[22] This longing (*Sehnsucht*) was widespread in postrevolutionary Europe as nations wrestled with rapidly changing political and cultural norms. One tactic for establishing a renewed sense of coherence and stability was to search for collective memories and forgotten narratives of so-called premodern and preliterate societies.[23] Perceiving modern,

---

[21] This lost trajectory may be attributable, in no small measure, to the world wars and the active disassociation of many scholars from the nationalistic enterprises of German institutions and thinkers. For more on the effect of the world wars on analyses of German Romanticism, see George S. Williamson, *The Longing for Myth in Germany: Religion and Aesthetic Culture from Romanticism to Nietzsche* (Chicago: University of Chicago Press, 2004), passim. Also see the Preface of this volume.

[22] The phrase "longing for myth" appears in a number of academic treatments on this subject. To the best of my knowledge, the first appearance of this phrase in English is George Mosse, *The Nationalization of the Masses: Political Symbolism and Mass Movements from the Napoleonic Wars through the Third Reich* (New York: Howard Fertig, 1975), 6.

Note that German neoclassicism in Germany during this period was distinct from the neoclassicism of the British and French. For more on this, see Williamson, *The Longing for Myth in Germany*, passim.

[23] See Eric Hobsbawm, "Introduction: Inventing Traditions," in *The Invention of Tradition*, ed. Eric Hobsbawm and Terence Ranger (Cambridge: Cambridge University Press, 2010), 1–14. As it concerns notable figures or other symbolic interests, the appropriation of ancestral figures like Boadicea or the "Aryan" race among Germans

Germanic culture to lack the kind of unifying mythology characteristic of the so-called orient (i.e., ancient Israel and ancient Greece), numerous eighteenth- and nineteenth-century thinkers including the Jena Romantics, the Brothers Grimm, Richard Wagner, and Friedrich Nietzsche sought to reclaim or create new mythologies for the German people via "rediscovered" folktales, hero stories, artwork, music, and so forth.[24] Given the porous disciplinary boundaries of the academy at the time, it was commonplace for the same methods used for recovering the oral stories of the preliterate *Volk* to be applied to the Greek and Latin classics and the Bible.[25] As George S. Williamson describes of German universities in this period, "it was not unusual for a single individual to [make] ... influential contributions to the study of the *Nibelungenlied*, the Homeric epic, and the textual history of the New Testament."[26] Indeed, great efforts were made to recover the folklore and parables favored by the illiterate, "primitive Christians" embedded in the gospels.

Coupled with this "longing for myth" was a rejection, particularly among Protestants, of the alleged corrupting influence of imperial Rome, both ancient and modern. Certain German philhellenes mourned the eclipse of ancient Greek culture (its literature, mythology, law, and perceived closeness to nature) by the excesses of "Roman tyranny, greed, love of luxury, and calculating pragmatism."[27] This anti-Roman sentiment also found expression in Germany's increasingly nationalist rhetoric as the educated classes (*Bildungsbürgertum*) and dilettantes alike labored to distinguish *Germania romana* from an imagined *Germania libera*.[28] These labors paralleled a contemporary and widespread rejection of papal authority and Rome's symbolic weight in the aftermath of the Reformation. Under these conditions, it is little wonder that the Romantic scholar

---

beginning in the nineteenth century loom large as constructed associations for nationalist movements (Hobsbawm, "Introduction," 7).

[24] See Jason Ā. Josephson–Storm, *The Myth of Disenchantment: Magic, Modernity, and the Birth of the Human Sciences* (Chicago: University of Chicago Press, 2017), 3.

[25] For more on the question of disciplinarity in the Romantic period, see John H. Zammito, *Kant, Herder, and the Birth of Anthropology* (Chicago: University of Chicago Press, 2002), 3–4 and passim.

[26] Williamson, *The Longing for Myth in Germany*, 13, speaking of the scholar Karl Lachmann.

[27] Suzanne L. Marchand, *Down from Olympus: Archaeology and Philhellenism in Germany, 1750–1970* (Princeton: Princeton University Press, 1996), 157, in reference to Herder.

[28] Marchand, *Down from Olympus*, 178. Also see Williamson, *The Longing for Myth in Germany*, 4, who notes that the educated classes were largely Protestant.

found it inconceivable that the gospel writers represented an elite social stratum of the Roman Empire.

Given this intellectual landscape, it becomes apparent how the idea of the poet or solitary "genius" as a pure and anonymous reflection of the *Volk* was persuasive in its moment in spite of its historical implausibility. This notion has been further reinforced, in part, by structuralist and deconstructionist approaches to the author in the twentieth century – sometimes referred to as the "death of the author." Although similar insofar as each brings to light questions of authorial agency and subjectivity, these approaches do not accurately represent the role of the author in the production of literature.[29] This is where Herder and Möhler's theories of language and culture come into sharper relief. While their discourses on *Volkspoesie* (popular poetry) and the *Geist* may seem, at first consideration, only tangentially tied to the later findings of Redaction and Form Criticism and the History of Religions School (*Religionsgeschichtliche Schule*), developments within allied fields like literary theory have reinforced certain Romantic methods. I discuss how concepts of oral tradition and community relate to the "death of the author" debates later on in this chapter.

"LONGING FOR MYTH"

Studies on German intellectual history and historical imagination have long been occupied with how to make sense of the politics and nationalism that animated the Third Reich and the Second World War. From the *Frühromantik* forward, scholars have mined the artifacts of German cultural heritage for evidence of the radical positions that culminated in National Socialism and "a peculiarly German cultural disorder" that privileged nostalgia over rationalism and warfare over liberalism.[30] One commonality often cited is the German enthusiasm for "myth," a somewhat amorphous term that signified an appreciation for the aesthetics (literature, art), practices, and cosmologies of premodern societies. As a variety of German artists, academics, and writers sought cultural artifacts that might express the unique and "essential spirit" of the German people,

---

[29] See Andrew Bennett, "Expressivity: The Romantic," in *Literary Theory and Criticism: An Oxford Guide*, ed. Patricia Waugh (Oxford: Oxford University Press, 2006), 48–58, cit. 57.
[30] Williamson, *The Longing for Myth in Germany*, 3.

or *Volk*,[31] the reclaiming of myths – or the forging of new ones – became common practice from the Renaissance onward.

From the vantage point of political science, I would be overstepping my bounds to comment on the soundness of theses that tie the German "use and abuse" of myth to the events of the twentieth century.[32] Certainly, there is something resonant about the Romantic idea that the German *Volk* were the "long-deprived heirs" of a storied history of a lost *Germania*; however, as Lincoln's formidable work on myth has demonstrated, the Germans were hardly alone in their pursuit of lost ancestors and mythic traditions upon which to build a nationalist furor; James Macpherson's invention of a Gaelic translation of Ossian poetry stands as but one example of this seemingly ubiquitous European project.[33] Setting aside the political implications of this observation, I detect twin issues with the way contemporary scholarship understands the role that "longing for myth" has played in shaping the field of ancient studies.

The first is the specter of the world wars in obscuring myth's central role in how eighteenth- and nineteenth-century thinkers analyzed the ancient world. We may recognize that the Romantic search for lost *Volk* or ancestors culminated in the unifying project of National Socialism, but we have been reticent to see its more benign influence in areas like classics and religious studies.[34] Recognizing, for instance, Romanticism's consuming focus on communities and "preliterate" storytelling helps to trouble our assumptions about the value of its model for describing how ancient literature was written, thus creating space for us to reconsider the role of literate elites and their networks. Moreover, a greater understanding of the role of myth in the minds of those who established the critical study of ancient texts crystallizes how, to paraphrase Hayden White, history is never disinterested.[35] In the case of German scholarship,

---

[31] Williamson, *The Longing for Myth in Germany*, 1, referencing Thomas Mann, *Pro and Contra Wagner*, trans. Allan Blunden (London: Faber and Faber, 1985), 201.

[32] A paraphrase of Nietzsche's *Sämtliche Werke: Kritische Studienausgabe*, 8:531: "Poetic invention can become myth if it finds widespread belief: how fluctuating is the use and abuse of a word." From Friedrich Nietzsche, *Sämtliche Werke: Kritische Studienausgabe*, ed. Giorgio Colli and Mazzino Montinari (Berlin: de Gruyter, 1988), 8:531.

[33] Lincoln, *Theorizing Myth*, 51. Also see Lincoln's work on Sir William Jones, chapter 4, "Mr. Jones's Myth of Origins," 76–100. James Macpherson, *Fingal: An Ancient Epic Poem in Six Books; Together with Several Other Poems, Composed by Ossian the son of Fingal*, 2nd ed. (London: T. Becket and P. A. De Honda, 1762).

[34] Thank you to Sarah Rollens for helping me to articulate this aspect of my project.

[35] I have in mind here White's work on historical consciousness. See, for instance, Hayden White, *Metahistory: The Historical Imagination in Nineteenth-Century Europe*

keen interest in ancient poetics, language, and autochthonous ancestors often signaled a desire to construct a noble and authorizing history for northern Europe that "broke the Mediterranean monopoly on antiquity."[36]

Second, historians who have documented Romanticism's influence on academic methods are often specialists in fields within which categories like "myth" or "religion" are undertheorized. As a result, terms designed to be categories of analysis can become conflated with their subjects of analysis, an issue addressed in the previous chapter. The key difficulty in identifying the role of myth in Romantic thought is that it concerns three distinct applications: (1) its inherited meaning and function in discourse from the Greek *"mythos"* forward, (2) the ways in which the term was employed and transformed over the course of the Romantic era, and (3) the word we have inherited in English that, for many, remains informed by Romantic thought.

For the Greeks, *mythos* signified a story understood to be, in some measure, invented or false – "fabulous (μυθῶδες)," according to Thucydides (1.22.4).[37] Notably, however, the ancient writers who invoked the speciousness of myth often did so before proceeding to tell arguably fictitious stories of their own (e.g., Plato, Hesiod, Herodotus).[38] The term was something of a rhetorical cudgel, a broadside to be used against one's competitors but recognized to be an authoritative, if fantastic, form of storytelling when done with skill, as with poets.[39] For German Romantics, *mythos* retained a sense of the fictive but also denoted a set of persistent, shared narratives (written or oral) deemed central to the self-identification of a given group of people; in other words, a narrative with representative information about supernatural beings, cosmology,

(Baltimore: Johns Hopkins University Press, 2014), and Hayden White, *The Fiction of Narrative: Essays on History, Literature, and Theory, 1957–2007* (Baltimore: Johns Hopkins University Press, 2010).

[36] Lincoln, *Theorizing Myth*, 48.

[37] Thucydides contrasts μυθῶδες with ὠφέλιμα, or "usefulness," in this passage. Also note his words concerning the poor reliability of memory (μνήμης) among eyewitnesses in 1.22.3. Thucydides is also cited by Russell T. McCutcheon, "Myth," in *Guide to the Study of Religion*, ed. Willi Braun and Russell T. McCutcheon (London: Cassell, 2000), 190–208, 191.

[38] As Wendy Doniger explains: "the myths Plato didn't like ... were lies and the myths he liked ... were truths." Cited from McCutcheon, "Myth," 192.

[39] The Romans, for their part, would adopt the word *fabulae* for such tales, signaling a lack of seriousness.

practices, landscapes, heroes, conflicts, laws, and so forth, held by a *Volk*.[40]

In the context of Romanticism's Protestant leanings, "myth" was increasingly associated with the peoples, culture, and literature that predated the perceived rise of Christianity. Despite Romanticism's rejection of Enlightenment rationalism, this tight correlation between myth and a "pre-Christian stage of culture" implied a certain theory of cultural evolution, including the conviction that myths were primarily an artifact of so-called preliterate communities. That said, it did not follow that these preliterate societies – sometimes called "pagan," sometimes "primitive" – were viewed disparagingly: the Greeks were heralded for embodying ideal piety and beauty and for their love of nature; the *Kinder- und Hausmärchen* of the Grimm Brothers brought to light the moral tales of a near-forgotten *Volk*;[41] and, to the extent that they were considered "products of a pre-Christian or preliterate mind-set," biblical writings represented the simple, unmediated, and divinely inspired expression of the "spirit" of the *Volk* who preserved them.[42] Colonialism would alter this affirmative perspective with terms like "myth," "primitive," "illiterate," and "barbarian" used malevolently to justify any number of ills and abuses. As with its use in antiquity, "myth" took on different valences, depending on to whom or what it pertained: the Old Norse Eddas were a proto-Jungian expression of a noble, collective unconscious, whereas Tartar literature was "as barren and dreary as that of their deserts."[43]

In modernity, "myth" continues to carry many of the same ambiguities about truth value, seriousness, and nostalgia. Narratives labeled as "myths" can be embraced and celebrated for their creativity and connection to an imagined past. Alternately, they can be dismissed as unscientific accounts of "how things came to be." They can be associated with

---

[40] "Myth" in German imagination also encompassed certain forms of artwork, music, and concepts of beauty. For more on this, see Williamson, *The Longing for Myth in Germany*, 4–18; Marchand, *Down from Olympus*, passim.

[41] On the proper genre classification of Grimm's *Kinder- und Hausmärchen*, see Christa Kemenetsky, *The Brothers Grimm and Their Critics: Folktales and the Quest for Meaning* (Athens: Ohio University Press, 1992), 184–88. There was an appreciable distinction between the *Volksmärchen* and the *Kunstmärchen* (although one not always apparent to those outside of the Grimm brotherhood); however, both forms of storytelling were considered part and parcel of the effort to preserve *Naturpoesie*.

[42] Williamson, *The Longing for Myth in Germany*, 6.

[43] "The Seventh Anniversary Discourse, on the Chinese, delivered 25th February 1790," in *Works of Sir William Jones*, vol. 3, ed. John Teignmouth (Cambridge: Cambridge University Press, 2013 [1807]), 81; also cited in Lincoln's *Theorizing Myth*, 90.

hallowed ancestors or shared social values, or they are seen as the foolish rationalizations of those who knew (or know) no better. In any case, they function as a strategy to "set off one kind of discourse from another,"[44] operating either to reject or to naturalize, reinforce, and advance socially constructed positions. In other words, they become "ideology in narrative form."[45] The difficulty with "myth" in contemporary usage is that it carries with it the implications of its past iterations as filtered through the discourses of the nineteenth and twentieth centuries. Depending on context, the term can imply Euhemerism, a Freudian collective anxiety, or an Eliadian expression of the sacred, among other associations. Its flexibility indicates the degree to which it functions as an "ordinary rhetorical device"; a myth has no special qualities per se, but it obtains significance depending on how it is accepted and perpetuated by social groups with a vested interest in its continuation.[46] Likewise, it is often the case that the further back such narratives can be traced, the more they are self-authorized by their continuity.

The desire for an anchor to a respected past is precisely what motivated Germany's search for the so-called lost narratives and material culture of northern Europe. This "longing for myth" was an expression of a need for social and political cohesion and legitimacy quite apart from any authenticity one might ascribe to the "myths" they adopted. The roots of this movement can be traced to the Renaissance. Following a period in which *mythoi* were considered little more than a trivial and even embarrassing foil to the "emphatically nonmythic" accounts of the Bible, the literature of Greece and Rome experienced a resurgence.[47] Among the recovered texts was Tacitus' *Germania*, a document that became something of a Rorschach test for those who cleaved to its descriptions of Rome and the Germanic tribes. It was made public (once again) by Aeneas Silvius Piccolomini (1405–1464) – later known as Pope Pius II – in 1457.[48] Piccolomini's conceit was to demonstrate that the German people of antiquity were little more than barbarians before the church's

---

[44] McCutcheon, "Myth," 191–92.   [45] Lincoln, *Theorizing Myth*, 147.

[46] McCutcheon, "Myth," 200. Such stories often support gender hierarchies and/or heteronormativity, emphasize opinion or impression over scientific knowledge, or claim social hierarchies or taxonomies based on categories like race, ethnicity, ableism, and so forth.

[47] Lincoln, *Theorizing Myth*, 47.

[48] Enea Silvio Piccolomini (Pius II), *De ritu, situ, moribus et condicione Germaniae descriptio (Beschreibung von Lage, Gebräuchen und vom Zustand Deutschlands)*, Repertorium Fontium 9, 259 (1457–58).

influence moved them to aspire to higher culture. As such, it was only natural, in Piccolomini's view, that "an appropriately grateful German empire ought submit to the Roman pontiff" in the present age.[49] The German empire, by contrast, read Tacitus' account as a chronicle of the manifold virtues (strength, courage, egalitarianism) and laudable isolationist tendencies of their ancestors, citing Tacitus' claim that Germania's inhabitants were "a nation uncorrupted by intermarriage with others (*nullis aliarum nationum conubiis infectos propriam*), a pure people and like no one but themselves (*sinceram et tantum sui similem gentem extitisse arbitrantur*)."[50]

Quite rightly, others have marked Piccolomini's text as the moment northern Europe was spurred to recover an ancient history of its own apart from the dominance of Greece and Rome in historical imagination. Even Alexander von Humboldt averred that the rediscovery of *Germania* opened the ancient world of the north in a manner comparable to what Columbus had done for the west.[51] With this new market established, entrepreneurial academes took advantage with an array of "rediscovered" ancient texts and genealogies, some genuine, some forged. The subtext of many of these translations and studies was to establish the north on an equal playing field with Israel, Greece, and Rome – this, despite the fact that none of these authorizing documents was in a language other than Hebrew, Greek, or Latin. In order to overcome this stumbling block, one strategy was to claim an antiquity greater than the texts in question via the medium of oral storytelling. Citing *Germania*, for instance, Annius of Viterbo (1437–1502) sought to establish Germany's intellectual antiquity through Tacitus' minor character Tuisco. Annius forged a manuscript by a certain Berosus of Babylonia, building on Tuisco as a founding figure for Germany and fashioning him as a son of the biblical Noah.

Tacitus' quote concerning Tuisco also contained a tantalizing thesis: the Germans "celebrate in ancient songs (*Celebrant carminibus antiquis*) – which are their sole means of memorializing and chronicling the past (*quod unum apud illos memoriae et annalium genus est*) – an earthborn god, Tuisco (*Tuistonem*), and his son Mannus (*Mannum*), as the

---

[49] Lincoln, *Theorizing Myth*, 48.
[50] Tac. *Germ.* 4; Latin text from Tacitus, *Agricola. Germania. Dialogue on Oratory*, trans. M. Hutton and W. Peterson, LCL 35 (Cambridge, MA: Harvard University Press, 1914).
[51] See Lincoln, *Theorizing Myth*, 48, n. 3, for more discussion of this passage and Humboldt, including his celebration of Dio Cass. *Annals* 2.10, 15–17, 88. Not mentioned by Lincoln is Martin Thom, *Republics, Nations, and Tribes* (London: Verso, 1995), 213, who makes a similar observation about Humboldt.

origin of their people and their founders (*originem gentis conditor-esque*)."[52] Not only could the Germans claim cultural parity with the heralded civilizations of the ancient Mediterranean through this fabricated genealogy of an "earthborn god"; they also could claim an older, oral tradition than the one represented by the extant manuscripts of the ancient Mediterranean.[53] As Annius asserts: "the beginning of philosophy is from the barbarians and not the Greeks (*Initium ergo Philosophiae a Barbaris non a Graecis fuerit*)."[54] Under this strategy, oral – not written – language takes precedence in determining the "true" origins of a cultural product. The use of oral tradition as a proving ground for both antiquity and authenticity would continue to characterize the Romantic project through to the fin de siècle and beyond.

The role of language as a unique expression of the fundamental character of a people or nation continued to capture the imagination of thinkers across Europe, particularly in the aftermath of the Thirty Years' War and French Revolution. The counter-Enlightenment figure Johann

---

[52] Tac. *Germ.* 2; Annius of Viterbo, *Berosi chaldaei sacerdotis Reliquorumque consimilis argumenti autorum: De antiquitate Italiae, ac totius orbis*, cum F. Ioan. Annij Viterbensis theology commentation (Lugduni: Ioannem Temporlae, 1554). I have cited Annius of Viterbo and Tacitus' Latin from Lincoln, *Theorizing Myth*, 49. Note that Lincoln cites 1512 as Annius' publication date for the Berosus manuscript. Elsewhere, the publication date is 1498, which corresponds more sensibly to Annius' death (1502). See, for example, Wilhelm Schimdt-Biggemann, "Antediluvian Wisdom and the Peoples' Genealogy: Annius of Viterbo's (1493–1502) Edition of 'Berosus,'" in *Philosophia perennis: Historical Outlines of Western Spirituality in Ancient, Medieval and Early Modern Thought* (Dordrecht: Springer, 2004), 421–34.

[53] Lincoln makes a slightly different argument in *Theorizing Myth*, claiming that Annius' implication is that the Germans could not have been illiterate, per Tacitus. This makes a great deal of sense on its face, given that Tuisco (= Tuyscon) becomes the "inventor of poetry, laws, and also writing"; however, it may be a step too far to claim that the ability to write automatically meant that the Germans were responsible for substantial literary production, as the paucity (some might say absence) of extant Roman-era Germanic writing attests. On the contrary, the claim to the superior quality of the *oral* traditions (storytelling, myth, philosophy, and so on) of the *Volk* is, in my estimation, a central argument of the proto-Romantic and Romantic movements and one more readily applicable to the case of Annius.

[54] The Latin text of Annius' Berosus manuscript is difficult to obtain and mostly preserved in fragments. The line cited above is found in Lincoln (without citation), as well as Herbert Jankuhn and Dieter Timpe's colloquium proceedings on the Berosus manuscript. Lincoln references Jankuhn and Timpe in a previous note in the same chapter (n. 4), so, lacking any further confirmation, I surmise that he obtained the quote from that source. See Lincoln, *Theorizing Myth*, 49 n. 6, and Herbert Jankuhn and Dieter Timpe, *Beiträge zum Verständnis der Germania des Tacitus: Bericht über die Kolloquien der Kommission für die Altertumskunde Nord- und Mitteleuropas* (Göttingen: Vandenhoeck & Ruprecht, 1989), 1:128–54, 138.

Georg Hamann (1730–88), for instance, did much to foreground the Romantic approach to language and poetry as a tool of the *Volk*. More than reason (as his later critiques of Kant refined), language mediated the human experience from one's relation to one's immediate surroundings, to one's interactions with one's social group(s) and, ultimately, God. With John 1:1 and Genesis in view, Hamann considered language a gift from God as well as a manifestation of the divine: "Everything ... in the beginning (*Anfang*) ... was a living word (*lebendiges Wort*), because God was the word (*denn Gott war das Wort*)."[55] For him, language was more than a system of abstract symbols secondary to rationality. It was the very means by which rational thought was obtained, and this was afforded by God's grace. As he later and quite dramatically stated: "Reason is language (*Vernunft ist Sprache*): *Logos*; I will eat this marrowbone and I will gnaw myself to death over it (*ich und werde mich zu Tod drüber nagen*)."[56] Moreover, one could detect through the Hebrew Bible, Ossian, and the Eddas that this God-given language was, in its first form, poetic (*Poesie*) – the "mother-tongue (*Muttersprache*) of the human race" – now degraded by the imposition of modernity.[57]

While language was an expression of God in human life, Hamann also maintained that it was communicated and learned through one's social group and therefore fundamentally communal. The formation of knowledge was an intimate process between self and neighbor in "hypostatic union." Thus, through the study of language, one could reveal the particular, collective experiences of a given people or *Volk*. Hamann explains, "the lineaments of language (*Die Lineamente ihrer Sprache*) correspond with the ... thought [of the *Volk*] ... and every *Volk* reveals them through the nature, form, laws, and customs of their speech (*Natur, Form, Gesetze und Sitten ihrer Rede*)."[58] Hamann's rhetorical union between divine revelation and human activity was plainly a defense for his Pietist views; however, his thoughts on language were also undoubtedly a reflection of nationalist concerns. In Königsberg, he was a proponent of the German spoken by the middle classes over the French that was used by the ruling courts and certain hubristic philosophers, and he

[55] Johann Georg Hamann, *Sämtliche Werke*, vol. 3, ed. Josef Nadler (Vienna: Thomas-Morus, 1949), 32.21–26.

[56] Johann Georg Hamann, *Briefwechsel*, ed. Walther Ziesemer and Arthur Henkel (Wiesbaden: Insel-Verlag, 1955), 5.177:18–20.

[57] Hamann, *Sämtliche Werken*, 2.197.15ff.

[58] Johann Georg Hamann, *Johann Georg Hamann: Lichtstrahlen aus seinen Schriften und Briefen*, ed. Heinrich Karl Hugo Delff (Leipzig: Brockhaus, 1874), 49.

actively argued against a movement to reform German letters in the French style. While these were not intended as explicitly political viewpoints, they were nonetheless a reflection of his deep-seated opposition to the imposition of one culture upon another.[59]

Hamann's concept of the *Volk* received greater expression in the work of his student and sometimes-interlocutor, Johann Gottfried Herder. Herder will feature prominently in the pages that follow, but a few words on his expansion of Hamann's theoretical framework illustrate the ways in which myth, language, and literature came to be so tightly associated with *Völker* in Romantic thought. Embracing Hamann's theological and linguistic premises, Herder further argued for a cultural relativism that saw distinction not only in the languages spoken by each *Volk* but also in the influence physical environments and climate have on a people's customs and practices, what he refers to elsewhere as *Nationalbildung* – "the development process through which groups acquire their cultural identity and individuals acquire identity as members of these groups."[60] This group-making and nation-building extends to myth insofar as myths are an expression of collectively held stories, values, and customs embraced by *Völker*. Lincoln usefully summarizes Herder's views:

if the environment impresses itself directly on the bodies of a *Volk*, it impresses itself on their customs and mores through the medium of myths, which *Völker* use to reflect on their surroundings and history and to transmit ancestral traditions from one generation to another. Acutely conservative, myths convey historic,

---

[59] See Robert Alan Sparling, *Johann Georg Hamann and the Enlightenment Project* (Toronto: University of Toronto Press, 2011), 172.

[60] Lincoln, *Theorizing Myth*, 53. Thus, in Herder's *Ideen zur Philosophie der Geschichte der Meschheit*, he argues that the landscape and temperature of a region dictate everything from a people's collective behavior to their physical bodies (skin color, skeletal structure, internal organs, and so forth). See Johann Gottfried Herder, *Ideen zur Philosophie der Geschichte der Menschheit* (Leipzig, 1786), 2.7.1–5, 2.8.1. Herder's perspectives on race may have interesting implications for later developments in New Testament studies, particularly when it comes to the so-called Judaism/Hellenism divide and related understandings of ethnic and religious groups in antiquity. Two notable books that treat the larger questions of the historical Jesus and nationalism are William E. Arnal, *The Symbolic Jesus: Historical Scholarship, Judaism and the Construction of Contemporary Identity* (Oakville: Equinox, 2014); Halvor Moxnes, *Jesus and the Rise of Nationalism: A New Quest for the Nineteenth-Century Historical Jesus* (New York: Tauris, 2012).

Note that for references to Herder's *Ideen zur Philosophie der Geschichte der Menschheit* (hereafter, *Ideen*) I have occasionally deferred to Lincoln's German transcription for clarification when manuscripts and/or scans of the eighteenth-century text were of poor quality. I have also elected to use gender-neutral language in certain cases in order to improve the readability of translated passages in English.

cultural, and practical knowledge while also guarding a *Volk's* distinctive values –
and errors – against forgetfulness and change.... Myths are thus a discourse of
differentiation: the distinctive stories *Völker* develop as they separate from one
another, through which they recall and reproduce their distinctive features.[61]

In Herder's estimation, recorded myths and so-called oral traditions of a
people – their shared poetry (*Poesie*), folktales or *Volkspoesie*, and literature – were the means by which they retained their distinctiveness as well
as their internal cohesion. This position comes into even starker relief
when Herder speaks of ethnicity and diversity.[62] He surmises that the
language and literature of a people are so specific to their collective
sensibility that both would be little more than nonsense to someone
positioned outside of the community:

The Brahmin would scarcely be able to comprehend if the Icelandic Voluspa were
read aloud and explained to him; the Icelander would find the Veda similarly
strange. Each nation has its own way of thinking, because it is its own, akin to its
own heaven and earth, sprouted from their way of life, handed down from fathers
and forefathers ... often the arbitrary national concepts and beliefs are such
cerebral-paintings, interwoven features of fantasy with the firmest connections
to body and soul. "Where did this come from? Has every single one of these tribes
of men invented their own mythology so that they love it as their own personal
property! By no means! He invented no part of it ... he inherited it."[63]

Herder imagines myth as a distinct and stable narrative (both oral and
written) passed from one generation to another. Counterintuitively, these
subjective interpretations and experiences are nonetheless shared or
imprinted as indelible markers of group homogeneity. The reliability
and consistency of these myths are never questioned by Herder or
Romantic thinkers of his ilk.[64] Nor are the mechanisms behind the

---

[61] Lincoln, *Theorizing Myth*, 53.

[62] Also see Jacqueline Vayntrub, *Beyond Orality: Biblical Poetry on Its Own Terms*
(London: Routledge, 2019), 51–54, on Herder on language and ethnicity.

[63] Herder, *Ideen*, 2.8.2: "Der Bramine würde sich kaum ein Bild denken können, wenn man
ihm die Voluspa des Isländer vorläse und erklärte; der Isländer fände beim Wedam sich
eben so fremde. Jeder Nation ist ihre Vorstellungsart um so tiefer eigenprägt, weil sie ihr
eigen, mit ihrem Himmel und ihrer Erde verwandt, aus ihrer Lebensart entsprossen, von
Vätern und Urvätern auf sie vererbt ist ... oft sind die willkürlichsten National-Begriffe
und Meinungen solche Hirngemälde, eingewebte Züge der Phantasie vom festesten
Zusammenhange mit Leib und Seele. 'Woher dieses? Hat jeder Einzelne dieser
Menschenherden sich seine Mythologie erfunden, daß er sie etwa sie sein Eigentum
liebe? Mit Nichten. Er hat nichts in ihr erfunden, er hat sie geerbt.'"

[64] Herder generally preferred terms like *Fabel* (fable), *Sage* (legend), or *Dichtung* (poetry)
when talking about the Bible. This preference was likely an effort to avoid unpleasant
comparisons with the likes of Homer and Hesiod.

transmission of these seemingly stable narratives adequately explained. Rather, the assumption is that these narratives somehow represent something original – that is, something pertaining to the *origins* – of the people in question.

Herder's schema for language and myth foregrounds my coming discussion of the common assumption that the gospels represent an oral tradition; if one takes for granted the existence of Christian communities, then it would seem sensible that texts like the gospels are comprised of "inherited" speech and are not "invented" literature. To the extent that language is a defining characteristic of *Völker*, for Herder and those sympathetic to his project the critical study of linguistics and literature should reveal the "origins" (*Ursprung/Ursprünge*) of a people. Indeed, much of Herder's body of work focused on questions of *Urvolk* and *Ursprache* and how to reconstruct the *original* myths, stories, and language of each unique community of *Volk*.[65]

For those who study the New Testament, this methodology should sound familiar relative to the way the gospels and their respective Christian communities are discussed and analyzed in the field (e.g., the "Markan community," the "Matthean community," and so forth). Yet there is very little concrete evidence to support the idea that early Christian literature is first and foremost a record of communal, oral storytelling. While certain texts associated with early Christian literature unquestionably shared content, it does not follow that the source or origin for this material is anything other than a normal literary exchange between individual writers. The effect of tying early Christian literature to the language and experiences of illiterate – or, in the Romantic imagination, preliterate – communities is to provide writings about Jesus a greater history (and cohesion) than they otherwise possess.

Again, I will return to Herder when I discuss Romanticism's influence on New Testament studies; however, this brief overview of his thought demonstrates the profound German interest in using language and myth as markers of *Völker*. Language and myth were the means through which one could locate not only the unique, lost narratives and gods of a

---

[65] See, for example, Johann Gottfried Herder, *Abhandlung über den Ursprung der Sprache* (Erstdruck: Berlin, 1772), passim.

Herder ultimately locates the origins of humankind in Asia. There is a great deal of academic literature on how Herder's theories on *Völker* informed the pernicious divisions that have been claimed historically between "Aryan" and "Semitic" peoples. See Williamson, *The Longing for Myth*, passim, and Lincoln, *Theorizing Myth*, 56–95, for a brief discussion and further bibliography.

homeland like Germany but also the origins of humankind itself. Using Genesis as a guide, philologists heavily debated the common origination point of all language and all *Völker*. The same deconstructive methodologies that guided so many thinkers in their attempts to claim earlier and earlier layers of the (now) formative narratives of their forefathers were also applied to linguistics. Thanks in no small measure to the efforts of men like Herder, F. Schlegel, and, crucially, Sir William Jones (1746–94), a consensus grew that the common origin for human language, and thus humankind, was in central Asia. Largely speculative, these etymological investigations argued that a family of "Indo-European" or "Aryan" languages (as well as Indo-European/Aryan gods) had emerged from the cradle of India and extended out into Egypt, Persia, Greece, Rome, and on through northern Europe.[66] These languages represented the earliest *Völkerwanderungen* – the migrations of *Volk* throughout the Western Hemisphere and into their present homelands. Good Herderians would understand that in the process of migration, these bands acquired distinctive national cultures as their travels took them to new environments, reshaping their languages, poetry, customs, and bodies in the process. Moreover, they would know that in their myths these people preserved memories of their origins and ancient *Völkerwanderungen*.[67]

Notably, while languages like German symbolized a rich and multilayered history of human development, migration, and thriving, many deemed languages like Arabic and Hebrew to be outliers that lacked the refinement and sublimity of the *Ursprache* Sanskrit.[68] Nationalistic and anti-Semitic prejudices unquestionably animated many such spurious theories about Aryan history and philology. Increasingly, the nineteenth century found thinkers like Feuerbach and Müller arguing for implicit contrasts between Aryan and Semitic history. Müller named Vedic India and Homeric Greece worthy members of the Aryan family tree; their poetry had given way to seductive myth, but, nevertheless, their speech

---

[66] These lists of Indo-European languages and territories often changed to suit the (scholarly) conversation. Take, for example, Jones' discussion of Jacob Byrant's *Analysis of Ancient Mythology* (1774–76): "We shall, perhaps, agree at last with Mr. Bryant, that *Egyptians, Indians, Greeks,* and *Italians,* proceeded originally from one central place, and that the same people carried their religion and sciences into *China* and *Japan*: may we not add, even to *Mexico* and *Peru*?" "On the Gods of Greece, Italy, and India," *Works of Sir William Jones,* 3:387.

[67] Lincoln, *Theorizing Myth,* 55.

[68] Not all theorists agreed on the poor aesthetic value of Hebrew, as I will discuss with Herder.

remained the spontaneous and unmediated expression of the wonders of creation. Languages like Hebrew were utilitarian – "less creative and more rigid" – and reflected concern for law and ritual.[69]

These spurious observations extended to other facets of defining *Volk*, such as whether or not post-*Völkerwanderungen* peoples had succumbed to foreign influence. The Germans, for instance, celebrated the material spaces and natural features of their homeland in folktales about forests, springs, and mountains, as chronicled by the likes of the Brothers Grimm. The Jews, by contrast, had abandoned their *Vaterland* long ago and were now a burden on other nations: "a race of crafty negotiators (*Geschlecht schlauer Unterhändler*) throughout almost the entire World (*ganzen Erde*), who, in spite of all oppression (*Trotz aller Unterdrückung*), nowhere longs for their own honor and living space (*Ehre und Wohnung*), nowhere for a fatherland (*Vaterlande*)."[70] Displaced, the Jews were arguably not even proper *Volk*, unable to properly preserve a continuing record of their homeland and kinship community. Christianity, on the other hand, was a great unifier and the culmination of Aryan antiquity.[71]

This particular aspect of Romantic history is too vast a subject to tackle in this chapter, but it is one that merits a great deal of attention as many of our assumptions in the fields of classics and religious studies may be more informed by racial prejudice than we presently recognize.[72] That said, in addition to emerging issues of race and ethnicity in the eighteenth, nineteenth, and early twentieth centuries, pressing political interests continued to inform methodological developments in how scholars read ancient texts, particularly those that attributed authorship to communities rather than individual writers. Because language was alleged to contain the "preserved memories" of various *Volk*,

---

[69] Lincoln, *Theorizing Myth*, 67.

[70] Johann Gottfried von Herder, *Ideen zur Philosophie der Geschichte der Menschheit* (Leipzig: Hartknoch, 1841), 2:12.3, p. 60.

[71] On the British construction of Aryan identity, see Thomas R. Trautmann, *Aryans and British India* (Berkeley: University of California Press, 1997). For a more expansive discussion on philology and constructions of anti-Semitism, see Maurice Olender, *The Languages of Paradise: Race, Religion, and Philology in the Nineteenth Century*, trans. Arthur Goldhammer (Cambridge, MA: Harvard University Press, 1992).

[72] On the British construction of Aryan identity, see Thomas R. Trautmann, *Aryans and British India* (Berkeley: University of California Press, 1997). For a wider-ranging discussion on philology and constructions of anti-Semitism, see Maurice Olender, *The Languages of Paradise: Race, Religion, and Philology in the Nineteenth Century*, trans. Arthur Goldhammer (Cambridge, MA: Harvard University Press, 1992).

comparative philology of the eighteenth and nineteenth centuries (including etymology, morphology, and so on) became increasingly aligned with the emerging fields of memory studies and the critical interpretation of ancient sources. As specific works became tightly associated with the history, national pride, and self-identification of various peoples, critics attempted to align these texts with an idea of "collective individuality" – that even a sole author is ultimately little more than a redactor of collective ideas.[73] This approach is reflected in our long-standing approaches to New Testament texts and is also evident in the Romantic treatment of other literature in the canon of classics, including Homer and the *Nibelungenlied*. These latter two cases offer compelling comparative data on how the notion of the New Testament redactor was able to achieve such ubiquity.

HOMERIC PRECURSORS

While debate over the nature of the *Iliad* and *Odyssey* was (and remains) long-standing among the Philhellenists of the Romantic era, the issue came to the forefront once more after the publication of Friedrich August Wolf's *Prolegomena ad Homerum* (1795). Accepting the premise that Homer and his audience were illiterate, Wolf suggested that the epics – like Ossian's poetry – must have been orally transmitted, going so far as to question the reliability of the Homeric *scholia* (Wolf being unaware that Ossian was Macpherson's invention).[74] Given his presumption that "the art of writing had not existed" for Homer, Wolf also doubted that such a lengthy and complex poem could be held in the mind of one man or that it would have been attentively received by the relatively low-brow

---

[73] Williamson, *The Longing for Myth in Germany*, 63.

[74] Friedrich August Wolf, *Prolegomena ad Homerum, 1795*, trans. Anthony Grafton, Glenn W. Most, and James E. G. Zetzel (Princeton: Princeton University Press, 1985). Wolf in fact argues that writing did not yet exist in Greece, contrary to the work of the philologist Jean-Baptiste Gaspard d'Ansse de Villoison. In drawing this conclusion, Wolf engaged Robert Wood's *Essay upon the Original Genius and Writings of Homer*. For more on Wolf and his influence on Homeric studies, see Gerard Passannante, *The Lucretian Renaissance: Philology and the Afterlife of Tradition* (Chicago: University of Chicago Press, 2011); Gregory Nagy, *Homer's Text and Language* (Urbana: University of Illinois Press, 2004); Barbara Graziosi, *Inventing Homer: The Early Reception of Epic* (Cambridge: Cambridge University Press, 2002); Anthony Grafton, *Defenders of the Text: The Traditions of Scholarship in an Age of Science, 1450–1800* (Cambridge, MA: Harvard University Press, 1991); Ian Morris and Barry B. Powell, eds., *A New Companion to Homer* (Leiden: Brill, 1997); Frank M. Turner, *The Greek Heritage in Victorian Britain* (New Haven: Yale University Press, 1981).

crowd to whom Homer would have been reciting.[75] His conclusion, then, was that the epics were orally composed by a series of poets and passed down through rhapsodes until formally redacted in Alexandria. This answer to the "Homer question" allowed Wolf to argue further that the *Iliad* was a collective work – "born and developed by accident and chance" by a like-minded people over the course of centuries.[76]

Wolf's findings were met with great fanfare and influenced broader analyses of Greek mythology as well as biblical literature. Of his interlocutors, Friedrich von Schelling is notable for considering the implications of the *Prolegomena* for the gospels, albeit not in terms of its historical or literary value. Schelling was not particularly concerned with determining the *Sitz im Leben* of the gospel authors or the early Christians. A lover of public expressions of religiosity, he sought a "new mythology" for the church that fully embraced modernity by unshackling itself from the Bible's letter of the law, decrying that "Living Authority (*der lebendigen Auktorität*) [has] given way to the authority of other books written in extinct languages (*in ausgestorbenen Sprachen geschriebener Bücher*)."[77] He even went so far as to support a ban on reading the Bible during liturgical services and criticized Protestants for their preoccupation with reconstructing the early church via the gospels. In his view, the gospels were not reliable sources for the details of Jesus' life but instead based on the messianic prophecies of the Hebrew Bible ("Christ is a historical person [*Christus sei eine historische Person*] whose biography [*Biographie*] was already recorded before he was born").[78] He deemed Jesus' depiction so lacking, in fact, that he was rumored to have declared the "snake" a much more interesting character.[79]

---

[75] Turner, *The Greek Heritage in Victorian Britain*, 138.

[76] Some notable critics of Wolf were Schiller, Goethe, and Nietzsche. Goethe even composed a scathing poem *Der Wolfische Homer*: "Sieben Städte zankten sich drum, ihn geboren zu haben; Nun da der Wolf ihn zerriß, nehme sich jede ihr Stück" ("Seven cities squabbled over which one gave birth to him; not that Wolf tore him apart, let each of them get a piece"). Schiller, for his part, accused Wolf of having "scattered Homer's laurel crown to the winds," according to Nietzsche. Wolf and Nietzsche quoted from Passannante, *The Lucretian Renaissance*, 121.

[77] Friedrich Wilhelm Joseph von Schelling, *Friedrich Wilhelm Joseph von Schelling sämmtliche Werke: 1802–1803*, ed. Karl Friedrich August Schelling, vol. 5 (Stuttgart: J. G. Cotta, 1859), 301. To the best of our knowledge, Schelling remained a Protestant throughout his life, although his deep sympathies for Catholicism are well noted in his various writings and personal correspondence.

[78] Friedrich Wilhelm Joseph von Schelling, *Werke. Auswahl in drei Bänden*, ed. Otto Weiss (Leipzig: Fritz Eckardt, 1907), 74.

[79] Williamson, *The Longing for Myth in Germany*, 65, n. 199.

Despite his displeasure with Protestant historiography and his reservations about the so-called historical Jesus, Schelling found that the gospels nonetheless offered an accurate depiction of the "grimy reality of first-century Palestine"[80] with its mass of "wretched and despised (*der Elenden und Verachteten*)" people.[81] Like the rough and rowdy crowd receiving the Homeric epics, he imagined that the gospels were composed under conditions that made the realism (read: poverty) of Judea almost too palpable, thus ruining their aesthetic quality.[82] He surmised that these vulgar masses corresponded with the social reality of the early church, reasoning that Christianity was able to establish and maintain its popularity by welcoming those on the margins. In this respect, Schelling accepted twin premises. First, the gospels offered a somewhat historically reliable account of the people and places of Galilee and Jerusalem. Second, these people were of the same kind of preliterate, premodern underclass sought after by many of his colleagues elsewhere in literature and linguistics.

What is evident even from Schelling's tepid appreciation for the gospels' historical value is the increasingly entrenched presumption that one could reclaim lost *Volk* by anatomizing a text. This anatomization could take the form of using literary details to draw broader conclusions about historical lacunae (e.g., the German reading of Tacitus) or identifying various layers of a text in order to argue for earlier and earlier historical strata. The Romantic treatment of the *Nibelungenlied* is a significant illustration of the latter, both for its form-critical methodologies and the debates it provoked between those loyal to the traditional idea of authorship and those seeking *Volkspoesie*.

---

[80] Williamson, *The Longing for Myth in Germany*, 65.

[81] Schelling, *Sämmtliche Werke*, 5:426. Schelling's full quote: "Just as Christianity originally drew its followers from the home of the wretched and despised (*der Elenden und Verachteten*), thus already demonstrating democratic leanings from the very beginning (*Ursprung schon die demokratische Richtung hatte*), so also did it continue to seek to maintain its popularity."

[82] This shabby reality did not correspond with Schelling's preferred vision of high classical antiquity. As Williamson explains: "Schelling combined a theological argument with an aesthetic argument: on the one hand, he sought to distance himself from both Judaism and the 'Bible religion' of the Protestant churches; on the other hand, he rejected the 'realism' of the biblical narrative as incompatible with good taste." Williamson, *The Longing for Myth in Germany*, 65–66.

THE *NIBELUNGENLIED* AND THE BROTHERS GRIMM

A Middle High German epic poem, the *Nibelungenlied* chronicles the exploits of Siegfried, a dragon-slayer who conspires with Gunther, King of Burgundy, to compete for the hand of Brünhild, Queen of Iceland. Paralleling a number of elements found in the Eddas and other old Norse tales, to the best of our knowledge the epic first appears in the Danube region before the royal court around 1200. Johann Jakob Bodmer was the first to publish a complete manuscript of the poem in 1757. This precipitated a renewed interest in the piece followed by a call to foreground the epic within German schools and among the German people writ large as a central text on par with the *Iliad* and *Odyssey*. Johannes von Müller and August Zeune, for instance, called for it to form the basis of all German education, and Schlegel praised it as a "return to the womb of the *Vorzeit* (*Rückkehr in den Schooß der Vorzeit*), the great means for a rebirth (*Mittel der Wiedergeburt*) of an original language (*ursprünglichen ... Sprache*), never separated from its roots (*von ihrer Wurzel niemals abgetrennten*)."[83] Although seemingly a product of the twelfth or eleventh centuries, there were those who, like Schlegel, believed certain elements of the text could be traced back as far as the fifth century CE and perhaps beyond. Informed by Wolf's *Prolegomena*, Schlegel argued that "Such a work is too great for one person (*solch ein Werk ist zu groß für einen Menschen*), it is the product of the entire power of an age (*der gesamten Kraft eines Zeitalters*)."[84] Likewise, it was open to the same scrutiny as to composition and authorship as Homer.

Within French-occupied Berlin, the drumbeat of enthusiasm for the *Nibelungenlied* continued. Numerous editions were published well into the nineteenth century, and colloquia were held on its essential role in developing German national identification. Discord emerged, however, once highly stylized editions of the epic began to appear, including a

---

[83] August Wilhelm Schlegel, "Mythologie des Mittelalters," in *Kritische Schriften und Briefe, vol. 4: Geschichte der romantischen Literatur*, ed. Edgar Lohner (Stuttgart: Kohlhammer, 1965), 102–14; also see August Wilhelm Schlegel, "Ueber das Lied der Nibelungen," in *Deutsches Museum*, ed. Friedrich Schlegel, vol. 1 (Vienna, 1812), 18.

[84] August Wilhelm von Schlegel, *Kritische Ausgabe der Vorlesungen: Vorlesungen über Ästhetik 1803–1827*, ed. Ernst Behler and Frank Jolles (Paderborn: Schöningh, 2007), 91. Schlegel ultimately argued that there may have been a final redactor of the *Nibelungenlied*, whom he identified as the thirteenth-century poet Heinrich von Offerdingen. The Grimms bitterly rejected this proposal. See Williamson, *The Longing for Myth in Germany*, 89, which cites A. W. Schlegel, *Kritische Schriften und Briefe*, 4:113.

rendering by Baron Friedrich de la Motte Fouqué reimagining the *Nibelungenlied* in the form of an Aeschylean trilogy. Fouqué was met with the ire of the Grimm brothers, who objected to the notion that national myths could be rewritten to suit contemporary tastes. Jacob Grimm compared such efforts to trying to extricate exotic animals to new locations, exclaiming: "Whoever wants to get to know the wretched kangaroos (*unglückseligen Känguruhs*) must travel to Australia."[85] In other words, one could only truly appreciate epic poetry like the *Nibelungenlied* through careful examination of its historical epoch.

Although rarely noted within the field, the Grimm Brothers enter into this schema as, arguably, two of the most influential figures aside from Herder for New Testament studies. Their insistence on the ability of scholars to reclaim lost, communal narratives through literature and oral stories solidified an understanding of the role of the author that persists to this day. The descendants of Protestant preachers and scribes (*Justizamtmann*), Jacob (1785–1863) and Wilhelm (1786–1859) remained close throughout their lives, pursuing careers in comparative linguistics largely through the preservation of a variety of medieval manuscripts and *Naturpoesie*, as well as the development of a comprehensive German grammar and dictionary.[86] Jacob in particular exhibited an interest in philology from an early age at Lyceum Fridericianum in Kassel and later worked under the noted philologist Franz Bopp (1791–1863).[87] The brothers' involvement in the Heidelberg group and their defense of Ossian and the *Nibelungenlied* incited some of their Romantic contemporaries; however, they are often credited with establishing folklore studies as a legitimate field of inquiry when "more refined, higher and later literature"

---

[85] Letter from Jacob to Wilhelm Grimm (October 18, 1809), in *Briefwechsel zwischen Jacob und Wilhelm Grimm aus der Jugendzeit* (Weimar: H. Böhlau, 1881), 98.

[86] For example: *Hildebrand und Hadubrand* (1812), *Das Weißenbrunner Gebet* (1812), *Kinder- und Hausmärchen* (1812–15), *Elder Edda* (1815), *Deutsche Grammatik* (1819–37), *Deutsche Sagen* (1816–1818), *Geschichte der deutschen Sprache* (1818), *Über deutsche Runen* (1821), *Deutsches Rechts-Alterthümer* (1828), *Die deutsche Heldensage* (1829), *Deutsche Mythologie* (1835, 1844), *Deutsches Wörterbuch* (1852). Interestingly, Wilhelm used his own wife, Dortchen, as a source for a number of the entries in *Kinder- und Hausmärchen* on the authority that she was the granddaughter of a noted philologist.
    Of note: the Grimms maintained a Herderian view of language, linking it to a shared, Aryan origin.

[87] Burton Feldman and Robert D. Richardson, *The Rise of Modern Mythology, 1680–1860* (Bloomington: Indiana University Press, 1972), 408–15.

had previously been the prime focus of academics.[88] They accomplished these feats despite remaining somewhat outside the academy proper for the majority of their lives. They advanced their viewpoints through a strategic campaign of letter writing and critical commentaries, never hesitating to confront their dissenters, and publishing prodigious amounts of material in the process.[89]

The work of the Grimms paralleled, in many ways, the efforts of those who mined Tacitus (or forged Berosus) for evidence of a heretofore lost – but hallowed – German past on par with Israel, Greece, and Rome. Their collections of poetry, folktales, and etymologies took Herder's methodologies on the exceptionalism and exclusivity of certain *Völker* and applied them to their native Germany. Their goal was twofold. First, they wished to celebrate the degree to which God inspired the poetry of the *Volk* from the earliest stages of their development.[90] Relatedly, they understood popular narratives like the *Nibelungenlied* to be an expression of a collective *Naturpoesie* impossible to attribute to a single origin, that is, to a single writer or author. Rather, these tales were emblematic of the shared *Geist* or spirit of the German people.

The Grimms also advocated an approach whereby one could scrutinize a text for evidence of its oral foundations. Their interest in oral tradition theory is perhaps best evident in their *Kinder- und Hausmärchen*, although their shared interest in preliterate narratives was by no means restricted to domestic fables. Their emphases on source material and philology were reminiscent of Wolf's *Prolegomena* in that they privileged the telling of myths as an oral phenomenon among primitive social groups.[91] The Grimms also influenced Karl Lachmann (1793–1851), the man generally considered the founder of *Germanistik*. Their close professional relationship with Lachmann helped inform his *Über die*

---

[88] August Schlegel referred to their work as a "devotion to triviality." See Feldman and Richardson, *The Rise of Modern Mythology*, 409.

[89] Jacob, for instance, took Schlegel to task for his analyses of the authorship of the *Nibelungenlied* – perhaps, not coincidentally, after Schlegel published a rather pointed review of their *Altdeutsche Wälder* (1813–15). For more on the letter-writing prowess of the Grimm brothers, see Williamson, *The Longing for Myth in Germany*, 83–84. Also see Marchand, "Excavating the Barbarian," in *Down from Olympus*, 152ff., for more on the composition of the academy and patronage in this period.

[90] Jacob Grimm, "Gedanken über Mythos, Epos und Geschichte," in *Deutsches Museum*, ed. Friedrich Schlegel, vol. 3 (Vienna, 1813), 56.

[91] Incidentally, this would be a description of history, language, and society that persisted through the work of sociologists like E. B. Taylor (1832–1917), Émile Durkheim (1858–1917), and Arnold van Gennep (1873–1957).

ursprüngliche Gestalt des Gedichts von der Nibelungen Noth (1816), which argued through Form Criticism that the *Nibelungenlied* consisted of sixteen song units arranged together by a twelfth-century redactor. Even after the *Nibelungenlied* fell out of favor outside of Berlin, Lachmann's interpretation would remain a stalwart reading of this "classic" German text.[92]

The *Nibelungenlied* lost its prominence after the fall of Napoleon and the coalition of the Holy Alliance. In effect, it became an unfashionable symbol of a past (and very specific) nationalistic fervor. Moreover, its themes of violence, monsters, trickery, and vice were increasingly seen as incompatible with Christian principles. Fredrich Heinrich von der Hagen, for instance, declared that "the Nibelungen are in no way our Homer or our *Iliad*; because we have something higher (*Höheres*) [and] sublime (*Erhabenes*), something beyond comparison, the Gospel and the Bible."[93] Indeed, as Germany gained political power, a discourse emerged that saw the *Geist* as the chief animating force in human history. France had collapsed, just like the Roman empire, as a result of its own decadence. And, as with Rome, part of this downfall involved the *Geist* ushering forward the revelation of Christ. Germany saw fit to claim that the "*Geist* had completed its process of self-formation in the 'Germanic-Christian' world," evinced by Germany's military victories, increased intellectual influence, and overall social standing in Europe.[94]

A dichotomy underscoring the inherent differences between Germany and Rome persisted throughout the nineteenth century as "'Rome' more than ever, came to signify antinationalist tyranny, elitism, and ultramontanism, and its symbolic defeat grew increasingly important to the establishment of German cultural autonomy."[95] In Suzanne Marchand's masterful work on German cultural history and classical antiquity, she details the extent to which *Vorgeschichte* was characterized by misplaced nationalistic pride. It was simple enough to construct a narrative that linked the German people to a long history of opposition to Rome's

---

[92] Of note, Lachmann stands as an early proponent of G. E. Lessing's theory of a "Nazarene Source" or ur-gospel. For more discussion, see Christopher Tuckett, *From the Sayings to the Gospels*, WUNT 328 (Tübingen: Mohr Siebeck, 2014), 88ff.; John S. Kloppenborg, *Excavating Q: The History and Setting of the Sayings Gospel* (Minneapolis: Fortress Press, 2000), 295–97.

[93] Friedrich Heinrich von der Hagen, *Die Nibelungen: Ihre Bedeutung für die Gegenwart und für immer* (Breslau: Josef Max, 1819), 207.

[94] Marchand, *Down from Olympus*, 159.

[95] Marchand, *Down from Olympus*, 159–60.

excesses. From Tacitus' biting account to Luther's valor, thinkers like Madame de Staël (1766–1817), Heinrich von Kleist (1777–1811), and Ernst Curtius (1814–1896) were emboldened to claim that Rome never faced a more hated and resistant enemy than proud *Germania*.[96] As Ossian and the *Nibelungenlied* rose, Vergil became little more than a "witty courtier."[97] The methods of the Grimm brothers and their disciples helped to establish a richer pre-Roman past populated with virtuous ancestors. Novels like Felix Dahn's *Ein Kampf um Rom* (1876) elevated the notion of the noble, German "barbarian" as Dahn's Gothic hero bravely faces certain death against an insurmountable Roman foe. The elite Roman oppressor was a stand-in for any number of perceived enemies to Germany's cultural autonomy and sense of superiority. As we have seen, this sense of German ascendency was inculcated in the academy as well.

In the years following the Holy Alliance, the various fields that studied the ancient Mediterranean were still relatively harmonious.[98] The study of Greco-Roman antiquity, German antiquity, and early Christianity remained intertwined and in continual conversation. To the extent that "Rome" symbolized Germany's cultural and moral antithesis, "Germany," and more specifically the German academy and German Protestantism, aligned itself with Rome's historic antagonists: Greece, Germania, and, crucially, the "primitive" Christians. In the case of critical studies of the New Testament, Romantic methodologies for detecting and retrieving oral narratives allowed scholars to reimagine the gospels as repositories for the lost early Christian communities or *Volk*. Thus, the gospel writers became the representative author-geniuses of their age: redactors of the greatest universal epic in modernity.

THE ROMANTIC GENIUS

The concept of "genius" or "the genius" in Romanticism is not, as we might imagine in our contemporary understanding, a theoretical or

---

[96] For example, see Ernst Curtius, "Rom und die Deutschen," in *Alterthum und Gegenwart: Gesammelte Reden und Vorträge*, vol. 1 (Berlin: 1875), 41–58; Mme de Staël, *De l'Allemagne* (New York: Roe Lockwood & Son, 1860).

[97] Marchand, *Down from Olympus*, 157.

[98] For more on the internecine debates within philology and *Vorgeschichte* in the nineteenth century in Germany, see Marchand, *Down from Olympus*, passim.

conceptual extension of reason.[99] Following Kant, it is an unconscious expression of literary or other artistic meaning that transgresses the strictures of convention while still remaining aesthetically successful.[100] Kant referred to genius as the "innate mental predisposition (*ingenium*) *through which* nature gives the rule to art" thereby establishing a symbiotic and tautological relationship between the artist and nature itself.[101] Romantic thinkers like August Wilhelm Schlegel and the aforementioned Friedrich Schlegel would add to this doctrine a Romantic theory of literature.

F. Schlegel in particular brought to bear on Kant's foundation the autonomous activity of the poet, wherein poetry is described as an act of continuous creativity or imagination that subsumes all other past expressions of literary genius into its process of achieving "perfect totality."[102] For Schlegel, out of the "deepest depths of the Spirit (*tiefsten Tiefe des Geistes*)," poetry is an expression of "a progressive universal poetry (*Poesie ist eine progressive Universalpoesie*) ... Only it can, like the epic, become a mirror of the whole surrounding world, a picture of the age."[103] Poetry was an expression of its immediate milieu. However, this was not to suggest that the poet was engaged in articulating stages within a grand narrative of history. The linear progression of history was an

---

[99] I am not attempting to revive the author-genius or the Romantic-expressive model of authorship in this book. Nor am I going so far as to engage in structuralist lines of thought that would attribute the authorship as Roland Barthes does to "innumerable centres of culture" ("The Death of the Author," in *Image, Music, Text*, trans. Stephen Heath [New York: Macmillan, 1977], 142–48, cit. 146). I am instead proposing a rich and dynamic social context for ancient writers and other literate experts based on historical evidence of their activities. A brief overview of the contours of these theories will help explain why what I am proposing in this chapter and the next differs from these other models. Note that I presented an earlier version of the following discussion in Walsh, "Q and the 'Big Bang' Theory of Christian Origins," 491–504.

[100] Immanuel Kant, *Critique of the Power of Judgment*, ed. Paul Guyer, trans. Paul Guyer and Eric Matthews (Cambridge: Cambridge University Press, 2000), 317–18. Also see Andrew Bowie, "Romanticism and Music," in *The Cambridge Companion to German Romanticism*, ed. Nicholas Saul (Cambridge: Cambridge University Press, 2009), 243–55, cit. 250.

[101] Kant, *Critique of the Power of Judgment*, §46 (186). Emphasis in original. On genius as "nature's favorite," see §49 (191).

[102] Jürgen Klein, "Genius, Ingenium, Imagination: Aesthetic Theories of Production from the Renaissance to Romanticism," in *England und der Kontinent: Subjektivität und Imagination von der Renaissance bis zur Moderne* (Frankfurt: Peter Lang, 2008), 88.

[103] August Wilhelm von Schlegel and Friedrich Schlegel, *Athenaeum: Eine Zeitschrift*, vol. 2: *1798* (Berlin: Rütten & Loening, 1960), 204 (fr. 116).

Enlightenment position rejected by the Romantics, who instead understood historical development as a continuous, cyclical process of birth, growth, and decay (e.g., the fall of the Roman Empire). Past organic forms of history could inform present understandings and artistic productions (e.g., the dramas of the ancient Greeks, the poetry of the ancient Israelites), but each culture was uniquely expressed within its epoch and informed by its own particular historical circumstances.

The period in which allied ideas about the genius originated is generally referred to as the *Geniezeit*, the "age of the genius." It gave rise to significant innovations in political theory, ethics, and epistemology. It also provided the foundation for theories of language that abandoned the French neoclassicism and German *Kanzleistil* of previous generations. Instead, the *Geniezeit* favored the identification of literary figures who represented a less elite but more unifying notion of *"Deutsch."* The late eighteenth and early nineteenth centuries had seen "Lilliputian statelets" and other relatively autonomous regions coalesce into the Holy Roman Empire of the German Nation; however, this nation lacked many cohesive political, economic, or cultural keystones. Thus, it fell to Romantic thinkers like Herder to establish an invented tradition for Germany, one that demonstrated continuity between the present amalgamated culture and a conceptually unified past.[104] In attempting to reclaim that past, the search for German heritage ultimately extended beyond the borders of what then constituted Germany and past the "old fault line dividing Latin from Germanic Europe."[105]

Among the individual geniuses identified by *Sturm und Drang* and others in the Romantic movement, William Shakespeare stands out as a seemingly peculiar choice to represent the language of unified Germany. However, the treatment of Shakespeare by men like Herder is instructive to my project, which seeks to redescribe the individual ancient author as incommensurate with the Romantic genius. For the Romantics, locating German heritage entailed looking to poets and geniuses like Shakespeare who were unencumbered by the *délicatesse* of the French and, as such, better represented the unmediated spirit of the (non-elite) German people. Shortly before the Romantic movement took hold in earnest, Heinrich

---

[104] For more on later German nation-building and invented tradition, see William E. Arnal, "The Collection and Synthesis of 'Tradition' and the Second-Century Invention of Christianity," *Method and Theory in the Study of Religion* 23 (2011): 199–200.

[105] Moore, "Introduction," xi.

von Gerstenberg (1737–1823) described Shakespeare as presenting "living images of moral Nature (*lebendige Bilder der sittlichen Natur*)." Later, Herder heralded Shakespeare as a craftsman of *Volkspoesie* comparable to Homer, the poets of the Hebrew Bible, and Ossian.[106] In a play on the same kind of synecdochical language used by Emerson, Herder avers that in Shakespeare:

The *whole* world (die *ganze* Welt) is only body to this great mind: *all* scenes of nature limbs on this body (*alle Auftritte der Natur an diesem Körper Glieder*), as *all* characters and modes of thought traits to this mind (*wie alle Charaktere und Denkarten zu diesem Geiste Züge*) – and the *whole* (*Ganze*) may be named as that giant god of Spinoza "*Pan! Universum!*"[107]

What Herder means by this is that Shakespeare represents not only an expression of artistic genius but also a synthesis of history for the way his works pull together disparate characters, plots, languages, and circumstances into an organic whole.[108]

Elsewhere, Herder claims that "the proper subject of the historical sciences is the life of communities and not the exploits of individuals . . . great poets expressed the mind and experience of their societies."[109] Indeed, the anti-Enlightenment notion of society – and religion – as a unified organism animated by its own particular *Geist* was widespread in the Romantic period. In Romantic thought, Shakespeare was a genius representative of his broader cultural milieu. Like Sophocles before him, he reflected the social life and customs of his epoch.[110] But, crucially, that

---

[106] Heinrich von Gerstenberg's *Letters on Curiosities of Literature* (1768) quoted from Moore, "Introduction," xvi. Also see Moore, "Introduction," xvii–xx.

[107] Herder, "Über Shakespeare," in *Herder's Sämmtliche Werke*, ed. Bernhard Suphan (Berlin: Weidmann, 1891), 5:220–226. Emphases in original. Herder's reference to Baruch Spinoza in this passage is likely in respect to the latter's monist philosophy but may also signal the *Pantheismusstreit* controversy between Friedrich Heinrich Jacobi and Gotthold Lessing.

[108] Herder, *Sämmtliche Werke*, 5:219–20: "He took history (*Geschichte*) as he found it, and with his creative spirit (*Schöpfergeist*) he combined the most diverse material (*verschiedenartigste*) into a wondrous whole (*Wunderganzen*)."

[109] Berlin, *Three Critics of the Enlightenment*, 211.

[110] Herder would also call Shakespeare "Sophocles' brother" in these discussions. See Herder, *Shakespeare*, 49. For more on Herder and Shakespeare, see Robert Edward Norton, "The Ideal of a Philosophical History of Aesthetics: The Diverse Unity of Nature," in *Herder's Aesthetics and the European Enlightenment* (Ithaca: Cornell University Press, 1991), 51–81.

Of note, in his "Demythologizing: Controversial Slogan and Theological Focus," Rudolf Bultmann cites Shakespeare, *Tempest* IV, 1, and Soph. *Aj.* 125–26 as examples of "mythical eschatology," thereby maintaining the comparison generations later. See

social life was expressed not through the oppressive literary scruples of the period, but the pervasive and plain speech of the people. In his introduction to a translation of Herder's treatment of Shakespeare in *Von deutscher Art und Kunst* (*On German Character and Art*), Gregory Moore explains:

> although Sophocles and Shakespeare may be outwardly dissimilar, they have a spiritual kinship that all geniuses share: they are true not only to nature ... but also to the culture from which they emerged ... Both are mouthpieces of the collective soul of the nation, expressing its thoughts and sentiments, manners and morals; in each case their art is a development of indigenous species of expression.[111]

Thus, both the Germans and English could unify under the cultural banner of genius insofar as Shakespeare's work expressed the spirit of the common people, the *Volksgeist*. Regardless of respective language, the author-genius functioned as the inspired mouthpiece of the people and their collective experience.[112]

The Romantic notion of the author-genius serving as a spokesperson for their community is a model for literary production that shares much with the description of ancient authors in early Christian studies. Scholars of early Christianity regularly describe the gospel author as a redactor of sayings, teachings, and other materials deemed essential or representative of their community. As discussed in the previous chapter, this community is traditionally envisioned as a religious group of some stripe unified by their shared "mind and practice." Stowers, reflecting on the concept of community, notes that nineteenth-century ideas of *Gemeinschaft* (community) and *Gesellschaft* (society) were often associated with notions of "an essential and totalizing identity and commitment" akin to the idea of conversion.[113] This is the same kind of wholesale "turning" of allegiance augured in passages like Acts 4:32: "a great number

---

Rudolf Bultmann: Interpreting Faith for the Modern Era, ed. Roger A. Johnson (Minneapolis: Fortress Press, 1991), 295.

[111] Moore, "Introduction," 19.

[112] Herder would not live to see Napoleon Bonaparte conquer Austria and Prussia (1805); however, the civic reforms and rebellions that would follow stoked the proto-liberal nationalism articulated by Herder, with the abolishment of serfdoms and the rise of the peasant class. See Hans-Joachim Hahn, "Germany: Historical Survey," in *Encyclopedia of the Romantic Era, 1760–1850*, ed. Christopher John Murray (New York: Fitzroy Dearborn, 2004), 418–21.

[113] Stowers, "The Concept of 'Community,'" 239. Stowers cites the late nineteenth-century work of Ferdinand Tönnies.

(πλῆθους) of the faithful (τῶν πισευσάντων) were of one heart and one soul/ mind (ἦν καρδία καὶ ψυχή)." Thus, sociological approaches to nineteenth-century Europe dovetail with traditional, scholarly descriptions of the social worlds of early Christian writers.

It would be an oversimplification, however, to say that when scholars in the field of New Testament and early Christian studies use words such as "community" or "church" they are consciously engaging the paradigms of the Romantics. Likewise, not all scholarship on the social world of the early Christians has engaged in discourse about communities, and, where it has, some scholarship recognizes that the model is problematic.[114] Yet it remains the case that the study of early Christianity largely persists in appealing to concepts of community that are, at best, ill-defined or, more commonly, myopically focused on religious groups that reinscribe Acts' myth of origins in some measure.[115] Moreover, much like the author-genius Shakespeare speaking for the "illiterate, low-liv'd" Elizabethan,[116] the early Christian writer is often imagined within a coterie of illiterate fellow Christians or ill-defined group of specialist revolutionaries (e.g., scribes). This model for ancient authorship agitates against what we know about the practices of those with sufficient education and training to produce and circulate writings in the ancient Mediterranean world.

---

[114] For instance, John G. Gager, *Kingdom and Community: The Social World of the Early Christians* (Englewood Cliffs: Prentice-Hall, 1975), 10: "My view is that past failures to deal with the rise of Christianity in social terms have resulted in serious distortions of the historical realities. Despite all their talk about the need to determine the *Sitz im Leben* of a given passage … students of early Christian literature have given remarkably little attention to the social dimensions of these communities. Thus, the emphasis given here to the social aspect of world-construction stems from a basic conviction that the process of generating a sacred cosmos or a symbiotic universe is always rooted in concrete communities of believers. This conviction takes us beyond the standard claim that religious beliefs and institutions are subject to the influence of social factors in their environment, for it makes the assertion that without a community there is no social world and without a social world there can be no community."

Abraham J. Malherbe, *Social Aspects of Early Christianity* (Baton Rouge: Louisiana State University Press, 1977), 13: "We must, for instance, resist the temptation to see so much of early Christian literature either as a community product or as reflecting the actual circumstances of the communities with which the writings are associated. We too frequently read of communities that virtually produced one or another of the Gospels or for which they were produced."

[115] Stowers, "The Concept of 'Community,'" 239–49.

[116] Bettina Boecker, "Groundlings, Gallants, Grocers: Shakespeare's Elizabethan Audience and the Political Agendas of Shakespeare Criticism," in *Shakespeare and European Politics*, ed. Dirk Delabastita et al. (Cranbury: Rosemont, 2008), 220–33, cit. 221–22.

Anticipating the coming discussion on ancient authorship, the Romantic ideal of the author-genius is incommensurable with ancient Mediterranean and West Asian writers in three fundamental and interrelated respects. First, ancient writers possessed rich and complex reasons for composing their works as active agents, and their writings should not be understood myopically as the expression of the totalizing "mind and experience" of their societies or immediate communities.[117] Ancient authorship practices will be discussed at length in the following chapter.

Second, this is not to say that authors are not engaging certain genres or canons and literary traditions or attempting to represent particular kinds of discourse in their writing. On the contrary, writers self-consciously choose and craft their references and source materials in a rational way. Speaking of Romantic aesthetic values as they pertain to ancient literature, Tim Whitmarsh notes that Greek literary culture of the imperial period was for some time viewed by scholars as an "embarrassing epilogue" given that its writers were perceived as failing to embody the Romantic "obsession" with originality and inspiration characteristic of the author-genius.[118] Writers like those of the Second Sophistic, for instance, were prized in their milieu precisely for their ability to participate in the creative imitation of other texts or the "intertextual refashioning of earlier literary works."[119] Skill was judged by the author's ability to consciously select the traditions from which they wished to emulate and their ability to "play the game" of participating in that literary culture.[120] It was not judged according to what extent the author, propelled forward by the *Geist* of the age and their own aesthetic talents, could faithfully represent the *Volk*.

Last, it is misleading to associate writers exclusively with non-elites in an attempt to say something about the "common traditions and common memories" of the *Volk*.[121] Writers may reflect certain discernable aspects of the language, culture, politics, and concerns of their milieu, but they are not unvarnished mirrors of the imagined experiences, traditions, and needs of unique groups or other categories of people. A study of literary culture in antiquity clearly demonstrates that it is the author's social

---

[117] Berlin, *Three Critics of the Enlightenment*, 211.

[118] Tim Whitmarsh, *The Second Sophistic* (Oxford: Oxford University Press, 2005), 1.

[119] Whitmarsh, *The Second Sophistic*, 1.

[120] Robyn Faith Walsh, "Revisiting Paul's Letter to the Laodiceans: Rejected Literature and Useful Books," to appear in volume dedicated to François Bovon, ed. Brent Landau et al. (Tübingen: Mohr Siebeck), forthcoming.

[121] Berlin, *Three Critics of the Enlightenment*, 234.

networks of fellow writers and literate critics that establish the most immediate and formative social context for the production of literature.[122] There is no compelling reason to think that the writers of early Christian literature should be situated in a different environment.

THE DEATH OF THE AUTHOR

One of the central issues with the author-genius writ large is that it wrests agency away from the author as a rational actor. This approach to literature has much in common with twentieth-century structuralist and poststructuralist approaches to anti-authorialism. It is useful to pause for a moment and examine this turn in literary theory, in part because its missteps further demonstrate the historical implausibility of the author-genius model. In short, the twentieth-century "death of the author" debate (and its subsequent dismissal) demonstrates that this means of understanding authorship has exhausted itself. New models – such as the one I am proposing in this project – are necessary to take its place.

Born of the rejection of subjectivity by Roland Barthes, Michel Foucault, and Jacques Derrida, the so-called death of the author eradicated the authorial subject from the production of literature by positing that language and knowledge exist before the consciousness of the author translates them into a particular discourse. Seán Burke describes this development as the "expulsion of the subject from the space of language ... call[ing] into question the idea that [humankind] can properly possess any degree of knowledge or consciousness."[123] In other words, it is not a *self* or an *I* author who speaks in literature, but it is language. Barthes explains:

Linguistically, the author is never more than the instance of writing, just as I is nothing other than the instance of saying I: language knows a "subject" not a "person," and this subject, empty outside of the very enunciation which defines it, suffices to make language "hold together," suffices, that is to say, to exhaust it.[124]

---

[122] See, for example, William A. Johnson, *Readers and Reading Culture in the High Roman Empire: A Study of Elite Communities* (Oxford: Oxford University Press, 2010). Speaking of the literary communities of elite authors like Pliny, Johnson states: "The community is characterized by a reciprocity that mutually recognizes common values, 'of which the most important is the rhetorical mastery of language'" (52). These networks of authors will be discussed in the next chapter.

[123] Seán Burke, *The Death and Return of the Author: Criticism and Subjectivity in Barthes, Foucault and Derrida*, 3rd ed. (Edinburgh: Edinburgh University Press, 2010), 14.

[124] Barthes, "The Death of the Author," 145.

Thus, the author is not only excluded from literature, they are considered never to have existed in the first place. Informed by Russian formalists like Vladimir Propp – who, incidentally, were informed by Romantic poetics – the symbolic logic of the text and its cultural signifiers become the medium of composition.[125] Simply put, cultures write texts, not authors. Barthes, in particular, held that the individual author, the genius, was a purely "modern figure," that is, a product of nineteenth-century theocentrism.[126] It was this figure that Barthes and his sympathizers wished to eliminate from the text in order to foreground the neglected reader.

The work of Barthes, Foucault, and Derrida continues to hold enormous sway in contemporary literary theory.[127] Their collective approach to the author has become so formative that in structuralist and poststructuralist thought, it is often taken "almost as an article of faith."[128] However, critics of Barthes have noted that the elimination of the author has not so much destroyed the author-god as contributed to its construction by "creat[ing] a king worthy of the killing."[129] Moreover, those who continue to claim that the text belongs purely to language have offered few compelling rationales for "proceeding . . . from this calm insight to the claim that the author has no part to play in the processes of text formation and reception."[130] It is in this critique of the "death of the author" that I place my own project: texts are the products of authors engaged in certain practices and conventions that correspond with their social contexts; they are not disembodied or passive filters of broader cultural structures.

Bourdieu's notion of "habitus" is instructive on this latter point. Habitus signifies an unconscious socialization that takes place among

---

[125] For the Romantic influence on Vladimir Propp and other formalist critics, see Winfried Menninghaus, *In Praise of Nonsense: Kant and Bluebeard* (Stanford: Stanford University Press, 1999).

[126] Barthes, "The Death of the Author," 143. Ironically, *Sturm und Drang* thinkers like Hamann similarly held that the language of symbols and feelings are antecedents of the activity of the genius. In some important respects, the Romantics and structuralists were not alien to one another. See Burke, *The Death and Return of the Author*, 14, 22, 30, 46, 88, 204.

[127] For more on how Foucault fits into this schema, see Walsh, "Revisiting Paul's Letter to the Laodiceans."

[128] Burke, *The Death and Return of the Author*, 16.

[129] Burke, *The Death and Return of the Author*, 25.

[130] Gayatri Chakravorty Spivak, "Translator's Preface to *Of Grammatology*," in Jacques Derrida, *Of Grammatology*, trans. Gayatri Chakravorty Spivak (Baltimore: Johns Hopkins University Press, 1976), ix–lxxxvii, cit. lxxiv. Cited from Burke, *The Death and Return of the Author*, 26.

agents that drives them to the internalization of the various conditions (e.g., social, economic) that comprise their "field" or sphere of social and cultural existence. Another way to describe habitus might be to say that people act in ways that are both practical and plausible given their social location and context. Bourdieu focuses his theorization in terms of practices: "the practices of the members of the same group or, in a differentiated society, the same class, are always more and better harmonized than the agents know or wish."[131] More than an amorphous designation of "culture" on a broad scale, Bourdieu situates agents according to their relative power and cultural capital within specific fields of activity. Elsewhere, he describes habitus as a set of practices that are "internalized and converted into a disposition that generates meaningful practices and meaning-giving perceptions."[132] Rather than attributing something like authorship to a broad and amorphous concept like culture, Bourdieu's pillars of habitus and field allow for a "socialized subjectivity" that unites structures with agents.[133]

The implications of Bourdieu's theorization for understanding the ancient world are that it allows for authors to engage in literary practices that are expected or usual for their historical circumstances and social location. This means that authors participate in particular standards and practices that are dictated by their levels of education, social class, and background as well as established methods for the composition and circulation of their texts. They are rational agents who make decisions in and about their writings based on knowledge of certain literary conventions, relevant bodies of literature, and the kinds of issues being actively discussed within their historical field. Not dead, these authors are very much alive. Moreover, contra the Romantics, they do not produce literature that is inspired by the *Geist* and communal mind of an ill-defined social body. Their historical processes, literary fields, and social networks can be described and analyzed.

The example of Luke–Acts offered in the previous chapter helps to illustrate the rational activity of an author. Beyond an interest in cultivating a myth of Christian origins, Luke qua author demonstrates knowledge of the letters of Paul, Mark, and possibly the hypothetical Q source.

---

[131] Pierre Bourdieu, *The Logic of Practice* (Stanford: Stanford University Press, 1990), 59.
[132] Pierre Bourdieu, *Distinction: A Social Critique of the Judgment of Taste*, trans. Richard Nice (Cambridge, MA: Harvard University Press, 1996), 170.
[133] Pierre Bourdieu and Loïc Wacquant, *An Invitation to Reflexive Sociology* (Chicago: University of Chicago Press, 1992), 126.

Given the level of education indicated by the quality of his writing, he was also likely aware of Augustan-era literature such as Vergil and other forms of ancient epic. Like Vergil, Luke claims to have a patron; he has an interest in establishing the divine genealogy of a dynastic family; he interprets visions and prophecy; and he writes about a founding figure tasked with establishing a new community. He may have also read *bioi* of notable philosophers and statesmen or some of the writings of the Second Sophistic or Neopythagorean pseudepigrapha.[134] In short, Luke is an author situated within many interconnected networks of literacy. His prologue, in fact, alludes to others before him who have "undertaken to draw up an account" of the life of Jesus and that he has taken it upon himself to "write an orderly account" after consulting a variety of oral and literary sources. Scholars tend to focus on the possibility that Luke is offering evidence in this passage for the kinds of oral traditions and other gospels imagined in the Big Bang; however, what Luke is in effect saying is: "other writers and storytellers have tried to convey this story, but I can write a much better one." Luke is situating himself in a competitive field of other writers from the very beginning of his work. Why Luke employs the strategy of attributing his work to the *logos* is a subject I explore in subsequent chapters.

Having identified certain approaches to authorship and social structure in Romanticism that have contributed to a view of literature as a repository for the *Volkgeist*, I now turn to Romantic theories of language, oral tradition, myth, and "primitivism" that have had direct influence on the field of early Christian studies. By direct influence I mean that it is possible to trace an intellectual genealogy from the Romantic figures I have discussed thus far through to many of the theologians and secular scholars at the forefront of the historical study of scripture and biblical criticism.

HERDER, MÖHLER, AND THE STUDY OF BIBLICAL LITERATURE

A student of Kant and a Lutheran pastor, Herder is widely considered the originator of the notion of the *Volkgeist* – the spirit of the German people and nation.[135] His major contributions to post-Enlightenment and

---

[134] See Marianne Palmer Bonz, *The Past as Legacy: Luke–Acts and Ancient Epic* (Minneapolis: Fortress Press, 2000), and John T. Fitzgerald, *Passions and Moral Progress in Greco-Roman Thought* (New York: Routledge, 2007).

[135] Coincidentally, Herder's proto-nationalistic positions would have "fateful consequences for the twentieth century"; Livingston, *Modern Christian Thought*, 73. By the end of his

theological thinking were in his critiques of language and history. Considering language to be the "foundation of human consciousness" – and not, contra Hamann, principally of divine origin or, contra Rousseau, a human invention – his construction of the circle of language and thought in many ways prefigured Wittgenstein's "language-game," viewing language as "a series of developing revelations" of the human race.[136] To be clear, this is not to say that he held that language signaled a progression of history per se. Rather, each epoch of history – each "cultural phase" – was its own unique expression of what Herder termed *Humanität* (humanity).[137]

Herder's view of language had particular implications for his theories of religion. Each religion is embedded in a certain culture and unique to that context: "He who has noticed, what an inexpressible thing the individuality of a person is ... how different and particular all things will be to him because they are seen by his eyes, measured by his soul, and felt by his heart? ... As far as heat is from cold, and as one pole is from another, so the religions differ."[138] For Herder, each religion, like each individual nation and culture, is autonomous: "Every nation flourishes like a tree on its own root (*Jede Nation blüht wie ein Baum auf eigner Wurzel*)." That said, while maintaining that each religious tradition is its own unique and valuable representation of a given culture, he still viewed Christianity as "nothing but the pure dew of heaven for all nations (*nichts als der reine Himmelsthau, für alle Nationen*)."[139] In his *First Dialogue*

---

life, however, Herder reputedly rejected nationalism. See Berlin, *Three Critics of the Enlightenment*, 224–25.

[136] Livingston, *Modern Christian Thought*, 74.

[137] Herder's student, Goethe, would describe this theory as a case of nature evolving from "an unknown center" moving toward "an unknown boundary." J. W. von Goethe, *Goethes Werke, Naturwissenschaftliche Schriften 1, Hamburger Ausgabe*, 14 vols., ed. Erich Trunz (Munich: Beck, 1981), 13:35.

[138] Johann Gottfried Herder, *Sämmtliche Werke*, 33 vols., ed. Bernard Suphan (Berlin: Weidmann Verlag Anstalt, 1877–1913), 5:502, 32:146: "Wer bemerkt hat, was es für eine unaussprechliche Sache mit der Eigenheit eines Menschen sei ... wie anders und eigen Ihm alle Dinge werden nachdem sie sein Auge siehet seine Seele mißt sein Herz empfindet ... So weit die Hitze von der Kälte, und ein Pol vom andern absteht, so verschieden sind auch die Religionen." These passages are also noted by Livingston, *Modern Christian Thought*, 74.

[139] Herder, *Sämmtliche Werke*, 24:48–49. Herder extends his metaphor of the tree in this passage, stating that each nation and religion remains distinct: "[Universal Christianity] does not change any tree's character or its fruit (*der übrigens keines Baumes Charakter und Fruchtart*)" but rather brings peace ("Friede wird sodann auf der Erde, Friede!"). The Tübingen philosopher Carl August Eschenmayer would put an even finer point on the matter: the highest expression of *Geist* in human history is found not in art, contra

Concerning National Religion (1802), Herder constructs a conversation between two friends in which one friend asks the other, "Would you blame me ... if I nevertheless consider Christianity the religion of all religions, of all people (*die Religion aller Religionen, aller Völker*)?" This then leads into an extended discourse on language (*Sprache*) as that which "distinguishes peoples genetically (*Völker genetisch unterscheidet*)"[140] and, further, that he who "is ashamed of his nation and language (*sich seiner Nation und Sprache schämt*) has torn not only the religion of his people (*die Religion seines Volks*) but the bond that ties him to the nation (*das ihn an die Nation knüpfet*)."[141] Following Hamann, Herder equates "linguistic petrifaction" with a valley full of corpses "which only 'a prophet' [such as Socrates, St. Paul, Luther, and perhaps himself] could cover with flesh."[142] For Herder, the poetic language of biblical texts was the collective "mother tongue (*Muttersprache*)" of the people and, in this poetry, evidence of "our very own language of religion (*das ist unsre eigenste unsre Religionssprache*)."[143]

Yet one could not deny that human hands were at work on the composition of the Bible. Herder acknowledges that the text reflects God's words and intentions, albeit complying with the frailties and limitations of human comprehension.[144] Thus biblical poetry necessarily reflects the particular linguistic and cultural traits of the people by and for whom it was composed; the author is a mediator of "developing divine revelation" put into accessible language for God's people, not an autonomous or rational actor.[145] By studying the poetry and other writings of biblical authors, Herder proposed that one could know the "thinking and feeling (*Denkart und Empfindung*)" of the *Volk*: "how they were educated (*wie sie erzogen wird*), what objects (*Gegenstände*) they looked upon, what kinds of things they love with passion (*Leidenschaft liebt*) ... their dances and music (*Tanz ihre Musik*)."[146]

F. W. J. Schelling, but in the early stages of Christianity's development out of the dregs of antiquity.

[140] Herder, *Sämmtliche Werke*, 24:43.   [141] Herder, *Sämmtliche Werke*, 24:48.

[142] Berlin, *Three Critics of the Enlightenment*, 240.

[143] Herder, *Sämmtliche Werke*, 24:43.

[144] Herder, *Sämmtliche Werke*, 31:104: "Gott muß sich also den Menschen ganz menschlich, ganz nach ihrer Art und Sprache, ganz nach ihrer Schwachheit und Eingeschränktheit der Begriffe erklären."

[145] Livingston, *Modern Christian Thought*, 77.

[146] Johann Gottfried Herder, *Vom Geist der ebräischen Poesie: eine Anleitung für die Liebhaber derselben, und der ältesten Geschichte des menschlichen Geistes*, 2 vols. (Liepzig: J. A. Barth, 1825), 4–5.

Perhaps Herder's best illustration of the association between nature and language comes in his *Vom Geist der ebräischen Poesie* (On the Spirit of Hebrew Poetry) (1782–83).[147] In this two-volume work, he equates the sensory metaphors used by the Hebrew poets to the pure and child-like nature of their "savage nations (*wilder Völker*)."[148] "Savage" is intended not to be pejorative in this case (although it inescapably retains a derogatory tenor) but a reflection of the simplicity of the *Volk* and their closeness to nature. Herder explains: "The more savage (*wilder*), that is, the more alive (*lebendiger*) and uninhibited (*freiwürkender*) a people (*Volk*) is ... the more savage (*wilder*), that is, lively, free, sensuous [and] lyrically persuasive its songs must be (*lebendiger, freier, sinnlicher lyrisch handelnder müssen auch ... Lieder*)."[149] This is the framework through which Herder begins his investigation, opening with a celebration of the music he envisages accompanied the Hebrew poets: "The clatter of the ancient cymbals and kettle-drums ... of [those] savage peoples (*wilder Völker*) ... is still ringing in my ears. I still see David dancing in front of the Ark of the Covenant, or the prophets summoning [a minstrel] to inspire him."[150] Correspondingly, he posits that the first stage of this poetry was chiefly oral. It is the unmediated expression of *Geist* among the *Volk* and the "simplest [form] by which

---

[147] Herder's enthusiasm for the Hebrew poets (the *Naturmenschen*) should not be conflated with his views on eighteenth- and early nineteenth-century Judaism. Although he embraced the historical, national character and language of the Hebrew people represented by the scriptures, he was also adamant that epochs remain conceptually segregated and in essence that the modern Jew had little association with ancient Hebrew poetry and law. See Anders Gerdmar, *Roots of Theological Anti-Semitism: German Biblical Interpretation and the Jews, from Herder and Semler to Kittel and Bultmann* (Leiden: Brill, 2009), 59.

[148] This phrase (*wilder Völker*) and its derivatives are found throughout Herder's *Vom Geist der ebräischen Poesie*; see, for example, 2, 276, 306.

[149] Herder, *Sämmtliche Werke*, 5:164.

[150] Herder, *Vom Geist der ebräischen Poesie*, 2; *Sämmtliche Werke*, 11:224: "Das Geklapper der alten Cymbeln und Pauken, kurz die ganze Janitscharenmusik wilder Völker, die man den orientalischen Parallelismus zu nennen beliebt hat, ist mir dabei im Ohr, und ich sehe noch immer den David vor der Bundeslade tanzen, oder den Propheten Spielmann rufen dass er ihn begeistre."

I have elected to elide Herder's comments on "Janizary music" and orientalism in the translation above for the sake of brevity; however, that he draws a connection between the Hebrew Bible and these musical genres/traditions is potentially significant given Romantic theories of linguistic origins in this period. Similarly, I have taken certain liberties in translating his reference to "Spielmann" but have preserved the original phrasing in this footnote for reference.

the human soul expressed its thoughts (*die simpelsten Vorstellungsarten der menschlichen Seele*)."[151]

He goes on to describe the work of these poets as "imperfect," full of "far-fetched images (*die weit hergesuchten Bilder*)" and parallelisms so "monotonous (*eintönig*)" they create an "eternal tautology (*eine ewige Tautologie*)."[152] He also suggests the active verb (*Verbum*) is "almost everything (*beinahe alles*)"[153] in Hebrew, offering the caveat: "but for this beggar-folk (*Bettlervolk*) ... from what sources could they form a language (*Sprache bilden*)?" However, as with the concept of the "savage," these observations are not designed to be detractions. The language expressed by these poets is the "living language of Canaan, during the period of its greatest beauty and purity, before it was mixed with the Chaldee [and the] Greek (*die lebendige Sprache Kanaans war, und auch hier nur von ihren schönsten reinesten Zeiten, ehe sie mit der Chaldaischen Griechischen ... vermischt ward*)."[154] Its active verbs and sensory metaphors combined "form and feeling (*Bild und Empfindung*)"; unlike Homer, the words "creak and hiss (*knarren und zischen*)" and are a product of sensation (*Empfindung*) and heartfelt emotion (*und gleichsam in der Region des Herzens gebildet*), not logic and refinement.[155]

According to Herder, eventually these oral traditions would be recorded as *Volkspoesie*, thus experiencing the process of being converted into literature. While Hebrew poetry was embedded in the language of its *Volk*, Herder was also aware that it passed through the "weaving of the book according to a later way of thinking (*Das Gewebe des Buchs nach späterer Denkart*)" – that is, it passed through the hands of redactors.[156] Naturally, this would result in a certain amount of degradation of the "purer" forms of the original *Poesie*. However, an enterprising analyst could recover elements of the pretextual oral/folk traditions of the "nation" represented by the text. Herder's model for an oral tradition behind the development of literature would later inform Romantic

---

[151] Herder, *Sämmtliche Werke*, 11:293: "All sensuous peoples (*sinnliche Völker*) know the nature (*Natur*) of which they speak [their poetry]; yes, they know her more vibrantly (*lebendiger*) and for their purposes [have a better knowledge of it]."

[152] Herder, *Vom Geist der ebräischen Poesie*, 5.

[153] Herder, *Vom Geist der ebräischen Poesie*, 7.

[154] Herder, *Vom Geist der ebräischen Poesie*, 9.

[155] Herder, *Vom Geist der ebräischen Poesie*, 12. Likewise, just as Herder considered the language of the Hebrews more simplistic and closer to a "pure (*reiner*)" state of nature, he considered the cognitive functions and morals of this *Volk* to be similarly "child-like (*so kindlich*)." See Herder, *Vom Geist der ebräischen Poesie*, 81.

[156] Herder, *Sämmtliche Werke*, 32:204.

folklorists like Wilhelm and Jacob Grimm. His methods would also influence later Redaction Criticism and Form Criticism in the field of New Testament studies, particularly members of the History of Religions School, including Hermann Gunkel and Johannes Weiss.

More immediately, Herder's theoretical reconstructions would impact the work of other nineteenth-century thinkers like Johann Adam Möhler. Möhler was part of the Roman Catholic theological renewal of the early nineteenth century at Tübingen until he left to become chair of New Testament exegesis at Munich. Influenced by Herder's conception of society and religion as organic forms, Möhler would develop a theology that traced the *Geist* from its expression in the oral teachings of Jesus through to Möhler's present day. He equated the presence of the *Geist* to an understanding of tradition wherein there is no distinction between written scripture and the oral or "living" gospel passed on by the apostles to the early Christians:

> The written scriptures (*Die heiligen Schriften*) were therefore not distinguishable from the living gospel (*dem lebendigen Evangelium verschiedenes ausgesaßt*) or ... the oral tradition (*die mündliche Tradition*) ... from the written gospels ... both were the Word (*das Wort*) of the Holy Spirit (*heiligen Geistes*), as both were handed over to the faithful by the apostles (*wie beides von den Aposteln den Gläubigen übergeben worden*), so both types of Words were regarded (*so wurden beide Arten des Wortes*) ... as completely *Die Einheit in der Kirche* inseparable (*als durchaus untrennbar*).[157]

Thus, he understood the canonical gospels to be a record of the oral teachings of Christ or the "first *written* document of that tradition."[158]

Building on Herder's organic forms, in his *Die Einheit in der Kirche* (*The Unity of the Church*) (1825), Möhler stressed the presence of the *Geist* within the Christian community, stating, "The Church (*Die Kirche*) ... is the body of the spirit of the believers ... forming from the inside out (*der Körper des von innen heraus sich bildenden Geistes der Gläubigen*)."[159] Moreover, he identified the gospels as the "embodied expression (*verkörperte Ausdruck*)" and "first link (*das erste Glied*)" of the *Geist* at the "beginning of Christianity."[160] The notion of an "embodied expression" would become increasingly central to scholarship on early Christian texts that concerned itself with recovering the teachings, experiences, and other holdings of imagined Christian communities.

---

[157] Johann Adam Möhler, *Die Einheit in der Kirche*, §15, 51–52.
[158] Livingston, *Modern Christian Thought*, 193. Emphasis in original.
[159] Möhler, *Die Einheit in der Kirche*, vi.   [160] Möhler, *Die Einheit in der Kirche*, 56.

James Livingston explains: "Möhler's ecclesiology is ... influenced by the Romantic conception of an organic, evolving, living tradition and a united and unbroken community consciousness that is guided by the Divine Spirit, *in and through which alone* the individual person can understand and appropriate the mysteries of Christian life and belief."[161] In challenging his Protestant interlocutors, however, Möhler – like Herder – did not see the gospels as infallible. Rather, he viewed them as a record of the *Geist* at work in human history, mediated through the selective choices of the gospel writers on which oral and written materials to preserve.

Möhler and Herder each represent lines of German Romantic thought that can be found in later Redaction and Form Criticism. For Form Critics, early Christian communities possessed oral stories and a small collection of written texts that preserved Jesus' teachings alongside elements of the community's collective interpretations and interpolations. In this construction of history, the notion of an autonomous author was absent. Authorship was fundamentally communal. Certain scholars would later associate the notion of communal *Geist* with the posited folk literature of Christian communities to claim that the gospel writer was a mere redactor of agreed-upon, shared materials. Moreover, many notable early Christianity and New Testament scholars saw in the idea of folk literature a window onto the preliterary, oral traditions of early Christian communities. Bultmann, for instance, proposed that one could demonstrate through "critical investigation ... that the whole tradition about Jesus which appears in the three synoptic gospels is composed of a series of layers which can on the whole be clearly distinguished."[162] He maintained that it could be "easily proved" that "many sayings originated in the church itself; others were modified by the church." One merely needed to separate content attributable to the "Aramaic tradition of the oldest Palestinian community" from content attributable to the manifestly distinct "Hellenistic Christian community" of the later gospel writers and their fellow Christians.[163] This Hellenistic brand of Christianity was seen as imbued with Platonism, Stoicism, pneumatology, and other elements that made it palatable to its Gentile audience.[164]

---

[161] Livingston, *Modern Christian Thought*, 193.

[162] Bultmann, *Rudolf Bultmann: Interpreting Faith for the Modern Era*, 97.

[163] Bultmann, *Rudolf Bultmann: Interpreting Faith for the Modern Era*, 97.

[164] Rudolf Bultmann, "Primitive Christianity as a Syncretistic Phenomenon," in *Primitive Christianity: In Its Contemporary Setting*, trans. R. H. Fuller (London: Thames & Hudson 1956), 209–13: "On other occasions the Christian missionaries went direct to the Gentile population, and then, in the first instance, to the lower classes in the cities.

Such interpretive moves would have monumental influence on interpretations of Q as well. Bultmann proposed that the supposed sayings-source was "a primary source from which we can reconstruct a picture of the primitive community in which the *Logia* [the sayings] arose."[165] Again, the significance of this shift in methodology was that the group rather than the autonomous author was now largely considered the primary actor in the course of authorship. The idea of a discrete writer of the canonical gospels, or Q, was rarely discussed in early Christian literature outside references to a representative scribe, redactor, or some similar figure. The notion of collective authorship became the norm, or at the very least, scholars spoke in terms of the communities that produced these materials rather than of individual writers.

Redaction Criticism introduced into this schema the notion of a redactor compiling disparate remnants from past Christian communities into a text reflecting not only elements of a more "authentic" Christian past but also the redactor's *Sitz im Leben*. This move found scholars interrogating the relative theology of the redactor: how the redactor's thought was a communal product simultaneously reinforcing and differentiating the group's unique perspectives and theological outlook. The choices made by the redactor as to which stories about Jesus' life to include were also offered as representative of the interests of each individual community. Once again, the poet – the author-genius – was the voice of the dissected whole.

For some, the community-writer perspective is simply cited in conjunction with the idea that authors are embedded within particular social or cultural contexts (*Sitze im Leben*) or that their writings are socially constructed products. That said, it is rare to find a study that does not deem the author's presumed *Christian community* to be the most immediately formative and relevant social framework. Miraculously cohesive and unified in "mind and practice," this Christian community is theorized in lieu of other kinds of social contexts or environments.[166]

There were probably churches of Gentiles only.... Christianity found itself in a new spiritual environment: The Gospel had to be preached in terms intelligible to Hellenistic audiences and their mental outlook, while at the same time the audience themselves were bound to interpret the gospel message in their own way, in light of their own spiritual needs. Hence the growth of diverse types of Christianity."

[165] Rudolf Bultmann, "The New Approach to the Synoptic Problem," *Journal of Religion* 6 (1926): 337–62, cit. 341.

[166] Stowers, "The Concept of 'Community,'" 238.

In recent years the social sciences have added to the conversation questions about the social organization of the early Christian communities – were they egalitarian, sectarian, patriarchal, economically or socially "stratified"? – but "community" has remained the starting point of analysis. This has been an extremely limiting – yet durable – approach to early Christian literature and one that has allowed "normative theological concepts [to parade] as descriptive and explanatory social concepts."[167] Gerd Theissen offers one representative example with his analyses of the relative ethics of the early Christian communities depicted in Paul and the Synoptics, often using Acts to anchor discussion of the Gentile Antioch community, the radical Matthean community, and so forth.[168] Helpfully, Theissen has argued against the "romantic idea of a proletarian Christian community" for the Pauline canon and recognizes that economic and social elites were likely also members of these Christ groups and not just the poor and disenfranchised. However, he continues to take the idea of the bounded, religious community for granted in most cases, debating their internal "stratification" and how they reflect the urban centers with which they are traditionally associated.[169] This approach was later heralded by Abraham Malherbe, Wayne Meeks, and others in their assessments of Paul and, by extension, the gospels.[170]

We also see the legacy of this thinking in the later work of scholars like Richard Horsley. Although Horsely has done much to demonstrate how to employ interdisciplinary methods and insights from allied fields like anthropology and sociolinguistics, the core questions he brings to the gospels still center on folk and oral traditions or communal language.

---

[167] Stowers, "The Concept of 'Community,'" 245–46. Reflecting on methodological approaches in the field more broadly, Stowers suggests, "The form critics and many of their heirs have continued to deny that the early Christian writings are properly literature. Letters and Gospels are rather deposits of folk speech or so-called oral tradition. The Gospels contained the *Geist* of the preaching, teaching and primitive churches because they are residues of oral speech."

[168] For example, Gerd Theissen, *Die Religion der ersten Christen: Eine Theorie des Urchristentums* (Gütersloh: Gütersloher Verlagshaus, 2000). Also translated into English as *The Religion of the Earliest Churches: Creating a Symbolic World*, trans. John Bowden (Minneapolis: Fortress Press, 1999).

[169] Gerd Theissen, "Social Stratification in the Corinthian Community: A Contribution to the Sociology of Early Hellenistic Christianity," in *The Social Setting of Pauline Christianity*, ed. and trans. John H. Schütz (Philadelphia: Fortress Press, 1982), 70.

[170] For a good review of this trajectory, see David G. Horrell, "Aliens and Strangers? The Socio-Economic Location of the Addressees of 1 Peter," in *Becoming Christian: Essays on 1 Peter and the Making of Christian Identity*, Library of New Testament Studies 394 (London: Bloomsbury T&T Clark, 2013), 100–132.

A survey of his body of work demonstrates that his analyses are never terribly far from talk of "the people's communal spirit"[171] or descriptions of the "community meetings in which the Gospel of Mark or Q was recited" and how the gospels function "as oral communication in community contexts" and our need to "transcend the modern assumptions of print culture" despite the only evidence for these writings being that they were a part of ancient Mediterranean book culture.[172] In short, the collective, illiterate proletariat – the "primitive Christian" – remains a tantalizing model of Christian exceptionalism in analyses of the ancient world, even when that model is recognized as problematic. That the gospel authors may have been elite Roman writers is almost inconceivable outside this attendant group of imagined *Volk*.

THE "PRIMITIVE" CHRISTIANS

I must preface this section by acknowledging that my study maintains a narrow and strategic focus on the works of Rudolf Bultmann (1884–1976) and Helmut Koester (1926–2016). Our field has been so singularly focused on a community model for reading the gospels that it would hardly be constructive for me to identify a host of instances over the decades where this social model was assumed. Moreover, as I account in my Preface, the Protestant-Catholic concern for reviving *Geist* among the people in Germany and elsewhere in Europe was such a complex and fraught enterprise at the fin de siècle that outlining its contours is a task worthy of its own study. Thankfully, Marchand's excellent *German Orientalism in the Age of Empire: Religion, Race, and Scholarship* has done much of this work already and, for the purposes of the present argument, the Bultmanian school represents the more immediate influence on our field, bridging the gap between the fin de siècle and its search for origins and the present day.[173]

Whenever concepts like community, oral tradition, illiteracy, "primitive," urban, poor, and the like are invoked without justification, the scholar has largely taken for granted the social circumstances of the gospel writer and is tailoring their subsequent analyses to fit this

---

[171] Richard Horsley, *Jesus and the Politics of Roman Palestine* (Columbia: University of South Carolina Press, 2014), 126; Richard Horsley, *Jesus and Empire: The Kingdom of God and the New World Order* (Minneapolis: Fortress Press, 2003), 126.

[172] Horsley, *Jesus and Empire*, 68.

[173] Marchand, *German Orientalism in the Age of Empire*, esp. 252–91.

foundational supposition. This includes studies that attempt to place these writers in a sociocultural tier more consummate with the traditional model of the non-elite "Christian community," despite historical evidence suggesting compositional prose would be beyond the education level of these segments of society. Even among scholars of the so-called new consensus perspective who maintain that the supposed urban Christians included "wealthy, elite, ruling-class members," literacy does not necessarily correspond with economic affluence.[174] Nor does participation in *paideia* or certain literate preparation guarantee the competency to write plot narrative. While scribes, for instance, could be hired to write an inscription, send a letter, or use their access to literary materials to help copy or produce a piece of writing like a contract, they did not necessarily possess the training, skill, and literacy necessary to write an original composition at the level of sophistication we see with the Synoptics.[175] This is an issue I address further in the following chapter.

Studies that aim to draw conclusions about ancient texts that are *external to the process of writing itself* are problematic. In the absence of more information about an author, their social circumstances, training, and so forth, one must begin from the perspective of what we know about writing practices and book culture and then proceed from this baseline. To begin from any other premise runs the risk of seeking evidence to support a predetermined conclusion. Returning to a maxim from the previous chapter, expertise is also a matter of "more or less"; either we acknowledge our Synoptic writers are engaging in a relatively complex level of literary exchange and intertext or we import idiosyncratic parameters on our evidence. Scholars of early Christianity cannot have it both ways. We cannot continue to idealize socially marginal Christ-followers, passing along the oral stories of the church, at the expense of concrete historical models of literacy. In addition to asking ourselves how the early Christians engaged in literate culture, we should be asking why a literate cultural producer would be interested in the subject of a Judean

---

[174] The "new consensus" is a term coined by Horrell to describe the ongoing debate about the economic and education levels of the early Christians. This scholarship ostensibly begins with Edwin Judge's work on Paul in the mid-twentieth century and is carried forward by Theissen, Malherbe, and Meeks. It is a perspective later challenged by Justin Meggitt, among others. Horrell suggests that "Paul and the earliest Christians shared in the absolute material poverty that was the lot of 99 per cent of the Roman empire's inhabitants," essentially dividing ancient society into a binary of have and have-nots. For more on this line of research, see Horrell, "Aliens and Strangers?," 101–2.

[175] Catherine Heszer, *Jewish Literacy in Roman Palestine* (Mohr Siebeck, 2001), 119–20.

wonder-working son of God. Rather than ask what makes the gospels exceptional, we should demonstrate how are they utterly commonplace imperial writings produced by ordinary Greco-Roman writers. Instead of scouring the ancient world seeking a social model that fits the Christian community narrative we have inherited from Acts, the church fathers, and Romanticism (e.g., the literate spokesperson, the rogue scribe, the unauthored and disembodied gospel "voice"), we should let historical research and the texts speak for themselves.

I want to be clear that I am not attempting to indict my colleagues who have employed the community model or its terminology. Rather, I am seeking a reevaluation of some of our long-standing approaches. Bultmann and Koester are useful touchstones because aspects of their methodologies stem from German Romantic thought and their work has remained influential through the twentieth and twenty-first centuries. This is not to say that they did not recognize the gospels as forms of Greco-Roman literature or that they were inattentive to the social fabric of the first century Mediterranean world – far from it.[176] But I do maintain that, fundamentally, they understood the literature of the Jesus movement to be representative of Christian *communities* and not of *writers*.

The use of the term "primitive" by scholars like Bultmann and Koester in reference to the "Christians" and "churches" of the first century indicates that strains of Romantic thinking persist within the field. In German, the word that is most often used in reference to the Jesus movement of the first century is *Urchristentum*, sometimes translated into English as "early" or, in the case of twentieth-century German scholarship, "primitive" Christianity; correspondingly, the word for the "primitive Christians" is *Urchristen*. Depending on context, terms such as these generally take different valences. Possible meanings include the sense that one is speaking of the earliest stages and people of the movement that will

---

[176] For example, see Helmut Koester, *Introduction to the New Testament*, 2nd ed., vol. 1, *History, Culture, and Religion of the Hellenistic Age* (Berlin: de Gruyter, 1995). This multiset volume does an excellent job using interdisciplinary methods (e.g., classics, archaeology) to evaluate the social world of the ancient Mediterranean. That said, discussion of Greek culture, the Roman Empire, Judaism/Judea are conducted in such a way that there is little sense of how the gospel writers may have functioned within these constructs; rather, "Christianity" as such is discussed as a separate phenomenon (e.g., how Christians would later understand Vergil as an eschatological poet prefiguring the coming of Christ, to be discussed). Perhaps of note, this book was dedicated by Koester "To the memory of my teacher, Rudolf Bultmann."

come to be known as Christianity or of the kinds of "uneducated and ordinary men" referenced in Acts 4:13; or, relatedly, the terms might indicate that one is speaking of a group of people akin to the Romantic Savage – simple, illiterate peasants who represent a seemingly more "authentic" or "pure" form of the moral teachings of Jesus. In the case of references to the uneducated *Urchristen*, they are typically imagined as Galilean peasants or representatives of the "primitive Christianity [that] arose from the band of Jesus' disciples" or the first Hellenized communities that emerged out of the eschatological Palestinian Judaism of the Jerusalem church.[177]

Again, this is a model that relies heavily on Acts. Bultmann provides an explanation of this pattern of development that is worth quoting at length:

The eschatological community did not split off from Judaism as though it were conscious of itself as a new religious society.... The decisive step was taken when the good news of Jesus ... was carried beyond the confines of Palestinian Judaism, and Christian congregations sprang up in the Graeco-Roman world. These congregations consisted partly of Hellenistic Jewish Christians, partly of Gentiles, wherever the Christian sought its point of contact in Hellenistic synagogues ... the Christian missionaries went direct to the Gentile population, and then, in the first instance, to the lower classes in the cities.... By and large, the chief differences between Hellenistic Christians and the original Palestinian version was that the former ceased to be dominated by ... eschatological expectation.[178]

In this description of the development of *Urchristentum*, Jesus' disciples carefully preserved his spoken teachings, and an eschatological sect of Judaism was founded. Subsequently, communities of other Jesus followers began to manifest explosively throughout the lower classes of the ancient Mediterranean as products of the missionizing activity of itinerant preachers and prophets.[179] As these communities emerged, the oral teachings of the original Palestinian *Urchristen* were filtered through *koinē* Greek and the Platonic and Stoic philosophical frameworks familiar to the Gentiles. As the Christian movement grew, the eschatological imperative of the earlier and more "original" message began to recede.

---

[177] Bultmann, *Primitive Christianity*, 209.

[178] Bultmann, *Primitive Christianity*, 209–12.

[179] On itinerant preachers and early Christianity, see William E. Arnal, *Jesus and the Village Scribes: Galilean Conflicts and the Setting of Q* (Minneapolis: Fortress Press, 2001). Arnal includes a short discussion on the influence of Germany and Protestant missionizing activity (*Wandervögeln*) on the interpretation of the New Testament.

In essence, the urbanization of Christianity led to certain philosophical adaptations of its earliest teachings. However, the central inspiration of Jesus' moral philosophy remained, and Jesus' words continued to be translated, circulated, and developed among these urban communities. This oral transmission closely resembled the collective speech of the Romantic *Volkspoesie*. In certain cases, the continued growth of Christianity would be attributed to the presumed progression of history, which was synonymous in many respects with the notion of Romantic *Geist*.

According to Bultmann's representative model, certain communities sought to record their oral teachings and developing theology either in collections of sayings like Q or in the writings we now call the gospels. For this, they employed an author or redactor who incorporated into an account of Jesus' life the teachings that the community held dear. Often, this writer is imagined to be part of the community, perhaps as a member of the *ekklēsia* who had enough education to write these oral traditions down. In some cases, thanks in part to the urbanization of Christianity, the gospel writer may have come from a more privileged background and is recognized as a well-educated and affluent member of the church. Occasionally, even the church itself is imagined to be a community of affluent Christians.[180] In any case, these writings expressed the community's collective experiences and concerns. Therefore, the author acted as a mouthpiece for his fellow Christians, his *Volk*. Later, in the second century, the canonical gospels would come to be associated with specific urban hubs of Christianity, such as Antioch, Rome, Ephesus, and so on.

Bultmann's description of the history of Christianity does not speak for early Christian scholarship writ large, but the picture he paints of the social world of *Urchristentum* continues to be prevalent. The contours of this model of "primitive Christianity" are reinscribed when scholarship persists in imagining the production of early Christian literature in terms of presumed or accepted religious communities, authentic oral traditions, and provincial *ekklēsiai*. Such models of the first century are informed in the main by Romantic ideas about the author-genius and related constructions that rob agency away from the writers of these texts and reinscribe a mystified idea of Christian beginnings.

Bultmann's historical description of Christianity and its literature also follows the ahistorical and ideological procedures imagined by second-

---

[180] For example, see Raymond E. Brown and John P. Meier, *Antioch and Rome: New Testament Cradles of Catholic Christianity* (New York: Paulist Press, 1983), 23.

century thinkers like the author of Acts, Papias, or the author of the *Apocryphon of James*. Koester, for example, cites the *Apocryphon of James* as a model for how we might rely on the "trustworthiness of the oral tradition" in the canonical gospels as remembered by the most primitive Christians: "the twelve disciples [were] all sitting together at the same time and remembering what the Savior had said to each one of them, whether in secret or openly, and [putting it] in books."[181] Interestingly, Koester goes on to mention that in the second-century context of the *Apocryphon's* production, "controversy" had been rife with so-called Gnostics, "writers ... composing their written documents on the basis of the claim that they remembered well from the apostles and from those who had followed them."[182] What Koester is in fact describing is an interconnected network of writers engaging with various first-century texts and oral stories and competing with one another in order to develop – again, to borrow a term from the previous chapter – an "invented tradition." Yet his overall analysis maintains a stark and anachronistic contrast between orthodoxy and heresy while also preserving the notion of an early Christian Big Bang.

When discussing non-Christian sources, Koester is more inclined to acknowledge historically plausible literary networks and forms of exchange. In a detailed overview of imperial Roman poetry in his *Introduction to the New Testament*, for example, he describes the literary networks of Plautus, Ennius, Terence, and Menander; Cicero and Varo; Vergil, Horace, Livy, and Maecenas; Propertius, Tibullus, and Ovid; Petronius, Persius, Cornutus, and Lucan; Cato, Caesar, and Sallust; Arrian and Dio Cassius; and the imperial Stoics and the writers of the Second Sophistic, considering their mutual influences and effects on the development of various literary genres. Throughout, he maintains a light focus on thematic issues including prophetic speech (e.g., Vergil), apocalypticism (e.g., Horace), moralizing narratives (e.g., Cicero), theology

---

[181] *Nag Hammadi Corpus* I 2, 7–15, cited from Helmut Koester, *Ancient Christian Gospels: Their History and Development* (Harrisburg: Trinity Press International, 1990), 34. This model also depends on accepting the Pauline version of Christian beginnings. In his *Introduction*, Koester reiterates this history: "Wherever Paul went, he was soon confronted with other Christian preachers who tried to outdo him with their performances. Much information about these marketplace philosophers comes to us only through their more educated literary opponents, because the philosophers who went out into the streets relied on the spoken word, just as Christian wandering preachers entrusted themselves not to the written word but to the effect of their oral message." Koester, *Introduction*, 341. This passage is also discussed below.

[182] Koester, *Ancient Christian Gospels*, 34.

(e.g., Plutarch), and a denial of imperial deification (e.g., Ovid). He expects his reader to intuit that these are salient *topoi* because they represent the intellectual interests of the early Christians; however, the only "educated literary" elite Koester sees fit to reference is Paul.[183] The gospel writers are not mentioned. Rather, the implication is that the gospel writers simply recorded the "spoken word" of the "Christian wandering preachers" who "entrusted themselves not to the written word but to the effect of their oral message."[184] Compare this with his analysis of the so-called Church Fathers like Clement of Alexandria openly reading and preserving the works of Plutarch and Marcus Aurelius.[185] Adherence to the Romantic oral tradition thesis and an acceptance of Acts' myth of origins prevented Koester from treating the gospels in the same manner as any of the other Greco-Roman writers he describes, not even Paul.

CONCLUSION: WHAT IS A CLASSIC?

Our inheritance from German Romanticism in the field remains strong and persistent, at times more evident in our approaches and conclusions than others. Periodically, scholars have acknowledged our problematic inheritance from our Romantic forebears, but our methods and

---

[183] Koester, *Introduction*, 343. One might argue that this is because his chief concern in this chapter is to provide a general, historical context for Christian literature; however, the structure of his argument is such that Christianity is illustrated as the fulfillment of the work of the Roman writers (e.g., the "salvific potential" of Vergil). See Koester, *Introduction*, 326. A survey of the book also reveals the use of general "Romantic" terminology of the kind discussed above (e.g., "The Spirit of the Hellenistic Age," 148, passim). He also repeatedly notes the superiority and influence of the Greeks on derivative Roman literature and education.

Koester did endorse close comparative studies between the New Testament and related literature and the Roman canon. One of Koester's students, Marianne Palmer Bonz, published her dissertation under the title *The Past as Legacy: Luke–Acts and Ancient Epic*, also referenced above. The overall theme of Palmer Bonz's monograph is that Luke's gospel can be considered a "sacred" epic in the same vein as the *Aeneid*. Therefore, as this chapter has reviewed, despite its excellent use and discussion of sources, Palmer Bonz's study maintains a Romantic focus in terms of characterizing certain texts as representative of a particular culture.

[184] Koester, *Introduction*, 341.

[185] Koester, *Introduction*, 345–46. He identifies Plutarch as a "kindred spirit" of the Greek fathers in his embrace of the world's "social and religious institutions" and "a life which finds true, spiritual happiness in the mastery of the moral demands of marriage, family, the education of children, as well as in the faithful fulfillment of the duties of religion." Koester explicitly lists these as values in contradistinction to "contemporary Christian Gnostics" who, presumably, expressed more misanthropic ideals.

assumptions about the social world of early Christianity remain static in ways that are, at times, so entrenched as to be almost imperceptible from inside the field. Throughout this chapter, I have mapped a genealogy of how these terms and methods have passed from mentor to mentee, Romanticism to poststructuralism, German to English, and so on. There remains a certain subtext to this discussion about how we construct history and how we establish and accept particular canons of literature as representative of a religion, a people, or what we call a tradition.

In a sense, I could have framed this chapter by asking the question: What is a classic? Whether the Synoptics, the *Nibelungenlied*, *Germania*, or the works of Bultmann and Koester, we collectively make decisions about the texts that represent our interests and tribe. It does not follow, however, that the authors of these texts should be eclipsed in favor of the groups that have adopted their texts – particularly if we are in the business of redescribing history. As Burton Mack cautions:

The task [for the scholar should] be to account for the formation of the gospel itself in the context of a later social history, not to use it as a guide to conjure up chimeras at the beginning ... [and it is only in this manner that] [t]he fantasy of an order of things without precursor might actually be capable of explanation.[186]

We need to describe the history and social networks of these writers and consider their methods and rhetoric before attempting to reconstruct the subsequent communities that adopted them.

---

[186] Burton L. Mack, *A Myth of Innocence: Mark and Christian Origins* (Minneapolis: Fortress Press, 1988), 9.

3

Authorship in Antiquity

Specialization and Social Formations

One of the more amusing accounts of how literature was consumed in antiquity is from the rhetorician Athenaeus Naucratita's *Deipnosophistae* (The Sophists at Dinner).[1] Comprised of a series of vignettes, Athenaeus combines verse and prose satire, philosophical reflection and biography with lexica of literary works, authors, sayings, and other sundry, in the sympotic style of Plato.[2] It is an eclectic storehouse of familiar literary genres and figures. Among the imagined guests in attendance are P. Livius

---

[1] A native of Egypt but located in Rome, Athenaeus of Naucratis is writing in the late second and early third centuries CE on the basis of his literary and imperial references. His other lost works include *On the Kings of Syria* and *On the First of Archippus*. His style is in the register of Plutarch, Lucian, and Galen.
   A discussion of the *Deipnosophistae* also appears in Robyn Faith Walsh, "Q and the 'Big Bang' Theory of Christian Origins," in *Redescribing the Gospel of Mark*, ed. Barry S. Crawford and Merrill P. Miller (Atlanta: SBL Press, 2017), 483–533, cit. 505–7.

[2] In addition to his reliance on Plato and Lucian's *Symposium* and *Lexiphanes* and Plutarch's *Table Talk*, Athenaeus employs a version of prose and verse satire popularized by Menippus the Cynic. For more on his possible literary influences, see Derek Krueger, "The Bawdy and Society: The Shamelessness of Diogenes in Roman Imperial Culture," in *The Cynics: The Cynic Movement in Antiquity and Its Legacy*, ed. Robert Bracht Branham and Marie-Odile Goulet-Cazé (Berkeley: University of California Press, 1996), 222–39; Ronald F. Hock, "A Dog in the Manger: The Cynic Cynulcus among Athenaeus's Deipnosophists," in *Greeks, Romans, and Christians: Essays in Honor of Abraham J. Malherbe*, ed. David Balch, Everett Ferguson, and Wayne Meeks (Minneapolis: Fortress Press, 1990), 20–37; Christian Jacob, *The Web of Athenaeus*, trans. Arietta Papaconstantinou, ed. Scott Fitzgerald Johnson (Cambridge, MA: Harvard University Press, 2013).

Larensis, Galen of Pergamum, Ulpian of Tyre, and Cynulcus the Cynic, to name a few.[3] And, naturally, the subject on everyone's mind is food.

Beyond the various delicacies, recipes and drinking cups his diners discuss, Athenaeus' food-talk is also an occasion for exploring the moral constitutions – the virtues and vices – of a variety of noteworthy figures. For instance, Athenaeus relates the *chreia* of a third-century BCE poet, Machon, on Philoxenus of Cythera and his unfortunate experience with an octopus:

They say that Philoxenus the dithyrambic poet was fond of delicacies (ὀψοφάγον). One day in Syracuse he found an octopus as big as his forearm. He cooked it and devoured almost all of it, except for the head (καταφαγεῖν ὅλον σχεδὸν πλὴν τῆς κεφαλῆς). Overcome with indigestion, he was terribly ill. A physician went in to him and, seeing how poorly he was, said: "If any of your affairs are not in order, arrange them quickly (εἴ τί σοι ἀνοικονόμητόν ἐστι διατίθου ταχύ), Philoxenus, for you will die before the seventh hour." That man replied, "All of my affairs are in check, doctor, and were long ago. With the help of the gods, I leave my dithyrambs behind grown into men (τοὺς διθυράμβους σὺν θεοῖς καταλιμπάνω ἡνδρωμένους) and all of them crowned with garlands (καὶ πάντας ἐστεφανωμένους), and I dedicate them to the Muses who reared me. Aphrodite and Dionysus are their guardians. My will makes this all plain. But since Charon does not allow leisure but, as in Timotheus' *Niobe*, cries that the ferry-boat is leaving (χωρεῖν δὲ πορθμίδ' ἀναβοᾷ).... So that I have all my things with me [for] when I am sent down below (ἵν' ἔχων ἀποτρέχω πάντα τἀμαυτοῦ κάτω), give me back the rest of my octopus!"[4]

The gluttony of Philoxenus is well attested elsewhere in ancient literature, including in the fragments of Aristotle and Theophilus.[5] He is among a number of character-types favored by *bios*-writers, who looked to subversive figures to explore "discourse on excess and temperament." Philoxenus' example also engages the theme of ignoble death found in biographical writings like Diogenes Laertius', whose philosophers often

---

[3] Several of the dinner guests correspond with known individuals. P. Livius Larensis was a pontifex minor (*CIL* 6.212); Galen of Pergamum fills the role of the Platonic physician; Ulpian of Tyre refers to either the well-known jurist or his son; the Cynic Cynulcus acts as Ulpian's foil. Other dinner guests include Myrtilus the Thessalin, who routinely attacks the Stoics, and a host of fictitious persons, such as Plutarch of Athenaeus. See John Paulas, "How to Read Athenaeus' *Deipnosophists*," *American Journal of Philology* 133 (2012): 403–39; Pauline A. LeVen, "Reading the Octopus: Authorship, Intertexts, and a Hellenistic Anecdote (Machon Fr. 9 GOW)," *American Journal of Philology* 134 (2013): 23–35; Jacob, *The Web of Athenaeus*.

[4] Ath. 8.341b; Machon fr. 9.

[5] See LeVen, "Reading the Octopus," 30; Arist. fr. 83; Theophilus, *FHG*, 5 vols., ed. C. Müller and T. Müller (Paris, 1843–70), iv. 6. Also see Ath. 8.341d, which cites Machon's account of Philoxenus desiring "a four-foot long throat so as to be able to enjoy food and drink all at the same time."

come to unceremonious ends. Such episodes recall Plutarch's preface to the *Vitae Parallelae: Alexander et Caesar* or *Life of Alexander*:

For it is not histories we are writing (ἱστορίας γράφομεν) but lives (βίους); it is not always the most famous deeds which illuminate a man's virtues and vices (ἀρετῆς ἢ κακίας); often a clearer insight into a man's character is revealed by a small detail, a remark, or a joke (πρᾶγμα βραχὺ... ῥῆμα... παιδιά), than by battles where tens of thousands die, or by the greatest of conflicts, or by the siege of cities (Plut. *Vit. Alex.* 1.2).

Certain biographical subjects are a useful foil for considering dominant ethical principles, both positive and negative in scope.

A comparison of literary references to a figure like Philoxenus also demonstrates that, in many cases, writers are well aware of other works that employ the same characters or ethical types. For example, a favorite at symposia for his racy subject matter, Machon engages a variety of literary allusions in his bons mots.[6] In the case of Philoxenus, his final words are a play on the last words of Socrates: Socrates asks Crito to fetch a cock for Asclepius; Philoxenus asks the doctor to fetch him an octopus' head.[7] Machon makes an explicit reference to Philoxenus' contemporary and literary conversation partner, Timotheus, as Philoxenus ponders his final moments. Likewise, Diogenes Laertius cites Timotheus' *Niobe* in his account of the philosopher Zeno's suicide, precipitated by a stubbed toe.[8] Given that both Timotheus and Philoxenus rely on the linguistic and thematic elements of epic to help formulate their dithyrambs, it is likely that Machon also has Priam's fast in *Iliad* 24 in mind. And then there is Athenaeus writing centuries later, incorporating these *chreiae* into his larger program of, as Pauline A. LeVen explains, "Hellenistic scholarly

---

[6] See LeVen, "Reading the Octopus," 25: "Under the Roman Empire, *chreiae* will be used as preparatory exercises in rhetorical schools, but Machon's *chreiae* seem to be of a different ilk, for their often-vulgar themes make them a poor fit for a school curriculum, and evidence suggests that they were performed at symposia ... 'there are elements that suggest that these witty sayings of parasites and prostitutes are not just crude popular entertainment but a literate, learned version thereof (and in that sense, typically 'Hellenistic')."

[7] See Plato, *Euthyphro. Apology. Crito. Phaedo. Phaedrus*, trans. Harold North Fowler, LCL (Cambridge, MA: Harvard University Press, 1914). Also see Pauline A. LeVen, *The Many-Headed Muse: Tradition and Innovation in Late Classical Greek Poetry* (Cambridge: Cambridge University Press, 2014), 139–40.

[8] Diog. Laert. *PMG*, ed. D. L. Page (New York: Oxford University Press, 1962), 786. Coincidentally, Zeno is also killed off by Athenaeus, via raw octopus (8.341c).

modes of *bios*-writing, reading poetic works and connecting texts, figures, and life."[9]

On the whole, Athenaeus' *Deipnosophistae* is a fine example of a writer producing a piece of literature informed by his educational training and in conversation with other writers and literary works of his milieu. Moreover, and though featuring a number of different types of *chreiae*, Athenaeus writes within an expected genre – that is, what he produces makes reference to known and established literary conventions.[10] He does not craft an unprecedented or sui generis piece of literature. His points of reference and literary aims are intelligible and represent his social location as an author exchanging ideas with members of his intellectual circle. While something of a parody, his composition nonetheless offers a window into the practices of writers and writing culture of the imperial period.

Athenaeus' dinner guests also offer a sense of the manifold ways literature could be engaged. The personal libraries of the *deipnosophistae* recall Philodemus' library at Herculaneum or the caches of book collectors and "bibliomaniacs" like Trimalchio.[11] Ulpian speaks of his quest for rare volumes from booksellers in Rome in a manner reminiscent of the characters in Aulus Gellius' *Noctes Atticae* (Attic Nights) who frequent bookshops and encounter there "true and fake scholars ... reading out loud and discussing textual criticism and interpretation of difficult texts."[12] The *deipnosophistae* are able to recite certain quotations from memory, although only if the excerpt is relatively fresh in their minds and not something read long ago.[13] Sometimes, with help, a forgotten text

---

[9] LeVen, "Reading the Octopus," 26.

[10] "Genre" is a modern designation. The ancients did not possess the same taxonomies that contemporary scholarship identifies for academic purposes. That said, ancient readers were aware that there were distinguishing features between kinds of literature (e.g., the novel, letter writing), even if they did not always use the same categories. When I use the term, I am indicating that writers conformed to certain literary conventions. While writers were perfectly capable of innovation, there are still certain rhetorical standards and training that are reflected in the works they produce. I will discuss the question of genre further in the next chapter. Also see Jennifer Eyl, "Why Thekla Does Not See Paul: Visual Perception and the Displacement of Erōs in the Acts of Paul and Thekla," in *The Ancient Novel and the Early Christian and Jewish Narrative: Fictional Intersections*, ed. Marília P. Futre Pinheiro, et al. (Groningen: Barkhuis Publishing; Groningen University Library, 2012), 3–12, cit. 3, n. 1.

[11] See Jacob, *The Web of Athenaeus*, 56–57, esp. n. 7; Ath. 13.556b, 7.276a; *Sat.* 48.4; Sen. *Tranq.* 9.4–7; Plin. *Ep.* 1.8, 2.17.

[12] Jacob, *The Web of Athenaeus*, 59. Gell. *NA* 5.41, 13.31, 18.4.

[13] Ath. 3.126b; 8.359d–e.

could be recalled – albeit not always properly.[14] "Living libraries" like Longinus or Porphyry were understood to have reached a "culminating point of *paideia*, at the summit of grammar and rhetoric" within their literary circles.[15] Indeed, training received in *paideia* to memorize and critique classical authors like Homer, Hesiod, and others was known to serve a writer well when composing their own works. Philo of Alexandria, for instance, while clearly knowledgeable of the Hebrew scriptures, also indicates his knowledge of the Homeric epics, citing the *Iliad* and using a number of Homeric expressions in his writings.[16]

The portrait painted by Athenaeus reveals that writing was a specialist's activity.[17] While one might be trained in certain scribal practices or memorization techniques, the ability to compose "original" poetry or prose required an advanced rhetorical education.[18] Moreover, a writer's most immediate and formative social network was his circle of fellow

---

[14] Ath. 3.83a–c. Slaves were often prized for their ability to help a master recall facts and passages. Trimalchio, for instance, heaps praise and affection on a young slave who is able to "do division and read books at sight" (*Sat.* 75).

[15] Jacob, *The Web of Athenaeus*, 79: Longinus "embodies Alexandria's erudition and critical authority, and his works fill the libraries of others." Eunap. *VS*, 455. For more on the Greek and Roman recitation of poetry, see Gordon Williams, "Political Patronage of Literature in Rome," in *Literacy and Artistic Patronage in Ancient Rome*, ed. Barbara K. Gold (Austin: University of Texas Press, 1982), 3–27, esp. 9–10.

[16] Philo, *Contempl.* 17; *Abr.* 10; *Conf.* 170; *Fug.* 31; *Somn.* 2:53, 2:275. Also see Maren R. Niehoff, *Jewish Exegesis and Homeric Scholarship in Alexandria* (Cambridge: Cambridge University Press, 2011), 2–3, cit. 3: "Other anonymous exegetes in Alexandria explicitly compared the biblical story of the Tower of Babel to a similar enterprise of the sons of Aloeidae recorded in the *Odyssey* (*Conf.* 4–5). Such references are not at all surprising given the known acculturation of Alexandrian Jews. They not only spoke and wrote in Greek but quickly read even their Scriptures only in the Greek translation. Homer's epics, which constituted the most important pillar of Greek education in Hellenistic Egypt, were obviously familiar to them."

[17] Some recent studies have begun to catalogue literary practices among less elite segments of Greco-Roman society with a great deal of success. See Paul Robertson, *Paul's Letters and Contemporary Greco-Roman Literature: Theorizing a New Taxonomy* (Boston: Brill, 2016). Teresa Morgan confirms that much of our evidence for literary practices is from high Roman culture in *Literate Education in the Hellenistic and Roman Worlds* (Cambridge: Cambridge University Press, 1998). Also see Tim Whitmarsh, *Greek Literature and the Roman Empire: The Politics of Imitation* (New York: Oxford University Press, 2001).

[18] Seneca, for example, speaks of a Calvisius Sabinus "who had bought high priced slaves trained to be living books: each one had learned one classical author by heart – Homer, Hesiod, or the Lyrics – and had the suitable quotations ready at the disposal of their forgetful master during the banquet conversations." Jacob, *The Web of Athenaeus*, 79; Seneca, *Ep.* 3.27.5. To what extent "by heart" means by memory or through quick reference to a written source is an open question.

writers and literary critics – an interconnected network of authors and literate consumers with particular kinds of intellectual knowledge and skill. In these works, points of reference (like a character's manner of death) might be borrowed from another writer and elaborated upon; imaginative school exercises like *imitatio, aemulatio,* or *suasoriae* (declamation) lent themselves to writers creatively supplementing accounts of well-known figures or subjects. In her work on "Roman fakes," Irene Peirano traces the frequency with which Roman writers engaged in the practice of creating "quasi-fictional scenarios centered on untold episodes and unexplored possibilities" or generating new fictions designed to supplement existing narratives.[19] She also describes the iterative process of writers building upon existing narratives/literary works in terms of a network of written and oral exchange: "In this literary culture, canonical texts are 'open works,' and 'reception' is to be envisaged not as an abstract phenomenon, but as a process in which, through a series of performative and textually mediated responses, canonical texts are routinely 'overwritten' and supplemented."[20] I take this to mean no subject in antiquity was entirely static and all writings were subject to change. Imitation, invention, and innovation were not only expected but also encouraged.

This chapter provides a redescription of first-century literature about Jesus that recognizes authors as elite cultural producers. Writing was ultimately a product of an author's education, training, and range of literary and other interests – as well as the feedback received from relative peers. Pliny describes his own literary circle as a group of "friends dedicated to the literary enterprise ... characterized by a reciprocity that recognizes common values, 'of which the most important is the rhetorical mastery of language.'"[21] Thus, I argue that ancient writers were engaged

---

[19] Irene Peirano, *The Rhetoric of the Roman Fake: Latin Pseudepigrapha in Context* (Cambridge: Cambridge University Press, 2012), 18.

[20] Peirano, *The Rhetoric of the Roman Fake*, 23. Elsewhere she also reiterates that in Roman imperial culture "narratives that integrate and supplement other narratives are far from being a peripheral phenomenon" (*The Rhetoric of the Roman Fake*, 13).

[21] William A. Johnson, *Readers and Reading Culture in the High Roman Empire: A Study of Elite Communities* (New York: Oxford University Press, 2010), 52. Johnson is summarizing Pliny, citing Florence Dupont, "*Recitatio* and the Space of Public Discourse," in *The Roman Cultural Revolution*, ed. Thomas Habinek and Alessandro Schiesaro (Cambridge: Cambridge University Press, 1997), 44–59. Also see Craig A. Williams, "Love and Friendship: Authors and Texts," in *Reading Roman Friendship* (Cambridge: Cambridge University Press, 2012), 174–258, particularly the sections on the letters of Cicero and Fronto.

in an intellectual practice that made their literary circle of fellow writers their most significant and formative social group – that is, the social group with whom the author shared significant and reciprocal "common values."

This is not to deny that when an author explores subjects concerning the gods and associated practices, ethics, and so on that they are not potentially involved with what we might term a "religious" group of some sort. However, this association and the degree to which it is instrumental must be demonstrated. Our understanding of an author's social environment should not be limited to the subjects explored in their writings in the event that the author is engaged in an ideological exercise of group-making, ethnicity-making, or religion-making. Such activity may be a reflection of aspiration or imagination, not reality. So-called religious topics are no more determinative of an author's network of social engagement than any other discourse. To limit our studies to such a narrow field of analysis risks uncritically accepting a writer's ideological categories as an accurate reflection of their social world, or allowing our own assumptions to determine what we regard as thinkable. What *is* determinative is the author's habitus and field, meaning the practices that we know are probable given a writer's historical location.

In what follows, I demonstrate how a continued focus on Christian communities has resulted in implausible descriptions of social exchange for the gospel writers. I preface this discussion with an overview of what we know about relevant ancient literary practices in antiquity, including among first-century Judean writers like Philo. Philo offers a particularly pertinent point of comparison in that he is addressing a number of interrelated themes in his writings also common to the gospel writers, such as the proper interpretation of the Hebrew scriptures, the works of other writers, politics, and so on. Using Bourdieu's theorization on fields, I propose an alternative approach to categorizing ancient

Also see Johnson, *Readers and Reading Culture in the High Roman Empire*, 33: "Pliny also had luminary literary connections. Quintilian was his teacher ... he counted among his *amici* Tacitus ... and Suetonius ... and Martial; he was less familiar but well acquainted with Silius Italicus ... of the previous generation. He does not mention Plutarch directly, but they shared two close consular friends." Also see *Vergil, Philodemus and the Augustans*, ed. David Armstrong, Jeffrey Fish, Patricia A. Johnson, and Marilyn B. Skinner (Austin: University of Texas Press, 2004); Elaine Fantham, *Roman Literary Culture: From Cicero to Apuleius* (Baltimore: Johns Hopkins University Press, 1996); H. Gregory Snyder, *Teachers and Texts in the Ancient World: Philosophers, Jews and Christians* (New York: Routledge, 2000).

literature – and early Christian literature in particular – that does not rely on the notion of communities.

By classing ancient writings in terms of fields and subfields that represent an author's rhetorical training, social location, and the established literary conventions for addressing particular subjects (e.g., ethnic literature, esoteric literature, moral philosophy), we can more accurately situate individual authors and their associated networks without appealing to their imagined audiences. The subsequent chapters of this study will demonstrate how first-century writings about Jesus can be reread in light of this proposed framework and how such rereadings reveal the gospels as a set of texts concerned with Judean practices and sacred writings, philosophy, subversive teacher-types, the perceived utopia of rural and exotic spaces, and paradoxographical subjects, among other interests, previously obscured by the need to account for Christian communities and Christian origins.

SETTING THE STAGE: ANCIENT WRITERS AS LITERATE SPECIALISTS

As illustrated by the example of an Etruscan haruspex in Chapter 1, religion is a second-order category that can be assessed in light of other kinds of social practices so that it functions as a matter of "more or less." This paradigm also pertains to the act of writing. When writers engage a topic like religion (e.g., talk of the gods), it is one among a number of overlapping interests and should be considered in tandem with the other subjects being raised. Authors possess the creative agency to address a variety of matters simultaneously: gods, ancestors, politics, war, food, ethics, daily life, the interpretation of other texts, issues of social class, and ethnicity. Their reasons for doing so can be multivalent and reflect a number of strategic interests. Moreover, their use of certain categories or exempla, like "communities," can also be imagined, ideal, or rhetorical. Awareness of the author's rhetorical aims, literary field, conversation partners, historical context, and other frames of reference helps the scholar analyze the ways in which discourse about religion functions within a text, as well as its relative purpose.

Talk of the gods and related subjects does not mean that an author is necessarily relating information about historical or "real," on-the-ground social activities or associated social groups. We must pay attention to what the author tells us about their social world while also recognizing that some

of their claims may be strategic or aspirational. This follows Rogers Brubaker's caution that we "take vernacular categories and participant's
understandings seriously, for they are partly constitutive of our objects of
study. But we should not uncritically adopt the engaged *categories of
ethnopolitical practice* as our *categories of social analysis*."²² As such,
groupness cannot be uncritically accepted or assumed, but should be
considered in tandem with a variety of other social and historical factors.

Likewise, we must consider acts of ancient writing in terms of our
historical knowledge of literary culture. That is, we must look to what we
know about ancient writing practices in their milieu in order to speak
accurately about what kinds of social networks a writer may have found
formative in the production of their literature, in addition to considering
what they tell us about their own interests and activities. Even if authors
situate themselves clearly in an established ethnic or religious tradition –
for example, first-century Judean literature – this kind of intellectual
activity must be contextualized and understood in terms of what we know
about the social conditions for authorship in the ancient Mediterranean.
Any act of writing requires a certain institutional structure, training, and
other "social conditions," both to legitimize and to support the specialists
involved.²³ Evaluations of ancient literary practices, therefore, cannot
treat the author myopically as a mouthpiece or a mirror on one particular
kind of social group. To do so risks mischaracterizing an author's fields of
influence and social membership.

A DAY IN THE LIFE OF A CULTURAL PRODUCER

A survey of ancient Roman education and rhetorical training demonstrates the degree to which being able to compose a piece of literature in
antiquity was a specialists' activity. Literate culture was, by and large, the
purview of men and of the elite – although those with limited financial
means would still strive to provide some schooling. With no mandated or
state education, the families of young men would pay a local *litterator* or
ludi magister a monthly fee to teach initial skills in reading, writing, and
math. This kind of instruction was usually restricted to the senatorial or

---

²² Rogers Brubaker, *Ethnicity without Groups* (Cambridge, MA: Harvard University Press,
   2004), 10. Emphasis in original.
²³ See Stanley K. Stowers, "The Ontology of Religion," in *Introducing Religion: Essays in
   Honor of Jonathan Z. Smith*, ed. Willi Braun and Russell T. McCutcheon (Oakville:
   Equinox, 2008), 434–49, cit. 447.

decurion class or greater (i.e., the governing or aristocratic classes) as the
Roman adaptation of Greek *paideia* came to reflect a "highly competitive
world of elite ambition."[24] The likely apocryphal *De liberis educandis*
(On the Education of Children) cautions specifically against hiring inex-
pensive tutors who lack sufficient expertise ("pursuing cheap ignorance
[εὔωνον ἀμαθίαν διώκοντες]"; Plut. *Mor.* 7F4). Greek tutors were preferred
as well as those who were established "scholar-poets," that is, tutors who
were already creative writers in their own right.[25] Stoics were also highly
prized for their perceived "discipline and high principles, frugality of life,
and courage," all ideal Roman virtues.[26]

The wealthy might also call upon an educated slave or employ a private
grammaticus to instruct members of the household, which Suetonius
indicates offered the best education.[27] Livius Andronicus is perhaps one
of the earliest and most famous examples of a Greek tutor given his
freedom for his effective work with the children of Livius Salinator.[28] On
the whole, literate slaves were represented "disproportionately ... among
the educated."[29] Cicero laments when one of his enslaved *anagostae* or
readers runs away (*Fam.* 5.9.2, 13.77.3), and we know Livia Drusi had a
lectrix.[30] The educated elite may in fact have been a target for this kind of
enslavement in the aftermath of war as prisoners from Roman imperial
campaigns were known to populate the households of the military and
aristocratic victors. Although not a slave, Josephus' role in the Flavian

[24] Whitmarsh, *Greek Literature and the Roman Empire*, 5. Also see Alex Scobie, *Apuleius and Folklore: Toward a History of ML3045, AaTh567, 449A* (London: Folklore Society, 1983), 8–9.

[25] Stanley Bonner, *Education in Ancient Rome: From the Elder Cato to the Younger Pliny* (Berkeley: University of California Press, 1977), 20–21.

[26] Bonner, *Education in Ancient Rome*, 109.

[27] Suet. *Gram. et rhet.* 9. Also see Elaine Fantham, *Roman Literary Culture: From Cicero to Apuleius* (Baltimore: Johns Hopkins University Press, 1996), 24.

[28] Bonner, *Education in Ancient Rome*, 20.

[29] Stanley K. Stowers, "Kinds of Myth, Meals, and Power: Paul and the Corinthians," in *Redescribing Paul and the Corinthians*, ed. Ron Cameron and Merrill P. Miller (Atlanta: Society of Biblical Literature, 2011), 105–49, cit. 120. Stowers explains: "A literate slave was very valuable to a master, and owners often educated them just to increase their value. Because Roman education developed under the influence of Greek education and by the first century CE most aristocratic and prosperous families wanted their sons to be educated bilingually, Greek-speaking urban slaves were considered ideal tutors and teachers. Slaves and freedmen, then, in some sense, dominated most areas of learning, but they faced a glass ceiling that kept them from the ranks of the aristocratic dominant culture of people like Vergil, Pliny, and Aelius Aristides."

[30] See Jane Stevenson, *Women Latin Poets: Language, Gender, and Authority, from Antiquity to the Eighteenth Century* (New York: Oxford University Press, 2005), 44.

household comes to mind as an allied scenario. Well before the Flavian period, thousands of captives arrived in Rome following the third Macedonian War; Polybius, for example, was conscripted into the household of Aemilius Paullus in order to educate his sons Fabius and Scipio.[31] This is the same Scipio of the famed (and possibly fantastic) Scipionic Circle, a social network of rhetoricians, philosophers, poets, playwriters, satirists, and historians who reputedly gathered to discuss their works.

Outside economically privileged households, for the few who could afford to do so, boys would remain enrolled in basic, public instruction – "street school" – until about the age of twelve.[32] Dio Chrysostom describes teachers holding court on street corners before their pupils with passersby joining in (*Or.* 20.9–10). Formally, this schooling was very much dependent on the needs and means of the family. Prosperous tradesmen or artisans, for instance, might send their children for instruction just long enough to learn the fundamentals of bookkeeping, at which point they would return to the family business. There are indications from extant papyri that *epheboi* who were members of a gymnasium enjoyed elevated social status within Egypt and may have been exempt from certain taxations, but the procedure for this dispensation is not clear.[33] Given the expense, the majority of Romans were not instructed beyond a very basic literacy, if at all. William A. Johnson explains:

One can well imagine that these merchants as a matter of course began with traditional elementary reading and writing instruction before being trained to full "literacy" in the specialty task; and yet it is also probably that most ... were not "literate" in the sense of being competent to read a book roll containing Plato or Sophocles, and perhaps not even so much as to be able to write and read a brief letter.[34]

There were no set parameters for what "literacy" entailed within *paideia*; however, the ability to read and write was likely beyond the purview of free-persons of the lower classes if not necessary for their profession or day-to-day activities.

---

[31] Bonner, *Education in Ancient Rome*, 23.   [32] Fantham, *Roman Literary Culture*, 23.

[33] For more on the *laographia* and possible interpretations of the so-called Boule-papyrus and their implications for Jews in Alexandria, see Erich S. Gruen, *Diaspora: Jews amidst Greeks and Romans* (Cambridge, MA: Harvard University Press, 2009), 75ff.; E. Mary Smallwood, *The Jews under Roman Rule: From Pompey to Diocletian: A Study in Political Relations* (Boston: Brill, 2001), 232.

[34] William A. Johnson, "Learning to Read and Write," in *A Companion to Ancient Education*, ed. W. Martin Bloomer (Malden: Wiley Blackwell, 2015), 137–48, cit. 147.

It is estimated that less than 20 percent of the Roman Empire was literate, and, when considered alongside the technical procedures for producing literature, this estimate may be generous.[35] Our material remains suggest that something as basic as papyri was often a specialist's tool. From the classical period forward, ostraca, for instance, were preferable to papyrus for their affordability and availability. In Egypt, ostraca were used for "private writing" either by etching or in ink, with papyri reserved for official publications.[36] Papyri were still favored for writing letters, in part because, when folded or rolled, they offered a measure of privacy; however, other media such as wooden or wax tablets were equally common tools for correspondence, school exercises, and so forth.[37] The relative status afforded by the use of papyri is evident in sources like Apuleius' *The Golden Ass*, which begins with the narrator inviting the reader to pore over "this Egyptian papyrus (*papyrum Aegyptiam*) written with a reed-pen from the Nile (*Nilotici calami inscriptam*)" (Apul. *Met.* 1.1), an invitation designed to impress.

While there were certain opportunities for education within small provincial towns, quality teaching was found primarily in cities. Horace, for example, tells us that his father took him to Rome to study under the *grammaticus* Orbilius.[38] Apuleius' Lucius boasts of his facility with Latin, albeit achieved through his own ingenuity and not with the famed schoolteachers of Rome (Apul. *Met.* 1.1). In a letter to Tacitus, Pliny laments that the boys of Como are forced to travel to Milan for better teachers and offers to contribute funds toward hiring proper instructors so that the young men can stay at home (*Ep.* 1b 4.13). In general, literacy decreased the further one traveled away from urban centers; the focus of basic education was on the "elementary learning of letters" and then rote exercises designed to improve oral communication.[39] More focused training and contact with social peers and literate networks required traveling to more densely populated areas.

For those trained in literary skills, Quintilian describes both public and private education involving tutoring in Greek, beginning with reciting

---

[35] Heszer, *Jewish Literacy in Roman Palestine*, 24–25. Also see Sarah Rollens, *Framing Social Criticism in the Jesus Movement: The Ideological Project in the Sayings Gospel Q* (Tübingen: Mohr Siebeck, 2014), 127, n. 100, for further bibliography.

[36] Antonia Sarri, *Material Aspects of Letter Writing in the Graeco-Roman World: 500 BC–AD 300* (Berlin: Walter de Gruyter, 2018), 53–86.

[37] Sarri, *Material Aspects of Letter Writing in the Graeco-Roman World*, 79.

[38] Hor. *Sat. I* 6.76–78. Also see Fantham, *Roman Literary Culture*, 23–24.

[39] Johnson, "Learning to Read and Write," 139–42.

Greek phrases, and then reading and writing through imitation of the alphabet.[40] The Greek language was the medium of training, and, without it, no student "could embark on any kind of advanced education."[41] This "advanced education" was undertaken only by the few who made it through the years of initial instruction. Once a basic knowledge of Greek was obtained, a pupil would be ready for more sophisticated rhetorical training – namely, beginning to read Greek texts with a *grammaticus*. These texts might include poetry or histories. Lessons at this point would include recitation and word study, often of Homer. This work was accomplished with the aid of commentaries that would offer "grammatical analysis, explanation of rare or poetical vocabulary, mythological or factual information, and moral interpretation of the text for discussion." In lieu of whole texts, whatever portions were available were read and complemented with synopses. The emphasis in this instruction was not on writing but on "functional literacy." This functional literacy included being able to read basic texts, assess judicial speeches, or, perhaps later in life, record political or military memoirs.[42] The Romans "favored practical eloquence over imaginative literature." By and large, the "ability to speak would be enough," and the individual could make a "career in the courts or the Senate without further exposure to the culture of books."[43] That said, recent work by AnneMarie Luijendijk on the "diverse bookish milieu" of Oxyrhynchus has brought to light some of the possible holdings of educated professionals like businessmen and managers (*pronoetai, phrontistai, boethoi*).[44] Within their libraries were the usual suspects – Homer, the *Medea*, Plato, Isocrates, legal texts, love spells, medical recipes – along with copies of "Christian texts" such as the letters of Paul, the Gospel of Matthew, the Gospel of Mary, the Gospel of

---

[40] Apul. *Met.* 1.1: Lucius speaks of his initial instruction in Attic Greek; Fantham, *Roman Literary Culture*, 24–25.

[41] Fantham, *Roman Literary Culture*, 27.

[42] On writing *hypomnēmata*, see Matthew D. C. Larsen, *Gospels before the Book* (New York: Oxford University Press, 2018), 11–77, esp. 24–25. Larsen attempts to attribute this kind of writing to those who fall short of the highest levels of literacy but nonetheless have professional experience that may have dictated a certain level of literacy (e.g., doctors, military men); however, writers like Cicero were also known to compose this kind of material under certain circumstances.

[43] Fantham, *Roman Literary Culture*, 29.

[44] AnneMarie Luijendijk, "The Gospel of Mary at Oxyrhynchus (P. Oxy. L 3525 and P. Ryl. III 463): Rethinking the History of Early Christianity through Literary Papyri from Oxyrhynchus," in *Re-Making the World: Christianity and Categories*, ed. Taylor G. Petrey (Tübingen: Mohr Siebeck, 2019), 391–418, cit. 389.

Thomas, and so forth. One flax merchant, a man by the name of Leonides, appears to have owned at least portions of Paul's letter to the Romans.[45] How these books operated as a tool of social and cultural membership is an open question (for example, might they have been "for show"?); however, that the Synoptic gospels may have stood on the proverbial shelf alongside Plato and *Medea* nonetheless speaks to the role of writings like the gospels in the culture of books.

It is unclear whether students at the advanced stage of rhetorical training received any meaningful instruction on writing in Greek. Elaine Fantham suggests: "After his education with the *grammaticus*, a boy might still find considerable difficulty writing formal Greek, and his ability to read and comprehend Greek literature would probably be limited to Homer, to classical Attic prose, and to such poetry as he had been taught."[46] To be able to compose original pieces of literature, a writer required continued instruction or independent study. This continued instruction might take place under a notable philosopher, rhetorical specialist, or in some cases in later antiquity, a rabbi. Self-instruction was dependent on financial means, proper social connections, and a considerable investment of time that would have been required to obtain and study literature and then learn to produce one's own writings.

One option for further study was to gain entry into a library or the *scholasterion* ("study house") of a willing patron. Cicero, for instance, describes going to the country home of Lucullus at Tusculum and seeing Cato in the library, "with many Stoic books piled up around him (*multis circumfusum Stoicorum libris*)."[47] Plutarch also paints a picture of Lucullus and his library as a meetinghouse for intellectual pursuits:

His libraries (βιβλιοθηκῶν) were open to all, and the walkabouts and study-rooms (σχολαστηρίων) surrounding them, and the Greeks, who constantly returned to that place like a lodging house of the Muses (Μουσῶν), were welcomed without restriction and spent the day with one another in glad escape (ἀσμένως ἀπο-τρέχοντας) from their other obligations. Often Lucullus himself spent his leisure time (συσχολάζω) there with them, walking about with the lovers of words (φιλόλογος) and politicians, assisting them in whatever they needed.[48]

Judeans who wished to continue with higher education would attend study houses like the kind described by Cicero and Plutarch where they

---

[45] Luijendijk, "The Gospel of Mary at Oxyrhynchus (P. Oxy. L 3525 and P. Ryl. III 463)," 399.

[46] Fantham, *Roman Literary Culture*, 30–31.   [47] Cic. *Fin.* 3.2.7.

[48] Plut. *Vit. Luc.* 42.1–2.

would train with Greek and Roman texts in addition to the Torah. Like their Gentile counterparts, they "had been educated in the Greek language by Greek private tutors" and were "likely to have proceeded to higher studies with *grammatici*, rhetors, and philosophers"[49] or to have sought instruction from local or well-known rabbis; "[in] the Roman Empire three intellectual topics were dominant, *grammatica*, rhetorics, and philosophy, and all three were of Greek origin."[50] Knowledge of and participation in Greek literary culture was therefore a necessity for anyone who pursued advanced literacy in the Roman period regardless of ethnic association. Moreover, as with Lucullus and his conversation partners, the social practices of the *scholasterion* were largely regarded as *otium* – a leisure activity.[51] In other words, intellectual engagement that involved the close reading, interpretation, production, and circulation of literature was perceived as an activity of those within elite circles.

After receiving sufficient training to try their hand at an original piece of writing, authors required the aid of a network of other literate specialists who might sponsor the production of a particular text, circulate writings for critique, gather for recitations or other private readings, and ultimately publish works.[52] Although representing a high register of Roman literary culture, the social interactions of writers like Pliny and his cohort are instructive for recognizing the complexity involved in producing writings that ultimately circulate widely. Descriptions of their literary exchanges and writing processes reveal "a larger fabric of social negotiations relating to literary production" than, for instance, simply recording popular oral stories, memory traditions, or other folk speech.[53]

The publication process began with men like Pliny, Verginius Rufus, Vestricius Spurinna, Titinius Capito, and Octavius Rufus gathering in a private setting to read their compositions aloud and elicit comments from their colleagues. Adrian Sherwin-White describes this activity as a "popular form of initial publication" among an educated audience.[54] After

---

49 Catherine Heszer, *Jewish Literacy in Roman Palestine* (Tübingen: Mohr Siebeck, 2001), 103.
50 Hezser, *Jewish Literacy in Roman Palestine*, 107.
51 Hezser, *Jewish Literacy in Roman Palestine*, 108.
52 The Roman Empire occasionally offered tax breaks for philosophers, teachers, and other elite cultural producers. See Whitmarsh, *Greek Literature and the Roman Empire*, 16.
53 Johnson, *Readers and Reading Culture*, 52.
54 Adrian Nicholas Sherwin-White, *The Epistles of Pliny: A Historical and Social Commentary* (Oxford: Clarendon Press, 1985 [1966]), 115; Johnson, "Pliny and the Construction of Reading Communities," 52–53.

discussing the material and making any necessary adjustments, the next stage for an author was to "publish" their work by allowing copies to be made. In this respect, publication as a concept is rather more fluid than our concept in modernity where it denotes a sense of finality.[55] Even at this stage there were no guarantees that a work would be read, continue to be copied, or circulate: "Since there were no 'publishers,' the only clear route to recognition as an author was by attachment to, and promotion by, one of these [literary] circles ... by word of mouth, written letters, and by recitations to which a larger acquaintance was invited."[56] As such, the most important social network for an individual writer was other writers and associated groups that participated in the interpretation and circulation of literature.[57]

According to Pliny, knowledge and even memorization of excerpts, phrases, or other passages from the works within one's circle of literary *amici* was a "surprisingly common expectation." Thus, an author or writing might come to be known to a wider network of associated consumers through word of mouth or fragments – for example, an excerpt from a poem that is repeated and discussed.[58] This process gives an entirely new meaning to the concept of "oral tradition." Pliny's letters also demonstrate that discussion of literature, encouragement for authors to "concentrate on their own literary efforts," and the circulation of texts between writers for comment were fundamental elements of social exchange.[59] As such, the author's *literary* community was central and formative. I return to the specific question of Pliny's intellectual circle – and its knowledge of the gospels – in the following chapter with a discussion of the *Satyrica* and the gospels.

Again, a writer like Pliny represents truly elite literary culture and is not necessarily representative of the activities of all imperial-era writers. As a "leisure activity," not all authors were able to luxuriate in the mastery of language like members of Roman high society. The modest skills of the

[55] See Bernard A. von Groningen, "ΕΚΔΟΣΙΣ," *Mnemosyne* 16 (1963): 1–17; Raymond Starr, "The Circulation of Literary Texts in the Roman World," *The Classical Quarterly* 17, no.1 (1987): 213–23; Larsen, *Gospels before the Book*, 11–36.

[56] Johnson, *Readers and Reading Culture*, 53.

[57] Stanley K. Stowers, "The Concept of 'Community' and the History of Early Christianity," *Method and Theory in the Study of Religion* 23, nos. 3–4 (2011): 238–56, 247.

[58] For an illustration of this process, see Johnson, *Readers and Reading Culture*, 55.

[59] For a comprehensive list of these references in Pliny, see Johnson, *Readers and Reading Culture*, 57, nn. 59–61.

author of the Gospel of Mark or the Latin *Historia Apollonii Regis Tyri* (History of Apollonius King of Tyre), for instance, demonstrate that there were varying degrees to which a writer possessed expertise. However, with functional literacy the purview of so few, the processes of training and intellectual development – as well as the nature of social exchange involved in the production and circulation of writings – likely followed along a similar trajectory in other literary (sub)fields. It therefore follows that authors like the gospel writers were constrained by the same practical aspects of writing ancient literature as any other writer in the ancient world; that is, they required the same relative levels of education, necessary training, and associated social networks. They possessed a certain habitus and composed their writings under the same plausible and practical conditions as other writers within their field of literary production in antiquity.

LOCATING EXPERTISE

We must account for the obvious distinction in skill level between authors who represent dominant literary registers like Vergil and an author like Mark. Following Bourdieu, an author is an elite "producer of cultural goods."[60] As an agent located within a particular field of social activity (in this case, writing and literary production) the author possesses habitus – a disposition to participate in practices based on an internalized understanding of convention and expectation. Each field possesses its own standards for what constitutes desirable cultural goods and, likewise, how social and symbolic capital is generated and obtained. Another way to illustrate this activity within fields is to say that certain practices or performances "constitute a game that has its own distinctive order of power, of social and symbolic capital, through the skills, productions, and prestige of its practices."[61] Each agent within the field participates in this game in some manner.

For Bourdieu, fields exist independently of each other and are stratified or hierarchically structured. In order to understand the conditions for participation in each field, one needs to identify its boundaries and the kinds of capital that can be obtained. He accomplishes this task by proposing we envision practices functioning on a sliding scale between

---

[60] Pierre Bourdieu, *The Field of Cultural Production: Essays on Art and Literature*, trans. Randal Johnson (New York: Columbia University Press, 1993), 115.
[61] Stowers, "Kinds of Myth, Meals, and Power," 121.

two poles. The "autonomous pole" represents cultural producers whose work is most dictated by the forms of capital specific to a given field – that is, the autonomy of the pole is determined by the "extent to which it manages to impose its own norms and sanctions on the whole set of producers."[62] Here we might situate Vergil or Pliny as members of the literate elite with a highly developed skill set and investment in the social capital afforded by engagement with *paideia*. This "autonomous" or dominant aspect of the field is located on an axis along with what Bourdieu calls the "heteronomous pole." The heteronomous pole represents cultural products that remain within a specific field while also demonstrating influence from other, overlapping fields.[63] So, for example, we might imagine an author who was able to receive instruction from a *grammaticus* for a certain period of time, but whose level of advancement was at least partially determined by economic or political forces outside the literary field.[64] "Poles" help demonstrate how disparity can exist among cultural products within a field (e.g., Mark's limited vocabulary and writing talent), despite the conditions for membership in that field (e.g., a certain level of mastery of the skills and learning necessary to produce literature) remaining constant.

Bourdieu's notion of "positions" is also useful for understanding the role of actors within fields. Positions are related to the idea of "structures"; for instance, an agent's habitus represents their "subjective structure" – it is a disposition acquired through the conditioning that comes with participation in the field coupled with their own position-takings or sense of place within the social or cultural dynamic. However, fields also possess "objective structures," which are the common positions or sets of relations and relative capital in the field that exist regardless of an agent or subject's expectations, will, or intentions. For example, there are certain objective structures that exist in the production of literature in antiquity (e.g., *paideia*) that affect whether an individual is capable of becoming an author. In this respect, positions represent the "intersection

---

[62] Bourdieu, *The Field of Cultural Production*, 40.

[63] Bourdieu, *The Field of Cultural Production*, 164: "The social universe functions somewhat like a prism which *refracts* every external determination: demographic, economic or political events are always retranslated according to the specific logic of the field."

[64] Pierre Bourdieu and Loïc Wacquant, *An Invitation to Reflexive Sociology* (Chicago: University of Chicago Press, 1992), 107.

of the structured social world with the dynamic agency of actors."[65] That is, there are objective structures that undergird any given field, and agents take suitable positions within that field according to their habitus, relative skill, and so on.

This overview of Bourdieu's theory offers an alternative social description of writing practices in antiquity that does not rely on an overly broad notion of communities. It also does not imagine historical or social conditions for authors that are outside what is typical for those able to produce and circulate writings. In particular, his categories of field, habitus, and position-takings make clear that participants come to a given field with a variety of dispositions that must be assessed in terms of what is both plausible for their relative position in the field and in light of what the agents themselves reveal about their interests and relative positions to one another. This model is useful for reconsidering the social landscape of early Christian literature. Reconsidering the nature of these social exchanges and writing practices helps us fine-tune our understanding of how literature like the Synoptics may have developed and does so without assuming that their later reception among religious groups mirrors the social conditions of their authorship.

I have already discussed some of the social conditions necessary for writers in the ancient world; however, they are not the only agents engaged in the field. While the production of literature was limited to a relatively small segment of society, this does not mean that people who were unable to read and write were likewise unable to participate in literary culture in some measure. Non-specialists could attend public recitations or engage in debate over the interpretation of a particular text read aloud. Those with very basic rhetorical training would likely have sufficient ability to interrogate a piece of writing, a theatrical performance, or a speech. Certain writings may also have lent themselves to different kinds of reception depending on their place within the hierarchy of literature in the field – that is, relative to the culturally dominant autonomous pole. David Konstan, in his work on the "Active Reader," for instance, suggests that in second and third centuries CE "there arose, in response to a sharp increase in popular literacy, a new kind of text ... This new literature was addressed to middle levels of society, as opposed to the elite that formed the readership for earlier

---

[65] Anne F. Eisenberg, "Negotiating the Social Landscape to Create Social Change," in *Illuminating Social Life: Classical and Contemporary Theory Revisited*, 5th ed., ed. Peter Kivisto (Thousand Oaks: Pine Forge Press, 2011), 371–94, cit. 380.

texts," including items such as cooking manuals, riddles, binding spells, "narratives of pagan martyrs and much Christian material," or romantic novels like Chariton's *Callirhoe*.[66] These texts did not elicit the same *scholia* as Homer or the *Aeneid*, but readers likely approached them with the same "interrogative relationship to the text for which we have found evidence in Plutarch, Synesius, and other sources."[67] In other words, this literature may not have been ranked among the "classics," but it was engaged in the same manner as the poetry and prose encountered in *paideia*.

To be clear, possessing enough popular literacy to interrogate a text, write a receipt, create *defixiones*, or draft a bill of divorce is not the same thing as writing literature. Studies of early Christian literature that confuse a projected audience with the social conditions of the author have struggled to account for this distinction.[68] Authorship was a specialist's activity that required significant training and rhetorical skill. Again, while they may fall short of the literary prowess of a Homer, Vergil, or Hesiod, authors of the romantic novels or second-century hagiographies were producing literature in a particular social and historical context in which the attendant practices and conditions for authorship still applied. Konstan notes that "the expansion of literacy thus gave rise to two reading publics with distinct levels of cultural competence, and the texts they read differed accordingly in content, style, and organization."[69] While geared to a less socially elite audience, this literature was by no means a product *of* or produced *by* these newfound readers. It was written by a trained specialist and designed to appeal to a field of consumers for the purposes of entertainment and edification as well as to engage those for whom participation in literate practices – including the interpretation and circulation of writings – conferred a certain social capital, even if one did not hold a high degree of literacy. The following chapter offers some suggestions for what strategic *topoi* and other literary elements may have been included in the Synoptics in order to appeal to audiences primed for this kind of literature and entertainment.

---

[66] David Konstan, "The Active Reader and the Ancient Novel," in *Readers and Writers in the Ancient Novel*, ed. Michael Paschalis, Stelios Panayotakis, and Gareth Schmeling (Groningen: Barkhuis Publishing; Groningen University Library, 2009), 1–17, cit. 6.

[67] Konstan, "The Active Reader and the Ancient Novel," 7.

[68] For example: Larsen, *Gospels before the Book*; Richard Bauckham, *The Gospel for All Christians: Rethinking Gospel Audiences* (Grand Rapids: Eerdmans, 1998).

[69] Konstan, "The Active Reader and the Ancient Novel," 6.

While the cultural field of literacy contains both authors and readers, their relative interests and practices within the field differ. For ancient writers, higher education was not something pursued solely for the sake or love of learning, perhaps save in the truly elite levels of society. Again, many engaged the discipline only to the extent that it aided their professional and social advancement or was perceived to improve moral character.[70] But overall, Greek *paideia* was a source of great cultural capital in Roman society, meaning that it conferred onto its participants a certain quality of influence and prestige. Greek literature, learning, and cultural symbols had a profound and increasingly prominent place within Roman cultural imagination throughout the Empire – from the literary tradition of the Second Sophistic to the imperial sponsorship of Greek intellectuals to Hadrian's beard. The representative value of *paideia* was that it demonstrated one's participation in this complex of elite social practice; "'Greekness' (*Hellēnismos*) was constituted by an aggregation of civilized and intellectual values: *praiotēs* ('gentleness'), *sōphrosynē* ('self-control'), *epieikeia* ('decency'), *philanthrōpia* ('benevolence') and – most importantly – *paideia*."[71]

In this respect, *paideia* itself was a habitus within which social capital was exchanged. For the writer, it showcased their engagement with the predominant trends and literature of the age. For the consumer, it offered the chance to participate in a field that represented elite cultural ideals of affluence, self-possession, and moral psychological fitness, among other virtues.[72] The attendant activities of these potential readers were not value-neutral. As demonstrated by the *deipnosophistae* or, perhaps, our flax merchant mentioned previously, participation in the activities and interests of the dominant culture held particular kinds of purchase for those who desired prestige and upward mobility. The perennial illustration of the cultural cachet of literacy is the *Satyrica*'s Trimalchio, who amasses an impressive library and opens it up as a *scholasterion* but is, himself, unable to read (*Sat.* 48.4).

The activities of Paul also demonstrate how social capital can be conferred through engagement with literate practices. To the best of our knowledge, Paul is a Pharisee of the retainer class with a skill level that

---

[70] Hezser, *Jewish Literacy in Roman Palestine*, 108.
[71] Whitmarsh, *Greek Literature and the Roman Empire*, 21.
[72] Thomas Schmitz, *Bildung und Macht: zur sozialen und politischen Funktion der zweiten Sophistik in der griechischen Welt der Kaiserzeit* (Munich: Verlag C. H. Beck, 1997), 26–31.

suggests knowledge of Greek *progymnasmata*. His familiarity with and interpretation of Judean texts and Middle Platonic philosophy offers potential patrons access to a divine lineage and special wisdom. Among the people to whom he writes are the heads of households as well as slaves or freed-persons. While it was not uncommon for slaves to be well-educated in order to act as teachers or tutors, they nonetheless "faced a glass ceiling that kept them from the ranks of the aristocratic dominant culture" given their social status. The alienation of educated slaves from the dominant culture might help explain the attraction to Paul's message of "alternative wisdom" to the autonomous pole of the cultural field.[73] Paul offered an alternative means of achieving prestige and cultural capital within an otherwise limiting field. Similarly, for the elite head of the household, having financial means and social status "might allow one to give hospitality and patronage to a specialist, but that status alone did not confer an aptitude for skillful learning and literate practices."[74] Yet, in supporting and consuming the kinds of intellectual (and other) products Paul offered, even an illiterate head of a household could hold some distinction in the fields of learning and literate culture.

This description of ancient literary practices illustrates that in order to compose and circulate a piece of writing, an author required a level of education, rhetorical training, and social exchange that made their activity highly specialized. Approaches to first-century Christian literature, like the Synoptics, often conflate what is at stake for participants in this field, imagining that both the gospel writer and their assumed "community" are unified in their desire to record and share the oral traditions of their group, the teachings of Jesus, or the like. This approach to early Christian literature has contributed to an ahistorical and misleading view of the social conditions for these writings that continues to reinscribe mystified Romantic frameworks. As discussed in the Introduction and Chapter 2, this mystification is particularly evident in approaches to the gospels that attempt to classify them as "less authored" or "fluid." Certainly, acts such as publication were not the definitive undertakings they are in modernity. Again, any piece of writing in circulation was subject to a "performative and textually mediated" process by which it could be supplemented, overwritten, claimed by others, accepted, or rejected. But this does not mean these writings were authorless. Each text represents

---

[73] Stowers, "Kinds of Myth, Meals, and Power," 120.
[74] Stowers, "Kinds of Myth, Meals, and Power," 121.

the interests, knowledge, and efforts of a rational agent. This agent may have some implied or explicit audience in view while composing their works; however, our ability to determine the exact parameters of that audience's influence – not to mention the degree to which a work has been "overwritten" or "supplemented" – is extremely (if not fatally) limited.[75] Our only secure footing is analysis of the practice itself (writing) and evidence for certain kinds of engagement with literate culture (e.g., use of certain rhetoric, *topoi*, etc.). That said, subject matter or content alone does not determine the social location of an author.

PHILO OF ALEXANDRIA: A CASE STUDY

Philo of Alexandria is another example of an ancient author interested in "religious" topics, but for whom an associated community is not considered central. A first-century Judean concerned with, among other things, the proper interpretation of sacred writings, he is treated by scholars as a traditional, autonomous writer and not a spokesperson for the beliefs of something like a "Philonic" group. Evidently trained in *paideia*, Philo does represent a literary practice emblematic of the autonomous pole of the dominant culture. Yet he also engages a class of literature not traditionally associated with the culturally dominant *paideia* in the Hebrew Scriptures. In this respect, he is a player in a subfield of ancient literature with its own habitus and associated rules for obtaining capital. I will return to this latter point in a moment.

A prolific writer connected with the Roman administration and a member of one of the wealthiest families in Alexandria, Philo is certainly a representative of the cultural elite.[76] Famously, he headed an embassy to Rome and spent at least two years in the capital. Maren R. Niehoff notes that this time within elite Roman intellectual circles was formative for Philo as he began "assuming positions strikingly similar to those of his contemporary Seneca. His *Exposition* indicates a significant transition from his early Aristotelian environment in Alexandria to a distinctly more Roman as well as Stoic context."[77] Among the indicators of Philo's Greek

[75] Peirano, *The Rhetoric of the Roman Fake*, 23.

[76] Maren R. Niehoff, *Jewish Exegesis and Homeric Scholarship in Alexandria* (Cambridge: Cambridge University Press, 2011), 15.

[77] H. Gregory Snyder, for example, notes that "much of Philo's writing activity was an individual pursuit, not simply a transcript of or a script for school or synagogue activity." Snyder, *Teachers and Texts in the Ancient World*, 123. See Niehoff, *Jewish Exegesis and*

education are his use of Homer, as well as his knowledge and advancement of Greek philosophy and rhetorical methods for interrogating texts. Ranked among the so-called Middle Platonists of the first century, Philo "engaged Aristotelian methods of Homeric scholarship ... His own exegetical approach can be understood as a new synthesis of Aristotelian and Platonic notions ... a highly significant predecessor of Longinus and Porphyry."[78] In his allegorical commentaries, for instance, he systematically evaluates Moses' writings and their allegorical meanings, considering their potential inconsistencies, stylistic elements, and merit as compared with the Greek poets; any perceived irregularities, errors, or redundancies he suggests are stumbling-blocks (*Conf.* 14) indicative of improper literal interpretation on the part of the reader.[79] Rather than be "astonished (θαυμάσῃς) by the rules of allegory (ἀλληγορίας κανόνας)" (*Somn.* 1.73), he advises approaching the Hebrew Scriptures according to custom and established interpretation.

Because he represents an aristocratic segment of society, in some respects Philo – like Pliny and Quintilian – provides only a snapshot of an elite stratum of literate practices and education. But he also offers some perspective on the activities and training of a Judean writer in the first century. The majority of our knowledge in this area comes from rabbinic sources, which indicate that elementary education did not include "practical writing skills" and, instead, focused on the reading of the Torah. Such schools may have been a rarity before the third century CE, with increased access to education coinciding with an increase in the number of synagogues. Torah instruction was primarily offered by certain scribes and rabbis who could provide more specialized training; however, it remains unclear to what extent the idea of an exclusively "Jewish education" is even a useful notion as "Greek Jewish scholars may have been indistinguishable from non-Jewish Greek intellectuals."[80]

Despite the apparent discrepancy in social location and training between Philo and the authors of early Christian literature, Philo's body of work is compelling *comparanda*. Philo demonstrates how an author can write about issues such as the proper interpretation of Judean scripture, ideal Israel, food laws, gender roles, moral psychology, politics, and

Homeric Scholarship in Alexandria, for more on Philo's network of fellow Alexandrian intellectuals.

[78] Niehoff, *Jewish Exegesis and Homeric Scholarship in Alexandria*, 14.

[79] Niehoff, "Literal Exegesis in the *Allegorical Commentary*," in *Jewish Exegesis and Homeric Scholarship in Alexandria*, 133–51, cit. 150.

[80] Hezser, *Jewish Literacy in Roman Palestine*, 497.

a variety of other shared subjects and not be considered a mouthpiece for a discrete community. Of his extant works, *De vita contemplativa* (On the Contemplative Life) is particularly noteworthy for its depiction of the practices and beliefs of a group of like-minded Judeans: the Therapeutae. Philo's illustration of this group is routinely read by scholars in concert with related examples from Greco-Roman literature and is understood to be, in at least some measure, rhetorical. While the Therapeutae are occasionally associated with the Essenes (as described elsewhere by Philo and Josephus), they are also understood to be a product of Philo's literary imagination.[81] Scholarly approaches to *On the Contemplative Life*, therefore, provide a model for how texts like the Synoptics might be similarly analyzed.

Ross Shepard Kraemer offers an excellent overview of the scholarly debate over the Therapeutae in her 2010 *Unreliable Witnesses: Religion, Gender, and History in the Greco-Roman Mediterranean*. Kraemer concedes that the social formation Philo describes is either "entirely invented" or "so radically shaped [by Philo's] representation of some actual persons" that the historical group is now "virtually inaccessible to us." She also suggests that Philo may have had elements of Genesis 1–3, Exodus 15, and other Judean scriptures in mind when constructing his portrayal.[82] Whether *On the Contemplative Life* is a "philosopher's dream"[83] in the tradition of Plato's utopian society or Aristotle's lives of moral philosophers or is an inversion to the sympotic works of Xenophon and Athenaeus, it is difficult to assess whether Philo is employing some rhetorical license (perhaps as an apologetic in anticipation of his impending journey to Rome) or if he has some concrete outsider knowledge of this group.[84] Nevertheless, scholars are able to locate Philo within the field of ancient literature in terms of his relative skill and training as an author, the literature of the autonomous pole that may have informed him, and his social standing as an allied member of the Roman elite.

---

[81] Joseph. *AJ* 13.171, 13.298, 13.311–13; *BJ* 2.119–61. Also see Ross Shepard Kraemer, *Unreliable Witnesses: Religion, Gender, and History in the Greco-Roman Mediterranean* (London: Oxford University Press, 2010), 65, nn. 35–37.

[82] Kraemer, *Unreliable Witnesses*, 66.

[83] Kraemer, *Unreliable Witnesses*, 67. Kraemer is describing Troels Engberg-Pedersen, "Philo's *De vita contemplativa* as a Philosopher's Dream," *Journal for the Study of Judaism* 30 (1999): 40–64.

[84] Kraemer, *Unreliable Witnesses*, 68.

In addition to these associations, Philo is recognized as a writer engaged with what we might term a literary subfield: ethnic Judean literature. Bourdieu's theorization allows for subfields as both large and small-scale semi-autonomous products. They represent a distinct position in relation to the dominant field and can relate to one another, offering a source of symbolic capital that is a subset of the kind of cultural capital characteristic of the larger field.[85] Literature that engages Judean thought and practice constitutes a subfield to the extent that it is concerned with issues that are not typically represented by the dominant field (e.g., Vergil, Pliny, Lucian). To illustrate how Philo participates in a subfield of ethnic literature, consider the ways in which the two writings I have discussed in this chapter – *Legum allegoriae I–III* (Allegorical Interpretation) and *On the Contemplative Life* – subvert the dominant cultural field: Philo employs certain Aristotelian methods for interrogating the scriptures but does so while maintaining that they contain no inherent contradictions; he goes into painstaking detail describing the Therapeutae but does so in such a way that he inverts the sympotic themes of vice in favor of depicting Judean virtues. Both Philo and Josephus make allied claims concerning Judean superiority elsewhere in their *corpora*, repeatedly "rewriting" the history of the Gentiles by arguing that the true origins for the predominant intellectual, philosophical, and religious traditions of Greek and Roman culture were the (more ancient) Hebrew people and scriptures.[86] In this respect, these Judean authors represent not only a subfield but also a subversion of the dominant pole.

The concept of "subversion" emerges as one of a number of potential field strategies for either the maintenance or acquisition of status within a Bourdieusian field. Subversion is usually the domain of those outside the dominant group and is designed to challenge its position and legitimacy "to define the standards of the field."[87] So-called ethnic literature, esoteric literature, paradoxography, certain popular romantic novels, or even first-century writings about Jesus are all types of literature that subvert

---

[85] See Bourdieu, *The Field of Cultural Production*, 53; Pierre Bourdieu, *Distinction: A Social Critique of the Judgment of Taste*, trans. Richard Nice (Cambridge, MA: Harvard University Press, 1996 [1979]), 170.

[86] See Arthur Urbano, *The Philosophical Life: Biography and Crafting Intellectual Identity in Late Antiquity* (Washington: Catholic University of America Press, 2013).

[87] David Swartz, *Culture and Power: The Sociology of Pierre Bourdieu* (Chicago: University of Chicago Press, 2012), 125. Emphasis in original. Also see Pierre Bourdieu and Loïc Wacquant, *An Invitation to Reflexive Sociology* (Chicago: University of Chicago Press, 1992), 106.

dominant cultural paradigms. Again, we must be cautious about conflating subject matter with author; material about Judean antiquity, customs, or sacred texts need not to have been produced by a Judean, for example. Subversive writings can nonetheless serve as commentary on the dominant field and its players (e.g., the Roman Empire), sanctioned literature (e.g., Vergil), or culturally dominant figures (e.g., civic biographies). Considering the gospels under this paradigm makes a good deal of sense; Jesus, John the Baptist, Judea, rural Galilee, wonder-working, Judean practices, texts, interpretation, ignoble death, and anonymity are all tools of subversion. A writer exploring these subjects is still bound by habitus to produce a work that engages best practices, including adhering to the expectations of genre, signaling *topoi*, rhetoric, tropes, and so forth, even if their literary ability falls short of the pinnacle of the field. Engagement with Roman book culture and the literate practices of an autonomous pole still confers capital to the participant, regardless of specific social location. I explore the theme of subversion in more depth in Chapter 5.

LITERARY SUBFIELDS AND THE GOSPEL WRITERS

By way of conclusion, let us engage in an exercise that imagines the author of a text like the Gospel of Mark – or any other first-century writings about Jesus – without placing undue emphasis on the notion of communities. With a patent interest in the interpretation of Judean literature, our gospel writer, living postwar, is allied to Judaism in some measure and has read, among other things, a good deal of Greco-Roman literature (e.g., Homer, some philosophy, *bioi*). Presumably male, his ability to read and write at a reasonably high level indicates that he has received a Greek education and possesses both a specialist's knowledge of texts and an awareness of current issues being discussed among other cultural producers – such as the significance of the destruction of the Temple, Stoic physics, genealogies, territories under imperial control, legislation, and the Mediterranean gods. He is also interested in certain kinds of esoteric or paradoxographical materials: riddles, teachings, signs, and wonder-workings. He is outside the dominant cultural field; he is not Vergil. But he has enough skill, means, and training to try his hand at a creative piece of writing.

Aware of the civic biographical tradition of distinguished statesmen, philosophers, and other leaders, he wants to engage that literary genre, offering a *bios* of another notable figure and philosopher who came to an ignoble and untimely end. However, here is he faced with a problem. He would like to write about a Judean figure – perhaps one of the many rural teacher-types and wonder-workers who claimed to be a son of god – but none of them (John the Baptist, Honi the Circle Drawer, Jesus of Nazareth) is a member of the dominant leadership or aristocracy. Yet, among his collected texts, our author has some material expressing an interest in Jesus, including copies of the letters of another elite cultural producer who is a Pharisee and a divination specialist by the name of Paul. There he finds talk of Jesus as Christ, possessing divine *pneuma* (Rom. 8:9; Mark 1:10); a divine lineage of Abraham (Rom. 3, 4, 9; Mark 1); "pneumatic" demonstrations (1 Cor. 2:4–5; Mark 2:8, 5:1ff., 5:41ff.), including divination; demonstrations of power over demons, archons, and unclean *pneuma* (Rom. 8:38–39; 1 Cor. 15:24; Mark 1:23, 39, 5:2ff., 7:25); Jesus as a prophet for a new age (Rom. 3:21–22; Mark 1:1–15) or a New Adam (1 Cor. 15:45; Mark 1:12ff.); a failure to recognize Jesus as the messiah during his lifetime (1 Cor. 2:6–8; Mark 4:41, 6:2, 8:29, 11:27ff.); and an active principle of God's *pneuma* bounding people "in Christ" through baptism (Rom. 6; Mark 1). He even finds talk of fellowship meals and a meal hosted by Jesus anticipating his death (the so-called Last Supper) with dialogue (1 Cor. 11:23–25; Mark 14:22–25) and mention of other characters like James and Peter (e.g., Gal. 2; Mark 3:20–21, 31–35, 8:31–33, 14:26, 66). The proper interpretation of Judean law and allegory also looms large in these letters (e.g., Gal. 1:6–11; Rom. 1:16–17; 1 Cor. 9:16; Mark 1:1, 2:18ff.), as one might expect from a Pharisee. Perhaps our writer also finds through exchanges within his literary network other Jesus material or a collection of related teachings in the style of Pythagoras' *Golden Verses*.

He then begins to write his *bios* engaging a certain set of issues that are important to him. Those issues might include esoteric teachings, food laws, Stoic ethics, or constructing a new, divine genealogy that subverts the one continually being reified by the Roman imperial family (e.g., *the Aeneid*). Any gaps in his narrative can be filled with references to other *bioi* of heroes, philosophers, or divine figures like Alexander the Great, or other established literary authorities (e.g., Plut. *Mor.* 718a: "[Plato instructs that beings born of God] do not come to be through seed [οὐ διὰ σπέρματος], surely, but by another power of God [ἄλλῃ δὲ δυνάμει τοῦ θεοῦ]"). As for other demonstrations of pneumatic ability or power, there is no shortage of testimony about afflictions and healings at the hands of gods like Isis and Asclepius (*IG*, *IV* 1.121.3–9; Mark 5:24–26), including in popular literature (Apul. *Met.* 1.9). He may even add some original plot device or anecdote to demonstrate literary skill. Something like the so-called Messianic Secret conveys to the reader why they may have never heard of Jesus before, while also arguably acting as a *thauma* in the tradition of paradoxography, Horace, or Vergil's Camilla.[88] Luke's worldwide census under Augustus, passing reference to the Syrian governor Quirinius (2:1–7), and convoluted references to Capernaum (4:31) are all seemingly fallacious details, but they make for great storytelling. Like Philoxenus' octopus, elements of Jesus' *bios* like his location, teachings, wonder-working, and death provide ample opportunity for the practice of literary allusion.

Our author may be aware of other "Jesus people." He may even loosely or strongly hold an identification with a particular group who share an interest in Jesus, the writings of Paul, the significance of Jesus' death, and so on. However, this group alone does not dictate the content of his writings. Instead, he is engaged in a writing practice that views other literature and fellow writers as chiefly formative. He exchanges his work among these other writers for comment, critique, and discussion. Some within this network begin to make copies of his writing for circulation. The issues he addresses attract a variety of different kinds of readers – for instance, those interested in subversive figures or in examples of Judeans who offered teachings that were not centered on Temple cult. These writings might even catch the attention of someone in an intellectual circle like Pliny the Younger's – someone who is flummoxed by those with an interest in this figure called Christ and who wants to know more, perhaps for his own writing. Thus, our imagined author goes on engaging with a network of readers and writers. The following chapters will now investigate how this social model for understanding the gospel authors alters the way we assess their motivations for writing, their conversation partners, and their level of engagement with the elite, literate book culture of the period.

---

[88] Thank you to my colleague in classics at the University of Miami, James R. Townshend, for bringing this connection to my attention through his unpublished work on the aesthetics of the grotesque. For more on the tradition of *thauma*, see Barbara Weiden Boyd, "Vergil's Camilla and the Traditions of Catalogue and Ecphrasis (Aeneid 7.803–17)," *The American Journal of Philology*, 113, no. 2 (Summer 1992): 213–34.

4

Redescribing Early Christian Literature

The Gospels, the Satyrica, and Anonymous Sources

To this point, I have argued that the Synoptic gospels are conventional literary artifacts of the imperial period, not records of oral tradition and Christian exceptionalism. Writing was a specialist's activity that required a great deal of training and an associated social network of literate conversation partners. This historical reality, coupled with the implausibility of the "communities-as-authors" model, opens up a host of new questions for the field. Among these questions is whether this shift in primary social setting – from religious communities to a network of elite cultural producers – reveals previously unconsidered or underconsidered literary *comparanda* for the gospels. Free from the artificial constraints of an implied Christian audience, the gospel writers are resituated within a dynamic, social interplay with other writers of their era. In this frame, the content of the gospels can be read not as a record of the historical Jesus and an implied, early Christian audience, but as a literary artifact using traditional techniques of allusion and elaboration in order to craft a compelling narrative about an ethical teacher and Judean wonder-worker named Jesus. Just as Philoxenus is a figure good "to think with" for Athenaeus' *deipnosophistae* in Chapter 3, Jesus offers numerous possibilities for employing literary training and skill in conversation with other writings (and writers) of the imperial period.

I am by no means the first scholar to acknowledge parallels between the gospels and works like the Greek and Roman novel, philosophical treatises, ancient historiographers, biographers, and so forth.[1] Indeed, in

---

[1] A version of the following argument about the *Satyrica* appears in Robyn Faith Walsh, "The *Satyrica* and the Gospels in the Second Century," *The Classical Quarterly* 70, no. 1 (2020): 356–367. There are multiple examples of this kind of comparative scholarship, and I will

the following chapter, I build on these previous studies in order to suggest that the gospels should be classified as a form of ancient biography.[2] Traditional approaches to the gospels, however, tend to attribute common literary *topoi* or rhetorical strategies like anonymous writing, divine genealogies, healings, teachings, fellowship meals, and empty tombs to received – that is, "communal" – oral tradition. Such idiosyncratic readings fail to recognize the gospels and their subject matter as the rational choices of educated Greco-Roman writers working within a circumscribed field of literary production.[3] Literary borrowing is

---

continue to cite examples throughout this chapter, including the work of G. W. Bowersock, David Konstan, Troels Engberg-Pedersen, Ilaria Ramelli, and Stanley Stowers. A few additional representative selections for reference: David R. Cartlidge and David L. Dungan, eds., *Documents for the Study of the Gospels* (Minneapolis: Fortress Press, 1980); Abraham J. Malherbe, *Paul and the Popular Philosophers* (Minneapolis: Fortress Press, 1989) (esp. chapter 3, "Gentle as a Nurse: The Cynic Background of 1 Thessalonians 2"); Adela Yarbro Collins, *Is Mark's Gospel a Life of Jesus?: The Question of Genre* (Milwaukee: Marquette University Press, 1992); Marcia L. Colish, "Stoicism and the New Testament: An Essay in Historiography," *ANRW* 26, no. 1 (1992): 334–79; Abraham J. Malherbe, "Hellenistic Moralists and the New Testament," *ANRW* 26, no. 1 (1992): 267–333; Richard A. Burridge, *What Are the Gospels?: A Comparison with Graeco-Roman Biography* (Cambridge: Cambridge University Press, 1992); Dennis R. MacDonald, *The Homeric Epics and the Gospel of Mark* (New Haven: Yale University Press, 2000); Johan Thom, "Cleanthes Hymn to Zeus and Early Christian Literature," in *Antiquity and Humanity: Essays on Ancient Religion and Philosophy*, ed. Adela Yarbro Collins and Margaret M. Mitchell (Tübingen: Mohr Siebeck, 2001), 477–99; Marianne Palmer Bonz, *The Past as Legacy: Luke–Acts and Ancient Epic* (Minneapolis: Fortress Press, 2000); Tuomas Rasimus, Troels Engberg-Pedersen, and Ismo Dunderberg, eds., *Stoicism in Early Christianity* (Grand Rapids: Baker Academic, 2010); Richard C. Miller, "Mark's Empty Tomb and Other Translation Fables in Classical Antiquity," *Journal of Biblical Literature* 129, no. 4 (2010): 759–76; Ilaria Ramelli and David Konstan, "The Use of *Xapa* in the New Testament and Its Background in Hellenistic Moral Philosophy," *Exemplaria Classica* 14 (2010): 185–204; Runar Thorsteinsson, *Roman Christianity and Roman Stoicism: A Comparative Study of Ancient Morality* (Oxford: Oxford University Press, 2010); Karl Olav Sandnes, *The Gospel "According to Homer and Virgil": Cento and Canon* (Leiden: Brill, 2011); M. David Litwa, *Iesus Deus: The Early Christian Depiction of Jesus as a Mediterranean God* (Minneapolis: Fortress Press, 2014); C. Kavin Rowe, *One True Life: The Stoics and Early Christians as Rival Traditions* (New Haven: Yale University Press, 2016).

[2] For example, see *The Ancient Novel and Early Christian and Jewish Narrative: Fictional Intersections*, ed. Marília P. Futre Pinheiro, et al. (Groningen: Barkhuis Publishing, 2012). Broadly, there is a tendency to focus on later Christian literature in such studies rather than the gospels.

[3] Here I am consciously invoking the language of Bourdieu referenced in the last chapter. I also have in mind Stowers' discussion of Heracles and myth-making in Stanley K. Stowers, "Kinds of Myths, Meals, and Power: Paul and Corinthians," in *Redescribing Paul and the Corinthians*, ed. Ron Cameron and Merrill P. Miller (Atlanta: Society of Biblical Literature, 2011), 146–48.

recognized without hesitation when it comes to the gospels citing one another or in their use of the Hebrew Bible – the same should be true for adaptations from broader Greek and Roman book culture. Similarly, if the gospel writers are producing their work within networks of literate intellectuals, there should exist discernible evidence of the gospels in conversation – and competition – with these other *amici* past and present.

In what follows I argue that a number of themes typically associated with the "incomparable uniqueness" of the gospels are commonplace elsewhere in our extant literature, notably in the *Satyrica* (hereafter, *Sat.*).[4] The *Sat.* is a compelling piece of *comparandum* in that it shares *topoi* and terminology with the gospels in distinctive combination, including communal meals, anointing rituals, crucifixion, missing bodies, and empty tombs. Yet relatively little has been made of these connections in scholarship.[5] Traditionally dated to the mid-first century CE, the most recent scholarship on the *Sat.* situates it in the second century, possibly in the social circle of Pliny the Younger.[6] Identifying shared *topoi* between the gospels and the *Sat.* also speaks to a more conventional process of composition and distribution for works like the gospels, placing these

---

[4] Stowers, "Kinds of Myths, Meals, and Power," 105.

[5] Notable exceptions: Ilaria Ramelli, "The Ancient Novel and the New Testament: Possible Contacts," *Ancient Narrative* 5 (2007): 41–68, and Richard I. Pervo, "Wisdom and Power: Petronius' *Sat.* and the Social World of Early Christianity," *Anglican Theological Review* 67 (1985): 307–25.

Note that there is no reason to presuppose that a Latin author in this period would be unable to engage Greek literature, particularly given the nature of *paideia*. In the specific case of the *Satyrica*, the author demonstrates knowledge of Greek texts, including Homer and, possibly, the Greek novel. See P. G. Walsh, *Petronius: The Satyricon* (New York: Oxford University Press, 1996), xiii–xxxiv. There is also possible evidence of Greek terminology in the text. See Gareth Schmeling, *A Commentary on the Satyrica of Petronius* (Oxford: Oxford University Press, 2011). For more on the literacy of Petronius and his characters, see Niall W. Slater, *Reading Petronius* (Baltimore: Johns Hopkins University Press, 1990), 146ff. The Latin commentary of Sage and Gilleland also argues that the title may have been a Latin spelling of the Greek neuter genitive plural (σατυρικων). See Evan T. Sage and Brady B. Gilleland, eds., *The Satiricon* (New York: Appleton-Century-Crofts, 1969).

For more on the knowledge of Greek by Latin authors, see Williams, "Political Patronage of Literature in Rome," which discusses Cicero's claim that "anyone who thinks Greek verse less valuable than Latin is wrong, for Greek is read all over the world, Latin only within narrow boundaries," cit. 9; *Arch.* 23.

[6] Andrew Laird, "The True Nature of the *Sat.*?," in *The Greek and the Roman Novel: Parallel Readings*, ed. M. Paschalis et al. (Groningen: Barkhuis, 2007), 151–67; Ulrike Roth, "Liberating the *Cena*," *The Classical Quarterly* 66, no. 2 (2017): 614–34; Ulrike Roth, "An(other) Epitaph for Trimalchio: *Sat.* 30.2," *The Classical Quarterly* 64, no. 1 (2014): 422–25.

writings within a social context more akin to the intellectual networks discussed in the previous chapter than a community of illiterate Christians.

Along these lines, I also reexamine authorial anonymity and claims to supernatural knowledge in the gospels as strategies of authorization, not as evidence of oral tradition or communal speech. I argue that assertions about divinely inspired sources (e.g., the *logos*) and anonymous writing are part of a larger trend toward "anti-intellectualism" that becomes increasingly prevalent in the imperial period.[7] Exemplified by the novel, certain lives (*bioi*), and the gospels, this "anti-intellectualism" attributes special knowledge, virtue, and wit to innate skill or blissful ignorance of the corruptions of urban life. In the case of the gospels, this strategy serves to reinforce the central conceit of the Jesus story – that Jesus and his followers are humble, divinely inspired, illiterate peasants. As argued in Chapter 2, invocations about "primitive" Christ followers should not be confused with the social context or literary processes of the gospel writers. When examined alongside similar rhetoric about the superior ethics and piety of unlettered, country folk, these claims make a great deal of sense as they engage a larger literary idealism of the utopian and pastoral – hallmarks of literature throughout this period, including in epic, philosophy, biography, and the Greek novel.[8]

Reexamining the relevant *comparanda* and literary strategies of the gospel writers foregrounds their status as rational actors. It is an approach that ties them more concretely to a known social context and

---

[7] Scholars have often acknowledged the existence of anonymous literature in the Jewish literary tradition and linked the gospels either to this phenomenon or to the notion of "protective anonymity" as exemplified by Gerd Theissen – namely, that the gospel writers were careful to avoid self-incriminating statements out of fear of persecution. See Gerd Theissen, *The Gospels in Context* (Minneapolis: Fortress Press, 1991); Paul N. Anderson, Felix Just, and Tom Thatcher, eds., *John, Jesus, and History: Aspects of Historicity in the Fourth Gospel*, vol. 2 (Atlanta: Society of Biblical Literature, 2009); Richard Bauckham, *Jesus and the Eyewitnesses: The Gospels as Eyewitness Testimony*, 2nd ed. (Grand Rapids: Eerdmans, 2017).

[8] For more on the pastoral as a genre in the ancient world, see Kathryn J. Gutzwiller, *Theocritus' Pastoral Analogies: The Formation of a Genre* (Madison: University of Wisconsin Press, 1991). Of note, Gutzwiller remarks concerning the connections between pastoral literature and "folk" narrative: "The connection between folk songs and literature or between religious experience and aesthetic pleasure is a proper, even fascinating, concern for scholars. But all too often it has been assumed that influence is origin and origin is meaning. Strict adherents of the popular and ritual theories thus make a fundamental mistake about what constitutes the nature of literature.... Theocritus' pastorals are *representations* of the speech acts of herdsmen, their conversations and songs"; Gutzwiller, *Theocritus' Pastoral Analogies*, 5. Emphasis in original.

habitus not predicated on anachronisms about communities or inherited models like the Romantic Poet. By disrupting the social paradigm of the Christian community, we are better positioned to break down the old dichotomies of religious/secular, orthodoxy/heresy, and religious studies/ classics that have so dominated our fields of study. Thus, this chapter presents a new perspective on how and why the gospels were written and the discourses with which they are in conversation.

THE GOSPELS IN CONVERSATION: THE *SATYRICA*

The *Sat.* has long been associated with a Neronian courtier named Petronius, mentioned by Tacitus in his *Annals.*[9] As such, the text is usually dated to the mid-first century CE. This view is so established that certain scholars have suggested that it is "little short of perverse not to accept the general consensus and read the *Sat.* as a Neronian text of the mid-60s AD."[10] In recent years, however, there has been a groundswell of support for reevaluating this long-held position. Andrew Laird, after comparing the "form and content" of the text to the Greek novel, came to the "unattractive" conclusion that the text may be from the second century.[11] Similarly, Ulrike Roth argues that the manumission scene in the *Cena* establishes a new *terminus post quem* for the text; she suggests that the freedoms granted by Trimalchio closely parallel – and parody – descriptions of awarding *ciuitas* found in the letters of Younger Pliny.[12] Indeed, the three slaves manumitted in the novel are associated with a boar (*Sat.* 40.3–41.4), Dionysus (*Sat.* 41.6–7), and a falling star (*Sat.* 54.1–5); likewise, the three slaves that are the subject of Pliny's letter are C. Valerius Aper (boar), C. Valerius Dionysius (god of wine), and C. Valerius Astraeus (stars).[13] Roth's argument suggests that the author

---

[9] Gilbert Bagnani, *Arbiter of Elegance: A Study of the Life and Works of C. Petronius* (Toronto: University of Toronto Press, 1954); K. F. C. Rose, *The Date and Author of the* Sat. (Leiden: Brill, 1971); Niall W. Slater, *Reading Petronius* (Baltimore: Johns Hopkins University Press, 1990); Gareth Schmeling, "Petronius and the *Satyrica*," in *Latin Fiction: The Latin Novel in Context*, ed. Heinz Hofmann (London: Routledge, 1999), 23–37; Edward Courtney, *A Companion to Petronius* (Oxford: Oxford University Press, 2001).

[10] "Introduction," in *Petronius:. A Handbook*, ed. J. Prag and I. Repath (Oxford: Oxford University Press, 2009), 9.

[11] Laird, "The True Nature of the *Sat.*?," 154.

[12] Roth, "Liberating the *Cena*," 624–30; Roth, "An(other) Epitaph for Trimalchio: *Sat.* 30.2," 422–25. Note that in "Liberating the *Cena*," 616, Roth does not address the possibility of multiple compositional strata.

[13] Pliny *Ep.* 7.16.3–4; 7.29; 10.104–5.

of the *Sat.* was not Nero's contemporary but a member of Pliny's intellectual circle, offering strong circumstantial evidence that troubles accepted
tradition on the work's authorship and date.

For our purposes, it is ultimately of little consequence whether the *Sat.*
is a first- or second-century composition given current scholarly consensus on the dating of the gospels; either argument sustains the possibility
that the *Sat.* and the gospels are in dialogue. This is not to suggest that the
issue of dating is inconsequential, particularly for understanding the *Sat.*'s
awareness of Christianity writ large. If the *Sat.*'s author is a member of the
intellectual and literary network of Younger Pliny, for example, this
might cast Pliny's letters to Trajan about Christians in Bithynia in a new
light (*Ep.* 10.96–97). Definitively dating the piece beyond current scholarly debate is simply not possible given existing evidence. The points of
literary contact between the *Sat.* and the gospels, however, demonstrate
that they are, at the very least, engaged with similar issues and elaborating
on similar motifs. In this respect, a comparison between these works
functions on two registers. The first identifies their common literary
themes and explores their level of agreement and creative license within
that paradigm. The second explores the possibility these writings are, in
some measure, aware of, alluding to, or, in the case of the *Sat.*, satirizing
one another as evidenced by the number of shared *topoi*, vocabulary, and
so forth. At end, identifying shared literary elements between these
writings challenges the implicit notion that writings about Jesus had
limited currency within the broader writing culture of Rome. Moreover,
expanding our understanding of which literary *comparanda* may be at
play for a second-century author of the *Sat.* adds greater complexity to
the potential interests, ambitions, and resources of this author.

The emerging debate over the date for the *Sat.* also exposes certain
preconceptions about which pieces of ancient writing are worthy of
comparison. For the vast majority of scholars who maintain that Petronius wrote the *Sat.* under Nero, it remains inconceivable that this work
had anything to do with the gospels.[14] In his 2001 study of the *Sat.*,
Edward Courtney, for instance, continually acknowledges parallels with
the gospels, yet dismisses them out of hand ("I cannot see it as compelling"; "it is not likely"; "other attempts to see parallels ... have been
rejected").[15] Courtney's disavowal has to do with his conjecture that the

---

[14] See, for example, Rose, *The Date and Author of the Satyricon*, esp. 1–20.
[15] Courtney, *A Companion to Petronius*, 121, n. 67. Also see Courtney, *A Companion to
Petronius*, 212, 548.

"circle of St Peter" in Rome was still composing the Gospel of Mark at the time of Petronius, a claim found in 1 Peter 5:13 and perpetuated by Papias (via Eusebius) and Irenaeus.[16] Courtney passively adopts this theological tradition, in spite of more critical scholarship on the subject that recognizes these claims as myth-making.[17] His position is representative of a trend elsewhere in scholarship on the *Sat.* that either relies on outmoded understandings of gospel transmission (via figureheads and in urban centers) or remains silent on the gospels entirely.[18]

Scholars who are more optimistic about a concrete connection between the *Sat.* and the gospels have also been stymied by the "Petronius timeline."[19] J. Allen Cabaniss attempts to resolve the conflict by suggesting that Petronius either had firsthand knowledge of Christianity from his time in Palestine and Bithynia or had a general awareness of the oral traditions of the early church. These conjectures do not sufficiently account for the degree of literary agreement he then posits between the *Sat.*, Paul's letters, the canonical gospels, and Acts.[20] Ilaria Ramelli likewise cites oral tradition theory, speculating that the imperial court demanded a written account of the "oral form" of Mark of which Petronius was aware.[21] Brenda Deen Schildgen, after marveling that

---

[16] See Euseb. *Hist. eccl.* 3.39.15–16; Irenaeus, *Adv. Haer.* 3.1.1–2; Courtney, *A Companion to Petronius*, 121, n. 67.

[17] Mark's association with Peter/Rome is questioned as early as the late nineteenth century; see B. W. Bacon, *Is Mark a Roman Gospel?* (Cambridge, MA: Harvard University Press, 1919), for a summary of scholarship. See also D. Peterson, *The Origins of Mark: The Markan Community in Current Debate* (Leiden: Brill, 2000), 13–16. For a counter-perspective, see A. Winn, *The Purpose of Mark's Gospel: An Early Christian Response to Roman Imperial Propaganda* (Tübingen: Mohr Siebeck, 2008), which notes that the "the ancient witness of a Roman provenance for Mark is worthless" (78).

[18] See Bagnani, *Arbiter of Elegance*, passim; Allen Cabaniss, "The Satiricon and the Christian Oral Tradition." *Greek, Roman, and Byzantine Studies* 3, no. 1 (1960): 36–39, 36; Cabaniss, "A Footnote to the 'Petronian Question,'" *Classical Philology* 49, no. 2 (1954): 98–102.

[19] Petronius is reported to have committed suicide at the behest of Nero in 66 CE; Tac. *Ann.* 16.17–20; Plin. *HN* 37.20; Conte, "Petronius," 454–55. The vast majority of scholars date Mark to around 70 CE; I see no compelling reason to trouble this consensus. For more on Mark's dating, see Adela Yarbro Collins, *Mark: A Commentary*, ed. Harold W. Attridge (Minneapolis: Fortress Press, 2007), 591–619.

There are other examples of scholars acknowledging parallels between the *Sat.* and the gospels (Mark in particular) that I do not address in this chapter, but are recognized by the authors cited, the earliest being Erwin Preuschen, "Die Salbung Jesu in Bethanien," *Zeitschrift für die neutestamentliche Wissenschaft* 3, no. 1 (1902–3): 67–70.

[20] For a list of minor agreements, see Cabaniss, "The *Satiricon* and the Christian Oral Tradition."

[21] Ramelli, "The Ancient Novel and the New Testament: Possible Contacts," 43.

"[d]espite obvious parallels ... no scholar of the genre has suggested a relationship" between the *Sat.* and Mark, vaguely proposes that both texts would have "appeared" in Rome around the same time (67 CE), but she offers no further evidence or discussion.[22] G. W. Bowersock and others tepidly accept the Petronius attribution but then cleverly speak of "resemblances" and "portent[s]" between the story collections without committing to which came first, effectively discounting that socially marginal or "primitive" Christians might share the interests of the literary elite of Rome that Petronius represents.[23]

Each of these approaches makes the problematic assumption that one must account for the gospels' beginnings as an internal Christian oral tradition before any literary comparison is possible. In other words, any semblance of shared thematic material between writings about Jesus and a work like the *Sat.* must be explained through a complex transmission theory of Christian figureheads, communities, and their shared oral teachings. This standard is applied to no other writing of the period. If we are to treat the gospel writers like any other literate intellectuals in this cultural field, their writings are simply one more example of imperial literature interested in the gods, philosophy, paradoxographical subjects, travelogues, socially marginalized people, capital punishment, and so forth. Liberated from strict adherence to oral traditions or Christian communities, we are better able to assess *topoi* the gospels share with other first- and second-century writings.[24]

Because the *Sat.* has been treated as a "normal" piece of Greco-Roman literature, we are well aware of its intertextual references. This offers a dual benefit. Comparing the gospels with the *Sat.* instantly opens up the former to a wider range of literary conversation partners, as scholars have

---

[22] Brenda Deen Schildgen, *Crisis and Continuity: Time in the Gospel of* Mark (Sheffield: Sheffield Academic, 1998), 32, 33.

[23] Pervo, "Wisdom and Power: Petronius' *Sat.* and the Social World of Early Christianity," 307–8, cit. 308. Bowersock adheres to the first-century dating for the *Sat.* and acknowledges associations between the Last Supper and Eumolpus' request to be served cannibalistically after death; G. W. Bowersock, *Fiction as History*: Nero to Julian (Berkeley: University of California Press, 1994), 135–40, cit. 137, 138; on 138–39, Bowersock also suggests that the author of Acts may have been aware of the *Sat.* and the ancient novel in general. Courtney explicitly denies Bowersock's thesis in Courtney, *A Companion to Petronius*, 212.

[24] Robyn Faith Walsh, "Q and the 'Big Bang' Theory of Christian Origins," in *Redescribing the Gospel of Mark*, ed. Barry S. Crawford and Merrill P. Miller (Atlanta: SBL Press, 2017), 483–533; Robyn Faith Walsh, "IVDAEA DEVICTA: The Gospels as Imperial 'Captive Literature,'" in *Class Struggle in the New Testament*, ed., Robert J. Myles (London: Lexington Books, 2019), 89–114.

long associated the *Sat.* with Homer, the Milesian Tales, philosophical treatises, Lucan, Vergil, and Ovid, to name a few.[25] As discussed in the previous chapter, all acts of writing are habituated by concrete processes of composition, intratextuality, publication, and dissemination. The gospels are not outliers to this dynamic as many of their seemingly unique features are long- and well-attested elsewhere in Greek and Roman literature. Moreover, the degree of specificity with which many of these gospel *topoi* are also shared with the *Sat.* suggest that these *corpora* were in dialogue beyond what might be accomplished through oral transmission. Thus, if the *Sat.* has direct knowledge of the Jesus movement, it is through written material that is circulating among literate elites, like all other Greco-Roman literature.

My focus in this comparison will be on passages from the *Sat.* that engage key elements of the Jesus story. To begin, there are several scenes involving anointing (*Sat.* 27, 70, 77–78), including the *Cena* in which Encolpius and his companions, reclining at the table, have their feet anointed with ointment in what is described as a peculiar fashion (*inaudito enim more, Sat.* 70.8). This scene evokes Jesus anointed at the table in Mark 14:3–9, Matt. 26:6–13, Luke 7:36–50, and John 12:1–8. In Mark and Matthew, Jesus' head is anointed with ointment (μύρον; Matt. 26:12; Mark 14:3) or pure nard (μύρου νάρδου; Mark 14:3; John 12:3). In Luke and John, it is his feet. More compelling is the anointing of Trimalchio later on in the dinner scene. He demands his graveclothes and "some ointment (*unguentum*), and a sample out of that jar (*amphora gustum*) which has to be poured over my bones (*ossa mea*)" (*Sat.* 77.7). After receiving the nard (*nardi, Sat.* 78.3), Trimalchio begins anointing all in attendance, proclaiming: "I hope I will like this as much in death as in life.... Imagine yourselves all invited to my funeral" (*Sat.* 78.4). Likewise, Jesus in Mark, Matthew, and John announces that his anointing at the table anticipates his funeral: "she has anointed my body (μυρίσαι τὸ σῶμά μου) beforehand for its burial" (Mark 14:8). According to Ramelli, Trimalchio's "funeral anointing" in the *Cena* is the only example "in all of classical literature," other than the gospels, in which a protagonist is given an ointment – and *nardum* specifically – in a banquet setting as a funerary rite.[26] Commentaries on the *Cena* have rightly noted that the "mock-funeral belongs to an established topos and that the early imperial

---

[25] See Gian Biagio Conte, "Petronius," in *Latin Literature: A History*, trans. Joseph Solodow (Baltimore: Johns Hopkins University Press, 1999), 453–66.

[26] Ramelli, "The Ancient Novel and the New Testament: Possible Contacts," 44–45.

mock-funerals must be understood against the 'background of the cortège as a participatory spectacle.'"[27] The curious addition of the *Sat.*'s multiple anointing scenes narrows this motif even further.

Before Trimalchio's banquet takes its turn into a self-imposed funeral, he is disarmed by the crowing of a rooster, which he takes as an omen of impending death.

> While he was saying so, a cock crowed (*gallus gallinaceus cantavit*). Trimalchio got upset and had some wine poured under the table and even sprinkled on the lamp. He transferred his ring to his right hand and said: "It is not without reason that this trumpeter gave a sign ... there will surely be a fire or someone close by will give up the ghost (*aut aliquis in vicinia animam abiciet*)...." And before he could finish speaking, the cock was brought in ... and Trimalchio ordered that he should be cooked in a bronze vessel. (*Sat.* 74.1)

The rooster portending death is also featured in the Synoptic gospels shortly after the Last Supper as Jesus predicts Peter will deny him three times "before the cock crows twice" (Mark 14:30; Matt. 26:34; Luke 22:34). Ramelli suggests that this depiction of the rooster as a "negative and funeral event"[28] is exclusive to the gospels and the *Cena*; however, there is precedent for roosters alerting human beings to danger.[29] The role of the rooster in prognostication, divination, and supplication is multivalent – including Socrates' last wishes on his death bed (*Phd.* 118a 7–8).[30]

---

[27] Schmeling, *A Commentary on the Satyrica of Petronius*, 328, citing John Bodel, "Death on Display: Looking at Roman Funerals," in *The Art of Ancient Spectacle*, ed. B. Bergmann and C. Kondoleon (New Haven: Yale University Press, 1999), 258–81, cit. 262. Also see John Bodel, "The *Cena Trimalchionis*," in *Latin Fiction: The Latin Novel in Context*, ed. Heinz Hofmann (London: Routledge, 1999), 38–51. Elsewhere, Schmeling cites Seneca and Tacitus in reference to the mock funeral motif: Seneca *Ep.* 12.8; Tac. *Hist.* 4.45; Schmeling, *A Commentary on the Satyrica of Petronius*, 545.

[28] Ramelli, "The Ancient Novel and the New Testament: Possible Contacts," 47.

[29] As Trimalchio indicates, roosters are associated with fires and death; Ter. *Phorm.* 708 (*gallina cecinit*); see Schmeling, *A Commentary on the Satyrica of Petronius*, 310, for further bibliography on the subject. There is also the long tradition of the divinatory and supernatural powers of birds, which, in literature, is notable in Homer and elsewhere. John Gager lists four curse tablets that invoke the rooster and, in one case, specifically petition it not to crow; John Gager, *Curse Tablets and Binding Spells from the Ancient World* (Oxford: Oxford University Press, 1999), 165 (#75).

[30] Interpretations of this passage have been greatly skewed by Nietzsche's influential reading of Socrates bemoaning the "disease" of life (*das Leben ist eine Krankheit*) in *Die fröhliche Wissenschaft* (The Gay Science); Friedrich Nietzsche, *Die fröhliche Wissenschaft* (Chemnitz: Verlag von Ernst Schmeitzner; New York: E. Steige, 1882), 253, §340. For more on Socrates' last words, see Glenn W. Most, "A Cock for Asclepius," *The Classical Quarterly* 43, no. 1 (1993): 96–111. For more on Nietzsche and his influence on North American philosophy and popular culture, see Jennifer Ratner-Rosenhagen, *American*

Possible associations between Jesus and Socrates as condemned teachers have long been acknowledged, including multiple similarities in the circumstances and manner of their trials and executions.[31] Connections between Socrates' death and that of Philoxenus are also reported in Athenaeus (8.341b). At a minimum, there are precedents in literature and in popular perception for each of these references to philosophers/teachers, anointing, funerary meals, and so on that extend well into the second century. The gospels are well situated in the center of this established literary conversation.

Later in his journey, Encolpius encounters another meal with a mock-funerary motif. The poet Eumolpus, a recurring character in the latter half of the *Sat.*, announces an unexpected codicil to his will. After a brief invocation of Socrates, he declares that his beneficiaries will have to divide and eat his body:

All those who are beneficiaries in my will (*testamento*), apart from my freedmen (*libertos*), may take what I have given only under the following condition: that they divide my body into parts (*corpus meum in partes*) and eat it in the presence of the people.... I advise my friends not to refuse what I order, but to eat my body (*corpus*) with the same enthusiasm with which they have cursed my spirit (*spiritum*). (*Sat.* 141.1–4)

Within the context of Eumolpus' request, he regales his audience with a discourse on "certain nations (*gentes*)" that endorse the practice of cannibalism. Each of his references is to a territory formerly "barbaric" and now under imperial Roman control.[32] Arguably, Herodotus' account of

---

Nietzsche: A History of an Icon and His Ideas (Chicago: University of Chicago Press, 2012).

[31] For instance, Joseph Priestly, *Socrates and Jesus Compared* (Philadelphia: P. Byrne, 1803).

On the trial of Jesus as a topic of debate among late antique thinkers and the church fathers, see Hal A. Drake, *A Century of Miracles: Christians, Pagans, Jews, and the Supernatural, 312–410* (New York: Oxford University Press, 2017), 157–58. Jesus' silence at his trial is unfavorably compared by some to the impassioned and learned speeches of Socrates and Apuleius.

Incidentally, comparisons between Jesus and Socrates were quite popular among English Romantic-era poets, such as Percy Shelley (e.g., *Epipsychidion*, line 33: "[Socrates] the Jesus Christ of Greece"), John Keats, George Gordon, and Lord Byron. Benjamin Franklin also refers to these figures as paragons of humility in his autobiography. See Benjamin Franklin, *The Autobiography of Benjamin Franklin: A Genetic Text*, ed. J. A. Leo Lemay and P. M. Zall (Knoxville: University of Tennessee Press, 1981).

[32] That is, Saguntum, Spain (219 BCE); Petelia, Italy (third century BCE); Numantia, Spain (133 BCE).

the Padaeans also looms large – a group who eat the sick among them (despite emphatic protests from the sick that they are on the mend).[33] The implication is that Eumolpus views his legatees as vultures or bandits awaiting his death for their personal gain. Shades of this trope are rife elsewhere, including (later) in Diogenes Laertius, Lucian, and Gellius.[34]

Bowersock suggests we view cannibalism as a larger, commonplace trope in imperial literature, stating: "when we find cannibalism playing a very conspicuous role in imperial fiction, it is no more likely to be there accidentally than the proclamation of Dionysus about the blood of his grape."[35] To the *Sat.* he adds the Boukoloi in Achilles Tatius, Lollianus' Phoenician novel, the *Toxaris* of Lucian, and the gospels.[36] He omits references to cannibalism found in Polybius, Diodorus Siculus, Livy, Pliny, Lucan, Frontinus, Josephus, Juvenal, Suetonius, and Athenaeus.[37] Cannibalism also appears as a specific theme in invective against Christians in several second- and third-century Greek and Roman sources, including Tacitus, Pliny, Justin Martyr, Tertullian, Origen, and Minucius Felix.[38] These allegations and refutations are often muddled in their details and variously represent strategic disputes over the changing social status of Christians, their perceived "foreignness" and ties to Judaism.[39] They also demonstrate that Christianity and cannibalism were easily linked from an early period.

Bowersock notably draws a direct correlation between the will of Eumolpus and the testament (διαθήκη) of Jesus in the Last Supper in Mark, Matthew, and Luke, arguing that "Greek speakers to whom

---

[33] Hdt. 3.99.

[34] Diog. Laert. 6.1.4; Luc. *Nigr.* 30; Gell. *NA* 20.1.39–49. See Schmeling, *A Commentary on the Satyrica of Petronius*, 546, for further discussion.

[35] Bowersock, *Fiction as History*, 132.   [36] Bowersock, *Fiction as History*, 132–33.

[37] Polyb. 7.1.3; Diodo. Sic. 34.2.20; Livy 23.30.1–4, cf. Ath. 21.528; Plin. *HN* 4.88, 6.53, 6.195; Luc. 1.41; Frontin. *Str.* 4.5.18; Joseph. *BJ* 6.199; Juv. 15.13; Suet. *Ner.* 37.2. For additional bibliography, discussion, and references, see Schmeling, *A Commentary on the Satyrica of Petronius*, 546–47. Of note, Schmeling suggests references to cannibalism could be a parody of the vegetarianism of the Pythagoreans, citing Ov. *Met.* 15.60.

[38] Tac. *Ann.* 15.44; Plin. *Ep.* 10.96; Justin, *Apol.* 1.26, *Apol.* 2.12; Tert. *Ad nat.* 1.7, *Apol.* 7, 8; Origen, *C. Cels.* 6.27; Min. Fel. *Oct.* 9, with reference to Fronto. To this list we may arguably add Athenagoras, *Leg.* 3.

[39] A. McGowan, "Eating People: Accusations of Cannibalism against Christians in the Second Century," *Journal of Early Christian Studies* 2 (1994): 413–42; J. Rives, "Human Sacrifice among Pagans and Christians," *Journal of Roman Studies* 85 (1995): 65–85; J. N. Bremmer, "Early Christian Human sacrifice between Fact and Fiction," in *Sacrifices Humaines: Dossiers, discours, comparaisons,* ed. A. Nagy and F. Prescendi (Turnhout: Brepols, 2013).

Christian doctrine was unfamiliar would certainly have heard in these phrases the word for 'testament' or 'will,' and understood in Jesus' instructions to eat and drink the testamentary stipulations of a man about to die."[40] While a reader of the gospels might also be aware of references to blood covenant in the Hebrew Bible, Bowersock's observation is well founded.[41] Directly preceding his *testamentum*, Eumolpus discusses his soul in reference to Protesilaus, the leader of the Thessalians who was the first to be killed at Troy and then resurrected by Hermes for three hours in order to see his widow Laodamia.[42] As such, Eumolpus' meditations on *spiritus* are more complex than his passing rebuke concerning cannibalism. That his larger framework includes an implicit reference to resurrection is a subject to which I will return.

Perhaps one of the more striking stories within the *Sat.* is that of the Widow of Ephesus, also related by Eumolpus. Inspired, in part, by a Milesian Tale, it chronicles a bereaved widow's (initially) virtuous vigil inside the tomb of her departed husband.[43] Watching over his body and weeping "night and day," she refuses food and drink in a public display of "chastity and love (*pudicitiae amorisque*)" that continues for several days (*Sat.* 111.5). During this time, adjacent to the tomb, the governor condemns a number of robbers to death by means of crucifixion (*crucibus*). A soldier is stationed at the crosses, there to prevent "anyone from taking down a body for burial." Hearing distant moans and detecting a light shining from the tomb, the soldier peers into the vault and is shocked to see a beautiful woman. Initially thinking her a ghost,[44] he quickly realizes that she is in mourning. In an attempt to console her, he brings her his dinner and encourages her to recognize that "all men make the same end" eventually.[45] Undeterred, the widow's displays of grief increase while an attending maid partakes in the soldier's offerings. After some time, the maid joins the soldier in calling for an end to the widow's

---

[40] Bowersock, *Fiction as History*, 132–37.

[41] Cf. Ex. 24:6–8; Jer. 31:31; Zech. 9:11; Heb. 9:15–16.

[42] *Sat.* 140, cf. Hom. *Il.* 2.695; Eur. *Protesilaus, frag.* 657N²; Ov. *Her.* 13.

[43] See G. Schmeling, "The *Satyrica* of Petronius," in *The Novel in the Ancient World*, ed. G. Schmeling (Leiden: Brill, 1996), 457–90, esp. 479–81.

[44] Compare this passage with Euripides *Alc.* 1127; Luke 24:37; Chariton 1.9.4.

[45] Schmeling, *A Commentary on the Satyrica of Petronius*, 430, provides a list of crossreferences to mourners encouraged to end fasts, as well as a list of "consolation literature."

outbursts.[46] Outnumbered, she finally concedes and accepts the food and wine.[47]

Then the tale takes a turn. Our author reminds the reader that "temptation generally assails human beings on a full stomach" (*Sat.* 112.1); the soldier begins to make his move and the widow finds herself receptive to his good looks and clever speech. For three nights, the soldier and the widow lock themselves away in the tomb, making love, and indulging in "all of the fine things his means permitted" (*Sat.* 112.4).[48] On the third night,[49] the soldier's post abandoned, the family of one of the crucified men steal his body off of the cross in order to provide a customary burial. In the morning, realizing his grievous error, the soldier returns to the widow in the tomb "in terror of punishment" and threatens suicide. It is at this point that the widow conspires to "make a dead man useful" rather than "send a live man to death." Together, they remove the corpse of her husband from his tomb and affix *him* to the cross instead. Eumolpus closes his yarn with the climatic line: "the next day the people wondered by what means the dead man had [ascended] the cross" (*Sat.* 112.8).

There are many striking elements to the Widow of Ephesus if one has the gospels in view. The robbers, crucifixion, guards, three nights in the tomb, missing crucified corpses, ascending the cross, and so forth are all shared *topoi*. If the Widow of Ephesus is indeed a Milesian Tale, characters like the ravenous widow, the cuckolded husband, and the rambunctious soldier may have been found in combination as far back as the first century BCE, if not in New Comedy. There is also a strong argument to be made that the author had a parody of Vergil's Dido and Aeneas in mind (*Aen.* 4). However, with the gospels in view, the added elements of the careless Roman soldier, the libidinous widow, and an alternative crucifixion are an ignominious play on the symbolic core of the gospel plot. The episode also evokes the motif of the empty tomb with the widow's husband ascending the cross.

---

[46] She is described as tearing out her hair, likely in reference to Vergil's Dido (*Aen.* 4.590).

[47] If the soldier's *vini* is a mixture of vinegar and water (*posca*), this may signal a further association with the gospels and Jesus' crucifixion (cf. Matt. 27:34, 48). The implication is no longer clear.

[48] There are a number of ancient witnesses to the notion that prostitutes ply their trade in graveyards. See Catull. 59; Mart. 1.34.8, 3.93.15; Juv. 6. O16.

[49] The themes of death, resurrection, sex, and three nights in the tomb also appear in Phlegon of Tralles' story of Philinnion and Machates; Phlegon of Tralles, Περὶ θαυμασίων ['On Marvels'] X [*FGrH* 257 F 36 X].

Beyond a narrative quip about a dead man ascending the cross, we never learn what those outside the unconventional love triangle featured in the Widow of Ephesus make of the missing crucified man and the sudden disappearance of the widow's husband from his final resting place. The unseemly series of events – culminating in an empty tomb – stand in humorous contrast to the usual, auspicious associations with spontaneously absent corpses. As satire, that the tomb remains empty in order to save the widow's lover is a humorous inversion of expectation.

Missing corpses were a very common occurrence in antiquity.[50] Throughout Mediterranean literature (and material culture), more often than not, these missing dead were understood to have experienced some form of apotheosis, resurrection/rebirth, or transition into a supernatural state. This is also how the gospel writers understand the phenomenon. For Mark it punctuates his overall narrative:

When the Sabbath was over, Mary Magdalene and Mary the mother of James and Salome brought spices, so that they might go and anoint him. And very early on the first day of the week, when the sun had risen, they went to the tomb. ... As they entered the tomb, they saw a young man, sitting on the right hand, dressed in a white robe; and they were astounded. But he said to them, "Do not be alarmed; you are looking for Jesus of Nazareth, the crucified. He was woken; he is not here. Look, there is the place they laid him. But go, tell his pupils and Peter that he is going ahead of you to Galilee; there you will see him, just as he told you." So they went out and fled from the tomb, for fear and amazement had gripped them; and they said nothing to anyone, for they were afraid. (Mark 16:1–8)

Others have critiqued the tendency among scholars to limit *comparanda* for this passage to the Hebrew Bible or Judean figures without due consideration of the empty tomb motif elsewhere in imperial biography, the novel, and paradoxography.[51] Richard Miller attributes this tendency to "a fundamental misapprehension of the processes and principles governing Hellenistic literary production" in antiquity.[52] Specifically, he cites a resistance among biblical scholars to recognize the literary habit of "creatively and consciously applying a variegated pastiche of Hellenic

---

[50] There are too many cases to detail here; however, a few representative examples include Aeneas (Dion. Hal. *Ant. Rom.* 1.64.4–5), Diomedes (Strab. *Geogr.* 6.3.9), Basileia of Uranus (Diod. Sic. 3.57.8). For more discussion, see Miller, "Mark's Empty Tomb and Other Translation Fables in Classical Antiquity," passim.

[51] Miller, "Mark's Empty Tomb and Other Translation Fables in Classical Antiquity," 759.

[52] Miller also attributes this myopic tendency to "a rather non-scholarly insistence on a 'pristine,' 'non-pagan' well from which the academy ought to draw nearly all cultural, literary, and ideological antecedents"; Miller, "Mark's Empty Tomb," 759.

conventions and cultural codes, often drawn from the Greek classical canon" among writers through the Second Sophistic and beyond.[53] By this measure, the empty tomb implied by the Widow of Ephesus is yet one more element with cultural currency among imperial writers and with which the gospels and the *Sat.* freely engage.

Empty tombs and the resurrected dead were particularly popular conventions of paradoxography, a genre that experienced a resurgence in the first and second centuries CE.[54] These "marvels" or "wonders" were themselves a pastiche – a thematic compilation of fantastic tales and facts presented with little or no clarification and with only a loose narrative structure. In many respects they resemble the gospels and the *Sat.* in their episodic descriptions of remarkable events (e.g., miracles) that seemingly defy the natural order. Comparatively few collections survive – the *admiranda* of Kallimachos of Cyrene, Cicero, and Varro, for instance, have been lost. Those that remain are largely derivative in the sense that they reference many of the same wonders chronicled by earlier authors of the ethnographies, histories, and travelogues that became increasingly popular from the fifth century BCE forward.[55] William Hansen explains:

From the fourth century BC onwards published collections of different sorts began to appear, such as the collection of Aesopic fables made by Demetrios of Phaleron, compilations of wit in the form of jokebooks, and in particular gatherings of ethnographic, biological and other data made by Peripatetic philosophers for the purpose of study and research. Collections of such information by Aristotle's successors reveal a growing enjoyment in remarkable information for its own sake, especially rarities, abnormalities and marvels of nature.[56]

The popularity of these tales fostered an increasing number of volumes dedicated to the miraculous. We know of more than twenty paradoxographers writing between the third centuries BCE and CE through allusions and fragments.[57] The surviving work of someone like Phlegon of

---

[53] Miller, "Mark's Empty Tomb," 760.

[54] A specific genre called "paradoxography" did not exist in antiquity and is a modern classification. On the development of the term "paradoxography," see William Hansen, trans. and ed., *Phlegon of Tralles' Book of Marvels* (Exeter: University of Exeter Press, 1996), 2–3. On writing about marvels, see Emilio Gabba, "True History and False History in Classical Antiquity," *The Journal of Roman Studies* 71 (1981): 50–62; Loveday Alexander, "Fact, Fiction, and the Genre of Acts," *New Testament Studies* 44 (1998): 380–99.

[55] Hansen, *Phlegon of Tralles*, 2; Gabba, "True History and False History," 50–52.

[56] Hansen, *Phlegon of Tralles*, 2–3.

[57] For a partial list of these authors, see Hansen, *Phlegon of Tralles*, 3.

Tralles, a second-century CE paradoxographer and reputed freedman of Hadrian, helps us contextualize what kind of phenomena typically populated these writings. His Περὶ Θαυμασίων (Book of Marvels) characterizes the genre and includes tales of preternatural births, medical oddities, fantastic creatures, lists of the exceptionally or rapidly aged, accounts of the resurrected and walking dead, and even excerpts from the Sibylline Books.

Among Phlegon of Tralles' marvels are the resurrection or revivification of Polykritos the Aitolian, Eurynous of Nikopolis, Rufus of Philippi in Thessalonica, and Philinnion of Amphipolis (*Mir.* 1.1–2.1). Each of these reanimated dead was said to be tasked with a particular mission or entrusted with a carefully guarded secret about the afterlife to motivate their return. Rufus of Philippi, for instance, a high priest in Thessalonica (ἐν Θεσσαλονίκη μεγίστης ἀρχιερωσύνης), was noteworthy for dying and rising on the third day after his death (τριταῖον ἀναβιῶναι), according to the will of the chthonic gods (χθονίων ... θεῶν). Sent in order to perform certain ritual tasks or spectacles (τὰς θέας ἐπιτελέσθαι τῷ δήμῳ), he succumbed to a final death once these demonstrations were complete.[58]

Philinnio of Amphipolis also experiences death for a second time, but under far more salacious circumstances. Similar to the Widow of Ephesus with its themes of sexually voracious women, empty tombs, and cuckolded husbands, the newlywed Philinnio passes shortly after her marriage to Krateros and is locked in the family tomb. Six months later, she rises from the grave in order to seduce her parents' houseguest, Machates. Over the course of three days and nights (ἐπὶ τρεῖς ἡμέρας), she visits Machates in his chambers, eating and drinking with him, exchanging gifts, generally canoodling, and accidentally leaving her breast band behind (*Mir.* 1.1–2). Eventually, a maid catches on to the situation and arranges a sting operation in order to catch Philinnio in the act. On the third night, her parents confront the loved-up duo. Philinnio reacts poorly, accusing her parents of "meddling" (πολυπραγμοσύνην) in her affairs. Cautioning them that it was "not without divine will (οὐ γὰρ ἄνευ θείας βουλήσεως)" that she had been revived, she elects to punish them with renewed grief by dropping dead (παραχρῆμα ἐγένετο νεκρά; *Mir.* 1.11). Word of these events travels fast, and a large crowd rushes to the girl's tomb in order to assess whether or not it is empty. There they find decomposing corpses and bones lying on biers, but on Philinnio's bier

---

[58] Procl. *In R.* 614B (2.115–16 Kroll).

lie only Machates' gifts. "[A]stonished and amazed (θαυμάσαντες δὲ καὶ ἐκπλαγέντες)," everyone returns to the house and confirms that Philinnio's corpse is still lying in Machates' bed (*Mir.* 1.14–18).

Each of these stories demonstrates how a writer could take a set of conventional elements from broader Greco-Roman literary habit, preserve anticipated aspects (e.g., three days inside or outside a tomb), yet still innovate and elaborate on a theme. The "empty tomb" or supernaturally missing corpse, for instance, is quite intelligible as a "convention in Hellenistic and Roman narrative" acknowledged by ancient writers and critics.[59] Plutarch discusses the motif at length, citing the missing Alcmene, Aristeas of Proconnesus, Cleomedes the Astypalaean, and Romulus, calling it an established mythic tale among writers and one that "all the Greeks tell ('Ελλήνων περί ... μυθολογουμένοις)" (*Vit. Rom.* 28.4). Indeed, Plutarch's subsequent analysis of Romulus' missing corpse, and its associated motif, elicits numerous points of contact with literary and popular imagination, including the gospels. From cataclysms and darkness[60] to an ascension and/or deification,[61] recognition of divine status as a "son of god,"[62] brilliant or shining manifestations,[63] awe and fear over the events,[64] a commission to report what transpired,[65] and eyewitnesses,[66] the formulaic elements of these stories were well-established.[67]

To Plutarch's exhaustive list of missing mortals, Miller compiles no fewer than twenty-nine additional examples throughout Hellenistic and Roman literature of figures who have "disappeared and were worshipped as a ... god," many of which have more than one known literary

---

[59] Miller, "Mark's Empty Tomb," 761.

[60] Livy 1.16.1; Ov. *Met.* 14.816–22; Dion. Hal. *Ant. Rom.* 2.56.2–6; Plut. *Vit. Rom.* 27.6–7; Mark 15:33, 38; Matt. 27:45–57; Luke 23:44–45.

[61] Livy 1.16.3, 6; Cic. *Rep.* 2.1.20b; Ov. *Met.* 14.820–24; Ov. *Fast.* 2.475–511; Dion. Hal. *Ant. Rom.* 2.56.2–6; Plut. *Vit. Rom.* 27.7, 28.3; Matt. 27:54; Luke 24:51.

[62] Livy 1.16.3; Dion. Hal. *Ant. Rom.* 2.56.2; Mark 15:39; Matt. 27:54.

[63] Ov. *Fast.* 2.475–511; Plut. *Vit. Rom.* 28.1–2; Mark 9:3; Matt. 17:2; Luke 9:29

[64] Livy 1.16.2; Ov. *Fast.* 2.475–511; Plut. *Vit. Rom.* 28.2; Mark 16:8; Matt. 28:5, 10; Luke 24:37–38.

[65] Livy 1.16.6; Ov. *Met.* 14.811, 815; Ov. *Fast.* 2.475–511; Plut. *Vit. Rom.* 28.2; Dion. Hal. *Ant. Rom.* 2.63.4; Matt. 28:18–20.

[66] Livy 1.16.1–8; Cic. *Rep.* 2.10; Ov. *Fast.* 2.475–511; Dion. Hal. *Ant. Rom.* 2.63.3–4; Plut. *Vit. Rom.* 27–28; Luke 24:35.

[67] Cited from Miller with some modifications. Miller detects twenty firm points of comparison excluded here, including "Mountaintop speech," "Immortal/heavenly body," "The people flee (*populifugia*)," "All in sorrow over loss," and so forth. See Miller, "Mark's Empty Tomb," 762, 772.

reference.[68] Of this list he does not cite examples from the novels, which include embellishments and details also echoed in the gospel accounts, such as the displaced stone at the grave's entrance. Take, for instance, Chaereas' initial reaction to Callirhoe's empty tomb, compared with Mark's account above:

When he reached the tomb, he found that the stones had been moved and the entrance was open. He was astonished at the sight and overcome by fearful perplexity at what had happened.... [Chaereas] hunted through the tomb, he could find nothing ... [he] looked towards the heavens, stretched up his arms, and cried: "Which of the gods is it, then, who has become my rival in love and carried off Callirhoe and is now keeping her with him – against her will, constrained by a more powerful destiny? ... It looks as if I have a goddess for a wife without knowing it." (Chariton, *Chaereas and Callirhoe* 3.3.1–5)

Whether or not Petronius wrote the *Sat.*, the *Sat.* is satirizing the gospels, or the Greek novel mirrors the account of the empty tomb in the gospels, the significant literary overlap between these writings demonstrates that the gospels are engaged in the same discourses, imagery, and style of creative elaboration as their peers. This kind of literary invention is most characteristic of literate cultural producers in conversation with the writings of their age, and indicative of their relative levels of education and training.

The remarkable ubiquity of this motif and, evidently, the frequency with which it was recognized in popular imagination demonstrates that, while the bodily ascension of Moses or Elijah may have been one point of reference for Jesus' empty tomb, the *topos* was also well established elsewhere in Greek and Roman literature.[69] Later church fathers like Justin Martyr, Origen, Tertullian, Minucius Felix, Arnobius, and competitors like Celsus all acknowledged that "the early Christians patterned

---

[68] A few representative examples include Aeneas (Dion. Hal. *Ant. Rom.* 1.64.4–5), Diomedes (Strab. *Geogr.* 6.3.9), Basileia of Uranus (Diod. Sic. 3.57.8); Miller, "Mark's Empty Tomb," 764, cites A. S. Pease, "Some Aspects of Invisibility," *Harvard Studies in Classical Philology* 53 (1942): 1–36, cit. 13.

[69] On this motif in Judaean literature, see Litwa, *Iesus Deus*, 141–79. Miller, "Mark's Empty Tomb," 766–72, argues that to understand the empty tomb motif in Mark as a resurrection is a misreading of the eschatological understanding of resurrection within Judaism. In terms of popular imagination, this *topos* was also featured in imperial iconography, notably the apotheosis of the deified Caesar found in the vault of the Arch of Titus (81 CE). For more on this element of the Arch, see M. Pfanner, *Der Titusbogen* (Mainz am Rhein: Philipp von Zabern, 1983); Penelope Davies, *Death and the Emperor: Roman Imperial Funerary Monuments from Augustus to Marcus Aurelius* (Cambridge: Cambridge University Press, 2000), 68–74, 142–48.

Jesus' resurrection tale after the Roman imperial and Greek heroic, mythographic tradition."[70] The empty tomb trope in particular was a compelling and dramatic touchstone for communicating the "translation fable" of the mortal who becomes a hero-sage or god. Notable "missing" figures like Romulus, Alexander the Great, Castor and Pollux, Herakles, or Asclepius helped to make the empty tomb palatable for readers of the gospels – a clear illustration of Jesus' new supernatural status. In his work on Paul and myth-making, Stowers notes that myths like that of Herakles, his missing body, and conquering of death would have helped contextualize Paul's message about the new, pneumatic body of Christ.[71] For creative writers, this kind of association also generated an opportunity for novel approaches to an established *topos*. The rolled-away stone from the tomb in the gospels and Chariton's novel heighten mystery and expectation. The missing body illustrates that the absent corpse is now a god or godlike with or without explicit explanation. This signaling demonstrates that a writer like Mark is beholden to the conventions of his craft but with a certain latitude for elaboration and exploring overlapping interests.

That Mark is employing a certain, well-worn illustration of the supernatural status of his subject encapsulates the degree to which he is a writer bound by the standards of imperial writing practices. Literary allusions to other supernatural leaders, gods, heroes, and so forth helped to create a symbolic universe for the Jesus of the gospels that indicated his status and importance through established conventions of Roman book culture.[72] Again, this is an approach to writings like the gospels that does not mystify their origins as manifestations of oral speech or special knowledge. Each of the *topoi* just discussed and the subject matter it evoked was quite intelligible within the literary field of the imperial period.

The story of a Galilean peasant resurrected like Romulus was also timely. Beyond engaging the *topoi* of historiography, *bioi*, the novel, and paradoxography, the gospel writers are crafting their narratives after the Jewish War (66–73 CE) in an era when, as discussed in the previous chapter, Judean sacred texts and interpretation were of evident great interest to the rest of the Empire. Roman imperial campaigns offered

---

[70] Justin, *1 Apol.* 21; Origen, *C. Cels.* 3.22–31; Tert. *Apol.* 21.2–23; Min. Fel. *Oct.* 21.9–10; Arn. *Adv. nat.* 6.1.41; Miller, "Mark's Empty Tomb," 774.

[71] Stowers, "Kinds of Myths, Meals, and Power: Paul and Corinthians," 146–47; cf. Litwa, *Iesus Deus*, 147.

[72] For *comparanda* to Jesus' birth narrative in literature in this period, see Litwa, *Iesus Deus*, 37–67.

ample opportunity for cultural elites to engage in creative projects aimed at critiquing or propagandizing the Empire. Flavian material imagery famously championed the victories of the Jewish War, while authors like Josephus offered companion commentary on certain events. Other literary examples are legion, including Tacitus' *Germania*, Suetonius' *Divus Claudius*, and Cassius Dio, to name a few. In each case, the conflicts, trials, deaths, and moral psychological states of generals, soldiers, citizens, captives, so-called barbarians, and so on acted as a convenient foil for writers aiming to explore the people, places, and gods of the rapidly expanding state, while simultaneously providing an opportunity to showcase literary skill. Elsewhere, I have classified this kind of writing as engaged in "imperial curiosity" – works that reflect on the places and persons in conflict with and in subjugation to the Empire.[73]

The canonical gospels – writings about Judea and its inhabitants – necessarily engage Judean sacred books, Judean customs, and the territory of Palestine, even if their details are, at times, vague or mistaken, as I will discuss below. The figure of Jesus serves as a "literary vehicle and emblem" of a fallen people and constitutes a subject matter sufficiently compelling for an imperial writer, with or without an attendant "community" of fellow Christians to motivate their writing.[74]

Miller also acknowledges that allusions to tropes like the empty tomb invited what he terms "optional appendages" in support of the primary *topos*. In the case of the missing corpse or '"translation fable" convention, this was more often than not the supporting detail of eyewitness testimony.[75] Whether Jesus or Romulus, a risen figure required bystanders. These bystanders are not necessarily "real" but woven into the fabric of the storytelling in order to confirm the writer's account and add

---

[73] Walsh, "IVDAEA DEVICTA," passim.

[74] Miller, "Mark's Empty Tomb," 771. Miller identifies a "broader cultural-literary" objective in Mark, one that dovetails with the idea that the gospel writers are actively combining their knowledge of and interest in Judean sacred books, Judea, and the war with the larger literary *topoi* discussed above: "Mark applies indigenous cultural coloring, while artfully adapting his work, weaving it with Near Eastern motifs and nimble mimetic transvaluations; or, at other moments, Mark has with ingenuous superficiality assigned Palestinian nomenclature and cultural flourish (as though foreign decals placed upon a model). Such Judeo-Oriental dress [is] ... a signification by abstraction and association" (760–61). The notion that Mark is employing a certain expertise by "abstraction and association" nicely encapsulates the activity of a writer obliged by the standards and literary tropes that characterize imperial writing practices, who is also interested in exploring an innovative and timely subject matter.

[75] Miller, "Mark's Empty Tomb," 761.

authenticity to their work. Claiming the authority of eyewitnesses, divine knowledge – or even authorial anonymity – was a strategic move on the part of the ancient writer to give weight to their work and attention to their claims. Indeed, the anonymity and divine status invoked by the gospel writers fit well within this strategic paradigm.

In the context of the subject matters discussed and the setting in which they have placed their primary object of consideration (Jesus), the gospel writers' citing of eyewitnesses and invocation of the *logos* or other super-natural authority confirms the central conceit of their stories: Jesus is a wonder-working son of God who possesses supernatural knowledge and power. Unsullied by mortal concerns and corruptions, he becomes a character that embodies ideals we see elsewhere in literature of the period, including the Greek novels, biographies, and Greek and Roman philoso-phy (particularly Stoicism). In this respect, the claims of the gospel writers combine to generate an authorizing "anti-intellectualism" that simultan-eously embraces the tactics of history and *bios* writing along with the idealism of bucolic or utopian fiction. Thus, these features of the gospels – eyewitnesses and anonymity – are not evidence of the manner by which these writings were produced or their uniqueness among other literature of the age. They are a commonplace, rhetorical invocation on the part of the gospel author.

EYEWITNESSES AND ANONYMITY AS LITERARY STRATEGY

For the Romantic scholar, the idea that the early church was comprised of the same kinds of illiterate followers found in the Synoptic gospels made a good deal of sense. The "primitive" Christian community was imagined to look like the *Volk* being sought after by the likes of Johann Gottfried Herder or the Grimm Brothers; therefore, bringing the same evaluative criteria to bear on the gospels as one might bring to German folktales seemed to have an unassailable logic and method. The gospels represented the roots and *Geist* of the Jesus movement – the oral stories passed on from one Christian group to another down to the literate spokesperson selected to record the community's knowledge. The gospels writers, then, were not dissimilar from the Grimm Brothers themselves, with the crucial distinction that no one of the Romantic era viewed *Aschenputtel* (Cinder-ella) or *Der Froschkönig* (The Frog King) as reliable German history. Hindsight reveals that the Grimms utilized questionable methods in cata-loging their folktales. As Chapter 2 illuminates, their "sources" for these tales were more often than not their social peers and not the "common people." The Grimms also incorporated into their fables numerous literary embellishments in order to make *Kinder- und Hausmärchen* more palatable to their audience.[76] Thus, the notion that the folktales and "fairytales" of the Grimms represented the commonly held narratives of the German people is nebulous at best and arguably a rhetorical invention. I contend something similar is at play with the Synoptic gospels.

If the gospels writers are aware of any oral tradition about Jesus, it is the position of this monograph that these elements are irretrievable to us, if they existed at all. Evidence of thematic engagement and borrowing from the literature of the age is not irretrievable, however, and demonstrates the extent to which the gospel authors are traditional Greco-Roman authors trained in *paideia* and participating in the dominant discourses of their fellow literate cultural producers. Through this prism, certain characteristics of the gospels previously cited as evidence of communal speech – like anonymity or testimony from eyewitnesses – are intelligible as the commonplace activities of writers attempting to compose a compelling story. Pseudepigraphic or divine attribution and formulaic references to eyewitnesses are not descriptions of authorial process, despite what Luke's preface may suggest or how it has often been read. Rather, they serve to enhance the premise that Jesus was a remarkable Judean teacher who emerged from the rural, bucolic, and divinely charged outskirts of the Empire to defeat death and achieve supernatural status. Spurious claims to eyewitness testimony are commonplace in Greek and Roman history; paradoxography similarly attempts to link fantastic or miraculous events to place and local lore in order to lend credibility to its anonymous claims. The Synoptic gospels fit well within this trajectory with their dramatic content and wonderous events, heightened by authorial claims to supernatural knowledge. In short, the anonymity of the gospels, and Luke's claims about eyewitnesses, need not signal the hallmarks of community – oral tradition and cohesive groups – but, instead, are demonstrative of clever writing.

The concept of unnamed or misnamed writing resists discrete definition among ancient commentators and contemporary scholars alike. Perhaps the most familiar examples are the pseudepigrapha of the Hebrew Bible and New Testament, a combination of anonymous texts and "authorial impersonations" that variously fall within the accepted

---

[76] Maria Tartar, *The Hard Facts of the Grimms' Fairy Tales* (Princeton: Princeton University Press, 1987), 24 and passim.

biblical canon. The Psalms of Solomon, for example, were a collection of anonymous pieces compiled and ascribed to the king. Deuteronomy, Fourth Ezra, and Third Enoch are understood to be anachronistic attributions. More broadly, the genre of Jewish apocalyptic literature was frequently anonymous or, more correctly, pseudonymous. In the Second Temple period, otherwise unattributed works were routinely connected to the prophets (e.g., 1 and 2 Kings; Jeremiah; 1 and 2 Samuel; Judges; Ruth; and so on).

Pseudepigraphic and anonymous writing practices were by no means limited to Judean literature. Dionysius of Halicarnassus first uses the word in his *Dinarchus*, distinguishing between his subject's authentic and "spuriously" attributed speeches ('Ιδιωτικοὶ ψευδεπίγραφοι; *Din.* 13.1). Plutarch and Lucian each discuss Xenophon's penchant for ascribing his histories to the enigmatic Themistogenes the Syracusan.[77] Diogenes Laertius reveals that most people regard Thales' *Nautical Astronomy* as belonging to Phocus of Samos.[78] Aelius Donatus elides forgery and plagiarism, labeling both forms of pseudepigrapha in his treatment of the *Eclogues*.[79] From Dionysius the Renegade's *Parthenopaeus*, to the pseudo-Vergilian *Catalepton*, the *Elegiae in Maecenatem*, or the *Consolatio ad Liviam* attributed to Ovid, these pseudepigrapha are understood variously as intentionally "deceitful" (*pseudes*) or passively "mistaken" (also *pseudes*). Indeed, pseudepigrapha can include intentional forgeries, simple imitations of an author's style, attempts to compose an autobiographical narrative about a famous figure, attempts at filling in lacunae in the literary or historical record, anonymous works set in an alternative time and space from the author's present, writings that are simply misattributed, or some combination thereof.

Some have attempted to delineate certain kinds of early Christian pseudepigrapha as self-consciously "lying and trying to deceive their readers."[80] It is certainly the case that one can identify subcategories of

---

[77] Luc. *Hist. Conscr.* 38–41. Also see Plut. *Mor.* 345E.

[78] Diog. Laert. 23. Diogenes also discusses some apothegms that are attributed to Thales in *Thales* 35.

[79] Donat. *Vit. Verg.* 48; also see Scott McGill, *Plagiarism in Latin Literature* (Cambridge: Cambridge University Press, 2012), 3, n. 10, in which McGill states that "[Aelius Donatus] is the sole instance I have found where a Roman source so conflates [forgery and plagiarism]," thus justifying his monograph's focus on plagiarism alone.

[80] Bart Ehrman, *Forged: Writing in the Name of God – Why the Bible's Authors Are Not Who We Think They Are* (New York: HarperOne, 2011), 25. I recognize that this is a book authored for a popular audience; however, as Ehrman is an established scholar in

pseudepigrapha; however, the characterization of forgery risks oversim-
plifying the range of motivations a writer might have for using a name
other than their own.[81] If an author uses a pseudonym in a direct exercise
of *mimesis* or *imitatio*, for example, their intention may be to emulate
their literary ideal with aplomb or even that their work might be mistaken
for the writer named, but perhaps only within a tight literary circle.
Quintilian and Pliny speak of using *aemulatio* – writing out lines imitating
and expanding upon the themes of a figure like Vergil – as a form of
private entertainment.[82] In his *Confessions*, Augustine recalls rewriting
Juno's speech from the *Aeneid* under duress as part of a school exercise –
and then characteristically ponders why his declamation so surpassed
those of his peers.[83] In the case of a text like the *Codex Salmasianus*, a
collection of reworkings from Vergil, it is not entirely clear what motivated its author(s), nor is it clear that they had any intention for their
works to circulate broadly.[84] Authorial intention – even if it is deception –
ultimately has little to do with how such texts are received, attributed, or
discussed.[85] The integration of pseudonymous literature into an established or developing corpus is not directly controlled by the individual
writer.

Peirano usefully suggests that "'pseudepigraphic' is better taken as an
indication of a text's problematic status within the canon than as a
descriptive label attached to writings that share specific formal characteristics."[86] Moreover, with the structured emulation of prized writings so
widespread as a fundamental literary practice, perhaps the more interesting question is not why pseudepigrapha exist but how they are used.[87]
Letters written in the name of Paul in the second century CE, for example,

---

the field, I read his trade books as a synthesis of arguments he makes elsewhere and I cite
him here with caution.

[81] Ehrman, *Forged*, 25.

[82] Quint. *Inst*.10.5.5; Plin. *Ep*. 7.9.3. Also see Irene Peirano, *The Rhetoric of the Roman
Fake: Latin Pseudepigrapha in Context* (Cambridge: Cambridge University Press, 2012),
esp. 14–15, for additional discussion and bibliography.

[83] August. *Conf*. 1.17.   [84] See Peirano, *The Rhetoric of the Roman Fake*, 14.

[85] See Peirano, *The Rhetoric of the Roman Fake*, 4, and her discussion of Ettore Paratore's
category of "pseudofakes."

[86] Peirano, *The Rhetoric of the Roman Fake*, 1–3, cit. 3; E. Paratore, "Il problema degli
Pseudepigrapha," in *La critica del testo. Atti del II Congresso internazionale della Società
Italiana di storia del diritto* (Rome: 1976), 5–32.

[87] For a useful overview of sources connected with *mimesis* and *imitatio* as literary practice
among both Greek and Latin authors, see D. A. Russell, "De imitatione," in *Creative
Imitation and Latin Literature*, ed. David West and Tony Woodman (Cambridge:
Cambridge University Press, 1979), 1–16.

stand as a reflection of Paul's transformation from an independent interpreter of Judean scripture to one of the founding fathers of Christianity.
"Homer," of course, is likely a construction.[88] Beginning in the sixth
century, a "hubbub" of untethered poems of "a religious, metaphysical,
or esoteric nature" came to be associated with Orpheus.[89] Hippocrates'
moniker similarly attracted a "diverse group of medical writings" that
were otherwise anonymous.[90] Iamblichus famously remarks that the
Pythagoreans "assigned everything to Pythagoras and did not keep as
their own any doctrines among those that they had discovered," and so
on.[91] Examining the strategic classification or "naming" of such texts –
whether by the author or by later consumers – reveals the degree to which
the incorporation of pseudepigrapha into a body of literature served as an
authorizing strategy for particular kinds of discourse.

In the case of anonymous writing, it is difficult to reconstruct a writer's
motivation for omitting their name (assuming that the writer even sought
anonymity and their name was not removed by others). Often, anonymous texts came to be associated with a particular author on the basis of
style or necessity. Peirano gives the examples of the Anacreon and Theognis in which "different kinds of anonymous texts written in a similar style
were gathered, some but by no means all of which can be described as
authorial impersonations" or the Sibylline oracles, which circulated both
as genuine prophecies of the seer and as broader imitations of the genre.
Such writings were often considered *adespoton* – "without a master" –
and the act of ascribing a name to them allowed them to be integrated into
a given discourse. As noted above, a leader of a movement (e.g., Pythagoras) or a perceived "founding father" (e.g., Paul) acted as a useful
"master" to authorize the content of an otherwise rudderless work.[92]
The scribes who later attributed "Mark," "Matthew," "Luke," and
"John" to the canonical gospels were likely engaged in such a practice
of authorization. Associating these anonymous writings about Jesus with
characters within the text itself established "august roots" for these
narratives, the developing canon, and the Jesus movement overall.

Scholars of the New Testament have often struggled to view this
practice of "anonymous naming" outside of assumptions about

---

[88] M. L. West, "The Invention of Homer," *The Classical Quarterly* 49, no. 2 (1999): 364–82,
cit. 364. Also see Josephus' discussion of the reliability of Homer in *Ap.* 1.12–16.
[89] Pl. *Resp.* 2; M.L. West, *The Orphic Poems* (Oxford: Clarendon Press, 1983), 5; Peirano,
The Rhetoric of the Roman Fake, 6 also cites West.
[90] Peirano, *The Rhetoric of the Roman Fake*, 6.   [91] Iambl. *VP* 198–99.
[92] Peirano, *The Rhetoric of the Roman Fake*, 5.

communities and oral tradition.[93] In the opening paragraph of his *Jesus before the Gospels*, Bart Ehrman summarizes the traditional approach to the question of gospel authorship: "stories about Jesus were in oral circulation, starting with tales told by those who were eye- and earwitnesses to the thing he did and said," and eventually these tales made their way to the gospel authors.[94] Richard Bauckham goes so far as to claim that "the usual ways of thinking of oral tradition are not appropriate at all ... Gospel traditions did not, for the most part, circulate anonymously but in the name of the eyewitnesses to whom they were due," suggesting that these texts were not "anonymous" in the usual sense of the term but inextricably tied to the historical persons to whom they were later ascribed.[95] Troubling Bauckham's position is the assumption that the notion of any kind of "oral tradition" is demonstrable. There is also the issue that the canonical gospel writers do not directly identify themselves; Luke's preface shrouds him in secrecy, even if he claims to base his account on the testimony of eyewitnesses in competition with "many (πολλοί)" others who endeavored to "draw up a narrative (ἐπεχείρησαν ἀνατάξασθαι διήγησιν)" in kind (Luke 1:1–2).[96] While this manner of "secrecy" is not unique among ancient authors – indeed, shockingly few of our extant ancient biographers name themselves in their titles or prefaces – particular literary habit cannot be taken as evidence for amorphous concepts like "oral tradition."[97] Both anonymity and the notion of the "eyewitness" are themselves rhetorical tropes that must be scrutinized before being taken literally.

---

[93] There is a great deal of literature on this subject, and I can only offer a few suggestions for further reading and counter arguments. See, for example, Simon Gathercole, "The Alleged Anonymity of the Canonical Gospels," *Journal of Theological Studies* 69 (2018): 447–76; Maurice Casey, *Is John's Gospel True?* (New York: Routledge, 1996), 140–77; Martin Hengel, *Between Jesus and Paul: Studies in the Earliest History of Christianity* (London: SCM Press, 1983); Martin Hengel, *The Four Gospels and One Gospel of Jesus Christ* (London: SCM Press, 2000). For a useful discussion of this matter, see James G. Crossley, *The Date of Mark's Gospel: Insight from the Law in Earliest Christianity* (London: T&T Clark, 2004), esp. 15–18.

[94] Bart Ehrman, *Jesus before the Gospels: How the Earliest Christians Remembered, Changed, and Invented Their Stories of the Savior* (New York: HarperOne, 2016), 1. As before, I cite a mass-market book here, from an established scholar, to indicate the prevalence of the perspective under discussion. See note 80 above.

[95] Richard Bauckham, *Jesus and the Eyewitnesses: The Gospels as Eyewitness Testimony* (Grand Rapids: Eerdmans, 2006), 8.

[96] Bauckham, *Jesus and the Eyewitnesses*, 6–9. Bauckham argues that John is written by an eyewitness rhetorically trading on this authority; however, the author nonetheless remains unidentified.

[97] See Gathercole, "The Alleged Anonymity of the Canonical Gospels," *passim*.

As a rhetorical trope, claiming access to eyewitness testimony is always superior to written accounts of past events. In the Phaedrus, reflecting on the art of letters, Socrates suggests that men have misplaced their affection for the act of writing, fostering "forgetfulness" (λήθην) among those who do not "practice their memory (μνήμης ἀμελετησίᾳ)" (*Phaed.* 275A). To rely on the written word also creates a false sense of authority in the reader who obtains only "the appearance of wisdom, not true wisdom (σοφίας δὲ τοῖς μαθηταῖς δόξαν, οὐκ ἀλήθειαν πορίζεις)" (*Phaed.* 275A). Socrates goes on to explain to Phaedrus that writing has a peculiar quality akin to a painting that features "living beings (ὡς ζῶντα)" that "maintain a solemn silence (σεμνῶς πάνυ σιγᾷ)" (*Phaed.* 275D) or, alternatively, "[indiscriminately] say only one and the same thing (σημαίνει μόνον ταὐτὸν ἀεί)" over and over again with no power to protect themselves (οὔτε βοηθῆσαι δυνατὸς αὑτῷ; *Phd.* 275D–E). Oral transmission of a narrative was vastly preferred. Polybius, citing Heraclitus, explains that both hearing and sight impart knowledge, but, of the two, "the eyes are much more accurate witnesses than the ears (ὀφθαλμοὶ γὰρ τῶν ὤτων ἀκριβέστεροι μάρτυρες)" (Polyb. 12.27.1). Using Timaeus as an example of the inferior approach, Polybius identifies reading as the path of least resistance, if not lesser accuracy:

On one hand, inquiries made of books involves no danger of hardship (ἐκ τῶν βυβλίων δύναται πολυπραγμονεῖσθαι χωρὶς κινδύνου καὶ κακοπαθείας) ... [with] a well-stocked library nearby (ὑπομνημάτων πλῆθος ἢ βυβλιοθήκην που γειτνιῶσαν). Then [you] can research lying down (κατακείμενον ἐρευνᾶν) and compare (συγκρίνειν) the accounts of different writers (συγγραφέων) without causing yourself any personal distress (κακοπαθείας). Personal inquiry, on the other hand, requires hard labor and great expense (ταλαιπωρίας καὶ δαπάνης). (Polyb. 12.27.3–5)

Citing Ephorus, Theopompus, and Homer on the subject, Polybius suggests that proper research into historical events requires being willing to travel far and wide to observe, inquire, and, ideally, experience great places and events worthy of documentation (Polyb. 12.27.11–28.7). Thus, he laments that Timaeus enjoys such a celebrated reputation, despite never leaving his library.

Polybius provides an idealized vision of the writer's task. Even if one relied on eyewitnesses, prejudice and bias were a continual risk; eyewitnesses might have an axe to grind, or an author might have cause to disparage a particular subject. In his introduction to the *Bellum Judaicum* (Jewish War), for example, Josephus remarks that many historians have chronicled the conflict, motivated by an interest in flattering the Romans or out of hatred for the Judeans (*BJ* 1.1–3). Personal relationships might encourage one to take liberties as well. In his letter to L. Lucceius, Cicero encourages his friend to "disregard the laws of historiography (*leges historiae neglegas*)" and "to let your affection (*amori*) for me take a degree of precedence over the truth (*ueritas*)" by incorporating some of Cicero's views into the historical account he was concurrently writing (*Fam.* 5.12).[98] Thus, claims about eyewitnesses are more aspirational and constructed than ultimately believable.

Concerning eyewitnesses, much like Polybius, Dionysius of Halicarnassus, and Plutarch, Josephus reiterates in *Antiquitates Judaicae* (Jewish Antiquities), *Contra Apionem* (Against Apion), and the *Jewish War* that "it is the duty of one who promises to present his readers with actual facts (παράδοσιν πράξεων ἀληθινῶν) first to obtain an exact knowledge of them himself (ἐπίστασθαι ταύτας πρότερον ἀκριβῶς), either through having been in close touch with the event, or by inquiry from those who knew them."[99] But Josephus' assurances that his historical accounts are unblemished demonstrates that writers were nonetheless concerned that they would be taken seriously, even if the presentation of their histories took on the proper-seeming form. As the poet and essayist Jaswinder Bolina summarizes on the rhetorical strength of lyric poetry: "The problem is that the authority of the lyric is contingent upon the audience's perception of credibility in the speaker. If an audience rejects that credibility at the outset for any reason, the power of the rhetoric evaporates."[100] Regardless of whether an author was in fact an eyewitness, engaged in the proper procurement of eyewitness testimony, or curtailed their innovations on literary style, it was essential that they professed to do so in order to be taken as an authority.

Beyond claims to sanctioned ethnic associations, eyewitness status, or the secure cataloging of eyewitness accounts, a writer might attempt to establish their bona fides through their title (e.g., Celsus' *A True Discourse* [Ἀληθὴς Λόγος] or, although a parody on the genre, Lucian's *True History* [Ἀληθῆ Διηγήματα]) or with a preface highlighting their motivations and methods, thereby situating their account within the trajectory of related discourses. As noted above, Josephus employs this strategy in abundance. Polybius infused his histories with references to the perils of bias, implying

---

[98] For discussion of this passage, see A. J. Woodman's lecture on Cicero in *Rhetoric in Classical Historiography: Four Studies* (Portland: Areopagitica Press, 1988), 70–116.

[99] *AJ* 1.1–26, 20.259–66; *Ap.* 1.53; *BJ* 1.1–30.

[100] Jaswinder Bolina, "Color Coded: On the Poetics of Donald Trump, the Progress of Poetry, and Reverse Racism," *Poetry Foundation* (accessed online May 11, 2016, at www.poetryfoundation.org).

that he was immune to the temptation (1.14.6, 7.12.3, 24.4.2). This kind of preface was not limited to history-telling. As Christopher Pelling notes in his critical analysis of narrative in Plutarch, prefaces, proems, and epilogues are "particularly important in the narrator's characterization of self, of narratees, and of the dynamic between the two. In proems, we often find a strong self-characterization, or characterization of the reading or writing process: a display of critical learning, or moral debate, or a setting of a hero's life in a wider ethical or historical perspective."[101] Longus' proem to *Daphnis and Chloe* includes an explanation of his impetus for writing: "But when I had seen with wonder (θαυμάσαντα) these and many other things having to do with the erotic/love (ἐρωτικὰ), I had a longing (πόθος ἔσχεν) to write a response to this image (ἀντιγράψαι τῇ γραφῇ) ... [in] four volumes (τέτταρας βίβλους)" (1.2).

As already discussed, Plutarch distinguishes between the act of writing a history and writing a *bios* in his *Life of Alexander*, relating history to the documentation of large-scale events and *bioi* to studies of character. The art of ancient biography will be discussed in more detail in the following chapter, but Plutarch's account of writing about lives – while attempting to create a taxonomy – betrays the degree to which writing about any event and the experiences of its protagonists signaled porous boundaries between genres. A good history, like a good *bios*, required identifying a fitting subject – someone or something "befitting a great person (μεγαλοπρεπεῖς)," according to Dionysius of Halicarnassus (*Ant. Rom.* 1.2).

The writer's subject matter was also a reflection of their larger moral choices. If motivated by anything other than the edification of the reader – for instance, by notoriety – a writer's account will be "neither fair nor true."[102] Similarly, the choice of a biographical subject was often based on the subject's relative virtues and vices. Beyond the traditional civic biographical types – usually great leaders of men – philosophers, teachers, and wonder-workers were also popular foils. Porphyry's *Vita Pythagorae* (Life of Pythagoras) appeared within his larger philosophic history, chronicling the lives and doxography of figures from Homer to Plato.[103]

---

[101] C. B. R. Pelling, "Plutarch," in *Narrators, Narratees, and Narratives in Ancient Greek Literature: Studies in Ancient Greek Narrative*, vol. 1, ed. Irene J. F. De Jong, René Nünlist, and Angus Bowie (Leiden: Brill, 2004), 403–21, cit. 406.

[102] Matthew Fox, *Roman Historical Myths: The Regal Period in Augustan Literature* (New York: Clarendon, 1996), 51.

[103] For more on Porphyry and Iamblichus, see Gillian Clark, "Philosophic Lives and Philosophic Life: Porphyry and Iamblichus," in *Greek Biography and Panegyric in*

Diogenes Laertius' subjects ran the gamut of virtue and vice, often shading into comedy. Philo's *De vita Moysis* (Life of Moses) is simultaneously a defense of the virtues of his subject and a defense of Judaism, as well as an invective against the Greeks and, akin to Josephus, a challenge to Gentiles who have failed to give worthy Judean figures their due. Even Lucian employs this same technique in his satire when he states that his writing references "things I have neither seen (μήτε εἶδον), nor have experienced (μήτε ἔπαθον) for myself, nor learned from others (μήτε παρ' ἄλλων ἐπυθόμην), and still things which, in fact, do not even exist at all (μήτε ὅλως)" (*Ver. hist.* 1.4), like so many other poets, historians, and philosophers who have written about places, people, miracles, and wonders they have never encountered for themselves.[104] Lucian's humorous approach to this well-known formula demonstrates both its pervasiveness and the expectation for its appearance in relevant literature.[105] Moreover, his ability to play with the expectations of what truth-telling meant to his audience augurs Cicero's claim that even writing history was a "rhetorical work," or *opus oratorium*.[106]

It is within this trajectory that a preface like that to Luke's gospel is intelligible as a rhetorical strategy, and not a concrete account of his writing process. He establishes his means and methods for writing about the events or "deeds" (πραγμάτων) that have taken place concerning the life of Jesus of Nazareth. Like Lucian and others, he references his literary competitors – the "many" who have also "set about composing an orderly account (πολλοὶ ἐπεχείρησαν ἀνατάξασθαι διήγησιν)" – and assures his patron that his account offers greater accuracy thanks to the "eyewitness" (αὐτόπται) testimony "passed down" (παρέδοσαν) from those

Late Antiquity, ed. Tomas Hägg and Philip Rousseau (Berkeley: University of California Press, 2000), 29–51.

[104] For more on Lucian, see Valentina Popescu, "Lucian's *True Stories*: Paradoxography and False Discourse," in *The Ancient Novel and the Frontiers of Genre*, ed. Marília P. Futre Pinheiro et al. (Eelde: Barkhuis: 2014), 39–58.

[105] Others have discussed examples from the *comparanda* mentioned in this chapter in reference to the Gospel of Luke, albeit not in precisely the same way I have framed it here. See, for example, Catherine Hezser, "Ancient 'Science Fiction': Journeys into Space and Visions of the World in Jewish, Christian, and Greco-Roman Literature of Antiquity," in *Christian Origins and Hellenistic Judaism: Social and Literary Contexts for the New Testament*, ed. Stanley E. Porter and Andrew W. Pitts (Leiden: Brill, 2013), 397–438, and Sean A. Adams, "Luke, Josephus, and Self-Definition: The Genre of Luke-Acts and Its Relationship to Apologetic Historiography and Collected Biography," in *Christian Origins and Hellenistic Judaism*, ed. Stanley E. Porter and Andrew W. Pitts (Leiden: Brill, 2013), 439–60.

[106] Cic. *Leg.* 1.5; Bowersock, *Fiction as History*, 12.

beholden to the *logos* (Luke 1:1–2). Luke proceeds to chronicle a series of historical facts and events – again, several of which do not hold up to scrutiny (e.g., a "world-wide census [ἀπογράφεσθαι πᾶσαν τὴν οἰκουμένην]" or the dates of Quirinius' rule in Luke 2:1–2) – aimed at justifying the nature of his writing, as well as his subject matter. As a writer, Luke is "playing the game" of establishing his bona fides, clearly aware of the literary tradition into which he is inserting himself. As such, his preface should not be taken as a reliable description of how information about Jesus or Judea came to him (i.e., via oral tradition) for it is incumbent upon him to make a claim of impartiality. Moreover, the anonymous nature of his narrative, and all of the canonical gospels for that matter, does not necessarily signal that Luke is representing communal knowledge or speech with his writing. The compelling feature of anonymous writing is not necessarily that an author withholds their name and why, but *how* anonymity functions in the ultimate reception and attribution of a work. In the case of the gospels, whether or not they were in their first composition anonymous, their later association with so-called founding figures of the Jesus movement codified them as representative accounts of Jesus' life.

Luke adds a compelling layer onto his preface, describing his sources as both eyewitnesses and beholden to the *logos* (1:2). Making an authoritative reference to *logos* is not exclusive to Luke or other writings about Jesus. Famously, in the prologue to the Gospel of John, *logos* is imagined to be an active principle, drawing certain associations to the Septuagint and the larger *corpora* of Judean literature in which the term is associated with creation (e.g., Gen. 1:1–5, 26–31; Proverbs 8; Wisdom of Solomon 9) and wisdom (e.g., Sirach 24). *Logos* also stands as more of a technical philosophical concept or even autonomous agent in other literature of the period.[107]

A useful parallel is the work of Philo in which the notion of *logos* as an active, creative principle is combined with a Stoic understanding of *logos* as a rational and directive agent. In *De opificio mundi* (On the Creation),

---

[107] There is a great deal of scholarship available on the concept of *logos* in early Christian literature writ large and in the Gospel of John in particular. For more discussion on the use of *logos* in Jewish scripture and Philo, see Kenneth Schenck, *A Brief Guide to Philo* (Louisville: Westminster John Knox, 2005), 86–95, cit. 87. For a discussion of Stoicism and its relevance for early Christian studies, see Tuomas Rasimus, Troels Engberg-Pedersen, and Ismo Dunderberg, eds., *Stoicism in Early Christianity* (Grand Rapids: Baker Academic, 2010).

for instance, Philo states that "the perceptible cosmos/world (νοητὸν κόσμον) is nothing other than the *logos* of God (θεοῦ λόγον) already engaged in making the cosmos (κοσμοποιοῦντος)" (*Opif.* 24). This *logos* is, in a Platonic sense, a reflection or image of God; however, Philo also conceives of it as a driving force in the universe. In *De Cherubim* (On the Cherubim), he frames *logos* or "divine reason (λόγος θεῖος)" as the "ruler and steersman of all things (ὁ δίοπος καὶ κυβερνήτης τοῦ παντός)." His position is clarified in his *Allegorical Interpretation* in his treatment of Genesis 1:27:

> God's shadow is his word (σκιὰ θεοῦ δὲ ὁ λόγος αὐτοῦ ἐστιν). By it he made the cosmos/world (ἐκοσμοποίει), using it as an instrument (προσχρησάμενος). And this shadow (σκιὰ) – this statue-like representation (ἀπεικόνισμα) – is an archetype (ἀρχέτυπον).... For just as God is the pattern of the image (ὁ θεὸς παράδειγμα τῆς εἰκόνος) that we have just called a shadow (σκιὰν), so this image (εἰκὼν) becomes a pattern of other things (εἰκὼν ἄλλων γίνεται παράδειγμα).

For Philo, the *logos* is a pervasive, rational agent that permeates the cosmos, associated with the creative strength and faculties of Yahweh. His position is akin to Stoics like Zeno, who viewed "*logos* [as] the ... maker of the universe (*artificem universitatis* λόγον) ... fate, necessity of things, god, and the mind of Zeus (*fatum et necessitatem rerum et deum et animum Iovis*)."[108] Scholarly literature on the concept of *logos* in Stoic thought is vast and need not be rehearsed here. But it is sufficient to note the ease with which Stoic principles on the power of *logos* dovetail conceptually with first-century Judean understandings of the Judean god. By extension, it is not difficult to see how the authors of the gospels may have had some of these same notions in mind when utilizing such technical philosophical terms. To the extent that the *logos* represents "divine reason," one can see how Luke may also understand it as an active principle in the perception of his reputed eyewitnesses. Recall that Georgias describes *logos* as a "powerful ruler" in the pursuit of evocative and emotionally charged descriptive writing. To cite *logos* as an authority in any measure for Luke signals a further appeal to the strategic authentication of his account.

One additional possibility is that Luke's preface signals a trope that would become standard among later Christian *bioi* and hagiographies: intellectual superiority despite a lack of formal education. Samuel Rubenson illustrates this pattern convincingly in his work on later Christian

---

[108] Lactanitus, *De vera sap.* 9 = 1.160. Cited from Alfred Chilton Pearson, *The Fragments of Zeno and Cleanthes with Introduction and Explanatory Notes* (London: C. J. Clay & Sons, 1891), 92, sec. 44.

monastic literature, summarizing that the ideal Christian was one "totally unaffected by schooling, a prophet taught by God alone, and himself a teacher of supreme wisdom."[109] From the opening of the *Life of Saint Antony*, for example, the idea of the Christian who is "both undefiled by human learning and wiser than Greek philosophers" is established and then reinforced:

When he was a child (παιδίον) he lived with his parents (γονεῦσι), aware of little else other than them and his home (πλέον αὐτῶν καὶ τοῦ οἴκου μηδὲν ἕτερον γινώσκων). As he grew and became a boy (παῖς), and was growing up (προέκοπτε τῇ ἡλικίᾳ), he could not bear to learn his letters (γράμματα ... μαθεῖν οὐκ ἠνέσχετο), wishing to remain separate (βουλόμενος ἐκτὸς) from companionship with other children (παῖδας συνηθείας). All his longing (ἐπιθυμίαν πᾶσαν), as it has been written of Jacob (γεγραμμένον περὶ τοῦ Ἰακὼβ), was for living in a natural state (ἄπλαστος οἰκεῖν) in his home (ἐν τῇ οἰκίᾳ αὐτοῦ). (*Life of Saint Antony* 1)

This is a trope among late antique Christian writers more broadly, building on the well-established tradition of prophetic dreams and visions in the Hebrew Bible, as well as the concept of *gnosis* within the developing Christian tradition after the second century CE. Arguably, this literary trend was also akin to the kind of cultural or ethnic competition discussed in this chapter, with Christianity – "a revelation handed down to simple fishermen" – asserting itself against the accepted "Greek intellectual elite." Moreover, any convincing apologetic for the developing Jesus movement would necessarily have to address the alleged humble origins of the earliest Jesus followers detailed in the gospels – a gaggle of founding heroes who are described as "unlettered rustics."[110] Claims about the "purity" or "truth" of what were later classified as Christian writings took a number of forms, including claims of divinely guided illiteracy (e.g., *Life of Saint Antony*; *The Shepherd of Hermas*, Vision 2.1[5]:4[111]) or invectives against Christians seeking classical education,

---

[109] Samuel Rubenson, "Philosophy and Simplicity: The Problem of Classical Education in Early Christian Biography," in *Greek Biography and Panegyric in Late Antiquity* (Berkeley: University of California Press, 2000), 110–39, cit. 110–11.

[110] Rubenson, "Philosophy and Simplicity," 111.

[111] *The Shepherd of Hermas*, Vision 2.1[5]: 4: "I took it (ἔλαβον ἐγώ,), and retiring to a certain spot in the country (τινα τόπον τοῦ ἀγροῦ ἀναχωρήσας) I copied it letter for letter (μετεγραψάμην πάντα πρὸς γράμμα); for I could not make out the syllables (συλλαβάς). When then I had finished the letters of the book (τὰ γράμματα τοῦ βιβλιδίου), suddenly the book was snatched out of my hand (ἐξαίφνης ἡρπάγη μου ἐκ τῆς χειρὸς τὸ βιβλίδιον); but by whom I did not see (ὑπὸ τίνος δὲ οὐκ εἶδον)."

lest any acquired knowledge damage "the purity of the Gospel."[112] Education through *logos* was deemed far superior to *paideia*.

What Rubenson's study reveals, beyond the fact that claims like those found in the introduction to the *Life of Saint Antony* were clearly literary tactics, is the willingness of scholars to accept such rhetoric as historical reality – notably in the ahistorical portrayal of the "pioneers of Egyptian monasticism as illiterate peasants."[113] This issue of mistaking literary claims for historical description is also tackled in the field of manuscript studies by S. D. Charlesworth in his work on the second- and third-century transmission of Christian papyri. Demonstrating in explicit detail the ways in which our earliest manuscript copies of the canonical and extracanonical gospels build on one another compositionally, Charlesworth argues that traditional scholarship on early Christian literature has displayed an "orality bias," preferring to adhere to "an idealistic folkloric" image of the illiterate, rustic, oral origins of the gospels, rather than face that intertextual study demonstrates that these writings were the work of educated, literate cultural producers. Discussing the intratextuality of the second-century Egerton Gospel, he explains that "*written sources*" would have been the primary reference point for a work like the gospels – whether other gospels, a sayings-source, or similar document.[114] To this *comparanda*, this chapter has added "sources" like the *Sat.* and paradoxography. Charlesworth explains that such intertextuality is by its very nature inter*textual* and not characteristic of oral transmission:

Once again intertextuality, the natural accompaniment of a well-read literacy, is textual, rather than oral, and stands in the wings while composition takes centre stage. The idea that the ancients were incapable of such a thing springs from a misunderstanding of the *realia* of ancient writers and their literary products. *It is rooted in an orality bias that paints early transmission of gospel tradition with an idealistic folkloric brush and, consequently, applies source-critical principles in speculative and unconvincing ways. It fails to recognize that there always were*

---

[112] See, for example, Hippolytus, *Traditio apostolica* 16.5; for more discussion on this trope, see Rubenson, "Philosophy and Simplicity," 111–14.

[113] See Rubenson, "Philosophy and Simplicity," 111, n. 2, for a list of secondary treatments of Antony that take the introduction to his *bios* at face value.

[114] S. D. Charlesworth, "The End of Orality: Transmission of Gospel Tradition in the Second and Third Centuries," in *Between Orality and Literacy: Communication and Adaptation in Antiquity, Orality and Literacy in the Ancient World*, vol. 10, ed. Ruth Scodel (Leiden: Brill, 2014), 331–55, cit. 347. Emphasis added.

some individuals who participated in the written transmission of gospel tradition.[115]

From the canonical gospels to second-century extracanonical texts to later *bioi*, each writer employs certain literary techniques designed to distinguish and authorize their works. These strategies have precedent in the rhetorical approaches of ancient historiographers and biographers; the use of technical terminology has precedence in Jewish, Greek, and Roman philosophical writings; and the manuscript tradition, albeit fragmentary, nonetheless establishes ongoing textual borrowing between writers. Despite this evidence, the myth of origins that Christianity tells about itself persists: the teachings of Jesus passed on orally from the illiterate eyewitnesses in Galilee to spontaneously formed and widespread communities of early Christians, later recorded by literate gospel authors. We continue to reify this narrative when we assume the anonymity of the gospels is relevant to the nature of their composition (not their reception), or when we take something like Luke's preface as tantamount to historical description. Assuming that all shared material in the gospels and Paul stem from the same oral tradition is what has fostered faulty notions about early Christian communities and their exceptionalism, severely limiting our understanding of Christian beginnings. In short, by accepting the Romantic reconstruction of the gospels, we fail to acknowledge the degree to which these writings fit perceptibly within a larger trajectory of imperial literature.

---

[115] Charlesworth, "The End of Orality: Transmission of Gospel Tradition in the Second and Third Centuries," 347. Emphasis added.

5

The Gospels as Subversive Biography

In this chapter, I carry forward a critique of the perceived exceptionalism of the gospels by offering a detailed examination of the genre of biography in antiquity. While some scholars maintain that the gospels were a literary anomaly without clear precedent, I argue that they are an innovative play on the civic biographical tradition.[1] By situating the gospels within this literary classification, I again work toward establishing an approach to these writings that does not seek the author's presumed religious "community" in its rhetorical framework. I begin with a brief discussion of the genre of biography followed by a rehearsal of the development of the civic biographical tradition in antiquity. This provides the basis for then outlining the trajectory of a form of writing lives that David Konstan and I have termed "subversive biography" – a type of "life" that emphasizes the capabilities of a figure perceived to be outside the dominant culture à la Pierre Bourdieu's "autonomous pole" in Chapter 3. Instead of a chronicle of the military pursuits of a great general, for instance, we have the *Vita Aesopi* (Life of Aesop) which tells the tale of a wily and bombastic slave, or the *Alexander Romance* which

---

[1] A portion of the following argument appears in David Konstan and Robyn Faith Walsh, "Civic and Subversive Biography in Antiquity," in *Writing Biography in Greece and Rome: Narrative Technique and Fictionalization*, ed. Koen De Temmerman and Kristoffel Demoen (Cambridge: Cambridge University Press, 2016), 26–43. I employ a similar approach to "subversive biography" in this chapter with Konstan's permission.

Some examples include Adela Yarbro Collins, *Is Mark's Gospel a Life of Jesus?: The Question of Genre* (Milwaukee: Marquette University Press, 1990), to be discussed. Also see Helmut Koester, *Ancient Christian Gospels: Their History and Development* (Harrisburg: Trinity Press International, 1990), 24.

portrays its resourceful and clever leader as something of an antihero. I place writings about Jesus within this same trajectory, which alternatively emphasize his wisdom, ready wit, and wonder-working as a strategy for demonstrating authority and gaining advantage when faced with challenges from more powerful figures. Viewing the gospels in this way demonstrates that there was a "market," so to speak, for this class of literature in the first and second centuries. Thus, specific characteristics of Jesus' portrayal in the Synoptics need not be a function of oral tradition, but a reflection of the rational interests of elite, imperial writers.

THE SCOPE OF BIOGRAPHY

Where today we speak of "biographies," the ancients, rather, used the term "lives" – *bioi* in Greek, *vitae* in Latin. In itself, the difference in terminology is seemingly inconsequential, but when it comes to usage, the equation between the English and the Greek or Latin words can be misleading. "Biography" in contemporary practice suggests a well-defined genre, with norms and conventions that are widely understood. A biographer offers a cradle-to-grave account of the life of a person (unless the work is explicitly limited to a certain period in their life) and professes to relate accurately the events in which the subject participated, often along with details of their character and thoughts. A certain amount of invention is allowed in reconstructing the psychology or inner life of the subject. This is particularly the case in literature of this kind produced in the past century. For instance, according to *The Oxford Dictionary of Literary Terms*:

[A] new movement emerged from 1918, known as the new biography ... in which biography was treated as an imaginative art in which invented dialogues, interior monologues and other techniques borrowed from the novel were employed.... The 20th century also saw the emergence of psychobiography, informed by psychoanalytic theories of development, and of sensational biographies exposing the sexual and other personal secrets of famous figures.[2]

Despite these innovations, all these types share certain readily recognizable conventions – even the most creative purport to represent the subject's life truthfully and offer evidence and sources to corroborate the story. Likewise, the boundary between biography and other narrative

---

[2] Christopher Baldick, "Biography," in *The Oxford Dictionary of Literary Terms* (New York: Oxford University Press, 2008).

genres, such as history or the novel, is typically clear. When this is not the case, one is usually conscious of deliberate experimentation or transgression that evokes, even as it disrupts, the standard generic markers.[3]

The case with ancient *bioi* is quite different. As Christopher Pelling observes in the article on Greek biography in *The Oxford Classical Dictionary*:

> Biography in antiquity was not a rigidly defined genre. *Bios*, "life," or *bioi*, "lives," could span a range of types of writing, from Plutarch's cradle-to-grave accounts of statesmen to Chamaeleon's extravagant stories about literary figures.... Consequently the boundaries with neighbouring genres – the encomium, the biographical novel on the model of Xenophon's *Cyropaedia*, the historical monograph on the deeds of a great man like Alexander the Great – are blurred and sometimes artificial.[4]

How is one to classify, for example, the manifestly fantastical *Alexander Romance*, which has a historical subject but, in many respects, seems as much a work of fiction as the anonymous *History of Apollonius King of Tyre*, usually regarded as a novel? Or what are we to make of the *Vita Homeri* (Life of Homer), ascribed to Plutarch, which bears a strong resemblance to a fairy tale? The Synoptic gospels may seem like biographies, but some scholars have defined them, rather, as histories, a form of apocalyptic narrative, or, often, as sui generis literature in a genre all their own.[5] All of these works are in some sense "lives," but it can be difficult

---

[3] An example is Per Wästberg, *The Journey of Anders Sparrman: A Biographical Novel* (London: Granta Books, 2010). In a *Times Literary Supplement* review under the title, "Life's Little Lacunae," Peter Parker observes: "A biographical novel ... is free to fill gaps, to speculate and invent; but this requires a true immersion in and understanding of the subject and the world in which he or she moved"; Peter Parker, "Life's Little Lacunae," *The Times Literary Supplement* (April 30, 2010), 20.

[4] Christopher Pelling, "Biography, Greek," in *OCD*, 232. Thomas Hägg, in *The Art of Biography in Antiquity* (Cambridge: Cambridge University Press, 2012), wonders about "the generic label" one might apply to the *Cyropaedia*, and observes that whether we call it "historical (or biographical or philosophical) novel, romanticized (or fictionalized) biography, mirror of princes ... its main topic is leadership and government, not the life of the historical King Cyrus the Great of Persia" (51).

[5] For full discussion with ample bibliography, see Collins, *Is Mark's Gospel a Life of Jesus?*, esp. 1–16; Collins herself argues that "Mark is an apocalyptic historical monograph" (27). Similarly, Willem Vorster, "Kerygma/History and the Gospel Genre," in *Speaking of Jesus: Essays on Biblical Language, Gospel Narrative*, ed. J. Eugene Botha (Leiden: Brill, 1999), 131, describe the so-called kerygma theory according to which "the gospel genre is something very unique" and "has no literary parallels prior to its origin and outside the canon." Based on the historical framework of 1 Cor. 15:3–7, 11:23–25; Acts 10:37–41 and 13:23–31 (among other passages), Vorster argues that "the gospel genre is not a product of the literary activity of Mark but ... of the apostolic preaching of Jesus from

to specify what else these writings may have in common with each other or with, for example, Plutarch's *Vitae Parallelae* (Parallel Lives) or, as mentioned in the previous chapter, Diogenes Laertius' *Lives of the Philosophers*.

Given this variety of biographical "types," it may seem fruitless to seek features that would lead one to be able to classify ancient *bioi* (or *vitae*) more coherently. However, certain elements stand out. Some *bioi*, for example, highlight the virtues of their subjects. Often these subjects are great statesmen or military heroes who exemplify justice and courage. Similarly, there are biographies of brilliant thinkers and writers, such as philosophers and poets, whose lives might serve as models even, at times, in a negative sense (when the subject was notorious for vices). Others endow their subjects with extraordinary abilities of a different kind – "superpowers," if you will – that involve what one might term "magic" or other sorts of wonder-working. This latter type often also emphasizes the sharp wit of the protagonist, whose clever ripostes and wise sayings, sometimes in the form of parables, catch their opponents off guard and turn the tables on them. Again, such lives tend to feature, in a somewhat picaresque fashion, a figure that is an outsider in some measure or a marginal member of society – often of a lower class or oppressed minority group – and, hence, a social underdog who must prove his worth to the more powerful people he (occasionally she) encounters.[6]

These latter elements, in combination, serve to identify a particular narrative form or strategy in the *bioi* that I characterize as "subversive," in contrast to the civic tradition of biography that focuses, rather, on powerful and respected individuals, such as those written by Cornelius Nepos, Plutarch, and Suetonius. In other words, this form of what David Konstan and I have termed "subversive biography" possesses distinguishing features that set it apart in the ancient biographical tradition from the dominant, civic variety. While the civic biography is a type that is

---

which it developed." See also Rudolf Bultmann, *The History of the Synoptic Tradition* (Peabody: Hendrickson, 1994 [1963]), 371–74; Helmut Koester, *Ancient Christian Gospels: Their History and Development* (Harrisburg: Trinity Press International, 1990), 26–31; Richard A. Burridge, *What Are the Gospels?: A Comparison with Graeco-Roman Biography* (Grand Rapids: Eerdmans, 2004); Richard A. Burridge, "Reading the Gospels as Biography," in *The Limits of Ancient Biography*, ed. Brian McGing and Judith Mossman (Swansea: Classical Press of Wales; Oakville: David Brown Book, 2006), 31–49.

[6] An example is the anonymous *Life of Aesop*, discussed below. For *bioi* of female characters, see the so-called *Lives of the Harlots*, a collection of Christian lives that illustrate the transition from extreme depravity to exemplary piety and repentance.

organized around the dominant social values, which are presupposed even in the breach (as in the case of imperfect or vicious subjects), subversive biography gives voice to those who are on the margins of power, and more or less subtly undermine or challenge the conventional ideology.[7]

To be clear, such a distinction, if indeed it is valid for ancient *bioi*, evolved and changed over time and differed in different places. As Tzvetan Todorov famously argued in the *Dictionnaire encyclopédique des sciences du langage*, genres do not exist in isolation: they are always defined in the context of a constellation of kindred forms and exist in a dynamic tension with them.[8] What is more, these forms are not given a priori but emerge historically; thus, the Russian formalist critic Boris Tomashevsky insisted that "no firm logical classification of genres is possible. Their demarcation is always historical; that is to say, it is correct only for a specific moment of history."[9] Nevertheless, I believe that the distinction Konstan and I have described remained stable, or at least relevant, from the classical epoch through late antiquity. In what follows, I rehearse the contours of the civic tradition and then demonstrate the parallel development of the subversive form of *bioi* which pertains to the gospels.[10]

XENOPHON AND THE CIVIC TRADITION

Two works that may be described as proto-biographies date to the fourth century BCE and are from Xenophon: an essay on the Spartan king Agesilaus and *Memorabilia* (Ὑπομνήματα), or *Reminiscences of Socrates*.

---

[7] There are, of course, other ways to classify ancient biographies, whose variety is neatly indicated the survey in Christopher Pelling, "Plutarch's Adaptation of His Source-Material," in *Essays on Plutarch's Lives*, ed. Barbara Scardigli (Oxford: Clarendon, 1995), 125–54.

[8] Oswald Ducrot and Tzvetan Todorov, *Dictionnaire encyclopédique des sciences du langage* (Paris: Éditions du Seuil, 1972), 193–97.

[9] Boris Tomashevsky, "Literary Genres," in *Formalism: History, Comparison, Genre*, ed. L. M. O'Toole and Ann Shukman (Oxford: Holdan Books, 1978), 55; cited in David Bordwell, *Making Meaning: Inference and Rhetoric in the Interpretation of Cinema* (Cambridge, MA: Harvard University Press, 1989), 147.

[10] Although the two types of biography did not achieve the status of formal genres, Konstan and I have argued that they represented recognizable options within the biographical tradition. A modern example is the distinction, within the genre of the detective novel, between the traditional sleuth in the style of Sherlock Holmes or Agatha Christie's Hercule Poirot and Miss Marple, and the hard-nosed version associated with the American writers Dashiell Hammett and Raymond Chandler.

Taken together, they may be regarded as the sources of the civic and subversive traditions. The *Agesilaus* is commonly described as an encomium, and it begins: "I know that it is not easy to write a praise (ἔπαινον γράψαι) worthy of Agesilaus' virtue (ἀρετῆς) and reputation (δόξης), but it must nevertheless be attempted; for it would be not be right if a man failed to obtain even inadequate praises just because he was consummately good (διὰ τοῦτο οὐδὲ μειόνων τυγχάνοι ἐπαίνων)" (*Ages.* 1.1). Xenophon proceeds to mention Agesilaus' outstanding ancestry, and the splendor of the city over which he ruled. He goes on to describe in detail his achievements during his reign, "since on the basis of his deeds (ἔργων), I believe that his character too will be most manifest (τοὺς τρόπους αὐτοῦ κάλλιστα νομίζω καταδήλους ἔσεσθαι)" (*Ages.* 1.6). With respect to his military abilities, Xenophon affirms: "How might one better demonstrate what kind of general he was than by describing just what he did (πῶς ἄν τις σαφέστερον ἐπιδείξειεν)?" (*Ages.* 1.9). During his incursions into the Persian empire, Agesilaus is shrewd enough to realize that he cannot sustain his army on a country that is laid waste, and so he furthers his aims not by force alone but also by gentleness (πραότης; 1.20), winning the favor of the local population and even making provision for children who are orphaned; "he frequently ordered his soldiers not to punish the conquered as criminals but to protect them as human beings (ἀνθρώπους)" (*Ages.* 1.21).

After recounting further triumphs (and glossing over some of his thornier entanglements), Xenophon turns from Agesilaus' deeds, which need no further proof, to "making manifest the virtue in his soul (τὴν ἐν τῇ ψυχῇ αὐτοῦ ἀρετὴν πειράσομαι δηλοῦν), by which he achieved all these things" (*Ages.* 3.1). He duly illustrates Agesilaus' piety; his justice in money matters; his extraordinary restraint with respect to the pleasures of food and drink, to heat and cold, and to sex; his courage and wisdom; his love for his city; his courtesy and good cheer; and his modest style of life. Xenophon concludes by insisting: "Let no one imagine that, because he is being praised after he has died, this is a funeral oration (τις τοῦτον τὸν λόγον νομισάτω), for it is much more an encomium (ἐγκώμιον)," since, Xenophon says, this is exactly the kind of thing that was said about him while he was still alive (*Ages.* 10.3). Thus, "encomium" here means not a one-sided eulogy but, rather, praise that is deserved. Xenophon is providing his readers with a true account of a man he deeply respects, and his essay may plausibly be described as biographical in intention.

Indeed, the emphasis on character was to mark the entire biographical tradition. Plutarch's aim, for instance, was self-consciously that of providing exemplary models of character in his *Lives*.[11] Like Xenophon, Plutarch supposed that character is revealed principally in actions, and he was conscious of the need to recount historical events as the backdrop to his illustrations of his subjects' *êthos*, whether good or bad. In this respect, history was important, and Plutarch's accounts had to be, if not veridical, then at least plausible. Nevertheless, Plutarch was more concerned to focus on the small detail that might shed light on a character's personality as opposed to narrating great wars and public events for their own sake; again, it was precisely this, according to Plutarch, that distinguished biography from historiography (cf. *Life of Alexander* 1.1). Likewise, in his life of Galba, Plutarch observes: "To relate each individual event exactly is the job of factual (πραγματική) history, but neither is it appropriate for me to pass over all the things worthy of mention that bear on what the Caesars did and suffered (ἔργοις καὶ πάθεσι)" (*Ages.* 2.3). Christopher Pelling raises the question: "Why this interest in character?" The answer, he explains (citing *Pericles* 1–2), is that Plutarch "hopes that his readers might be led by examples of virtue to become better themselves" and, correspondingly, that they may be deterred from wrongdoing by the instances of wickedness, just as he himself has been thanks to his own studies (cf. *Aem.* 1.1).[12] Whether or not Plutarch always followed his own introductory statements of intent in the biographies as a whole, he clearly conceived of his project in these terms.[13]

Cornelius Nepos, in his life of Agesilaus, was influenced directly by Xenophon's account. As he states in the opening sentence: "Agesilaus the Lacedaemonian has been praised (*collaudatus*) by various writers and outstandingly by Xenophon the disciple of Socrates" (*Ages.* 1.1). Nepos

---

[11] Of note, I also situate comparable *bioi* written by Judeans like Josephus and Philo in the civic tradition. Philo's *Life of Moses*, for example, presents Moses as a divinely sanctioned king, prophet, philosopher, lawgiver, and exemplar. Philo even describes his *bioi* on Abraham, Isaac, and Jacob as a study of three figures who are "nominally men but really, as I have said, virtues," *Abr.* 54–55. For more discussion on Philo's biographical treatment of notable figures, see Maren Niehoff, *The Figure of Joseph in Post-Biblical Jewish Literature* (Leiden: Brill, 1992), 54–83.

[12] Pelling, "Plutarch's Adaptation of His Source-Material," 143, apropos *Nicias* 1.

[13] D. A. Russell, "On Reading Plutarch's Lives," in *Essays on Plutarch's Lives*, ed. Barbara Scardigli (Oxford: Clarendon, 1995), notes that "By the time a man is grown up, his pattern of conduct is normally well enough established for predictions to be made about how he will behave in most circumstances.... Plutarch's normal procedure in writing a Life is to state his conclusions on this point fairly early ... and then justify them by the ensuing narrative" (82).

goes on to record Agesilaus' achievements, and, although he does not divide his biography into active accomplishments and moral excellences, as Xenophon had done, he concludes by contrasting Agesilaus' gifts of virtues of the mind (*animi virtutibus*) with its parsimony in regard to his physical attributes (namely, he was short and had a limp), though these in no way impeded his success (*Ages.* 8.1). There is, then, little to distinguish the genre in which Nepos was writing from that of Xenophon.[14] Plutarch, too, exhibits Agesilaus' moral qualities through his military and political achievements. As the second year of his war in Persia rolled round, Plutarch tells us that word of his abilities reached the Persian king, and "a wonderful opinion of his temperance, frugality, and moderation prevailed" (*Vit. Ages.* 14.1); Plutarch also commends his sense of justice and civic duty (πειθαρχία) in putting the interests of his city above his personal ambition (*Vit. Ages.* 15.4–5).

However, for all his concentration on character, and the effort to mark biography off from history precisely by this emphasis, Plutarch, like Nepos before him, found it handiest or most effective to present the events and deeds by which the characters of his subjects are revealed in roughly chronological order – and to this extent his lives resemble historical narratives. Suetonius has been accused of having driven the wedge between history and biography still further; thus, Andrew Wallace-Hadrill affirms: "Rather than let biography become history, he would write non-history."[15] To this end, he divided his narrative into subsections (*species*), among which were included segments on the virtues and vices of the several emperors, without respect to chronological order.[16] But if Suetonius to this extent transformed the genre of biography, which typically traced the life and career of a subject from childhood through maturity, he was in another sense returning to the model of Xenophon's

---

[14] Jeffrey Beneker, "Nepos' Biographical Method in the *Lives of Foreign Generals*," *Classical Journal* 105, no. 2 (December 2009/January 2010), remarks of Nepos' account of Agesilaus' physical deformities: "Nepos has already advertised in the Preface that he intends to elucidate the virtues of his subjects, and our judgment of Agesilaus ought therefore to be made on that basis" (113); in general, Nepos, while recognizing the importance of objective achievements, "warns that in coming to terms with a man's life, they are not to be given priority over virtue" (115). By distinguishing biography from history in this way, Nepos "anticipates Plutarch" (120).

[15] Wallace-Hadrill, *Suetonius*, 9.

[16] See M. J. Edwards, "Birth, Death, and Divinity in Porphyry's *Life of Plotinus*," in *Greek Biography and Panegyric in Late Antiquity*, ed. Thomas Hägg and Philip Rousseau (Berkeley: University of California Press, 2000), 52–71.

Agesilaus, with its division between the description of the Spartan king's military achievements and his moral qualities. If the chief purpose of such *bioi* is the revelation of character through deeds, then the question of chronological order becomes tactical – a matter of narrative strategy. The fundamental feature that underlies this biographical tradition is the exhibition of character by way of actions, and the actions are selected with this view in mind. These actions may be recounted more or less in temporal sequence, but this is not essential, and other ways of organizing the narrative, for example, around particular virtues, may do as well.

XENOPHON AND THE SUBVERSIVE TRADITION

The second strand in the biographical tradition may have also had its origins in Xenophon's *Memorabilia*: the collection of anecdotes or conversations featuring Socrates and various interlocutors.[17] Like Agesilaus, Socrates is a paragon of virtue, but even though some of his virtues are analogous to some of Agesilaus' – for example, moderation and wisdom – the context in which they are manifested, and the complex character that they exhibit, suggest a different kind of portrait. Whereas Agesilaus' personality was revealed in action, Socrates' is manifested solely through words. His excellences reside less in *erga* than in *logoi*, though there is testimony in Plato and elsewhere to his courage in battle and his physical hardiness (e.g., Pl. *Symp.* 219E–221C).[18]

However, a record of conversations, in contrast to heroic deeds in battle or successes in politics, does not so readily organize itself along chronological lines. One can, of course, proceed from signs of precocious brilliance in childhood to a representation of the subject's more mature wisdom, and the context for discussions may evolve in accord with the stages of a person's life; thus, nothing excludes the possibility of a more

---

[17] While a collection of dialogues and, therefore, not a biography in the traditional sense, the *Memorabilia* nonetheless embodies the same subversive literary type under consideration, and, indeed, these subversive kinds usually differ from the straightforward narrative characteristic of the civic variety (e.g., the *Life of Aesop*, the *Life of Homer*, the *Alexander Romance*, and so on).

[18] On the representation of Socrates in Xenophon's *Memorabilia*, Thomas Hägg observes: "it is important to note that much of the characterization of Socrates the individual is achieved through the *way* he speaks, his method of inquiry, his use of parables and examples from daily life, his irony and wit." Thomas Hägg, *The Art of Biography in Antiquity* (Cambridge: Cambridge University Press, 2012), 27. These are just the qualities that cast Socrates as the antithesis to the portrait Xenophon draws of Agesilaus.

strictly biographical frame for such a narrative (some ancient examples are considered below). Nevertheless, there is a certain "openness" inherent in such texts, in which any given episode of clever repartee may be added or omitted, or its position in the sequence altered, without noticeable effect on the coherence of the whole. This variability is characteristic of a certain tradition of ancient literature that Konstan and Christine Thomas have identified elsewhere as "open texts."[19] Once again, the form may be a narrative strategy in the service of a biographical aim, a way of relating certain qualities of the subject that lend themselves particularly, but not exclusively, to this style.

But the difference between the two biographical traditions is not solely a matter of emphasizing the subject's facility with words versus his capacity for action. For the active hero manifests his virtue in the public sphere, the world of war and statecraft; whether he wins or loses, the measure of his character is his conformity with the dominant ideals of society and culture. He is a central player, part of the system: he is a model for those who would govern. The Socratic type, on the contrary, is at the margins of society, puckish and nonconformist. In relation to the powers that be, he is the underdog despite his sharp wits; indeed, it is precisely because he is politically weak that he must rely on clever ripostes and arguments to defend himself. In so doing, he tends to upset inherited beliefs and thereby threatens the establishment ideology. Thanks to the critical edge of his commentary, he is seen as subversive, not because he may wrest political control from his adversaries but because he seems to undermine the values on which society depends.

Xenophon introduces the *Memorabilia* as a defense of Socrates designed to prove that the charges on which he was condemned to death were false, and that far from being a menace to society who challenged conventional piety and corrupted the young, Socrates was "never guilty in civic matters of a war that turned out badly or of civil faction or of treason, nor in private affairs did he ever deprive any person of good things or envelop anyone in evils" (*Mem.* 1.2.63). Thus, Xenophon sets out to demonstrate that "he benefitted those who associated with him both in deed, by showing the kind of person he was, and in conversation"

---

[19] See David Konstan, "The Alexander Romance: The Cunning of the Open Text," *Lexis* 16 (1998): 123–38; Hägg, *The Art of Biography in Antiquity*, 99–101; Christine M. Thomas, "Stories without Texts and without Authors: The Problem of Fluidity in Ancient Novelistic Texts and Early Christian Literature," in *Ancient Fiction and Early Christian Narrative*, ed. Ronald F. Hock, J. Bradley Chance, and Judith Perkins (Atlanta: Scholars Press, 1998), 273–91.

(*Mem.* 3.1.1). To be sure, Xenophon does what he can to present Socrates as an upstanding citizen, defending proper behavior in accord with social conventions; nevertheless, the corrosive nature of Socrates' critique of conventional attitudes constantly emerges. For example, at the end of the first book, Socrates argues that no one who is not competent to rule should seek office in the state. Basing his claim on the familiar appeal to the arts, such as flute-playing or piloting a ship, Socrates affirms that the greatest fraud is "the person who deceives others by persuading them that he is competent to rule the city, though he is worthless" (*Mem.* 1.7.5). The clear implication is that many current leaders are both unskilled in the craft of politics and disguise the fact. Therefore, it is natural that Socrates acquired enemies in high places. But hovering at the edges of his critique is the idea that the virtues, as popularly conceived, are faulty and that a revolution in values is needed. It is this proposed change in values that lends his views an air of unorthodoxy, and it is confirmed by his eccentric outward behavior – such as going shoeless, neglecting his household, and buttonholing people in the street with abstract inquiries.

If Xenophon attempted to soften the outlines of this countercultural image of Socrates, the Cynics took a much more aggressive tack. Through them, a type of life story entered the literature that was to have great influence on later biographies.[20] The two traditions, civic and subversive, took on further definition over time, in part by interacting with each other; indeed, the same figure could be represented in either mode, as we will see below. Whether collections of conversations like Xenophon's *Memorabilia* and dialogues like those of Plato took the form of a life or biography is uncertain, and various influences may have helped to shape them. Early on, a work such as Ion of Chios' "Visits" (*Epidemiai*), which apparently included a narrative by Sophocles on his own dramatic development, could have contributed to the stream and so too Socrates' own autobiographical sketch recorded in Plato's *Phaedo*. It is tempting to suppose that the emergence of lives in the style of Xenophon's *Agesilaus*

---

[20] In a nonbiographical context, one can see the posture of the subversive figure in Epictetus' *Discourses*, e.g., at 1.18–19, where a person is imagined as protesting Epictetus' doctrine that we accept all that is not under our control: "So am I only to have my throat cut?" To this Epictetus replies: "Do you want all people to have their throats cut?" The equivocation here is on the word *monon*, but the witticism recalls Socrates' retort, as reported in Xen. *Ap.* 28; when Apollodorus affirms that it is terrible to behold Socrates being executed unjustly, Socrates replies: "would you rather see me be executed justly?" These are the verbal tactics of the jester, which may seem frivolous to a modern reader but were part and parcel of the diatribe tradition in antiquity.

catalyzed competing efforts in the rival genre. A major influence, however, came from abroad, in the form of a Greek version of the Ahikar
romance.[21] The Greek form appears fully developed in the anonymous
Life of Aesop, in which the protagonist, who for much of the story is a
slave of the philosopher Xanthus, consistently flusters his master by
displays of his superior wisdom.[22] I will return to a discussion of Aesop
in a moment. First, the dual tracks of biography I have been discussing are
perhaps best illustrated by contrasting two works that purport to describe
the life of the same individual: Plutarch's *Life of Alexander* and the so-
called *Alexander Romance*.[23]

THE TWO FACES OF ALEXANDER THE GREAT

Plutarch's Alexander has, as one might have expected, the iconic virtues
associated with great men of action: courage and strategic brilliance (e.g.,
Vit. Alex. 6.1–5, 19.1–5, 20.1–8, 31.6–33.10) but also temperateness in
his way of life, mercy toward enemies (22.4–5, 23.1–6), and regal generosity (12.1–3, 30.1–3), though he is not without certain flaws in his
character, especially in his overly passionate disposition (4.3–4), with a
weakness for drink (4.3, 23.1, 38.1, 50.1–51.10, 67.4, 75.2–4), a suscep-
tibility to flattery (23.4), and, in his later years, a tendency toward
superstition (75.1–2). Chronicling Alexander's life from his boyhood to

[21] See William Hansen, *Anthology of Greek Popular Literature* (Bloomington: University of
Indiana Press, 1998), 106–10; Grammatiki A. Karla, *Vita Aesopi: Überlieferung, Sprach
und Edition einer frühbyzantinischen Fassung des Äsopromans* (Wiesbaden: Reichert,
2001), introduction; Ioannis Konstantakos, *Akicharos: He Diegese tou Ahikar sten
archaia Hellada*, 3 vols. (Athens: Stigme, 2008–13), on the Persian narrative; vol. 3
examines in particular its influence on the *Life of Aesop*.

[22] On Socrates in relation to the *Life of Aesop*, see M. Schauer and S. Merkle, "Aesop und
Sokrates," in *Der Äsop-Roman* (Tübingen: Gunter Narr Verlag, 1992), 90–96. Also see
Grammatiki A. Karla, *Fiction on the Fringe: Novelistic Writing in the Post-Classical Age*
(Leiden: Brill, 2009), 13–32, for discussion of the *Life* as a "fictional biography," as well
as Corinne Jouanno, "Novelistic Lives and Historical Biographies: The *Life of Aesop* and
the *Alexander Romance* as Fringe Novels," in *Fiction on the Fringe* (33–48), who
discusses similarities between *Life* and the *Alexander Romance*.

[23] Philosophers were particularly amenable to a double treatment, whereby, on the one
hand, they might stand out for their exemplary character, while, on the other, they could
be seen, like Socrates, as preaching against the grain of the dominant values. For a
detailed survey of the *topoi* that characterize the lives in Diogenes Laertius, including a
certain amount of charlatanism and wonder-working, see Sergi Grau Guijarro, *La imatge
del filòsof i de l'activitat filosòfica a la Grècia antiga: anàlisi dels tòpics biogràfics presents
a les Vides i doctrines del filòsofs més il·lustres de Diògenes Laerci* (Barcelona: Universitat
de Barcelona, 2009), esp. 251–428.

his death, Plutarch strings together a variety of scenes, some from daily life, others drawn from the battlefield, aimed at demonstrating Alexander's character traits. Thus, the young Alexander observes an exchange between his father, Philip, and Philonicus the Thessalian over the purchase of the "savage" and untamable horse Bucephalus (6.1). Bucephalus will not allow any of Philip's attendants to mount him. A frustrated Philip dismisses the animal, but Alexander intercedes and asserts that someone possessing the appropriate skill and courage can control the horse, wagering that he is up to the task or he will forfeit the horse's price to his father. Philip watches in amazement as Alexander, who realizes that Bucephalus is fearful of his own shadow, turns the horse toward the sun and masters him. The scene ends with Alexander dismounting the horse and his tearful father extolling his talents, exclaiming that he should seek another kingdom more worthy of his talents (6.5), foreshadowing Alexander's future greatness.

Alexander's perceptiveness and self-control are qualities that he exemplifies later in life as well. A noteworthy illustration of his aplomb in war follows the battle of Issus. When he learns that the mother, wife, and daughters of his enemy, Darius, are among his prisoners, Alexander makes sure they know that Darius has not been slain and arranges for them to live unmolested, with allowances befitting their former status; he also allows the women to bury their war dead according to custom. Here we see Alexander's ability to control his passions, as well as his clemency and a certain degree of compassion; as Plutarch notes, Alexander was "more affected by their affliction" than by his victories (21.1). Such leniency, however, would not be granted to all of Alexander's enemies. While in Persis, for example, he orders that the citizens be butchered (37.2) and, after the ensuing pillage, attacks an overturned statue of Xerxes as if it were alive (37.3). In another episode, he is incited by the nationalistic posturing of the Greek Thaïs to burn down Xerxes' palace – with a garland on his head and a torch in his hand, he leads the mob (38.3–4), though he subsequently has second thoughts and gives orders for the fire be extinguished.

Plutarch makes it clear, too, that Alexander's fondness for drink exacerbated his tendencies toward anger and impulsive action. Perhaps the most regrettable incident involved his officer and friend, Cleitus. At a drinking party, a quarrel between the two men escalates until Alexander, losing his temper, pelts Cleitus with an apple and has to be physically restrained by others from attacking him with his sword. He finally spears Cleitus and, feeling immediate remorse, has to be restrained once more, this time from slashing his own throat (51.1–6). Alexander spends the rest of the night and the following day weeping and lamenting his actions (52.1–3), and he recovers from his despair only with the help of Anaxarchus, a tough-talking philosopher (52.3–7).

Although Plutarch's Alexander displays some wit here and there (e.g., 14.3, 64.1–10), the emphasis is not on his ability to engage in clever exchanges so much as to exemplify his sagacity as a leader.[24] The *Alexander Romance*, by contrast, presents itself not as a display of its hero's virtues and vices but rather as an exhibition of Alexander's canniness, his ability to turn his adversaries' pretensions against them with a clever word or observation.[25] For example, according to the *Romance*, Alexander was the son not of Philip of Macedon but rather of the former king of Egypt, Nectanebo. Nectanebo is described as a magician who fled to Pella in Macedon when he perceived that the gods supported the foreign armies marching on his country (1.3). In Macedon, he seduces Olympias, the wife of Philip. When Alexander comes of age he decides to participate in the Olympic games, and Philip takes this opportunity to divorce Olympias and marry Cleopatra. Alexander appears at the wedding banquet and gives his father his victor's wreath with the words, "when in turn I give my mother, Olympias, to another king, I shall invite you to Olympias' wedding" (1.20). Lysias, the brother of Philip's new bride Cleopatra, in turn declares that Philip will now "have legitimate children (ἐπὶ τῇ νεότητι τῆς νῦν σοι γαμουμένης), not unlawfully conceived (ἧς παιδοποιήσεις γνησίους), looking just like you (ὁμοίους τῷ σῷ χαράγματι)" (1.21). Alexander throws a cup at Lysias and kills him, whereupon Philip draws his sword, but, as he rises, he trips over the foot of the couch. Alexander mocks this man so eager to conquer all of Asia and Europe, yet unable to take a single step forward, then seizes his father's sword and wreaks havoc among the guests. Some days later, Alexander manages to reconcile his father and mother, encouraging them to embrace (1.22).

---

[24] Hägg, *The Art of Biography in Antiquity*, treats Plutarch's *Lives* under the heading of "ethical biography," and he notes that in the *Lives*, as elsewhere in Plutarch, "moral value and usefulness take precedence over aesthetics" (277). We should be clear that, although figures like Coriolanus are subversive in the sense of undermining the state (something similar can be said of Catiline), his biography falls strictly within the civic type: he has vices that are to be avoided (an *exemplum negativum*); he is not a model of the weak turning the tables on the strong by virtue of their wits.

[25] As Hägg, in *The Art of Biography in Antiquity*, remarks, "Alexander is no conventional war hero, but a smart, witty, impulsive, rather contradictory figure whose success is more due to cunning and persistence than to courage or piety" (131).

The Macedonians are impressed by Alexander's wiliness, and Philip is sufficiently appeased to send his son with a large army to subdue the rebellious city of Methone, which he accomplishes through his keen power (δύναμιν) of persuasion (1.23). Once again, Alexander achieves his purpose with words rather than actions.

When Alexander, in his campaign against Persia, reaches the city of Tyre, he is initially repulsed by the Tyrians. A dream warns him not to present himself at Tyre, so he sends a letter demanding that the city surrender (1.35). The Tyrians flog the messengers in order to determine which of them is Alexander, and then slay them. A second dream, involving a contrived pun on satyr (*saturos*), cheese (*turos*), and the name of the city, Tyre, presages Alexander's victory, and he proceeds to take the town without further ado or explanation. The *Romance* evinces little interest in scenes of war and courage; rather, it consistently draws attention to the role of insight and interpretation, the ability to decipher or manipulate words – a technique more characteristic of the disempowered upstart than of a mighty general on the offensive.

Early in the war, Darius sends Alexander a strap, a ball, and a chest full of gold. The accompanying letter explains that the strap is for Alexander's chastisement, and the ball is a childish toy for him to play with. Alexander reads the letter aloud to his troops, then puts their minds at ease by comparing Darius to a small dog that is, essentially, all bark and no bite (1.37). With this, he orders Darius' messengers to be crucified, which provides the occasion for further repartee: Alexander explains that since Darius had described him as a bandit, "I am killing you as though you had come not to a king (βασιλεῖ), but to a scoundrel (ἀρχιληστῇ)." The messengers win reprieve by affirming that he is truly a great king. Alexander then writes back to Darius and proposes a counterinterpretation of his gifts: with the strap, he will beat the barbarians, while the ball signifies the world that Alexander will conquer (1.38). Once more, the emphasis is on verbal and intellectual, not military, skill.

When Alexander is encamped outside Persis, the seat of Darius' empire, he has a dream that instructs him not to send a messenger but rather to go himself to Darius, dressed as the god Ammon (2.13). In this disguise, Alexander is invited in for dinner by Darius, and at the table he stuffs all the cups that come his way in his pocket. When Darius asks what on earth he thinks he is doing, Alexander replies that he routinely makes a gift of cups at his own dinners, a yarn that in itself intrigues the banqueters (2.15). This episode is not intended to make Alexander seem greedy but simply to illustrate his clever way with language, as the author or redactor cannot refrain from noting.

Although the *Alexander Romance* follows a more or less chronological arrangement, what stands out is the emphasis not on its hero's conquests as such but on his uncanny ingenuity and mastery of language. The personality of the protagonist is constituted by his wit rather than by ethical qualities, which are the core of the virtue-based biographical tradition.[26] As mentioned above, a similar example is found in the extant *Lives of Aesop*, with Aesop in many respects representing the paragon of the witty and subversive biographical subject. Interestingly, however, some recent studies have attempted to align the more countercultural elements of Aesop with oral traditions from Greek "popular culture."[27] This search for a "nonelite strata" of "Aesop tradition" mirrors similar approaches to the gospels that have sought early Christian oral traditions about Jesus; this approach to Aesop, however, has been met with resistance among classicists for reasons that are similar to those I have put forward in this monograph.[28] As such, a review of Aesop's contribution to the subversive paradigm, as well as the critique that follows attempts to seek out strains of popular Archaic culture behind it, is a useful corollary to literature about Jesus.

AESOP AND ORAL TRADITION

The *Life of Aesop* stands as an early example of subversive biography from the Greek tradition, along with Xenophon's *Agesilaus*.[29] Organized loosely around the stages of his life, Aesop's story begins in Phrygia, with

---

[26] On the genre of the *Alexander Romance*, see also Richard Stoneman, *The Greek Alexander Romance* (London: Penguin, 1991), 17–23, who compares it, at least in its later redactions, with the apocryphal Acts of the Apostles, the *Life of Aesop*, and the *Vita Apollonii* (Life of Apollonius of Tyana).

[27] See, for example, the monograph by Leslie Kurke, *Aesopic Conversations: Popular Traditions, Cultural Dialogue, and the Invention of Greek Prose* (Princeton: Princeton University Press, 2011).

[28] Hayden Pelliccia, "Where Does His Wit Come From?" Review of Aesopic *Conversations: Popular Tradition, Cultural Dialogue, and the Invention of Greek Prose*, by Leslie Kurke, *New York Review of Books* (November 8, 2012), 36–40, cit. 37.

[29] These references to the text are based primarily on the "*Vita* G" (Grottaferrata) manuscript, with some additions from "*Vita* W" (Westermann). See John Esten Keller and Louis Clark Keating's version *Aesop's Fables: With a Life of Aesop* (Lexington: University Press of Kentucky, 1993).

him working as a field hand, suffering from a speech impediment, yet nonetheless clever and astute in his interactions.[30] As a thank-you for his generosity to a priest of Isis who had lost his way on the road, Aesop is granted the ability to speak all languages – including those of the animals – and to become a writer of many *logoi*.[31] He is also able to engage people openly with his cutting wit. He recognizes that his newfound gifts are due to his piety and charity, and, once endowed with them, he immediately begins to voice his opinions and verbally spar with those around him, beginning with admonishing an overseer who beats a slave without cause.[32]

Aesop clearly embodies some of the traditional concerns with virtue found in other lives; however, Aesop himself does not always act ethically – one case in point is when he beds his owner's wife ten times in a row in exchange for a new shirt.[33] In fact, the *Life* is laced with numerous examples of Aesop and the people he encounters behaving badly, with sexually explicit exploits and extremely violent imagery – from the severe and public beatings of slaves to the amorous attentions Aesop receives from various women to incest to obtaining pig's feet from live pigs to Aesop, having offended the locals, being forced to throw himself off a cliff at Delphi. Aesop acts as a foil at times for ethical behavior, but he is also a source of what one might term "comic relief." Hayden Pelliccia explains:

[S]tories such as these would not have been welcomed onto the classical reading lists of Victorian-era Eton; that does not mean, however, that they reflect non-elite Greco-Roman taste. Vases depicting the maniacally erect priapism of satyrs, for example, were unfailingly popular with the Greek upper classes. As for cruelty, slave-beating was a beloved staple of the comic stage. Even nonslaves could be turned to this purpose: for example, the unnamed protagonist of Aristophanes' *Women at the Thesmophoria*, identified only as "Euripides' kinsman," is literally crucified during the play's last two hundred lines, and the shrieks he emits as he is stapled to the cross seem to have brought the audience no end of delight.[34]

By the time his lives are being written, Aesop was already well known, earning mention in Herodotus and Aristophanes.[35] Our first record of his *logoi* dates to around the late fourth century BCE, and it is not clear how

---

[30] *Aesop's Fables*, 10.   [31] *Aesop's Fables*, 11.   [32] *Aesop's Fables*, 12–13.
[33] From *Life* chapter 75, cited from Pelliccia, "Where Does His Wit Come From?," 36.
[34] Pelliccia, "Where Does His Wit Come From?," 37.
[35] Ar. *Vesp.* 1448; Hdt. 2.134, which describes Aesop as a *logopoios*. Also see Kurke, *Aesopic Conversations*, 21, 371.

his sayings and details of his life were passed on in the decades prior.[36] Whether he ever existed is also something lost to us. But, regardless of our ability to retrieve the "historical Aesop," what is clear is that the figure adopted a dual aspect in literary imagination: he was a representative of ethical actions in some measure through his observations, teachings, and commentary yet, at the same time, he emerged as a subversive symbol who transgressed the norms of the dominant culture, to comedic effect.[37]

Aesop eventually finds himself a house slave again, this time of a philosopher named Xanthus, who, humorously, proves no match for Aesop's shrewd mind. Aesop's wit earns him his freedom and, like Phaedo, Menippus, and Epictetus, he rises from the position of slave to honored statesman hobnobbing with philosophers and the court of the Lydian King Croesus, who sends him on a number of diplomatic missions, including to Delphi. His death there is occasioned by the city's collective fear that Aesop, esteemed and ever-observant, would reveal to the outside world how morally corrupt their city had become. He is framed for theft, accused of impiety, and sentenced to death as a common criminal dragged through the streets from the safe house of the Temple to Apollo.[38] In the wake of his forced suicide, Aesop received many posthumous honors – Phaedrus, for instance, tells us that Lysippos crafted a statue of Aesop, standing in front of the Seven Sages in Athens.[39] And, of course, there is the long tradition of his treatment in literature.

---

[36] See, for instance, Pelliccia, "Where Does His Wit Come From?,": "The form of these citations does nothing to tell us if Aesop lore was circulating as written texts or only orally. The first clear evidence we have for a written collection of 'Aesopian' fables dates to the end of the fourth century BCE, and from that point on collecting and rewriting them becomes a busy side industry of classical culture" (36). Also see Kurke, *Aesopic Conversations*, esp. 1–49.

[37] Priapus is a useful *comparandum* for the dual model I am describing. Ralph M. Rosen and Catherine C. Keane, for instance, describe Priapus as "a jumble of conservative and subversive ideologies. On the one hand, Priapus celebrates the enforcement of social norms. He defends private property, penetrates others, and, using brash circular logic, brands his victims as sexual deviants. He therefore seems to represent the way the traditional power structure virtually 'stains' marginal figures … for easy identification. On the other hand, Priapus seems to celebrate transgression against decorum when he asserts that his realm sanctions, even demands, obscene speech and action. These two qualities are combined, to comic effect, in the sexualized Roman satirist figure." Ralph M. Rosen and Catherine C. Keane, "Greco-Roman Satirical Poetry," in *A Companion to Greek and Roman Sexualities*, ed. Thomas K. Hubbard (Malden: Wiley-Blackwell, 2014), 381–97, cit. 387.

[38] *Aesop's Fables*, 47–51.

[39] *Phdr.* 2.9.1–4; François Lissarrague, "Aesop, between Man and Beast: Ancient Portraits and Illustrations," in *Not the Classical Ideal: Athens and the Construction of the Other in*

As is often noted, Aesop's unjust death and posthumous admiration are biographical elements shared with the likes of Socrates and Jesus.[40] Bracketing Jesus for a moment, there is another characteristic shared by Socrates and Aesop that further demonstrates their ability to simultaneously engage certain ethical principles representative of the dominant culture, but in a distinctively subversive key: their physical appearance. Both are described as particularly unappealing. Socrates is likened to a satyr or a flatfish, with a "bald head, bulging, crab- or frog-like eyes, a protruding forehead, fleshy lips," and, like Aesop, a potbelly and large mouth.[41] Aesop, even more harshly, is described as deformed: "misshapen of head, snub-nosed, swarthy, dwarfish, bandy-legged, short-armed, squint-eyed, liver-lipped – a portentous monstrosity."[42] On its face, this shared, sorry depiction is unusual for a heroic subject, as heroes are usually depicted as handsome and possessing impressive physiques. Pseudo-Aristotle, for instance, states that "a well-proportioned body indicates an honest, valiant, and intelligent individual, while a badly-proportioned one reveals deceitfulness."[43] A survey of Greek and Latin literature indeed bears this out – unattractive figures like Homer's Thersites act in a base manner, while traditional heroes, like the virtuous men (and women) populating the ancient novel, are described as beautiful (*Il.* 2, 216–19).

The exception appears to be in the case of philosophers, like the Cynics, or men described as short in stature; in Aesop's *Life*, for example, one character remarks in reference to Aesop: "little fellows who are short on looks are long on brains (ταῦτα τὰ ἀνθρωπάρια τὰ λειπόμενα τῇ μορφῇ φρένας ἔχει)."[44] Likewise, in the *Alexander Romance*, Alexander stuns the Persians with his diminutive stature (1.18.9) and is challenged to a duel by a king, Poros, who judges him easy to beat on account of his size (2.15.1).

Greek Art, ed. Beth Cohen (Leiden: Brill, 2000), 132–49, cit. 137. Some traditions claim that the Delphians also dedicated a temple to Aesop and worshipped him as a hero. See Kurke, *Aesopic Conversations*, 5; P. Oxy. 1800.

[40] For a discussion and bibliography, see Emily R. Wilson, "Pain and Revelation: The Death of Socrates and the Death of Jesus," in *The Death of Socrates* (Cambridge, MA: Harvard University Press, 2007), 141–69.

[41] Iōannēs-Theophanēs A. Papadēmētriou, *Aesop as an Archetypal Hero* (Athens: Hellenic Society for Humanistic Studies, 1997), 35.

[42] Daly, *Aesop without Morals*; cited from Pelliccia, "Where Does His Wit Come From?," 36.

[43] Here I am citing Papadēmētriou, who provides the Greek text. See Papadēmētriou, *Aesop as an Archetypal Hero*, 16, n. 17.

[44] Cited from Papadēmētriou, *Aesop as an Archetypal Hero*, 24.

And, again, Xenophon tells us that Agesilaus was similarly proportioned. Thus, such unlikely "heroes" and leaders come to be recognized in this literature as possessing certain qualities on the basis of their appearance: "little guys" make for powerful leaders and sharp thinkers, while "ugly" characters are anticipated either to be unethical or, in some cases, to possess particularly impressive knowledge or wit. In other words, their physical form communicates something to the audience about their subversive qualities from the start.[45]

What is significant about this observation is not necessarily that this trope exists but that, along with the subversive biographical type, the physically unappealing hero develops in the literary tradition from Homer onward. It further demonstrates, much like Athenaeus' account of the *deipnosophistae* or in motifs like the empty tomb, that writers were trained with certain texts, engaged with interconnected networks of literacy and played off of one another's ideas. This is a particularly important point in the case of Aesop, given some recent studies that have attempted to attribute aspects of Aesop's *Life* – such as his appearance and more outrageous actions – to earlier, oral traditions about the figure. Scholarship of this type claims that particular characteristics of the subversive subject should be traced back to (illiterate) Greek "popular culture" and not attributed to the literary imagination of the elite writer.

Leslie Kurke's recent *Aesopic Conversations: Popular Traditions, Cultural Dialogue, and the Invention of Greek Prose*, for instance, argues that a first-century CE recension of the *Life of Aesop*, known as "*Vita G*" (after the monastery, Grottagerrata, where it was once known to be housed), preserves a "wisdom tradition" about Aesop that dates to around the sixth century BCE.[46] By "wisdom tradition," Kurke means "a native Greek conceptualization of Hesiod, Theognis, Pythagoras, and the Seven Sages (among others) as a coherent tradition, designated as *Sophia* ... [embracing] poetic skill, practical political wisdom, and religious expertise."[47] Elsewhere in her monograph, Kurke explains that she is chiefly concerned with what she terms "ancient Greek popular culture" – the folk traditions and interests of non-elites that heretofore have

---

[45] At another point in the *Life*, Aesop refers to himself as someone speaking "sensible" (*phrenêrês*) things, "in a cheap little body." The same term is also found repeatedly in the *Alexander Romance*. See Pelliccia, "Where Does His Wit Come From?," 37.

[46] The manuscript itself is from the tenth or eleventh century. The content was dated to the first century on the basis of philological evidence by Ben Edwin Perry in the early twentieth century. See Kurke, *Aesopic Conversations*, 4.

[47] Kurke, *Aesopic Conversations*, 95.

been able to be accessed only "through the finds of archaeology, nonliterary texts like papyrus documents, lead curse tablets, and funerary inscriptions."[48] Citing Peter Burke's work on early modern Europe, she also refers to this aspect of society as the "little tradition" that was necessarily excluded from elite culture (the "great tradition").[49]

In Kurke's estimation, there is a parallel track of non-elite popular thinking that developed alongside the elite ideologies exemplified by the remnants of high ancient literary culture. This distinct, non-elite track she believes marks the beginnings of later Greek prose writing. She further determines that elite culture was invested in erasing the memories of this more simplistic, rustic discourse – like the kind preserved in *Vita* G. This is evident, she claims, in the figure of Aesop himself. She states that "just as Aesop himself is poor, lowly, and marginal," he represents the comparatively lowly consumer of this literature.[50] Given that his *Life* was written in "colloquial" *koinē* and "highly permeable" (i.e., configured in a manner similar to what I have referred to as the "open text"), she suggests it is fundamentally unlike the canon of classics (e.g., Homer, Vergil) that were "treated with the greatest care and respect and transmitted in pristine form" by the ancients. Therefore, she suggests that a writing like *Vita* G is best understood to contain a record of certain "long-lived popular oral traditions."[51] She illustrates this difference with another comparison to Burke: "Thus we might imagine stories about Aesop continuing to circulate orally as 'old wives' tales' or popular tales told at festivals, while the written text in turn might even be read aloud in other public contexts where different social strata mixed (like Burke's 'tavern' or 'marketplace')." She also makes a comparison with the peasant folktales of prerevolutionary France, which she imagines were passed onto the literate elite from their "servants and wet nurses."[52] As such, she sees in *Aesop* the remnants of the folktales of the "little tradition" of Greek culture, later coopted and transmitted by those with the education and means to produce writings.

Kurke's folktale analogy is necessary precisely because she concedes, as I argue in Chapter 3, that the nature of producing literature in antiquity required an elite cultural producer and certain social conditions. To use

---

[48] Kurke, *Aesopic Conversations*, 3. I am not sure what Kurke means by "nonliterary" texts.

[49] Kurke, *Aesopic Conversations*, 7–8.　　[50] Kurke, *Aesopic Conversations*, 2.

[51] Kurke, *Aesopic Conversations*, 6–7.　　[52] Kurke, *Aesopic Conversations*, 9.

her words, "it [is] impossible to postulate an author who is not a member of an elite of wealth and education."[53] Herein lies the difficulty with the oral tradition thesis. As noted previously, Kurke turns to aspects of Aesop, such as his shabby appearance, vulgar speech, and explicit encounters, as evidence of a set of more "low-brow" or "little culture" interests. This is the "wisdom tradition" of Aesop, calibrated to a less learned audience. However, her model for retrieving oral tradition and popular culture is as fraught as it is for scholars of early Christian literature. Take, for example, what Hayden Pelliccia calls Aesop's, "certain literary pretentions" – namely, that after Aesop gains his voice, "he is able, in spite of the rustic isolation of his previous life, to name Euripides and quote his poetry verbatim ... all the more impressive if we consider that Euripides would not begin his career for another century." There are other examples where Kurke attempts to align certain Greek words and phrases myopically with a less-elite Greek culture (e.g., προστάτην as a "slave overseer," instead of as an honorific for Apollo). None of these efforts reveal why such references must come from an oral tradition rather than an author's literary imagination. Moreover, our knowledge of non-elite culture is so fragmentary that, if there is evidence of the lower classes in upper-class writings, it is unlikely we would know how to recognize it. With Aesop's supposedly "little tradition" references grounded in strong "great tradition" literary parallels or precedent, it would seem that the author of Aesop is not so much reliant on some oral stories about the figure; rather, "exuberant if heavy-handed plundering of the literary tradition is more his stock-and-trade."[54] This literary "plundering" would also go a long way in accounting for the somewhat fluid or open structure or organization of the text itself.

As I mentioned above, critiques of Kurke's work are compelling *comparanda* given that a similar approach to the "oral traditions" of the "primitive Christians" has been employed in scholarship on literature about Jesus so often. Kurke claims that one of the difficulties in studying Aesop's *Life* is that it has long been segregated or "in quarantine" from comparison with the traditional canon of classical literature, which is a fate some might argue is shared by the Synoptic gospels.[55] Of course, unlike Aesop, Jesus fails to deliver Euripidean speeches; however, his teachings nonetheless engage numerous ancient genres, including

---

[53] Kurke, *Aesopic Conversations*, 6.
[54] Pelliccia, "Where Does His Wit Come From?," 37.
[55] Kurke, *Aesopic Conversations*, 5.

biography, the novel, history, paradoxography, philosophy, and physics.[56] Accounts of his life also share many of the subversive elements that I have rehearsed thus far in this chapter. As such, more than a sui generis category of literature, first-century literature about Jesus can be situated coherently within the trajectory of the subversive biographical tradition.

THE GOSPELS AS SUBVERSIVE BIOGRAPHY

Odd as it may seem to subsume the *Alexander Romance*, the *Life of Aesop*, and the gospels under the same genre, the narratives of Jesus' deeds and sayings can be seen as pertaining to the same biographical tradition. Like Socrates or Aesop, Jesus is at the margins of society, a Judean peasant powerless in relation to the state. In his encounters with Pharisees or other interlocutors, he wins his victories by means of his wits and his ability to turn the words of his opponents against them – in this, resembling Alexander when he finds himself in the palace of Darius, alone and defenseless. Although we are not given a description of his physical appearance, he is depicted as an underdog from a lower class of society and of few means. He is followed by fisherman and teaches and interacts with other marginalized persons. He is baptized by John, who lives as a Cynic-like recluse in the desert, eating nothing but locusts and honey (e.g., Matt. 3:4). And he comes to an untimely end, accused of impiety, and publicly executed.

Yet scholars have often resisted comparing the gospels with the tradition of ancient biography. Adela Yarbro Collins, for instance, challenges the status of the Gospel of Mark as biography, preferring to read it as a version

---

[56] Erin Roberts, "Anger, Emotion, and Desire in the Gospel of Matthew" (PhD diss., Brown University, 2010); Stanley K. Stowers, "Jesus as Teacher and Stoic Ethics in the Gospel of Matthew," in *Stoicism in Early Christianity*, ed. Tuomus Rasimus, Troels Engberg-Pedersen, and Ismo Dundenberg (Peabody: Hendrickson, 2010). Also see Abraham J. Malherbe, "Hellenistic Moralists and the New Testament," *ANRW* II.26.1, 267–333. If the Gospel writers were indebted to Paul's letters as source material, then a further argument could be made for the presence of philosophical lines of thought (e.g., so-called Middle Platonism). See, for example, Abraham J. Malherbe, "'Gentle as a Nurse': The Lyric Background to I Thessalonians ii," *Novum Testamentum* 12 (1970): 203–17; Abraham J. Malherbe, *Paul and the Thessalonians: The Philosophic Tradition of Pastoral Care* (Mifflintown: Sigler, 1987); Abraham J. Malherbe, *Paul and the Popular Philosophers* (Minneapolis: Fortress Press, 1989); Troels Engberg-Pedersen, *Paul and the Stoics* (Edinburgh: Westminster John Knox, 2000); Troels Engberg-Pedersen, *Cosmology of the Self in the Apostle Paul: The Material Spirit* (Oxford: Oxford University Press, 2010).

of historical narrative. As Collins notes, comparisons between Mark and such works as the *Life of Aesop* or the *Life of Homer* have been drawn on the basis of their literary style as well as their structure and, in particular, their chronological organization.[57] She also cites Vernon Robbins' hypothesis that "the author of Mark conflated Jewish prophetic traditions about teachers, such as Socrates in Greco-Roman culture."[58] Collins objects, however, that "the argument that these similarities mean that Mark and the *Memorabilia* of Xenophon belong to the same genre is not compelling," on the grounds that "similarities in form do not outweigh differences in content." More particularly, Jesus is "introduced as an exorcist" with the ability to cast out demons, something absent in the Socratic tradition; Collins suggests that in this respect "he is more like Empedocles than Socrates."[59] It is by this process of elimination that Collins concludes that the gospel is a species of history-writing, with the closest analogy being Sallust's *De Catilinae coniuratione* (Conspiracy of Catiline).

Although Jesus' message is obviously different from that of Socrates, both run counter to prevailing ideologies and embody a position of relative weakness, at least in temporal terms. Jesus' wonder-working or miracles, like his gift for parables and subtle sayings, are precisely the weapons of choice in such a case. In this tradition, the moral excellence of the biographical subject is assumed, but it is not illustrated by an enumeration of the classical virtues, as in the civic type, which seeks by this means to delineate character. The focus is, rather, on how the protagonist demonstrates his superiority in spite of his humble or precarious position (the *Alexander Romance* contrives to place its subject in the latter situation). In Mark 5, for instance, Jesus demonstrates his supernatural status in rapid succession, first casting the "unclean *pneuma* (τὸ πνεῦμα τὸ ἀκάθαρτον)" Legion (λεγιὼν ὄνομά μοι) out of the Gerasene man and into a herd of pigs (χοίρους; Mark 5:1–20), then inadvertently healing a long-suffering hemorrhaging woman (γυνὴ οὖσα ἐν ῥύσει αἵματος δώδεκα,

---

[57] Collins, *Is Mark's Gospel a Life of Jesus?*, 20, citing David Aune, *The New Testament in Its Literary Environment* (Philadelphia: Westminster, 1987), 57. Richard I. Pervo, "A Nihilist Fabula: Introducing the Life of Aesop," in *Ancient Fiction and Early Christian Narrative*, ed. Ronald F. Hock et al. (Atlanta: Scholars Press, 1998), 81–82, proposes to read Aesop "as a gospel," classifying it as a novel with some possibly historical features and akin to the "popular narratives" concerning Alexander, Apollonius of Tyana, Jesus, the apostles, Daniel, Mordecai, and Tobit.

[58] Collins, *Is Mark's Gospel a Life of Jesus?*, 22, citing Vernon K. Robbins, *Jesus the Teacher: A Socio-Rhetorical Interpretation of Mark* (Minneapolis: Fortress Press, 1992), 53.

[59] Collins, *Is Mark's Gospel a Life of Jesus?*, 22.

Mark 5:21–34), followed by the resurrection of a young girl (ἀνέστη, Mark 5:35–42). From his precocious behavior in the Temple as a young man in Luke ("his mother asked him: 'Child [τέκνον], why have you treated [ἐποίησας] us like this? ...' He said ... 'Did you not know I must be in my Father's house?,'" Luke 2:41–52)[60] to his many clever teachings and ripostes (e.g., "a camel through the eye of a needle," Matt. 19:24), Jesus continually reifies his subversive perspective and humor against those perceived to be more powerful (e.g., the ruling elite, Caesar, other teachers, the rich, Rome). Moreover, what links Xenophon's *Memorabilia* and the gospels as biographical narratives are the way the subjects of both challenge conventional values and the character traits that underpin them. In these respects, the gospels are situated in conversation with the literary tradition of biography, demonstrating that certain details of Jesus' life may have been the product of an author's engagement with an established genre of writing lives, and not necessarily the reflection of an "oral tradition."

Yet the question still stands: To what degree are these *bioi* the creative activity of an author and to what degree are these authors obtaining their information about these figures from elsewhere? Unfortunately, beyond what we can assess in terms of literary borrowings from other pieces of literature, we have no way of knowing with absolute certainty. However, what we do know is that these biographies, whether full and cohesive narratives or more representative of the "open text" tradition, are the products of creative literary activity. This also holds for other forms of literature that purport to represent a particular figure or figures, their lives, or their thought in some manner – for instance, pseudepigrapha, *chreiai*, and so on. It is conceivable that this literature may hold some thread of "oral tradition"; however, as Pelliccia cautions about Aesop, how would we know that we are looking at it?[61] Given what we know about the training involved in producing a piece of writing in antiquity, it stands to reason that our first line of inquiry when approaching an ancient text should be to consider the ways in which it is engaging various literary conventions, precedents, and ongoing conversations – subversive biography among them.

---

[60] The alternative version of Jesus' reply is "Did you not know that I must be involved in my Father's business (οὐκ ᾔδειτε ὅτι ἐν τοῖς τοῦ πατρός μου δεῖ εἶναί)?" (Luke 2:49).

[61] Pelliccia, "Where Does His Wit Come From?," 37.

Conclusion

"Lions mate with lions": Creative License and Future Directions

In 2012, the Gagosian Gallery in New York City hosted an exhibition of the artwork of Pablo Picasso and Françoise Gilot. Curated by the late art historian John Richardson, "Picasso and Françoise Gilot: Paris–Vallauris 1943–1953" featured numerous drawings, paintings, sculpture, and ceramics produced by the pair during their relationship. The collection reacquainted the public with Gilot and her compelling biography, which includes romantic partnerships with Picasso and the vaccine pioneer Jonas Salk. Queried time and again on why these notable men sought her companionship, she has often quipped, "lions mate with lions . . . they don't mate with mice" – a clever riposte that gently reminds the inquirer that she is a celebrated artist in her own right.[1] Her response also acknowledges the social circles in which she has traveled for much of the twentieth century. Through Picasso, she forged friendships with Georges Braque and Henri Matisse. Her 1964 memoir *Vivre avec Picasso* (*To Live with Picasso*) narrates the couple's interactions with the likes of Georges Bataille and Charlie Chaplin. Gilot also details what Picasso told her about his past intellectual and artistic dialogues with the poet Guillaume Apollinaire or F. Scott and Zelda Fitzgerald.[2] The dynamic

---

[1] For example, Irene Lacher, "A Place of Her Own: Culture: Françoise Gilot, Picasso's Former Lover and Jonas Salk's Wife, Wants to Be Known Not as the Companion of Great Men, but as Their Equal," *Los Angeles Times* (March 6, 1991); Robert Fulford, "'Lions mate with lions': Introducing Françoise Gilot, the Woman Who Said No to Pablo Picasso," *National Post* (May 10, 2016).

[2] Françoise Gilot and Carlton Lake, *Vivre avec Picasso* (Paris: Calmann-Lévy, 1965), passim.

exchange of ideas and the creative process she describes reveal a network of cultural elites in dialogue across disciplines, educating one another and reflecting that influence in their work.

In a joint interview about the Gagosian exhibit, Richardson and Gilot had an interesting exchange about Picasso's *Winter Landscape, 1950* and Richardson's revelation that the painting was inspired by El Greco:

GILOT: First of all, that painting is extremely important because at ... the first sight, it is kind of desolate. It's winter ... the two trees in front seen without leaves, like skeletons ... there is a palm tree next to a square house and the palm tree, in my mind, stands for Matisse and his house called Le Reve – "the Dream" – which he had in Vence. And then the big tree, which is being tormented to the right is Picasso himself. And then to the left, there is a tree a bit smaller and a bit whitish as if it was anemic, that's for me....

RICHARDSON: What I discovered about this painting, which excited me, was it kept on reminding me of something and suddenly I realized when I was working on the show, of course, the El Greco in the Met.... And so I went up Madison Avenue and looked at it, and clearly Picasso knew it, so I did a bit of research and indeed the great El Greco "Landscape of Toledo" in the Met was in Paris belonging to a dealer from 1900 to 1910 when Picasso was living in Paris and would have seen it. And the color, the composition, the sort of feeling is straight out of El Greco. And we know at the time that he had done another version of El Greco ... a self-portrait of El Greco as a painter. And, so, he must have also had a book. [To Gilot] Do you remember what book he had on El Greco? He must have had a book around at the time.

GILOT: ... Also ... even when he was quite young, in Barcelona before he ever came to Paris, his friends, who were older than himself from Els Quatre Gats, one of them was an art critic and was the first one to buy some El Greco and bring them to Barcelona. So even in Barcelona he had seen some magnificent El Greco. So, he was interested

and knew El Greco much before other people. So, of
course, when he saw it later in France, he must have
been intrigued.[3]

Through observation and a bit of detective work, Richardson was able to
uncover yet one more conversation partner for one of Picasso's paintings.
In addition to engaging directly with Matisse and Gilot, Picasso paid
homage to a past master in El Greco. The comparison opens up an
entirely new perspective on the significance and history of influence for
this particular piece of Picasso's – including, with Gilot's help, recognition
of the artists, composers, poets, musicians, and other early patrons of the
Els Quatre Gats café who contributed much to Picasso in his formative
years. The interactions, exchanges, and processes of creative individuals
illustrated by the collective knowledge of Richardson, Gilot, and Picasso
demonstrate how the kind of literary production described in this book
was possible.

The persons responsible for our cultural artifacts across time do not
differ substantially in terms of social position, education, and their relative
social networks. As audience members, we may appreciate these artifacts
for their aesthetic quality or the symbolic meaning they acquire as representative objects of a received or "invented" tradition. But appreciation
and utility alone do not dictate process or history. Theoretical work must
be done on how we (re)describe the role of the author and their perceived
audience, particularly when it comes to objects we might describe as
possessing an element of "art" or creative license. This is ground that
was tread in some measure by the earlier "death of the author" debate(s).
However, I would like to foreground a slightly different point of emphasis:
how to account for creative license when "doing" history.

Artist creativity or creative license as a category of human activity is
something that sociologists, philosophers, and those who study aesthetics
have largely folded under the umbrella of "culture." Even the most
innovative acts of creativity or imagination are tied, in some measure, to
certain conventions of the medium in which they are expressed. However,
in studying the ancient world, it can be difficult at times to pin down the
influences, cross-references, motivations, or even technologies of certain
artists, writers, and so on. And when scholars attempt to use something
like an ancient text as data for asking or answering certain questions

---

[3] Françoise Gilot and John Richardson, interview by Charlie Rose, Charlie Rose LLC, May
17, 2012.

about the social practices or networks of the past, it is not always clear how to account for materials that might be a product of creativity or imagination. In terms of the ancient Mediterranean, many methodologies rely on the notion that one can read between the lines of a given text to detect usable information about its writer and the social world in which they lived. This is held in tension with an awareness that authors frequently fabricate various facets of their subject matter. The difficulty this poses is, if one cannot refute or corroborate certain information elsewhere, they are left questioning the reliability of the source material. This brings to the fore a broader question: In any creative production, how much can one rely on the creator to truthfully communicate anything about "real life"?

Increasingly, I find that making concrete claims about reality in literature and art is slippery business at best. Take one more minor example from Pablo Picasso's paintings of Françoise Gilot, his 1951 painting *Woman Drawing (Françoise)*. In this painting, Gilot is pictured drawing in a style once again reminiscent of El Greco (see El Greco, *Portrait of Jorge Manuel Theotokopulus*, c. 1600–1605). She is also pictured using an odd, rounded pencil affixed to her desk. Speculating on the deeper significance of this pencil, certain art historians have suggested that it faithfully represents how Gilot worked, tying her pencils to her desk in order to prevent her children from taking them or knocking them from her hand as they played. When presented with this academic proposal, Gilot dismissed it as a total misreading of Picasso's motivations: "That's hot air. Pablo imagined that pencil. It had nothing to do with anything he saw. He had such a fantastic visual memory, and most of the time he drew from what was in his mind.... I never used a pencil like that, so it's pure imagination."[4] Thus, according to Gilot, art historians have missed the mark with this particular feature of Picasso's work. If Gilot is to be trusted, not every element of a creative composition designates meaning beyond the creativity and aesthetic choices of its author.

Building on this latter point, allow me to offer another example from the world of poetry. Below is an excerpt from "Make Believe" by the poet mentioned in Chapter 4, Jaswinder Bolina:

We will eventually be archaeology, but now in America
I tell my young daughter the new headlights are a bluish-white instead
of the murky yellow of my upbringing.

[4] Dodie Kazanjian, "Life after Picasso: Françoise Gilot," *Vogue* (April 27, 2012).

She's busy with her bubble-making, her dig in the flower bed,
her pantomimed banquet, phantom guests
dining on her small handfuls of weeds and grasses
. . .
Brandy in soda water, a xylophone jingle of the ice, I sit in my Adirondack
without my minute, Midwestern wife
who Tuesday returns from her summit in Cleveland.
It's that time when I'm alone in America with my young daughter who startles
herself realizing the woodpile beneath that black oak is itself formerly a tree. . . .[5]

If I knew nothing about Bolina, his life, or his influences, I might understand by virtue of the title of this poem that he is playing with double
entendre and that the entire piece is a product of imagination. The use of
double entendre in itself would be a literary practice that one could
analyze as an element of cultural production and might signal a difference
in how to approach analyzing the text.

When Bolina reads this poem at various events, his audience, without
fail, asks him questions about his daughter and family life. In reality,
Bolina has a son and a wife from New England, but not even they were a
part of his life when this was written. This poem is engaging the language
play of John Ashbery and the appeals to intimacy characteristic of Robert
Hass. These are imagined characters, and the author is in conversation
with a network of fellow poets. It is this engagement with literary practices that I believe is where we must begin to account for creativity when
evaluating our cultural producers.

To draw an analogy between the approaches to Picasso, Bolina, and
the ancient world, imagine that I am reading Bolina's poem 2,000 years
from now in a context in which my material data is extremely limited.
Imagine I have no extant evidence of Ashbery and no biography of Bolina
at hand. But I am interested in saying something about rural American life
in the early twenty-first century. It would be tempting to cite Bolina's
poem. And, interestingly, even if the details he provides are a product of
imagination, they are not necessarily an inaccurate description of the
period and location I want to describe. But this does not mean I can
wholly separate Bolina from his social network of other writers. As a
scholar, I can no more assume that Bolina is offering a "true" representation of life than I can assume Gilot sketched with a strange, rounded
pencil.

---

[5] Jaswinder Bolina, *Phantom Camera* (Kalamazoo: Western Michigan University Press, 2013), 12–13.

Just like the scholars of modern art and culture who have realized that creative acts are expressions of their cultural milieu, scholars of history must remain attentive to the plausible and practical aspects of the creative *process*. Artists and writers tend to communicate and share their materials within fairly established networks. In both antiquity and modernity, the most immediate and formative social context for the production of any kind of cultural product tended to be circles of like-minded consumers and critics. These circles can be comprised of living contemporaries (e.g., Els Quatre Gats, the Algonquin Round Table), past exemplars of the field (e.g., Homer, Hesiod, or the authors associated with the Second Sophistic), or conversation partners across disciplines and time periods. When a poet adapts a line from a fellow poet, or a painter borrows from another painter, it gives us a clue as to the artist's process, social location, influences, and conversation partners – the field of cultural production. This is identifiable data. And perhaps this is as concrete as we can be in our evaluations of artists, writers, and texts if we are looking for data on social realities. If we speculate beyond these parameters, we risk "filling in the blanks," as it were, with anachronisms, assumptions, or the accumulated discourses associated with acts of history-making and tradition. And as time stretches between the evaluator and the artifact being evaluated, this risk increases.

When it comes to the ancient Mediterranean, these connections and conversations between authors and artists are more difficult to spot for a number of reasons. One, of course, as noted above, is a limited and fragmented historical record. The other is the veil that tradition can place over our sources. It is the contention of this monograph that the gospel authors are aware of a diverse range of literature (e.g., biography, paradoxography) and are in conversation with social peers (i.e., other writers), yet we continue to emphasize in scholarship that they are selecting their materials based on the desires of their fellow Christians. Why extract these writers from their *literary* networks when we imagine their social worlds? I suggest it is because we are hopeful to learn something about the early Jesus movement and the so-called earliest Christians, and our desire to find a touchstone to that tradition has influenced how we read these texts. But if we treat the gospel authors as authors with artistic license, we must contend with the possibility that these are writers acting as writers. This means that it is possible, even likely, that a good portion of what we read when we read the gospels is invention or part of a broader *literary* tradition.

Bibliography

Adams, Sean A. "Luke, Josephus, and Self-Definition: The Genre of Luke–Acts and Its Relationship to Apologetic Historiography and Collected Biography." In *Christian Origins and Hellenistic Judaism: Social and Literary Contexts for the New Testament*, edited by Stanley E. Porter and Andrew W. Pitts, 439–59. Leiden: Brill, 2013.

Adler, Eric. *Valorizing the Barbarians: Enemy Speeches in Roman Historiography*. Austin: University of Texas Press, 2011.

Aesop. *Aesop without Morals: The Famous Fables, and a Life of Aesop*. Translated by Lloyd William Daly. New York: Thomas Yoseloff, 1961.

Aesop's Fables: With a Life of Aesop. Translated by John Esten Keller and L. Clark Keating. Lexington: University Press of Kentucky, 1993.

Alexander, Loveday. "Fact, Fiction and the Genre of Acts." *New Testament Studies* 44 (1998): 380–99.

Ameriks, Karl, ed. *The Cambridge Companion to German Idealism*. Cambridge: Cambridge University Press, 2000.

Anderson, Paul N., Felix Just, and Tom Thatcher, eds. *John, Jesus, and History: Aspects of Historicity in the Fourth Gospel*. Vol. 2. Atlanta: Society of Biblical Literature, 2009.

Apuleius. *The Golden Ass, or A Book of Changes*. Translated by Joel Relihan. Indianapolis: Hackett, 2007.

Armstrong, David, Jeffrey Fish, Patricia A. Johnson, and Marilyn B. Skinner, eds. *Vergil, Philodemus and the Augustans*. Austin: University of Texas Press, 2004.

Arnal, William. *Jesus and the Village Scribes*. Minneapolis: Fortress Press, 2001.

"A Parting of the Ways? Scholarly Identities and a Peculiar Species of Ancient Mediterranean Religion." In *Identity and Interaction in the Ancient Mediterranean: Jews, Christians and Others: Essays in Honour of Stephen G. Wilson*, edited by Zeba A. Crook and Philip A. Harland, 253–75. Sheffield: Sheffield Phoenix, 2007.

"The Gospel of Mark as Reflection on Exile." In *Introducing Religion: Essays in Honor of Jonathan Z. Smith*, edited by Willi Braun and Russell T. McCutcheon, 57–67. London: Equinox, 2008.

"The Collection and Synthesis of 'Tradition' and the Second-Century Invention of Christianity." *Method & Theory in the Study of Religion* 23 (2011): 193–215.

The Symbolic Jesus: Historical Scholarship, Judaism, and the Construction of Contemporary Identity. Oakville: Equinox, 2014.

"Mark, War, and Creative Imagination." In *Redescribing the Gospel of Mark*, edited by Barry S. Crawford and Merrill P. Miller, 401–82. Atlanta: SBL Press, 2017.

Asad, Talal. *Genealogies of Religion: Discipline and Reasons of Power in Christianity and Islam.* Baltimore: Johns Hopkins University Press, 1993.

Ascough, Richard S. "Matthew and Community Formation." In *The Gospel of Matthew in Current Study: Studies in Memory of William G. Thompson*, edited by David E. Aune, 96–126. Grand Rapids: Eerdmans, 2001.

Ash, Rhiannon. "Fractured Vision: Josephus and Tacitus on Triumph and Civil War." In *Roman Rule in Greek and Latin Writing: Double Vision*, edited by Jesper Majbom Madsen and Roger Rees, 144–62. Leiden: Brill, 2014.

Aune, David E. *The New Testament in Its Literary Environment.* Philadelphia: Westminster, 1987.

Bagnani, Gilbert. *Arbiter of Elegance: A Study of the Life and Works of C. Petronius.* Toronto: University of Toronto Press, 1954.

Balch, David L. *Roman Domestic Art and Early House Churches.* Tübingen: Mohr Siebeck, 2008.

Baldick, Christopher. "Biography." In *The Oxford Dictionary of Literary Terms.* Oxford: Oxford University Press, 2008.

Barthes, Roland. "The Death of the Author." In *Image, Music, Text*, translated by Stephen Heath, 142–48. New York: Macmillan, 1977.

Bauckham, Richard. *The Gospels for All Christians: Rethinking the Gospel Audiences.* Grand Rapids: Eerdmans, 1998.

Jesus and the Eyewitnesses: The Gospels as Eyewitness Testimony, 2nd ed. Grand Rapids: Eerdmans, 2017.

Beneker, Jeffrey. "Nepos' Biographical Method in the *Lives of Foreign Generals*." *The Classical Journal* 105, no. 2 (2009): 109–21.

Bennett, Andrew. "Expressivity: The Romantic." In *Literary Theory and Criticism: An Oxford Guide*, edited by Patricia Waugh. New York: Oxford University Press, 2006.

Berlin, Isaiah. *Three Critics of the Enlightenment: Vico, Hamann, Herder.* Edited by Henry Hardy. Princeton: Princeton University Press, 2013.

Bieler, Ludwig. *Theios aner: Das Bild des "Göttlichen Menschen" in Spätantike und Frühchristentum.* Vienna: Höfels, 1935.

Bird, Michael F. "Sectarian Gospels for Sectarian Christians? The Non-Canonical Gospels and Bauckham's *The Gospels for All Christians*." In *The Audience of the Gospels: The Origin and Function of the Gospels in Early Christianity*, edited by Edward W. Klink, 27–48. London: T&T Clark, 2010.

Bloom, Harold. *The Ringers in the Tower: Studies in Romantic Tradition.* Chicago: University of Chicago Press, 1971.

Bodel, John. "The *Cena Trimalchionis*." In *Latin Fiction: The Latin Novel in Context*, edited by Heinz Hofmann, 38–51. London: Routledge, 1999.

"Death on Display: Looking at Roman Funerals." In *The Art of Ancient Spectacle*, edited by B. Bergmann and C. Kondoleon, 258–81. New Haven: Yale University Press, 1999.

Boecker, Bettina. "Groundlings, Gallants, Grocers: Shakespeare's Elizabethan Audience and the Political Agendas of Shakespeare Criticism." In *Shakespeare and European Politics*, edited by Dirk Delabastita, Jozef de Vos, and Paul Franssen, 220–32. Newark: University of Delaware Press, 2008.

Bolina, Jaswinder. *Phantom Camera*. Kalamazoo: Western Michigan University, 2013.

"Color Coded: On the Poetics of Donald Trump, the Progress of Poetry, and Reverse Racism." Accessed May 11, 2016. www.poetryfoundation.org.

Bonner, Stanley. *Education in Ancient Rome: From the Elder Cato to the Younger Pliny*. Berkeley: University of California Press, 1977.

Bonz, Marianne Palmer. *The Past as Legacy: Luke–Acts and Ancient Epic*. Minneapolis: Fortress Press, 2000.

Boorstin, Daniel. *The Lost World of Thomas Jefferson*. Chicago: University of Chicago Press, 1993.

Bordwell, David. *Making Meaning: Inference and Rhetoric in the Interpretation of Cinema*. Cambridge, MA: Harvard University Press, 1989.

Borgen, Peder, et al., eds. *The Philo Index: A Complete Greek Word Index to the Writings of Philo of Alexandria*. Grand Rapids: Eerdmans; Leiden: Brill, 2000.

Bourdieu, Pierre. *The Logic of Practice*. Translated by Richard Nice. Stanford: Stanford University Press, 1990.

The Field of Cultural Production: Essays on Art and Literature. Edited by Randal Johnson. New York: Columbia University Press, 1993.

Distinction: A Social Critique of the Judgement of Taste. Translated by Richard Nice. Cambridge, MA: Harvard University Press, 1996.

Bourdieu, Pierre, and Loïc J. D. Wacquant. *An Invitation to Reflexive Sociology*. Chicago: University of Chicago Press, 1992.

Bovon, François. *Luke 1: A Commentary on the Gospel of Luke 1:1–9:50*. Edited by Helmut Koester and translated by Christine M. Thomas. Minneapolis: Fortress Press, 2002.

Bowersock, G. W. *Fiction as History: Nero to Julian*. Berkeley: University of California Press, 1994.

Bowie, Andrew. "Romanticism and Music." In *The Cambridge Companion to German Romanticism*, edited by Nicholas Saul, 243–55. Cambridge: Cambridge University Press, 2009.

Boyd, Barbara Weiden. "Virgil's Camilla and the Traditions of Catalogue and Ecphrasis (Aeneid 7.803–17)." *The American Journal of Philology* 113, no. 2 (Summer 1992): 213–34.

Boyer, Pascal. *Tradition as Truth and Communication: A Cognitive Description of Traditional Discourse*. Cambridge: Cambridge University Press, 1990.

Braun, Willi. "Schooled Intelligence, Social Interests, and the Sayings Gospel Q." Paper presented at Westar Seminar on Christian Origins. Santa Rosa, October 2007.

Brown, Jonathan, ed. *Picasso and the Spanish Tradition*. New Haven: Yale University Press, 1996.

Brown, Raymond E., and John P. Meier. *Antioch and Rome: New Testament Cradles of Catholic Christianity*. New York: Paulist Press, 1983.

Brubaker, Rogers. *Ethnicity without Groups*. Cambridge, MA: Harvard University Press, 2004.

Brunt, P. A. *Roman Imperial Themes*. Oxford: Clarendon Press, 1990.

Bultmann, Rudolf. "The New Approach to the Synoptic Problem." *Journal of Religion* 6 (1926): 337–62.

———. *Theology of the New Testament*. Translated by Kendrick Grobel. New York: Scribner, 1951.

———. *Primitive Christianity in Its Contemporary Setting*. Translated by R. H. Fuller. London: Thames & Hudson, 1956.

———. *Rudolf Bultmann: Interpreting Faith for the Modern Era*. Edited by Roger A. Johnson. Minneapolis: Fortress Press, 1991.

———. *The History of the Synoptic Tradition*. Translated by John Marsh. Peabody: Hendrickson, 1994 [1963].

Burke, Seán. *The Death and Return of the Author: Criticism and Subjectivity in Barthes, Foucault and Derrida*, 3rd ed. Edinburgh: Edinburgh University Press, 2010.

Burridge, Richard A. *What Are the Gospels? A Comparison with Graeco-Roman Biography*, 2nd ed. Grand Rapids: Eerdmans, 2004.

———. "Reading the Gospels as Biography." In *The Limits of Ancient Biography*, edited by B. C. McGing and Judith Mossman, 31–49. Swansea: Classical Press of Wales, 2006.

Cabaniss, Allen. "A Footnote to the 'Petronian Question.'" *Classical Philology* 49, no. 2 (1954): 98–102.

———. "The *Satiricon* and the Christian Oral Tradition." *Greek, Roman, and Byzantine Studies* 3, no. 1 (1960): 36–39.

Cappon, Lester Jesse, ed. *The Adams-Jefferson Letters: The Complete Correspondence between Thomas Jefferson and Abigail and John Adams*. Chapel Hill: University of North Carolina Press, 1959.

Cartlidge, David R., and David L. Dungan, eds. *Documents for the Study of the Gospels*. Minneapolis: Fortress Press, 1980.

Casey, Maurice. *Is John's Gospel True?*. New York: Routledge, 1996.

Charlesworth, S. D. "The End of Orality: Transmission of Gospel Tradition in the Second and Third Centuries." In *Between Orality and Literacy: Communication and Adaptation in Antiquity, Orality and Literacy in the Ancient World*, edited by Ruth Scodel, 10:331–55. Leiden: Brill, 2014.

Clark, Elizabeth A. *History, Theory, Text: Historians and the Linguistic Turn*. Cambridge, MA: Harvard University Press, 2004.

Clark, Gillian. "Philosophic Lives and Philosophic Life: Porphyry and Iamblichus." In *Greek Biography and Panegyric in Late Antiquity*, edited by Tomas Hägg and Philip Rousseau, 29–51. Berkeley: University of California Press, 2000.

Clark Keating, Louis. *Aesop's Fables: With a Life of Aesop*. Lexington: University Press of Kentucky, 1993.

Clarke, John. "Augustus's and Trajan's Messages to Commoners." In *Art in the Lives of Ordinary Romans: Visual Representation and Non-Elite Viewers in Italy, 100 B.C.E. –A.D. 315*, 19–41. Berkeley: University of California Press, 2006.

Cody, Jane M. "Conquerors and Conquered on Flavian Coins." In *Flavian Rome: Culture, Image, Text*, edited by A. J. Boyle and W. J. Dominik, 103–23. Leiden: Brill, 2003.

Cohen, Shaye J. D. *Josephus in Galilee and Rome: His Vita and Development as a Historian*. Leiden: Brill, 1979.

Colish, Marcia L. "Stoicism and the New Testament: An Essay in Historiography." *ANRW* 26, no. 1 (1992): 334–79.

Collins, Adela Yarbro. *Is Mark's Gospel a Life of Jesus? The Question of Genre*. Milwaukee: Marquette University Press, 1990.

——— *Mark: A Commentary*. Edited by Harold W. Attridge. Minneapolis: Fortress Press, 2007.

Conte, Gian Biagio. "Petronius." In *Latin Literature: A History*, edited by Don Fowler and Glenn W. Most, translated by Joseph B. Solodow, 453–66. Baltimore: Johns Hopkins University Press, 1999.

Courtney, E. *A Companion to Petronius*. Oxford: Oxford University Press, 2001.

Crossley, James G. *The Date of Mark's Gospel: Insight from the Law in Earliest Christianity*. London: T&T Clark, 2004.

Curtius, Ernst. "Rom und die Deutschen." In *Alterthum und Gegenwart: Gesammelte Reden und Vorträge*. Vol. 1. Berlin, 1875.

Davies, Margaret. *Rhetoric and Reference in the Fourth Gospel*. Sheffield: JSOT Press, 1992.

Davies, Penelope. *Death and the Emperor: Roman Imperial Funerary Monuments from Augustus to Marcus Aurelius*. Cambridge: Cambridge University Press, 2000.

Deissmann, Adolf. *Licht vom Osten: Das Neue Testament und die neuentdeckten Texte aus dem hellenistisch-römischen Welt*. Tübingen: Verlag von J. C. B. Mohr Siebeck, 1908.

Delff, Heinrich Karl Hugo, ed. *Johann Georg Hamann: Lichtstrahlen aus seinen Schriften und Briefen*. Leipzig: Brockhaus, 1874.

Denzey Lewis, Nicola. "The Limits of Ethnic Categories." In *Handbook of Early Christianity: Social Science Approaches*, edited by Anthony J. Blasi, Paul-André Turcotte, and Jean Duhaime, 489–507. Walnut Creek: AltaMira Press, 2002.

Detering, Hermann. "The Dutch Radical Approach to the Pauline Epistles." *Journal of Higher Criticism* 3, no. 2 (1996): 169–93.

Dietler, Michael. "'Our Ancestors the Gauls': Archaeology, Ethnic Nationalism, and the Manipulation of Celtic Identity in Modern Europe." *American Anthropologist* 96, no. 3 (1994): 584–605.

Diggins, John P. *The Lost Soul of American Politics: Virtue, Self-Interest, and the Foundations of Liberalism*. Chicago: University of Chicago Press, 1986.

Douglas, Mary. *Natural Symbols: Explorations in Cosmology*. New York: Routledge, 2003.

Dowden, Ken. _Death and the Maiden: Girls' Initiation Rites in Greek Mythology._ London: Routledge, 1989.

Drake, Hal A. _A Century of Miracles: Christians, Pagans, Jews, and the Supernatural, 312–410._ New York: Oxford University Press, 2017.

Ducrot, Oswald, and Tzvetan Todorov. _Dictionnaire encyclopédique des sciences du langage._ Paris: Éditions du Seuil, 1972.

Duff, Tim. _Plutarch's Lives: Exploring Virtue and Vice._ Oxford: Oxford University Press, 1999.

Dupont, Florence. "_Recitatio_ and the Space of Public Discourse." In _The Roman Cultural Revolution_, edited by Thomas Habinek and Alessandro Schiesaro, 44–59. Cambridge: Cambridge University Press, 1997.

Edwards, M. J. "Birth, Death, and Divinity in Porphyry's _Life of Plotinus._" In _Greek Biography and Panegyric in Late Antiquity_, edited by Tomas Hägg and Philip Rousseau, 52–71. Berkeley: University of California Press, 2000.

Ehrman, Bart D. _Forged: Writing in the Name of God: Why the Bible's Authors Are Not Who We Think They Are._ New York: HarperOne, 2011.

Jesus before the Gospels: How the Earliest Christians Remembered, Changed, and Invented Their Stories of the Savior. New York: HarperOne, 2016.

The New Testament: A Historical Introduction to Early Christian Writings. 6th ed. Oxford: Oxford University Press, 2016.

Eisenberg, Anne F. "Negotiating the Social Landscape to Create Social Change." In _Illuminating Social Life: Classical and Contemporary Theory Revisited_, 5th ed., edited by Peter Kivisto, 371–394. Thousand Oaks: Pine Forge Press, 2011.

Emerson, Ralph Waldo. _The Annotated Emerson._ Edited by David Mikics. Cambridge, MA: Harvard University Press, 2012.

Engberg-Pedersen, Troels. _Paul and the Stoics._ Edinburgh: T&T Clark, 2000.

ed. _Paul beyond the Judaism/Hellenism Divide._ Louisville: Westminster John Knox, 2001.

ed. _Paul in His Hellenistic Context._ London: T&T Clark, 2004.

Cosmology and Self in the Apostle Paul: The Material Spirit. Oxford: Oxford University Press, 2010.

Eyl, Jennifer. "By the Power of Signs and Wonders: Paul, Divinatory Practices, and Symbolic Capital." PhD diss., Brown University, 2012.

"Why Thekla Does Not See Paul: Visual Perception and the Displacement of Erōs in the Acts of Paul and Thekla." In _The Ancient Novel and the Early Christian and Jewish Narrative: Fictional Intersections_, edited by Marília P. Futre Pinheiro, Judith Perkins, and Richard Pervo, 3–12. Groningen: Barkhuis Publishing; Groningen University Library, 2012.

"Semantic Voids, New Testament Translation, and Anachronism: The Case of Paul's Use of Ekklēsia." _Method & Theory in the Study of Religion_ 26, nos. 4–5 (2014): 315–39.

Signs, Wonders, and Gifts: Divination in the Letters of Paul. New York: Oxford University Press, 2019.

Fantham, Elaine. _Roman Literary Culture: From Cicero to Apuleius._ Baltimore: Johns Hopkins University Press, 1996.

Feldman, Burton, and Robert D. Richardson, eds. *The Rise of Modern Mythology, 1680–1860*. Bloomington: Indiana University Press, 1972.

Fitzgerald, John T., ed. *Passions and Moral Progress in Greco-Roman Thought*. London: Routledge, 2008.

Fox, Matthew. *Roman Historical Myths: The Regal Period in Augustan Literature*. New York: Clarendon, 1996.

Frazier, Françoise. *Histoire et morale dans les Vies parallèles de Plutarque*. Paris: Les Belles Lettres, 1996.

Frye, Northrop. *The Secular Scripture: A Study of the Structure of Romance*. Cambridge, MA: Harvard University Press, 1976.

Fulford, Robert. "'Lions mate with lions': Introducing Françoise Gilot, the Woman Who Said No to Pablo Picasso." *National Post* (May 10, 2016). Accessed February 16, 2020. https://nationalpost.com/entertainment/books/lions-mate-with-lions-introducing-francoise-gilot-the-woman-who-said-no-to-pablo-picasso.

Gabba, Emilio. "True History and False History in Classical Antiquity." *The Journal of Roman Studies* 71 (1981): 50–62.

Gadamer, Hans-Georg. *Truth and Method*, 2nd rev. ed. Edited by Joel Weinsheimer and Donald G. Marshall. New York: Continuum, 2004.

Gager, John G. *Kingdom and Community: The Social World of Early Christianity*. Englewood Cliffs: Prentice-Hall, 1975.

——. ed. *Curse Tablets and Binding Spells from the Ancient World*. New York: Oxford University Press, 1992.

Gathercole, Simon. "The Alleged Anonymity of the Canonical Gospels." *Journal of Theological Studies* 69 (2018): 447–76.

Gerdmar, Anders. *Roots of Theological Anti-Semitism: German Biblical Interpretation and the Jews, from Herder and Semler to Kittel and Bultmann*. Leiden: Brill, 2010.

Gerstenberg, Heinrich Wilhelm. *Briefe über Merkwürdigkeiten der Literatur*. Schleswig: Joachim Friedrich Hansen, 1766.

Gill, Christopher. *The Structured Self in Hellenistic and Roman Thought*. Oxford: Oxford University Press, 2006.

Gillespie, Gerald, Manfred Engel, and Bernard Dieterle, eds. *Romantic Prose Fiction*. Philadelphia: Benjamins, 2008.

Gilot, Françoise, and Carlton Lake. *Vivre avec Picasso*. Paris: Calmann-Lévy, 1965.

Gilot, Françoise, and John Richardson. Interview by Charlie Rose. Charlie Rose LLC, May 17, 2012.

Goethe, J. W. von. *Goethes Werke, Naturwissenschaftliche Schriften 1, Hamburger Ausgabe*. Edited by Erich Trunz. 14 vols. Munich: Beck, 1981.

Goodenough, Erwin. *Jewish Symbols in the Greco-Roman Period: Pagan Symbols in Judaism*. Vol. 8. New York: Pantheon Books, 1958.

Goodman, Russell B. *American Philosophy and the Romantic Tradition*. Cambridge: Cambridge University Press, 1990.

Gowers, Emily. *The Loaded Table: Representations of Food in Roman Literature*. New York: Oxford University Press, 1993.

Grafton, Anthony. *Defenders of the Text: The Traditions of Scholarship in an Age of Science, 1450–1800.* Cambridge, MA: Harvard University Press, 1991.

Grau Guijarro, Sergi. *La imatge del filòsof i de l'activitat filosòfica a la Grècia antiga: Anàlisi dels tòpics biogràfics presents a les Vides i doctrines dels filòsofs més il·lustres de Diògenes Laerci.* Barcelona: Universitat de Barcelona, 2009.

Graziosi, Barbara. *Inventing Homer: The Early Reception of Epic.* Cambridge: Cambridge University Press, 2002.

Grethlein, Jonas. *Experience and Teleology in Ancient Historiography: "Futures Past" from Herodotus to Augustine.* Cambridge: Cambridge University Press, 2013.

Grimm, Jacob. "Gedanken über Mythos, Epos und Geschichte." In *Deutsches Museum,* edited by Friedrich Schlegel, 3:53–75. Vienna, 1813.

Grimm, Jacob, Wilhelm Grimm, and Herman Friedrich Grimm. *Briefwechsel zwischen Jacob und Wilhelm Grimm aus der Jugendzeit.* Weimar: H. Böhlaus, 1881.

Gruen, Erich S. *Diaspora: Jews amidst Greeks and Romans.* Cambridge, MA: Harvard University Press, 2009.

Gunkel, Hermann. "Ein Notschrei aus Anlaß des Buches Himmelsbild und Weltanschauung im Wandel der Zeiten." *Die Christliche Welt* 14 (1900): 56–61.

Gutzwiller, Kathryn J. *Theocritus' Pastoral Analogies: The Formation of a Genre.* Madison: University of Wisconsin Press, 1991.

Hadot, Pierre. "Théologie, exégèse, révélation, écriture dans la philosophie grecque," edited by M. Tardieu, 13–34. Paris: Le Cerf, 1987.

Hagen, Friedrich, von der. *Die Nibelungen: Ihre Bedeutung für die Gegenwart und für immer.* Breslau: Josef Max, 1819.

Hägg, Tomas. *The Art of Biography in Antiquity.* Cambridge: Cambridge University Press, 2012.

Hahn, Hans-Joachim. "Germany: Historical Survey." In *Encyclopedia of the Romantic Era, 1760–1850,* edited by Christopher John Murray, 418–21. New York: Fitzroy Dearborn, 2004.

Hall, Edith. *Inventing the Barbarian: Greek Self-Definition through Tragedy.* New York: Oxford University Press, 1989.

Hamann, Johann Georg. *Sämtliche Werke.* Edited by Josef Nadler. Vol. 3. 6 vols. Wien: Thomas-Morus Presse, 1949.

Briefwechsel. Edited by Walther Ziesemer and Arthur Henkel. Vol. 5. 8 vols. Wiesbaden: Insel-Verlag, 1955.

Hammer, Dean. *Roman Political Thought: From Cicero to Augustine.* Cambridge: Cambridge University Press, 2014.

Hansen, William, trans. and ed. *Phlegon of Tralles' Book of Marvels.* Exeter: University of Exeter Press, 1996.

Anthology of Greek Popular Literature. Bloomington: University of Indiana Press, 1998.

Harnack, Adolf von, ed. *Die Lehre der zwölf Apostel: nebst Untersuchungen zur ältesten Geschichte der Kirchenverfassung und des Kirchenrechts.* Leipzig: Hinrichs, 1884.

Hengel, Martin. *Between Jesus and Paul: Studies in the Earliest History of Christianity.* London: SCM Press, 1983.

The Four Gospels and One Gospel of Jesus Christ. London: SCM Press, 2000.

Herder, Johann Gottfried von. *Abhandlung Über den Ursprung der Sprache.* Berlin, 1772.

Ideen zur Philosophie der Geschichte der Menschheit. Hartknoch, 1786.

Sämmtliche Werke: Ideen zur Philosophie der Geschichte der Menschheit. Berlin: Weidmann, 1877, 1887, 1891.

Hezser, Catherine. *Jewish Literacy in Roman Palestine. Texts and Studies in Ancient Judaism 81.* Tübingen: Mohr Siebeck, 2001.

"Ancient 'Science Fiction': Journeys into Space and Visions of the World in Jewish, Christian, and Greco-Roman Literature of Antiquity." In *Christian Origins and Hellenistic Judaism: Social and Literary Contexts for the New Testament,* edited by Stanley E. Porter and Andrew W. Pitts, 397–438. Leiden: Brill, 2013.

Hobsbawm, Eric J. *The Invention of Tradition.* Cambridge: Cambridge University Press, 2012.

Hodge, Caroline E. Johnson. *If Sons, then Heirs: A Study of Kinship and Ethnicity in the Letters of Paul.* New York: Oxford University Press, 2007.

Holzmeister, Angela. "*Ekphrasis* in the Ancient Novel." In *The Ancient Novel and the Frontiers of Genre,* edited by Marilia P. Futre Pinheiro, Gareth Schmeling, and Edmund P. Cueva, 411–23. Eelde: Barkhuis, 2014.

Hopkins, Keith. "Christian Number and Its Implications." *Journal of Early Christian Studies* 6, no. 2 (1998): 185–226.

Horrell, David G. "Aliens and Strangers? The Socio-Economic Location of the Addressees of 1 Peter." In *Becoming Christian: Essays on 1 Peter and the Making of Christian Identity,* 100–132. Library of New Testament Studies 394. London: Bloomsbury T&T Clark, 2013.

Horsley, Richard A. *Jesus and Empire: The Kingdom of God and the New World Disorder.* Minneapolis: Fortress Press, 2003.

Jesus and the Politics of Roman Palestine. Columbia: University of South Carolina Press, 2014.

Iggers, Georg G. *The German Conception of History: The National Tradition of Historical Thought from Herder to the Present.* Middletown: Wesleyan University Press, 1983.

Jankuhn, Herbert, and Dieter Timpe. *Beiträge zum Verständnis der Germania des Tacitus: Bericht über die Kolloquien der Kommission für die Altertumskunde Nord- und Mitteleuropas.* Göttingen: Vandenhoeck & Ruprecht, 1989.

Jay, Jeff. *The Tragic in Mark: A Literary-Historical Interpretation.* Tübingen: Mohr Siebeck, 2014.

Johnson, Luke Timothy. "On Finding the Lukan Community: A Cautious Cautionary Essay." In *Contested Issues in Christian Origins and the New Testament: Collected Essays,* 129–43. Leiden: Brill, 2013.

Johnson, William A. *Readers and Reading Culture in the High Roman Empire: A Study of Elite Communities.* Oxford: Oxford University Press, 2010.

"Learning to Read and Write." In *A Companion to Ancient Education,* edited by W. Martin Bloomer, 137–48. Malden: Wiley Blackwell, 2015.

Jones, William. *The Works of Sir William Jones.* Edited by John Teignmouth. Vol. 3. Cambridge: Cambridge University Press, 2013.

Josephson-Storm, Jason Ānanda. *The Myth of Disenchantment: Magic, Modernity, and the Birth of the Human Sciences.* Chicago: University of Chicago Press, 2017.

Josephus, Flavius. *Flavius Josephus: Translation and Commentary, Volume 10 against Apion.* Edited by Steve Mason and translated by John M. G. Barclay. Leiden: Brill, 2007.

Jouanno, Corinne. "Novelistic Lives and Historical Biographies: The Life of Aesop and the Alexander Romance as Fringe Novels." In *Fiction on the Fringe: Novelistic Writing in the Post-Classical Age,* edited by Grammatiki Karla, 33–48. Leiden: Brill, 2009.

Kamenetsky, Christa. *The Brothers Grimm and Their Critics: Folktales and the Quest for Meaning.* Athens: Ohio University Press, 1992.

Kant, Immannuel. *Kant's Critique of the Power of Judgment: Critical Essays.* Edited by Paul Guyer and translated by Paul Guyer and Eric Matthews. Cambridge: Cambridge University Press, 2000.

Karla, Grammatiki A., ed. *Vita Aesopi: Überlieferung, Sprache und Edition einer frühbyzantinischen Fassung des Äsopromans.* Wiesbaden: Reichert, 2001.

——— ed. *Fiction on the Fringe: Novelistic Writing in the Post-Classical Age.* Leiden: Brill, 2009.

Kazanjian, Dodie. "Life after Picasso: Françoise Gilot," *Vogue* (April 27, 2012). Accessed February 16, 2020. www.vogue.com/article/life-after-picasso-fra noise-gilot.

Kee, Howard Clark. *Community of the New Age: Studies in Mark's Gospel.* Macon: Mercer University Press, 1983.

King, Karen L. *What Is Gnosticism?* Cambridge, MA: Belknap Press of Harvard University Press, 2003.

——— "Factions, Variety, Diversity, Multiplicity: Representing Early Christian Differences for the 21st Century." *Method & Theory in the Study of Religion* 23, nos. 3–4 (2011): 216–37.

Kirk, G. S., J. E. Raven, and Malcolm Schofield, eds. *The Presocratic Philosophers: A Critical History with a Selection of Texts,* 2nd ed. Cambridge: Cambridge University Press, 1983.

Klein, Jürgen. "Genius, Ingenium, Imagination: Aesthetic Theories of Production from the Renaissance to Romanticism." In *England und der Kontinent: Subjektivität und Imagination von der Renaissance bis zur Moderne,* 47–97. Frankfurt: Peter Lang, 2008.

Kloppenborg, John S. *Excavating Q: The History and Setting of the Sayings Gospel.* Minneapolis: Fortress Press, 2000.

——— *Q, the Earliest Gospel: An Introduction to the Original Stories and Sayings of Jesus.* Louisville: Westminster John Knox, 2008.

——— "Greco-Roman *Thiasoi,* the *Ekklēsia* at Corinth, and Conflict Management." In *Redescribing Paul and the Corinthians,* edited by Ron Cameron and Merrill P. Miller, 187–218. Atlanta: Society of Biblical Literature, 2011.

Koester, Helmut. *Ancient Christian Gospels: Their History and Development.* Harrisburg, PA: Trinity Press International, 1990.

History, Culture, and Religion of the Hellenistic Age, vol. 1: Introduction to the New Testament, 2nd ed. Berlin: de Gruyter, 1995.

Konstan, David. "The Alexander Romance: The Cunning of the Open Text." *Lexis* 16 (1998): 123–38.

——. "The Active Reader and the Ancient Novel." In *Readers and Writers in the Ancient Novel,* edited by Michael Paschalis, Stelios Panayotakis, and Gareth Schmeling, 1–17. Groningen: Barkhuis Publishing; Groningen University Library, 2009.

Konstan, David, and Robyn Walsh. "Civic and Subversive Biography in Antiquity." In *Writing Biography in Greece and Rome: Narrative Technique and Fictionalization,* edited by Koen de Temmerman and Kristoffel Demoen, 26–43. Cambridge: Cambridge University Press, 2016.

Konstantakos, Ioannis. *Akicharos: He Diegese tou Ahikar sten archaia Hellada.* 3 vols. Athens: Stigme, 2008.

Kotrosits, Maia. *Rethinking Early Christian Identity: Affect, Violence, and Belonging.* Minneapolis: Fortress Press, 2015.

Kraemer, Ross Shepard. *Unreliable Witnesses: Religion, Gender, and History in the Greco-Roman Mediterranean.* New York: Oxford University Press, 2011.

Kurke, Leslie. *Aesopic Conversations: Popular Tradition, Cultural Dialogue, and the Invention of Greek Prose.* Princeton: Princeton University Press, 2011.

Kysar, Robert. "The Contribution of D. Moody Smith to Johannine Scholarship." In *Exploring the Gospel of John: In Honor of D. Moody Smith,* edited by R. Alan Culpepper and Carl Clifton Black, 3–17. Louisville: Westminster John Knox, 1996.

Lacher, Irene. "A Place of Her Own: Culture: Françoise Gilot, Picasso's former Lover and Jonas Salk's Wife, Wants to Be Known Not as the Companion of Great Men, but as Their Equal." *Los Angeles Times* (March 6, 1991).

Lachmann, Karl. *Betrachtungen über Homers Ilias.* Berlin, 1847.

Laird, Andrew. "The True Nature of the *Satyricon?*" In *The Greek and the Roman Novel: Parallel Readings,* edited by Michael Paschalis, Stavros Frangoulidis, Stephen Harrison, and Maaike Zimmerman, 151–67. Groningen: Barkhuis, 2007.

Larsen, Matthew D. C. *Gospels before the Book.* New York: Oxford University Press, 2018.

Last, Richard. "The Social Relationships of Gospel Writers: New Insights from Inscriptions Commending Greek Historiographers." *Journal for the Study of the New Testament* 37, no. 3 (2015): 223–52.

Law, Timothy Michael, and Charles Halton, eds. *Jew and Judean: A Marginalia Forum on Politics and Historiography in the Translation of Ancient Texts.* Los Angeles: Marginalia Review of Books, 2014.

LeVen, Pauline A. *The Many-Headed Muse: Tradition and Innovation in Late Classical Greek Poetry.* Cambridge: Cambridge University Press, 2014.

Lewis, James R., ed. *The Oxford Handbook of New Religious Movements.* Oxford: Oxford University Press, 2004.

Lincoln, Bruce. *Theorizing Myth: Narrative, Ideology, and Scholarship.* Chicago: University of Chicago Press, 1999.

Lissarrague, François. "Aesop, between Man and Beast: Ancient Portraits and Illustrations." In *Not the Classical Ideal: Athens and the Construction of the Other in Greek Art*, edited by Beth Cohen, translated by Jennifer Curtiss Gage, 132–49. Leiden: Brill, 2000.

Litwa, M. David. *Iesus Deus: The Early Christian Depiction of Jesus as a Mediterranean God.* Minneapolis: Fortress Press, 2014.

How the Gospels Became History: Jesus and Mediterranean Myths. New Haven: Yale University Press, 2019.

Livingston, James C. *Modern Christian Thought, vol. 1: The Enlightenment and the Nineteenth Century,* 2nd ed. Minneapolis: Fortress Press, 2006.

Luijendijk, AnneMarie, "The Gospel of Mary at Oxyrhynchus (P. Oxy. L 3525 and P. Ryl. III 463): Rethinking the History of Early Christianity through Literary Papyri from Oxyrhynchus." In *Re-Making the World: Christianity and Categories,* edited by Taylor G. Petrey, 391–418. Tübingen: Mohr Siebeck, 2019.

MacDonald, Dennis R. *The Homeric Epics and the Gospel of Mark.* New Haven: Yale University Press, 2000.

MacDonald, Margaret Y. "Rereading Paul: Early Interpreters of Paul on Women and Gender." In *Women and Christian Origins,* edited by Ross Shepard Kraemer and Mary Rose D'Angelo, 236–52. New York: Oxford University Press, 1999.

Mack, Burton L. *A Myth of Innocence: Mark and Christian Origins.* Minneapolis: Fortress Press, 1988.

"On Redescribing Christian Origins." *Method & Theory in the Study of Religion* 8 (1996): 247–69.

The Christian Myth: Origins, Logic, and Legacy. New York: Continuum, 2001.

Madsen, Jesper Majbom. "Patriotism and Ambitions: Intellectual Response to Roman Rule in the High Empire." In *Roman Rule in Greek and Latin Writing: Double Vision,* edited by Jesper Majbom Madsen and Roger Rees, 16–38. Leiden: Brill, 2014.

Malherbe, Abraham J. "'Gentle as a Nurse': The Lyric Background to I Thessalonians Ii." *Novum Testamentum* 12 (1970): 203–17.

Social Aspects of Early Christianity. Baton Rouge: Louisiana State University Press, 1977.

"Hellenistic Moralists and the New Testament." *ANRW* 26, no. 1 (1992): 267–333.

Mann, Thomas. *Pro and Contra Wagner.* London: Faber and Faber, 1985.

Paul and the Thessalonians: The Philosophic Tradition of Pastoral Care. Mifflintown, PA: Sigler, 1987.

Paul and the Popular Philosophers. Minneapolis: Fortress Press, 1989.

Marchand, Suzanne L. *Down from Olympus: Archaeology and Philhellenism in Germany, 1750–1970.* Princeton: Princeton University Press, 1996.

German Orientalism in the Age of Empire: Religion, Race, and Scholarship. Washington, DC: German Historical Institute; Cambridge: Cambridge University Press, 2009.

Mason, Steve. "Jews, Judaeans, Judaizing, Judaism: Problems of Categorization in Ancient History." *Journal for the Study of Judaism* 38, nos. 4–5 (2007): 457–512.

Josephus, Judea, and Christian Origins: Methods and Categories. Peabody: Hendrickson, 2009.

McCutcheon, Russell T. "Myth." In *Guide to the Study of Religion*, edited by Willi Braun and Russell T. McCutcheon, 190–280. London: Cassell, 2000.

Critics Not Caretakers: Redescribing the Public Study of Religion. Albany: State University of New York Press, 2001.

McGill, Scott. *Plagiarism in Latin Literature.* Cambridge: Cambridge University Press, 2012.

Meggitt, Justin. *Paul, Poverty and Survival.* Edinburgh: T&T Clark, 1998.

Menninghaus, Winfried. *In Praise of Nonsense: Kant and Bluebeard.* Stanford: Stanford University Press, 1999.

Miller, Richard C. "Mark's Empty Tomb and Other Translation Fables in Classical Antiquity." *Journal of Biblical Literature* 129, no. 4 (2010): 759–76.

Miller, Stephen G. "Excavations at Nemea, 1979." *Hesperia* 49, no. 2 (1980): 178–205.

Möhler, Johann Adam. *Die Einheit in der Kirche, oder das Princip des Katholicismus: Dargestellt im Geiste der Kirchenväter der drei ersten Jahrhunderte.* Tübingen: Laupp, 1825.

Symbolik, Oder, Darstellung der Dogmatischen Gegensätze der Katholiken und Protestanten nach ihren öffentlichen Bekenntnissschriften. Mainz, 1888.

Moore, Gregory. Introduction to *Shakespeare*, by Johann Gottfried Herder, translated and edited by Gregory Moore, vii–xlii. Princeton: Princeton University Press, 2008.

Morris, Ian, and Barry B. Powell, eds. *A New Companion to Homer.* Leiden: Brill, 1997.

Moss, Candida R. *The Myth of Persecution: How Early Christians Invented a Story of Martyrdom.* New York: HarperCollins, 2013.

Mosse, George L. *The Nationalization of the Masses: Political Symbolism and Mass Movements in Germany from the Napoleonic Wars through the Third Reich.* New York: H. Fertig, 1975.

Most, Glenn W. "A Cock for Asclepius." *The Classical Quarterly* 43, no. 1 (1993): 96–111.

Moxnes, Halvor. *Jesus and the Rise of Nationalism: A New Quest for the Nineteenth-Century Historical Jesus.* London: Taurus, 2012.

Mroczek, Eva. *The Literary Imagination in Jewish Antiquity.* New York: Oxford University Press, 2016.

Nagy, Gregory. *Homer's Text and Language.* Urbana: University of Illinois Press, 2004.

Nanos, Mark D. *The Irony of Galatians: Paul's Letter in First-Century Context.* Minneapolis: Fortress Press, 2002.

Nasrallah, Laura Salah. *Christian Responses to Roman Art and Architecture: The Second-Century Church Amid the Spaces of Empire.* Cambridge: Cambridge University Press, 2010.

Niehoff, Maren. *The Figure of Joseph in Post-Biblical Jewish Literature*. Leiden: Brill, 1992.

Jewish Exegesis and Homeric Scholarship in Alexandria. Cambridge: Cambridge University Press, 2011.

Nietzsche, Friedrich Wilhelm. *Die fröhliche Wissenschaft*. Chemnitz: Verlag von Ernst Schmeitzner; New York: E. Steige, 1882.

Briefwechsel: Kritische Gesamtausgabe. Edited by Giorgio Colli, Mazzino Montinari, and Helga Anania-Hess. Berlin: de Gruyter, 1975.

Sämtliche Werke: Kritische Studienausgabe. Edited by Giorgio Colli and Mazzino Montinari. Berlin: de Gruyter, 1988.

Nongbri, Brent. "Dislodging 'Embedded' Religion: A Brief Note on a Scholarly Trope." *Numen* 55, no. 4 (2008): 440–60.

Before Religion: A History of a Modern Concept. New Haven: Yale University Press, 2013.

God's Library: The Archaeology of the Earliest Christian Manuscripts. New Haven: Yale University Press, 2018.

Norton, Robert Edward. *Herder's Aesthetics and the European Enlightenment*. Ithaca: Cornell University Press, 1991.

"The Ideal of a Philosophical History of Aesthetics." In *Herder's Aesthetics and the European Enlightenment*, 51–81. Ithaca: Cornell University Press, 1991.

Novalis. *Schriften: Die Werke Friedrich von Hardenbergs, vol. 3: Das philosophische Werk II*. Edited by Richard Samuel, Paul Kluckhohn, Gerhard Schulz, and Gabriele Rommel.. Stuttgart: Kohlhammer, 1968.

Olender, Maurice. *The Languages of Paradise: Race, Religion, and Philology in the Nineteenth Century*. Translated by Arthur Goldhammer. Cambridge, MA: Harvard University Press, 1992.

Page, D. L., ed. *Poetae Melici Graeci*. New York: Oxford University Press, 1962.

Papadēmētriou, Iōannēs-Theophanēs A. *Aesop as an Archetypal Hero*. Athens: Hellenic Society for Humanistic Studies, 1997.

Paratore, E. "Il problema degli Pseudepigrapha." In *La critica del testo. Atti del II Congresso internazionale della Società Italiana di storia del diritto*, 5–32. Reprinted in *Romanae Litterae*. Rome, 1976.

Parker, Peter. "Life's Little Lacunae." *The Times Literary Supplement* (April 30, 2010). www.the-tls.co.uk/articles/private/lifes-little-lacunae/.

Passannante, Gerard Paul. *The Lucretian Renaissance: Philology and the Afterlife of Tradition*. Chicago: University of Chicago Press, 2011.

Patton, Kimberley C. *The Sea Can Wash Away All Evils: Modern Marine Pollution and the Ancient Cathartic Ocean*. New York: Columbia University Press, 2007.

Pearson, Alfred Chilton. *The Fragments of Zeno and Cleanthes with Introduction and Explanatory Notes*. London: C. J. Clay & Sons, 1891.

Pease, Arthur S. "Some Aspects of Invisibility." *Harvard Studies in Classical Philology* 53 (1942): 1–36.

Peirano, Irene. *The Rhetoric of the Roman Fake: Latin Pseudepigrapha in Context*. Cambridge: Cambridge University Press, 2012.

Pelliccia, Hayden. "'Where Does His Wit Come From?' Review of *Aesopic Conversations: Popular Tradition, Cultural Dialogue, and the Invention of Greek*

Prose, by Leslie Kurke." *The New York Review of Books* (November 8, 2012).

Pelling, Christopher. "Plutarch's Adaptation of His Source-Material." In *Essays on Plutarch's Lives*, edited by Barbara Scardigli, 125–54. Oxford: Clarendon, 1995.

——— "Biography, Greek." In *The Oxford Classical Dictionary*, 4th ed., edited by Simon Hornblower, Antony Spawforth, and Esther Eidinow, 232–33. Oxford: Oxford University Press, 2012.

Pervo, Richard I. "Wisdom and Power: Petronius' *Sat.* and the Social World of Early Christianity." *Anglican Theological Review* 67 (1985): 307–25.

——— "A Nihilist Fabula: Introducing the Life of Aesop." In *Ancient Fiction and Early Christian Narrative*, edited by Ronald F. Hock, J. Bradley Chance, and Judith Perkins, 77–120. Atlanta: Scholars Press, 1998.

——— *Dating Acts: Between the Evangelists and the Apologists*. Santa Rosa: Polebridge Press, 2006.

Peterson, Dwight N. *The Origins of Mark: The Markan Community in Current Debate*. Leiden: Brill, 2000.

Pfanner, M. *Der Titusbogen*. Mainz am Rhein: Philipp von Zabern, 1983.

Pinheiro, Marília P. Futre, Judith Perkins, and Richard I. Pervo, eds. *The Ancient Novel and Early Christian and Jewish Narrative: Fictional Intersections*. Groningen: Barkhuis, 2012.

Plato. *Euthyphro. Apology. Crito. Phaedo. Phaedrus*. Translated by Harold North Fowler. Loeb Classical Library. Cambridge, MA: Harvard University Press, 1914.

Plutarch. *Lives, VII*. Translated by Bernadotte Perrin. Loeb Classical Library. Cambridge, MA: Harvard University Press, 1914.

Poloczek, Sławomir. "Pusty grób Kalliroe i Chrystusa." *U schyłku starożytności - Studia źródłoznawcze* 13 (2014): 9–32.

Popescu, Valentina. "Lucian's *True Stories*: Paradoxography and False Discourse." In *The Ancient Novel and the Frontiers of Genre*, edited by Marilia P. Futre Pinheiro, Gareth Schmeling, and Edmund P. Cueva, 39–58. Eelde: Barkhuis, 2014.

Prag, J., and I. Repath, eds. *Petronius: A Handbook*. Oxford: Oxford University Press, 2009.

Preuschen, Erwin. "Die Salbung Jesu in Bethanien." *Zeitschrift für die neutestamentliche Wissenschaft* 3, no. 1 (1902): 67–70.

Priestly, Joseph. *Socrates and Jesus Compared*. Philadelphia: P. Byrne, 1803.

Pseudo-Callisthenes. *The Greek Alexander Romance*. Translated by Richard Stoneman. London: Penguin Books, 1991.

Pummer, Reinhard. *The Samaritans in Flavius Josephus*. Tübingen: Mohr Siebeck, 2009.

Ramelli, Ilaria. "The Ancient Novels and the New Testament: Possible Contacts." *Ancient Narrative* 5 (2007): 41–68.

Ramelli, Ilaria, and David Konstan. "The Use of Χαρα in the New Testament and Its Background in Hellenistic Moral Philosophy." *Exemplaria Classica* 14 (2010): 185–204.

Rasimus, Tuomas, Troels Engberg-Pedersen, and Ismo Dunderberg, eds. *Stoicism in Early Christianity*. Grand Rapids: Baker Academic, 2010.

Ratner-Rosenhagen, Jennifer. *American Nietzsche: A History of an Icon and His Ideas*. Chicago: University of Chicago Press, 2012.

Reardon, B. P., trans. *Collected Ancient Greek Novels*. Los Angeles: University of California Press, 2008.

Richard, Carl J. *The Founders and the Classics: Greece, Rome, and the American Enlightenment*. Cambridge, MA: Harvard University Press, 1994.

Richardson, John. "Picasso's Apocalyptic Whorehouse." *New York Times Review of Books* (April 23, 1987), 40–46.

Riggsby, Andrew M. *Caesar in Gaul and Rome: War in Words*. Austin: University of Texas Press, 2006.

Ripat, Pauline. "Expelling Misconceptions: Astrologers at Rome." *Classical Philology* 106, no. 2 (2011): 115–54.

Robbins, Vernon K. *Jesus the Teacher: A Socio-Rhetorical Interpretation of Mark*. Minneapolis: Fortress Press, 1992.

Roberts, Erin. "Anger, Emotion, and Desire in the Gospel of Matthew." PhD diss., Brown University, 2010.

———. *Emotion, Morality, and Matthew's Mythic Jesus*. Oxford University Press, forthcoming.

Robertson, Paul. *Paul's Letters and Contemporary Greco-Roman Literature: Theorizing a New Taxonomy*. Boston: Brill, 2016.

Robinson, James M., Paul Hoffmann, and John S. Kloppenborg, eds. *The Critical Edition of Q*. Leuven: Peeters, 2000.

Rollens, Sarah. *Framing Social Criticism in the Jesus Movement: The Ideological Project in the Sayings Gospel Q*. Tübingen: Mohr Siebeck, 2014.

Rose, K. F. C. *The Date and Author of the Satyricon*. Leiden: Brill, 1971.

Rosen, Ralph M., and Catherine C. Keane. "Greco-Roman Satirical Poetry." In *A Companion to Greek and Roman Sexualities*, edited by Thomas K. Hubbard, 381–97. Malden: Wiley-Blackwell, 2014.

Roth, Ulrike. "An(other) Epitaph for Trimalchio: *Sat.* 30.2." *The Classical Quarterly* 64, no. 1 (2014): 422–25.

———. "Liberating the *Cena*." *The Classical Quarterly* 66, no. 2 (2017): 614–34.

Rowe, C. Kavin. *One True Life: The Stoics and Early Christians as Rival Traditions*. New Haven: Yale University Press, 2016.

Rubenson, Samuel. "Philosophy and Simplicity: The Problem of Classical Education in Early Christian Biography." In *Greek Biography and Panegyric in Late Antiquity*, edited by Tomas Hägg and Philip Rousseau, 110–39. Berkeley: University of California Press, 2000.

Rudd, Niall, trans. *Juvenal: The Satires*. Oxford: Clarendon, 1991.

Russell, D. A. "*De imitatione*." In *Creative Imitation and Latin Literature*, edited by David West and Tony Woodman, 1–16. Cambridge: Cambridge University Press, 1979.

———. "On Reading Plutarch's Lives." In *Essays on Plutarch's Lives*, edited by Barbara Scardigli, 75–94. Oxford: Clarendon, 1995.

Sage, Evan T., and Brady B. Gilleland, eds. *The Satiricon*. New York: Appleton-Century-Crofts, 1969.

Saldarini, Anthony J. "Reading Matthew without Anti-Semitism." In *The Gospel of Matthew in Current Study: Studies in Memory of William G. Thompson*, edited by David E. Aune, 166–84. Grand Rapids: Eerdmans, 2001.

Sandnes, Karl Olav. *The Gospel "According to Homer and Virgil": Cento and Canon*. Leiden: Brill, 2011.

Sarri, Antonia. *Material Aspects of Letter Writing in the Graeco-Roman World: 500 BC–AD 300*. Berlin: Walter de Gruyter, 2018.

Schauer, M., and S. Merkle. "Aesop und Sokrates." In *Der Äsop-Roman*, 90–96. Tübingen: Gunter Narr Verlag, 1992.

Schelling, Friedrich Wilhelm Joseph von. *Friedrich Wilhelm Joseph von Schelling sämmtliche Werke: 1802–1803*. Edited by Karl Friedrich August Schelling. Vol. 5. Stuttgart: J. G. Cotta, 1859.

Werke. Auswahl in drei Bänden. Edited by Otto Weiss. Leipzig: Fritz Eckardt, 1907.

Schenck, Kenneth. *A Brief Guide to Philo*. Louisville: Westminster John Knox, 2005.

Schilbrack, Kevin. "Religions: Are There Any?" *Journal of the American Academy of Religion* 78, no. 4 (2010): 1112–38.

Schildgen, Brenda Deen. *Crisis and Continuity: Time in the Gospel of Mark*. Sheffield: Sheffield Academic, 1998.

Schlegel, August Wilhelm. "Ueber das Lied der Nibelungen." In *Deutsches Museum*, edited by Friedrich Schlegel, 1:9–36. Vienna, 1812.

Kritische Schriften und Briefe, vol. 4: Geschichte der romantischen Literatur. Edited by Edgar Lohner. Stuttgart: Kohlhammer, 1965.

Kritische Ausgabe der Vorlesungen: Vorlesungen über Ästhetik 1803–1827, edited by Frank Jolles and Ernst Behler. Paderborn: Schöningh, 2007.

Schlegel, August Wilhelm, and Friedrich Schlegel. "Fragmente." In *Athenaeum: Eine Zeitschrift*. Vol. 1.2:28–30 (frag. 116). Berlin: Rütten & Loening, 1960.

Schmeling, Gareth. "The *Satyrica* of Petronius." In *The Novel in the Ancient World*, edited by Gareth Schmeling, 457–90. Leiden: Brill, 1996.

"Petronius and the *Satyrica*." In *Latin Fiction: The Latin Novel in Context*, edited by Heinz Hofmann, 23–37. London: Routledge, 1999.

A Commentary on the Satyrica of Petronius. Oxford: Oxford University Press, 2011.

Schmidt-Biggemann, Wilhelm. *Philosophia Perennis: Historical Outlines of Western Spirituality in Ancient, Medieval and Early Modern Thought*. Archives Internationales d'histoire Des Idées = International Archives of the History of Ideas 189. Dordrecht: Springer, 2004.

Schmitz, Thomas. *Bildung und Macht: zur sozialen und politischen Funktion der zweiten Sophistik in der griechischen Welt der Kaiserzeit*. Munich: Verlag C. H. Beck, 1997.

Schultz, Rima, and Adele Hast, eds. *Women Building Chicago 1790–1990: A Biographical Dictionary*. Bloomington: Indiana University Press, 2001.

Sherwin-White, Adrian Nicholas. *The Epistles of Pliny: A Historical and Social Commentary*. Oxford: Clarendon Press, 1985 [1966].

Slater, Niall W. *Reading Petronius*. Baltimore: Johns Hopkins University Press, 1990.

Smallwood, E. Mary. *The Jews under Roman Rule: From Pompey to Diocletian: A Study in Political Relations*. Boston: Brill, 2001.

Smith, E. P. *Priestly in America: 1794–1804*. Philadelphia: Blakiston, 1920.

Smith, Jonathan Z. *Drudgery Divine*. Chicago: University of Chicago Press, 1990.

———. *Relating Religion: Essays in the Study of Religion*. Chicago: University of Chicago, 2004.

———. *On Teaching Religion*. Edited by Christopher I. Lehrich. New York: Oxford University Press, 2013.

Smith, Wilfred Cantwell. "The Study of Religion and the Study of the Bible." *Journal of the American Academy of Religion* 39, no. 2 (1971): 131–40.

Snyder, H. Gregory. *Teachers and Texts in the Ancient World: Philosophers, Jews and Christians*. New York: Routledge, 2000.

Sparling, Robert Alan. *Johann Georg Hamann and the Enlightenment Project*. Toronto: University of Toronto Press, 2011.

Spittler, Janet, *Animals in the Apocryphal Acts of the Apostles*. WUNT 247. Tübingen: Mohr Siebeck, 2008.

Spivak, Gayatri Chakravorty. Translator's Preface to *Of Grammatology*, by Jacques Derrida, translated by Gayatri Chakravorty Spivak, ix–lxxxvii. Baltimore: Johns Hopkins University Press, 1976.

Staël, Mme de. *De l'Allemagne*. New York: Roe Lockwood & Son, 1860.

Stark, Rodney. *The Rise of Mormonism*. Edited by Reid L. Neilson. New York: Columbia University Press, 2005.

Starr, Raymond. "The Circulation of Literary Texts in the Roman World." *The Classical Quarterly* 17, no. 1 (1987): 213–223.

Stevenson, Jane. *Women Latin Poets: Language, Gender, and Authority, from Antiquity to the Eighteenth Century*. New York: Oxford University Press, 2005.

Stoneman, Richard. *The Greek Alexander Romance*. London: Penguin, 1991.

Stowers, Stanley K. *A Rereading of Romans: Justice, Jews, and Gentiles*. New Haven: Yale University Press, 1994.

———. "The Ontology of Religion." In *Introducing Religion: Essays in Honor of Jonathan Z. Smith*, edited by Willi Braun and Russell T. McCutcheon, 434–49. Oakville: Equinox, 2008.

———. "The Apostle Paul." In *The History of Western Philosophy of Religion, vol. 1: Ancient Philosophy of Religion*, edited by Graham Robert Oppy and Nick Trakakis, 145–57. Durham: Acumen, 2009.

———. "Jesus the Teacher and Stoic Ethics in the Gospel of Matthew." In *Stoicism in Early Christianity*, edited by Tuomas Rasimus, Troels Engberg-Pedersen, and Ismo Dunderberg, 59–76. Grand Rapids: Baker Academic, 2010.

———. "The Concept of 'Community' and the History of Early Christianity." *Method and Theory in the Study of Religion* 23, nos. 3–4 (2011): 238–56.

———. "Kinds of Myths, Meals and Power: Paul and Corinthians." In *Redescribing Paul and the Corinthians*, edited by Ron Cameron and Merrill P. Miller, 105–49. Atlanta: Society of Biblical Literature, 2011.

———. "Paul and the Terrain of Philosophy." *Early Christianity* 6 (2015): 141–56.

Struck, Peter T. *Birth of the Symbol: Ancient Readers at the Limits of Their Texts*. Princeton: Princeton University Press, 2004.

"The Genealogy of the Symbolic." In *Birth of the Symbol: Ancient Readers at the Limits of Their Texts*, 1–20. Princeton: Princeton University Press, 2004.

Struthers Malbon, Elizabeth. "Galilee and Jerusalem: History and Literature in Marcan Interpretation." *Catholic Biblical Quarterly* 44, no. 2 (April 1, 1982): 242.

Tacitus. *Agricola. Germania. Dialogue on Oratory*. Translated by William Peterson and Maurice Hutton. LCL 35. Cambridge, MA: Harvard University Press, 1914.

Tartar, Maria. *The Hard Facts of the Grimms' Fairy Tales*. Princeton: Princeton University Press, 1987.

Temmerman, Koen de. *Crafting Characters: Heroes and Heroines in the Ancient Greek Novel*. Oxford: Oxford University Press, 2014.

Theissen, Gerd. *Sociology of Early Palestinian Christianity*. Translated by John Bowden. Philadelphia: Fortress Press, 1978.

"Social Stratification in the Corinthian Community: A Contribution to the Sociology of Early Hellenistic Christianity." In *The Social Setting of Pauline Christianity: Essays on Corinth*, translated by John H. Schütz, 69–119. Philadelphia: Fortress Press, 1982.

The Gospels in Context: Social and Political History in the Synoptic Tradition. Translated by Linda M. Maloney. Minneapolis: Fortress Press, 1991.

"The Wandering Radicals: Light Shed by Sociology of Literature on the Early Transmission of the Jesus Sayings." In *Social Reality and the Early Christians: Theology, Ethics, and the World of the New Testament*, translated by Margaret Kohl, 33–59. Minneapolis: Fortress Press, 1992.

The Religion of the Earliest Churches: Creating a Symbolic World. Translated by John Bowden. Minneapolis: Fortress Press, 1999.

Die Religion der ersten Christen: Eine Theorie des Urchristentums. Gütersloh: Gütersloher Verlagshaus, 2000.

Thom, Johan. "Cleanthes Hymn to Zeus and Early Christian Literature." In *Antiquity and Humanity: Essays on Ancient Religion and Philosophy*, edited by Adela Yarbro Collins and Margaret M. Mitchell, 477–99. Tübingen: Mohr Siebeck, 2001.

Thom, Martin. *Republics, Nations, and Tribes*. London: Verso, 1995.

Thomas, Christine M. "Stories without Texts and without Authors: The Problem of Fluidity in Ancient Novelistic Texts and Early Christian Literature." In *Ancient Fiction and Early Christian Narrative*, edited by Ronald F. Hock, J. Bradley Chance, and Judith Perkins, 273–91. SBL Symposium Series 6. Atlanta: Scholars Press, 1998.

Thomas, Richard F. *Lands and Peoples in Roman Poetry*, Cambridge Philological Society Supp. Vol. 7. Cambridge: Cambridge Philological Society, 1982.

Thorsteinsson, Runar M. *Roman Christianity and Roman Stoicism: A Comparative Study of Ancient Morality*. Oxford: Oxford University Press, 2010.

Tomashevsky, Boris. "Literary Genres." In *Formalism: History, Comparison, Genre*, edited by L. M. O'Toole and Ann Shukman, 52–93. Russian Poetics in Translation 5. Oxford: Holdan Books, 1978.

Trautmann, Thomas R. *Aryans and British India*. Berkeley: University of California Press, 1997.

Trevor-Roper, Hugh. "The Invention of Tradition: The Highland Tradition of Scotland." In *The Invention of Tradition*, edited by E. J. Hobsbawm and T. O. Ranger, 15–41. Cambridge: Cambridge University Press, 2012.

Tuckett, Christopher. *From the Sayings to the Gospels*. WUNT 328. Tübingen: Mohr Siebeck, 2014.

Turner, Frank M. *The Greek Heritage in Victorian Britain*. New Haven: Yale University Press, 1981.

Tyson, Joseph B. *Marcion and Luke–Acts: A Defining Struggle*. Columbia: University of South Carolina Press, 2006.

Urbano, Arthur P. *The Philosophical Life: Biography and the Crafting of Intellectual Identity in Late Antiquity*. Washington: Catholic University of America Press, 2013.

Vayntrub, Jacqueline. *Beyond Orality: Biblical Poetry on Its Own Terms*. London: Routledge, 2019.

von Groningen, Bernard A. "ΕΚΔΟΣΙΣ." *Mnemosyne* 16 (1963): 1–17.

Vorster, Willem S. "Kerygma/History and the Gospel Genre." In *Speaking of Jesus: Essays on Biblical Language, Gospel Narrative and the Historical Jesus*, edited by J. Eugene Botha, 129–38. Leiden: Brill, 1999.

Waite, Charles B. "Notes of Travel." In *Chicago Law Times*, vol. 2, edited by Catharine V. Waite, 326–28. Chicago: C. V. Waite, 1888.

Walbank, Frank W. "Profit or Amusement: Some Thoughts on the Motives of Hellenistic Historians." In *Polybius, Rome and the Hellenistic World: Essays and Reflections*, 231–41. New York: Cambridge University Press, 2002.

Wallace-Hadrill, Andrew. *Suetonius: The Scholar and His Caesars*. New Haven: Yale University Press, 1983.

Walsh, P. G. *Petronius: The Satyricon*. New York: Oxford University Press, 2009.

Walsh, Robyn Faith. "The Influence of the Romantic Genius in Early Christian Studies." *Relegere* 5, no. 1 (2015): 31–60.

——— "Q and the 'Big Bang' Theory of Christian Origins." In *Redescribing the Gospel of Mark*, edited by Barry S. Crawford and Merrill P. Miller, 483–533. Atlanta: Society of Biblical Literature, 2017.

——— "Religion Is a 'Private Matter.'" In *Stereotyping Religion: Critiquing Clichés*, edited by Brad Stoddard and Craig Martin, 69–81. London: Bloomsbury, 2017.

——— "IVDAEA DEVICTA: The Gospels as Imperial 'Captive Literature.'" In *The Bible and Class Struggle*, edited by Robert Myles, 89–114. London: Lexington Books, 2019.

——— "The *Satyrica* and the Gospels in the Second Century," *The Classical Quarterly*, 70, no. 1 (2020): 356–367.

——— "Revisiting Paul's Letter to the Laodiceans: Rejected Literature and Useful Books." To appear in volume dedicated to François Bovon. Edited by Brent Landau et al. Tübingen: Mohr Siebeck, forthcoming.

Wasserman, Emma. *The Death of the Soul in Romans 7: Sin, Death, and the Law in Light of Hellenistic Moral Psychology*. Tübingen: Mohr Siebeck, 2008.

Wästberg, Per. *The Journey of Anders Sparrman: A Biographical Novel.* London: Granta Books, 2010.

Wendt, Heidi. *At the Temple Gates: The Religion of Freelance Experts in the Early Roman Empire.* New York: Oxford University Press, 2016.

West, M. L. *The Orphic Poems.* Oxford: Clarendon, 1983.

"The Invention of Homer." *The Classical Quarterly* 49, no. 2 (1999): 364–82.

White, Hayden V. *The Fiction of Narrative: Essays on History, Literature, and Theory, 1957–2007.* Edited by Robert Doran. Baltimore: Johns Hopkins University Press, 2010.

Metahistory: The Historical Imagination in Nineteenth-Century Europe. Baltimore: Johns Hopkins University Press, 2014.

Whitmarsh, Tim. *Greek Literature and the Roman Empire: The Politics of Imitation.* Oxford: Oxford University Press, 2001.

The Second Sophistic. Oxford: Oxford University Press, 2005.

Wilamowitz-Moellendorff, Ulrich von. *Homerische untersuchungen.* Berlin: Weidmann, 1884.

Williams, Craig A. *Reading Roman Friendship.* Cambridge: Cambridge University Press, 2012.

Williams, Gordon. "Phases in Political Patronage of Literature in Rome." In *Literary and Artistic Patronage in Ancient Rome,* edited by Barbara K. Gold, 3–49. Austin: University of Texas Press, 1982.

Williamson, George S. *The Longing for Myth in Germany: Religion and Aesthetic Culture from Romanticism to Nietzsche.* Chicago: University of Chicago Press, 2004.

Wilson, Emily R. "Pain and Revelation: The Death of Socrates and the Death of Jesus." In *The Death of Socrates,* 141–69. Cambridge, MA: Harvard University Press, 2007.

Winn, Adam. *The Purpose of Mark's Gospel: An Early Christian Response to Roman Imperial Propaganda.* Tübingen: Mohr Siebeck, 2008.

Wolf, F. A. *Prolegomena to Homer, 1795.* Translated by Anthony Grafton, Glenn W. Most, and James E. G. Zetzel. Princeton: Princeton University Press, 1985.

Woodman, A. J. *Rhetoric in Classical Historiography: Four Studies.* Portland: Areopagitica Press, 1988.

Wrede, William. *The Messianic Secret.* Translated by J. C. G. Greig. Cambridge: J. Clarke, 1971.

Wright, N. T. *The New Testament and the People of God.* Minneapolis: Fortress Press, 1992.

Young, Iris Marion. "The Ideal of Community and the Politics of Difference." In *Feminism/Postmodernism,* edited by Linda J. Nicholson, 300–323. New York: Routledge, 1990.

Zammito, John H. *Kant, Herder, and the Birth of Anthropology.* Chicago: University of Chicago Press, 2002.

Index

CPSIA information can be obtained
at www.ICGtesting.com
Printed in the USA
LVHW101054160622
721218LV00027B/91